COMPUTER TECHNOLOGY FOR HIGHER EDUCATION

Volume One	:	**An Overview**
Volume Two	:	**The Indian Experience**
Volume Three	:	**The Canadian Experience**

COMPUTER TECHNOLOGY FOR HIGHER EDUCATION

A Design Model for a Computerizing University

Volume III

The Canadian Experience

W. David Chandler
Barbara Kaltz
Murray Knuttila
R. Brien Maguire
William A. Stahl
Larry R. Symes

Concept Publishing Company, New Delhi 110059 (India)

ISBN-81-7022-466-7 (Set)
ISBN 81-7022-469-1 (Vol. III)

First Published 1993

Published and Printed by
Ashok Kumar Mittal
Concept Publishing Company
A/15-16, Commercial Block, Mohan Garden
NEW DELHI-110059 (India)
Phones: 5554042, 5504042

TABLE OF CONTENTS

INTRODUCTION

This volume is part of a three volume report, entitled *A Design Model for a Computerizing University*. This volume presents results of several years of cooperative work and research by the Canadian team. The reader should refer to Volume I for an overview of the joint conclusions of the Canadian and Indian teams and to Volume II for the findings of our Indian colleagues. Together the three volumes represent the culmination of the research portion of a project that was conceived almost nine years prior to the seminar in India where these results were presented.

The term "model" is not used in the mathematical sense, nor does the design model present a detailed outline which can be explicitly followed in the computerization of a university. Rather, the research examines the various aspects of computerizing the three major functions performed at a university (teaching, research and administration), outlines the underlying objectives and assumptions associated with computerization, indicates critical issues which must be dealt with and explores the possible pathways which may be followed. As a result the model addresses the technical, the social and the organizational aspects of university computerization.

The idea of this collaborative research project involving a group of researchers in Canada and India was first discussed at the Spring 1984 board meeting of the Shastri Indo-Canadian Institute. A dinner held in conjunction with the board meeting brought together the Indian High Commissioner to Canada, Mr. Fabian, Dr. Roland Miller of Luther College, University of Regina and Dr. Alex Guy, Deputy Minister of the Saskatchewan Government's Department of Science and Technology. The idea of a collaborative project to study computerization in higher education was born. With the assistance of a start-up grant from the Saskatchewan Department of Science and Technology, four members of the University of Regina–Drs. Bruce MacDonald, Roland Miller, William Stahl and Larry Symes–attended a Shastri Institute sponsored conference in Montreal in June 1985. There they met Dr. Gunvant Shah of South Gujarat University, Surat who was also attending the seminar. Through Dr. Shah, Dr. Madhuri Shah, chair of the University Grants Commission (UGC) of India, was contacted concerning the sanctioning of a seminar on the topic of the use of technology in higher education.

The UGC agreed to fund the proposed seminar. The Canadians approached the International Development Research Centre (IDRC) and received funding to permit them to attend the seminar and to further develop the concept of a collaborative project. In January 1986, a year before the Surat Seminar, four faculty members from the University of Regina–Drs. Bruce MacDonald, Brien Maguire, William Stahl and Larry Symes, visited India to meet with individuals at seven universities and institutes. The seminar held at South Gujarat University, Surat in February 1987 brought the Canadian group into contact with a number of individuals. The resultant discussions led to a meeting in June 1988 at Gujarat University in Ahmedabad, at which time it was agreed that the Canadian and Indian groups would submit proposals to the Canadian International Development Agency (CIDA) and the UGC, respectively, to fund a joint collaborative project.

Proposals were developed and submitted to the respective funding agencies in July 1988 in India and October 1988 in Canada. Approvals for the project were received from CIDA in March 1989 and from UGC in November 1989. While the project was nominally a three-year project, its activities have taken place over almost five calendar years due to fiscal year-ends of the two granting agencies and the variation in the approval dates for the project. Just prior to receiving official confirmation of funding for the Canadian component of the project, the Canadian Team was expanded by three with the addition of Dr. W. David Chandler, Dr. Barbara Kaltz and Dr. Murray Knuttila. They joined Dr. Maguire, Dr. Miller, Dr. Stahl and Dr. Symes, developers of the project proposal. In December of 1989, Dr. Miller, who had been the Project Director, left the University on an extended leave and Dr. Symes assumed the role of Project Director.

The project had two major objectives. The first was the development of a design model which can be used as a guide when computerizing a university. The second was to increase the number of Indian academics and administrators who are aware of the potential of computer technology and the effect of computerization on a university. The former has resulted in the three volume document entitled *A Design Model for a Computerizing University* of which this is Volume III. Activities associated with the latter objective have resulted in three six week training programs being conducted at the University of Regina in May and June of 1990, 1991 and 1992 (*cf.* Appendix B). In 1991, with the assistance of the Digital Equipment of India Corporation, a training centre was established on the campus of Gujarat University, Ahmedabad–the Computer Training and Applications Laboratory (COMTAL). Through September 1992, seven training programs have been conducted there and more are planned. Thus, COMTAL will continue for some time to magnify the training activities of those who came to Canada for training, as their role changes from trainee to trainer.

Methodology

Since a range of different types of data were required in the preparation of this Design Model, a number of different research techniques were utilized. In some cases unstructured interviews were used, while other information was gathered using standard historical methods, document searches, library research and literature reviews. A field experiment was used in connection with the use of an electronic blackboard.

The baseline surveys relied on a self-administered mail survey instrument that had been pre-tested. The academic survey was sent to 957 faculty members at 13 universities across Canada. The sample was established using a modified stratified cluster sample. Since universities in Canada differ significantly in terms of size and resources, it was felt that there might also be important differences in accessibility to, use of, and attitudes relating to computers. This lack of overall homogeneity necessitated the establishment of three strata representing large (over 1000 faculty), medium (between 200 and 999 faculty) and small (less than 200 faculty) universities.

On the basis of a simple random sample, three universities were selected from each stratum and from within the faculty lists of these universities a further sample of individual respondents was drawn. The sample of individuals drawn from each university was also a simple random sample and the number drawn was equal to the university's proportion of faculty in that stratum. If, for example, a particular university represented 10 per cent of all faculty in its strata, a simple random sample of 10 per cent of that university's faculty was drawn.

The stratified cluster sample described thus far was modified to account for the several unique characteristics of Canadian society and the Canadian university system. In order to account for the fact that there is one very large university in Canada, the University of Toronto, whose size gives it unique characteristics, it was set aside in a strata of its own. The University of Waterloo has an established reputation as a pioneer and innovator in computerization and thus it was felt that it should be added because of its unique characteristics. It fell in the medium strata. Finally, in order to ensure a degree of regional representation an additional university was added to each of the large and small strata.

The survey instruments sent to admissions officers, registrars, directors of computer centres, and persons in charge of administrative computing were sent to all universities. A simple random sample of 33% of deans and student counsellors was drawn. The response rates were as follows (34, that is, 2.6%, of the questionnaires mailed to individuals were returned unopened):

Questionnaire	Number Sent	Number Returned	Percent Returned
Admissions Officers	78	36	46.2
Registrars	76	35	46.1
Director Computer Centre	57	12	21.1
Administrative Computing	65	28	43.1
Deans/Counsellors	99	50	50.5
Faculty			
University of British Columbia	163	34	20.9
Brock University	10	3	30.0
University of Calgary	82	24	29.3
Concordia University	71	17	24.0

University of Lethbridge	11	4	36.4
McMaster University	67	12	17.9
Memorial University	61	12	19.7
University of Moncton	10	1	10.0
Mount Allison University	10	3	30.0
Royal Military College	10	0	0.0
University of Sherbrooke	32	4	12.5
University of Toronto	329	80	24.3
University of Waterloo	101	28	27.7
Subtotal Faculty	957	222	23.2
Total Questionnaires	1,332	383	28.8

The six members of the Canadian Team brought a rich mosaic of experience in teaching, research and administration to the project. Dr. W. David Chandler, a Professor of Chemistry, was Head of the Department for 18 years, Chair of the Computer Users Advisory Committee and a member of the University Academic Review Task Force; Dr. Barbara Kaltz, an Associate Professor of French, was director of SCIL; Dr. Murray Knuttila, an Associate Professor and Head of Sociology and Social Studies, was Assistant Dean of the Faculty of Arts for four years; Dr. R. Brien Maguire, a Professor of Computer Science, was Head of the Department for 8.5 years and Director of Academic Computing; Dr. William A. Stahl, an Associate Professor of Sociology; and Dr. Larry R. Symes, a Professor of Computer Science, was Director of the Computer Centre for five years, Head of Computer Science for 11.5 years, Director of Academic Computing and Dean of Science for 10.5 years.

The findings presented in this volume are the result of both individual and team efforts. The issues to be dealt with in this study as well as the methodology to be used were determined by the team. As a result, the three major functions of a university–teaching, research and administration–are being examined here in the broader context of the role of universities within society and the social consequences of the computerization process. In addition, given that the rapid pace of technological change affects all functions of the university, a study of future trends in technology was also considered essential. As a result, the volume is divided into six chapters. The main responsibility for each chapter lies with the individual team member who prepared initial and final drafts:

Chapter 1	Dr. Murray Knuttila
Chapter 2	Dr. William A. Stahl
Chapter 3	Dr. Barbara Kaltz
Chapter 4	Dr. W. David Chandler
Chapter 5	Dr. Larry R. Symes
Chapter 6	Dr. R. Brien Maguire

The drafts of the individual chapters went through a process of review, critique and debate by the Canadian Team. In addition, research plans and results have been shared and debated with our colleagues on the Indian Team, at formal meetings in August 1989 in Regina, August 1990 in Ahmedabad and August 1992 in Regina, and thoughout the duration of the project by mail and telephone.

The appendices were developed by the following individuals: Appendixes A, D, E and J, Larry Symes; Appendix B, David Chandler and Murray Knuttila; Appendix C, David Chandler; Appendixes F, G and H, Murray Knuttila and Appendix I, William Stahl.

Acknowledgements

The project is indebted to Dr. Roland Miller for his valuable assistance and guidance in the development and formation of the project. The assistance and support of the Shastri Indo-Canadian Institute has also been significant; this includes Resident Directors–Dr. A Gupta, Dr. J. Hill, Dr. G. N. Ramu, Dr. J. R. Wood, Dr. B. S. Sahni and Dr. L. Anderson, and especially, the Administrative Director, Mr. P. N. Malik. The considerable assistance and encouragement of Professor S. K. Khanna, Vice-Chairman of the UGC must be noted along with that of Dr. L. I. Barber and Dr. M. N. Desai, the Vice-Chancellors of the University of Regina and Gujarat University who have taken the time to join their project team members on visits to meetings being held in the collaborator's country. We would also like to express our appreciation to our colleagues on the Indian Team–Dr. Sarla Achuthan, Dr. Binod C. Agrawal, Dr. Vimal P. Shah, Mr. R. P. Soni and Mr. S. R. Thakore. Without their efforts this project would not have been a success. We should also like to thank the numerous individuals that we met with in India on our visits while the project was being formulated and, later, during its execution. Some of these individuals are: Dr. A. K. Agrawal, Gujarat University, Dr. M. T. Ahmed, Aligarh Muslim University, Dr. J. N. Handoo, Central Institute of Indian Languages, Dr. K. Sarukesi, Barathiar University and Dr. M. M. Singh, North Eastern Hill University. We should also like to acknowledge the enthusiasm and patience of the trainees who joined us in Regina. The efforts of a number of individuals from Digital Equipment Corporation must be recognized, in association with the securing of the donation of the computer to COMTAL–Ms. S. Foster, Manager Regina Branch, Mr. T. DiCenzo, Digital USA, Mr. N. L. Hickerson, Digital Asia, and Mr. M. Shah, Digital India. We are indebted to the various students who assisted the project in many ways in Regina–Mr. S. Burt B. Christian, Mr. Vipin Gupta, Mr. B. Johnson, Mr. Sushil Manocha, Ms. Renée Misfeldt, Ms. Gayle Woloshyn, Mr. Jason Walters and Mr. Neng-Quan Wang, and to those who have worked at various times in what has become known as the CIDA/India Project office on campus–Ms. Bea Gropp, Mr. Don Irwin, Mrs. Ina Kurtz, Mrs. Myra

McKnight, Mrs. Laurel Ryder, and Ms. Lila Wendling. Other individuals who contributed to the success of the project include: Dr. C. Blachford, Dr. T. Bryant, Dr. R. Rystra-Bryant, Ms. P. Campbell, Mr. J. Fagan, Dr. R. Ghosh, Dr. D. Griffin, Mr. P. Hoffman, Dr. G. Moore, Mr. W. Clarke-Okah, Dr. R. Robinson, Dr. R. Shanker, Prof. N. Southam and Ms. P. Van Havere.

CHAPTER 1

THE UNIVERSITY AND SOCIETY

Human beings must be understood as cultural creatures whose characteristics and development are profoundly influenced by their institutional experiences. The process of formal education is an important part of the social processes by which the human personality is molded. As a part of the formal educational system the university is an important part of this process; however we must understand that the modern western university is not an island onto itself. Indeed it is clear that the structures, operation and role of the Western university have always been influenced by the larger social, cultural, political, and economic structures of the society within which the university exists; therefore, in order to understand the university we must locate it within this larger context.

In recent decades Canadian universities have been transformed by the introduction and application of computer technology. This new technology has had an impact on the two central functions of the university—teaching and research—as well as on its administrative operations. The various chapters in this report examine the impact of computers and computerization on teaching, research and the administration of universities. In order to provide a larger context for these discussions, this introductory chapter attempts to provide an historical account of the emergence of Western universities, with an emphasis on Canada. Though this historical overview is limited to data relating to the Western experience, we hope it illustrates the fact that changes in the educational system can only be understood by reference to much broader social, economic and political changes.

A second general objective which this chapter attempts to accomplish is to provide the reader with an introduction to the major theoretical perspectives or paradigms which have been utilized in order to explain and understand the nature, structures and functions of education. The discussion of theoretical approaches proceeds from the assumption that there is a fundamental difference between describing a phenomenon and explaining it. While the task of description is relatively easy and straightforward, providing an explanation and analysis of why particular processes or events occur is more difficult. In the case of social analysis of education and the university, the situation is complicated because we find that there is no generally agreed on or widely accepted way of explaining the characteristics, structures and functions that these institutions and actors have. As a result we are forced to consider different theoretical frameworks that have been used in analyzing the educational system and its role in society at large.

Though it may not seem immediately apparent why one would engage in an overview of social theory in a volume such as this, it is clear that many of the issues that emerge when we consider computerization do in fact relate to broader questions including:

1. What is the social role of the university? What are its objectives and priorities? Who sets these goals and priorities?
2. Whom should and does the university serve?
3. Who should provide resources for the university? What share of society's resources should be thus allocated?
4. How should the university be organized and structured? How are decisions in a university made?

Given the nature of these questions, it is obvious that many of the issues and topics which this document addresses will be wrought with controversy, argument and debate. In order to make sense out of some of the debates, we think it is useful to begin by understanding the basic issues that underlie some of the disagreements. It is our position that among the central issues that often inform these debates are different views concerning the very nature of society and the role of the educational system and the university in society. In this chapter we will attempt to sketch out two of the basic positions that inform different interpretations of the academy, its role, structure and operation. First, however, we want to establish the importance of the educational processes to the very survival of the species we know as homo sapiens.

1. Education and Species Homo Sapiens

Homo sapiens is a cultural creature and thus social learning, in the broadest sense of the term, is an integral dimension of being human and the human being. The educational process and the institutional arrangements associated with it obviously are linked to the essential human activity of learning.

We know that in recent millennia the precise form that human learning has taken has been diverse and varied. We also know that human learning has always been, and continues to be, a complex life long process. In modern industrial society some learning is formally organized and structured, while some is informal, even unintentional, and occurs without the participants even realizing that learning was occurring. For much of the time that our ancestors have inhabited the planet this latter form of learning was dominant. In more recent times education and learning has taken on a more formally organized character. In order to fully comprehend the social character and context of the modern Western university a few comments on the history of education in Western cultures are in order.

2. The Emergence of the Western University

The history of the modern Western university begins in the era of the collapse of the Roman Empire in the late fifth century. The decline of centralized political structures and systems of non-local economic activity, the increasing power of the church and the emergence of local centres of economic, social and cultural activity contributed to the emergence of several different forms of education. As described by Atkinson and Maleska (1965), some of these new educational structures were centered in the emerging Christian monasteries, while others developed in order to train the children of the developing aristocracies and of handicraft producers. The roles of the monasteries in preserving much of the classical knowledge of Greek and Rome and of guild-based education in preserving and developing new practical skills and knowledge are particularly noteworthy.

A series of processes that were to change the nature of education continued on from the thirteenth century. Among them were the economic changes associated with urban development, expanding trade, commerce, and handicraft production as well as the expansion of agriculture. The political fragmentation that had characterized the immediate post-Roman Empire era came to an end and the steady process of political consolidation that eventually created the modern nation state began. The new classes produced by these changes, an aristocracy with more political power and the merchants and craft producers, began to realize that a more systematic secular education was in their interests. As a result, key secular figures began to encourage specialized education. William Boyd describes the process that produced the first universities in the following manner:

> The "universities" in the original sense of the word were simply societies (or guilds) of masters and students, formed for the purpose of mutual help and protection, after the manner of the guilds of craftsmen which were rising into prominence with the great impulse to corporate life which made itself felt throughout Europe in the twelfth century. (1928:145)

Murray Ross notes that among the factors that gave rise to the emergence of the universities was the demand for trained administrators, physicians and lawyers (1976:5). The fact that a renaissance was underway throughout most of Western Europe must also have contributed to the stimulation of a new interest in knowing and knowledge.

As the gatherings of scholars and students that were to become universities grew in size, reputation and influence, they began to attract students from further and further away. Eventually this produced bodies of students with an "international" character though the formally organized nation states of Western Europe were just beginning to emerge. Some of the students began to gather in more and more formal organizations in order to facilitate learning, finance their studies and provide each other with physical security and protection. The entire student body was called the *Studium Generale* while those studying similar subjects became sub-groups called *facultas* (Atkinson and Maleska 1965:43).

Though there were significant differences between the more religiously oriented schools of the North and their more practical Italian counterparts, universities in their formative states were characterized by what Ross refers to as "a buoyancy and zestfulness" (1976:9). The teachers and students associated with the early universities established a tradition of searching for knowledge without particular concern about offending those who disagreed with the conclusions the scholars reached. Universities in a community brought with them prestige and wealth and as a result, teachers and students were able to avoid the power of the church and the local political rulers by playing them off against each other or threatening to use what was called "cessation" or "migration" if their activities were interfered with. Cessation referred to going on strike or ceasing activities and migrating meant simply moving to another locale where their activities were better appreciated.

Mulhern notes that "by the fifteenth century universities existed everywhere in Europe" (1959:279-280). Ross puts the number at about 70 by the year 1500. The early universities had no buildings and the teachers survived on the basis of fees collected from students. Though it first occurred in Italian cities, eventually a widespread system of public funding emerged. In the years that followed, significant conflicts developed as guilds, churches, city politicians and emerging monarchies all sought to control universities and its operation. As nation states emerged it seemed as if the monarch might become dominant; however the turmoil associated with the Reformation and post-Reformation period actually saw an increase in the influence of church on universities.

It was a period of decline in terms of the vitality and learning associated with universities as both church and state sought to control these institutions. Indeed Mulhern refers to the post-Reformation period as one in which the university was in bondage, as churches attempted to limit the intellectual activities that went on in the university while using it to promulgate particular beliefs (1959:400-401).

The rise of the nation states and the beginning of the overall decline of the church brought a new form of secular control of the universities in some nation states. In England, the uniting of religion and the state served to limit and control the activities and development of universities as the state established universities by statute but the Church of England set the limits and boundaries on what was taught. Ross notes that many of the great scientific discoveries of the period were made by scientists and thinkers not associated with the universities, indicating that universities were stultified. He further argues that the establishment of the Royal Society in 1662 resulted because the established universities of Oxford and Cambridge were not interested in advances in knowledge but rather in passing on established religious orthodoxy. Indeed he refers to them as the servants of the status quo catering to the needs of a male and upper class population (1976:17-26).

Quite different patterns of university development emerged in different nation states and geographical regions. By the nineteenth century in Germany we see the first systematic move to a form of academic freedom as universities there ceased being theological seminaries and broadened the range of subjects taught and issues considered (Mulhern 1959:402). Metzger (1955) reviews numerous factors that gave rise to a new attitude in Germany. Ross notes that among the great ideas that made German universities different were the notions of *Lernfreiheit*, referring to the student's right to choose a programme of study and move from one university to another and *Lehrfreiheit*, the freedom of the professor to investigate and teach without government interference (1976:27). Others such as Marcuse (1941) have noted that, ironically, the dominance of German idealism in the realm of philosophy allowed thinkers more freedom because ideas were not yet deemed to pose a threat to those with political power.

It was not until after several decades of aborted reform that universities in England began to break free of the control of the church. Until 1871 one had to subscribe to the tenets of the Church of England in order to receive a degree from Oxford or Cambridge. Such a situation prevented Roman Catholics and Jews from studying at these universities. It was not until after intellectual changes which, as was noted, largely occurred outside the universities that changes began in England. By the mid to late 1700's several new tendencies in Western thought were emerging, among them the modern philosophical schools associated with rationalism and empiricism.

Ross refers to the new way of approaching knowledge as the "rational-empirical" outlook (1976:34). This new outlook or approach to the production of knowledge was predicated on the assumption that scholarship and the search for truth must be independent, propelled by curiosity, disciplined in its rigor, unafraid of originality and unconcerned with offending those with authority. If universities were to become home to such forms of scholarship, then they had to change and indeed they did. Other factors were also at work.

Among the many radical ideas associated with the French Revolution, which had ramifications far beyond the borders of France, was the notion that the state should play a central role in education. As far as possible, education at all levels, it was deemed, should be universal, free and secular with the state playing a central role in molding the new citizens for the new order. It should be noted, as Diana Coole (1988) and others have pointed out, that "universal" in the ideology of the French Revolution was not in fact universal at all since women were often excluded from the discourse. For the university this meant the possibility of being freed from financial dependence upon and association with the church. However, care had to be taken not to simply create institutions which were now considered branches of the state apparatus from whence major financing was to come. The delays in establishing systematic patterns of state funding for universities in England meant that by the time this occurred, according to Ross during the World War II era, a set of established structures and practices were in place that attempted to ensure the academic and scholarly independence of the university regardless of the role that state financing played. More on these structures in a moment.

As European influence spread to the colonies the divergent views of the university prevalent in Europe came to impact education and the university. Harvard College was founded by the Puritans in 1636 with the explicit purpose of expounding and perpetuating Puritan teaching and providing a supply of clergy (Mulhern 1959:402). Other religious denominations were also important in starting and funding universities. However, the ideas concerning access to education appear to have been manifest in the provisions of the Ordinance of 1787 which provided for the granting of lands for the purpose of establishing universities in the Northwest Territory (Mulhern 1959:611).

3. Universities in Canada

The history and development of universities in Canada have been influenced by the nation's complex cultural, social, political and economic history. The educational system that developed in Canada reflects the influence of the French, British and the American models.

Three types of college and university institutions developed and each continues to influence the current system. The three major types of universities and colleges were: 1) those established by various churches; 2) government-funded institutions and 3) the privately endowed universities. The development of these various types of institutions into the system that exists today was the result of complex social, cultural, economic and political processes, only some of which can be mentioned here. To further complicate the picture the current scene is characterized by institutions that represent a blending and melding of these various types of arrangements.

3.1 Church and Denominational Colleges and Universities

The first formal schools and colleges in Canada were established by the French. Indeed several different types of formal educational institutions were established in New France or what is today Quebec. The *petites écoles* provided rudimentary and elementary education, focusing on a minimal degree of literacy and some competence in mathematics, organized mostly at the parish level. Needless to say, religious matters were an important part of these schools as well. The church oversaw the establishment of schools for craft producers at Montreal and Quebec. There were also classical colleges and the Petit Séminaire de Quebec established by Bishop Laval (Audet 1970). In later years, after the British conquest, education in French Canada languished for lack of funds, mistrust and concern by some in the French-speaking community concerning the role the pre-Confederation Assembly would play in education (Philips 1957:80, Audet 1970:154).

Between the British conquest and Confederation, Protestant denominations were active in establishing a series of universities and colleges throughout the British colonies that were to become Canada. For example, the Church of England established three King's Colleges, at Windsor, Nova Scotia (subsequently moved to Halifax), Toronto, and Fredericton. Bishops College at Lennoxville, Quebec and Western were established by the Anglican Church. Acadia and McMaster were originally started by people of Baptist faith while Mount Allison was founded by Methodists. While these and other church-operated and funded colleges continued to flourish well into this century, the problems associated with finances were eventually to result in affiliation with government-funded institutions (Stamp 1970:330).

3.2 Government-Funded Institutions

Debates surrounding the role of the state in education date back to pre-Confederation Canada. The issue emerged in the context of a period of industrial development that took place in Canada during the two decades between 1840 and Confederation. It was a time when the relationship between economic development and education became a matter of debate with one of the central figures being Egerton Ryerson. Donald Wilson summarizes Ryerson's view of education: "Ryerson looked on the school as a vehicle for inculcating loyalty and patriotism, fostering social cohesion and self reliance and ensuring domestic tranquillity" (1970:215). If the school were to perform these social roles it would have to be properly funded and, in Ryerson's opinion, this left government funding as the only option. Ryerson's idea of a school system supported by compulsory tax assessments on all properties became known as the "free school" movement. Wilson argues that it was in part informed by a pro-British stance in that such a system would be instrumental in promoting British values and institutions in the face of a perceived threat from the United States. Similarly, the arguments in favour of a university in Upper Canada put forward by Lord Simcoe, included providing opportunities for young men to study in Canada rather than having to go to the United States where the "pernicious influences" of republican and democratic ideals would lead them astray (Wilson 1979:226). Simcoe's efforts produced a sizable land grant that was to be used for funding grammar schools and a university. Though it took a series of political struggles, action was taken and in 1849 the nondenominational University of Toronto was created.

The establishment of the nondenominational university with government funding was the trend that was followed in the Western provinces of Saskatchewan and Alberta when they were created. The evolution of the University of Manitoba was a more complex process that involved the secularization of several church affiliated institutions and an injection of provincial government money.

3.3 Privately Endowed Institutions

Alternate patterns characterized the development of several Canadian universities in that they were funded and supported, in their initial period at least, by financial resources connected with foundations or independent wealth. The universities founded on independent, that is non-government or church wealth, followed a pattern more akin to the Scottish tradition by being more democratic and less aristocratic in their orientation. Hamilton (1970:37) notes that Dalhousie, McGill and Queen's tended to follow this pattern.

3.4 Variations and Blends

As universities in Canada developed, a blending of these various organizational and funding arrangements occurred. The province of Nova Scotia stopped all of its grants to universities in 1881 and as a result there were closings. Dalhousie University was exempted from the action and as a result of continued provincial government grants and private fund raising efforts and endowments it experienced considerable growth. In Ontario the government stopped all grants to denominational colleges in 1868 but after the University Federation Act of 1887 resumed funding the University of Toronto, with assistance going to those colleges officially affiliated with it. In response Queen's undertook a rigorous fund-raising campaign and greatly enhanced its already impressive endowments.

In Quebec, McGill continued to receive generous support from a variety of private sources including the Carnegie and Rockerfeller Foundations. Laval was officially split into two campuses in 1919. The Montreal campus became the University of Montreal and was granted a charter, receiving provincial government funds as well as church and private contributions.

Demands for more government assistance for universities and colleges began to become more systematic because of the activities of the National Conference of Canadian Universities. At one of its regular meetings the NCCU called for income tax credits for donations given to universities. In 1905 a Royal Commission on the University of Toronto had recommended that half of the province's succession duties should go to university funding. In 1929 another Royal Commission suggested annual grants be made to all nondenominational universities (Harris 1976:361). This was clearly to become the wave of the future.

4. Universities, Politics and the Economy

In Canada political developments have always had profound implications for the entire educational system, including the university. After Canada became an independent nation in 1867 major responsibility for education was in the hands of the provinces. Though Canada developed an educational system with a number of different mixtures and patterns of government, church and private involvement in different provinces, there were some common features. One common characteristic, at least prior to the First World War, was a university sector that was quite small, whose students were primarily drawn from the wealthy and who tended to study the subjects traditionally associated with an Oxford-style education (Ross 1976:40-41). Axelrod (1982) reports that the increasing pace of industrialization that characterized the latter half of the nineteenth century led to reform of the educational system so as to produce students better equipped for the new jobs, but the university sector remained untouched. In Alexrod's words, "universities retained their function of schooling the tiny and privileged elite who would occupy society's leading professions" (1982:11).

According to Axelrod the role of universities in Canadian society was altered radically by the Second World War and the economic boom which followed. During the war universities joined in the war effort in two ways. The first had to do with the ideological and public relations campaigns that tend to surround major war efforts. In addition, for the first time in Canadian history the universities became major centres of research. Working under the auspices of the National Research Council, Canadian universities worked alongside government and private sector researchers to produce an impressive body of knowledge, much of which had direct application to the war effort (Axelrod 1982:18-19).

The immediate postwar era was one of considerable uncertainty as many Canadians feared a return to the economic, social and political instability of the Depression. Several factors prevented any such reoccurrence, factors which also acted as a major stimulus to the expansion of the university sector. As some Canadians began to become concerned about their national identity amid growing American investment, a Royal Commission on the Development of the Arts, Letters and Sciences, the Massey Commission, recommended a greater and expanded role for the university sector. In North America a period of economic expansion was fueled by ripple effects associated with the Marshall Plan, postwar consumer demand, the "baby boom," and growing American investment in Canada. This economic growth was accompanied by a continuation of Keynesian economic policies by various Canadian governments. As a result, government expenditures on education grew steadily as new demands were placed on the universities, not only to educate returning soldiers but to prepare more and more Canadians for the high technology and specialized jobs that had become prevalent in the postwar era.

As the "baby boomers" began to mature, parents increasingly came to see the possibilities of their children having a better life, provided they had an adequate educational preparation. University education increasingly became seen as a route to upward mobility as well as economic and social stability. The emergence of the Cold War and the perceived Soviet superiority in terms of scientific education also spurred Western governments to spend more on education. For the first time in Canadian history attending university became a priority for many Canadians and for their children. The following enrollment data illustrates the trend:

	Total Full -Time	Total Part -Time
1971/72	320,992	151,761
1987/88	486,062	294,503

(Source: *Trends: The Canadian University in Profile*)

This represents an increase of 51 per cent in full-time students and 94 per cent in part-time. During about the same period there was a dramatic increase in the number of females attending Canadian universities. Between 1972/73 and 1987/88 the number of male full-time undergraduates went up 21 per cent, from about 177,000 to 213,000 while the number of female full-time undergraduate students increased from 109,000 to over 215,000, an increase of about 96 per cent.

Female university students in Canada seem to concentrate their studies in certain areas. In 1987-88 more than 60 per cent of undergraduate students in education, fine and applied arts, humanities and health professionals were women. In general arts and science, social science and agricultural and biological science programmes women accounted for more that 50 per cent of students, while in engineering, mathematics and the physical sciences about 25 per cent of students were women. It should be noted that the proportion of degrees granted to women declines the higher the level of the degree. The following data for 1989 illustrate the point.

Field of Study	% of bachelor/first prof degrees to women	% master's degrees to women	% doctoral degrees to women
Education	70	63	46
Humanities	62	57	42
Social Sci.	54	41	42
Agri/Biol Sci.	57	45	27
Math/Phys Sci.			
Engineering/	28	21	16
Appl. Sci.	13	13	6
Health Prof.	71	66	39

In terms of employment and career opportunities after graduation, a report by the department of the Secretary of State, *Profile of Higher Education in Canada* (1991), indicates that in 1987 88 per cent of 1982 college graduates were employed. Eighty nine per cent of 1982 graduates with undergraduate degrees were employed while 91 per cent of master's degree holders and 93 per cent of doctoral degree holders were employed. We have no precise data on whether or not those not employed were voluntarily out of the labour market; however, the report notes that the unemployment level for holders of doctoral and master's degrees was 3 per cent and 4 for those with undergraduate degrees.

It seems that the higher the level of education the greater the chance of securing jobs related to that education. Of those graduating with doctoral degrees in 1982, 98 per cent had work relating to their education and level of qualification in 1987, as compared to 94 per cent with master's degrees and 88 with undergraduate education. Lastly there seems to be a significant degree of satisfaction with educational choices. For example, 81 per cent of doctoral degree holders said that if they faced the same educational decisions again, they would take the same programme, indicating many believed they had made the correct choice.

The geographic and historical realities of Canada presented a potential problem to the idea that the university is the route to a better future. Canada is a nation in which there are distinctive regional patterns of wealth distribution, with more industrialized and populous regions generally enjoying higher standards of income and living. Clearly one's chance of attending university was influenced by the region in which one was born. Though the provinces control education, federal governments have sought to provide some semblance of a national system by attempting to provide equality in terms of the financial resources available for education. As a result, complex agreements to facilitate the transfer of federal moneys earmarked for education were eventually negotiated. The "Federal-Provincial Fiscal Arrangements and Established Programs Act, 1977" formally established these arrangements. Though amended in subsequent years, the system still operates to provide federal money for an area of provincial jurisdiction. In addition the federal government provides assistance to university students through the Canada Student Loan Act of 1964 (Canadian Education Association 1984:38-39). The system that evolved in Canada results in virtually all Canadian universities being dependent to a large measure on provincial and federal governments for funding and financial support at the operational, capital and research levels. The following data illustrate the current situation.

Total University Income (Current $ '000s)

	Gov't/Non-Gov' Grants	Fees	Gifts, Donations	Total
1977/78	1,981,035	328,383	12,391	3,220,021
1987/88	4,201,182	826,970	32,017	5,164,482

It is clear then that in the period after the Second World War universities in Canada took on a more important role in society. Rather than being viewed as the domain of the elite they became part of a system designed to provide all Canadians with an opportunity to attain the highest level of education they were capable of achieving. Such a view of the university both justified and demanded that governments spend money to adequately fund the university system. There were other reasons why the university was important and these had to do with its perceived role of creating new knowledge through the conduct of research.

The issue of the proper mix of teaching and research continues to be an important one. When, for example, decisions are to be made on the allocation of scarce resources for computing, which area has priority? Or is it even possible to argue that one is more important? In a paper at a recent conference on post-secondary education in Canada, R. L. Watts argues that the research and teaching functions are so closely integrated that they cannot be realistically separated for the allocation of priorities. In addition, both are linked, he argues, to the larger social role of the university as a "community service station" of higher learning, cultural transmission and knowledge production (Watts 1987, also see: Adelmann and Lee 1968).

The vision of the university in Canadian society that emerged by the late twentieth century is summarized in a recent statement of the fundamental mission of The University of Regina which captures the essence of how many see the Canadian university:

> A university is committed to the pursuit of truth and beauty; to the free development and exchange and debate of ideas; to careful and stimulating dissemination of knowledge and to scientific and social criticism. Each of these commitments involves teaching, research and service to the community in their various forms. (Academic Review Task Force 1988:6)

The question arises how this mission can be accomplished when the university is obviously connected to the larger structures of society and so dependent on governments and others for financial support. In order to answer this question we need to consider the governance of the Canadian university.

5. University Governance in Canada

The solution, if we can use this strong word, that has been worked out in many Western societies, including Canada, involves a careful structuring of the institution itself and the establishment of traditions and structures that build on the principles of academic autonomy, self-governance and the free dissemination of ideas (Brown 1969; Gorovitz 1967). This point can perhaps be better understood by first viewing some historical patterns and then focusing on the concrete example of the University of Regina.

5.1 Structure and Autonomy in Western Universities

Two different forces had an impact on the evolution of the governing structures of the early universities. As we have seen, both the teachers and the students were able to utilize the prestige of having a university in a community and the associated material benefits to establish a measure of autonomy. Eventually this autonomy resulted in the development of structures of an internal self-government. The precise form that self-government took was itself influenced by the organizational characteristics of the early monasteries. This meant that while there was recognition of a formal hierarchy, there was also a considerable degree of consultation. Though the precise forms varied, the system that emerged eventually was based on "the idea of self-government by the master or teachers . . . as the proper form of university organization" (Ross 1976:161).

The principle of self-government and university autonomy was lost or at least seriously diminished during the post-Reformation period when the universities were in "bondage" (Mulhern 1959:400). The rise of liberalism and eventually the liberal democratic state provided new opportunities for universities to once again free themselves from the state and the church. The liberal ideals of individual freedom and liberty may not have been realized in the actual operation and structures of early industrial society; however, they provided a philosophical framework for the unfettering of human thought (Gamble 1981). The concurrent existence of liberal philosophies, a liberal democratic state, a declining church and an emerging reliance on science all contributed to the spreading of the ideals of a university as a place of free, unfettered, critical and scientific thought.

In Germany and Scotland the traditions of freedom and critical inquiry that characterized earlier universities had not been lost, and these traditions began to reemerge in England and America. The fact that universities were becoming more than just teaching units raised certain structural problems, especially when state financial aid was becoming more important.

A commission, sponsored by the Canadian Association of University Teachers and the Association of Universities and Colleges of Canada, which investigated university government in Canada, noted that the modern mode of university organization began to emerge with the establishment of the

University of London in 1836. The system involved a two-tiered structure in which the non-academic affairs of the university were handled by a board of governors and the academic affairs by the community of scholars associated with the university (1966:12). Ross notes that the legislation which established the University of Manchester in 1870 established three levels of university government: 1) a court made up of the graduates; 2) a council composed of administrative heads and lay people, and some faculty; 3) a senate made up entirely of faculty members.

The formal legislation establishing the University of Toronto in 1906 set up a two-tiered system of university government under which a board of governors was responsible for the overall financial operation and a senate (with faculty councils) was responsible for academic matters. The structures which vest the board with ultimate responsibility and financial control and the senate with jurisdiction over academic matters became the model for most publicly funded universities in Canada. (Ross 1976:168)

The University of Regina emerged as a result of the integration of Regina College with the University of Saskatchewan (Pitsula 1988; Riddell 1974). In 1959 the University of Saskatchewan, Regina Campus, was given degree granting status. As enrollments and programmes continued to grow the campus at Regina became more autonomous. In 1964 a Faculty Council was established and granted the full power accorded such a body under the terms of the University Act in Saskatchewan. Finally on July 1, 1974, under the terms of an Act of the Saskatchewan Legislature, the University of Regina became an autonomous body.

The organizational and administrative model adopted for the University of Regina is a bicameral structure. In essence, the academic and the financial operations of the university are separated as much as possible. On the academic side the British model is in evidence. Although all major academic decisions are ultimately made by University Council, a body composed of all teaching staff (except special lecturers), senior administrators and elected student representatives, much of the "day-to-day" decision-making of council is actually carried on by an elected Executive of Council which represents all parts of the university. All of University Council's decisions are subject to approval of the senate. Senate is a body with broad public representation, some appointed, some elected and some *ex officio*. The teaching activities of the university are organized around faculties, and in some cases departments, which structure the actual curriculum. The teaching and research faculty of the university that comprise the departments and faculties along with the administrative staff, make up the department, faculty and Council committees that make the academic decisions upon which the university's operations depend. The academic operation is overseen by department heads (where applicable), deans and an academic vice-president. The university president presides over meetings of Executive of Council and the full University Council.

A separate set of structures operates on the financial or fiscal side of the operation. A twelve member board of governors, which includes one elected faculty member and six members appointed by the government, oversees the financial operations of the university. The role of the board is essentially financial and not academic, though an absolute separation of the two is impossible. The fact that the government is represented on the board and not the Council means that direct interference in matters academic is made as difficult as possible.

The development of universities in Canada has followed the normal Western pattern; it has been complex and convoluted. The task we now face is beginning to make some sense out of this process, that is, developing some way of explaining and understanding why and how these developments have occurred. This task requires a shift in the focus of our discussion.

6. Social Theory and the Study of Education

In order to fully understand the role of the university in society it is necessary to move beyond descriptions of the historical evolution and development of educational systems. An historical overview such as that presented above should establish the fact that educational systems are part of political, historical, and social structures and thus change and evolve as society does. If we are to understand the nature and causes of these changes and developments as well as contemporary processes such as computerization, we require a broader perspective on the relationship between the educational system and the larger society. This task is complicated by the fact that there are several alternate ways of understanding and explaining this relationship. We will briefly examine two of the more important alternate theoretical perspectives. While little of the literature on education, the educational system and the university actually mentions these theoretical approaches, they inform much of the thinking and analysis which is found in this literature.

6.1 The Functionalist or Consensus Approach

Much of the literature on the social functions or roles of education in general and the school system in particular has been influenced by what we can term the functionalist approach. Reduced to its most salient tenets, the functionalist perspective maintains that we can best understand human society if we think of it as a complex whole composed of many interdependent and interrelated parts. The parts, in turn, are best understood in terms of the functions they perform for the whole. A functionalist typically utilizes an analogy in order to understand human society.

The components that make up a society can be compared to the individual organs that compose a complex organism such as the human body. Social systems and living organisms are deemed to have certain basic needs that must be met if they are to survive. In the organic system the basic needs are met and problems are solved by the various organs. Thus the function of an organ is the problem it solves or the need it meets. As long as problems are solved and needs are met, the system will exist in its normal condition of stability and equilibrium.

Human society is understood as system with basic needs and problems that must be solved if it is to survive, prosper and continue to exist in an orderly fashion. Among the basic problems that a society must solve if it is to survive are cultural transmission, organizing material production, ensuring biological reproduction, looking after the spiritual needs of its members as well as developing some system of social decision making. In a society such as Canada we understand the political, economic, religious, educational and familial institutions in terms of their contributions to solving these basic social problems. A central problem for complex societies is the maintenance of social order and cohesion. As society becomes more complex and differentiated there is an ever-present danger of social conflict and disintegration, and some means of providing for social order and stability is essential. The functionalist perspective maintains that social order is usually based on an accepted, shared and widely held belief or value system which all members of society are taught and internalize into the structures of their personalities.

Societies are understood to have undergone an evolutionary developmental process, over time becoming more complex with differentiated and specialized structures. When examining the educational system a theorist adopting a functionalist perspective will argue that the educational system is best understood as performing a series of functions for society. The precise functions that the educational system will perform will vary from society to society and from historical epoch to historical epoch. Haralambos (1985:175-176) summarizes the essential functions of the educational system in an industrialized society such as Canada as including:

> Socialization of young people to ensure acceptance of the basic value system of society. Education facilitates social order and stability by providing the basis of a value consensus.
>
> In an advanced industrial society great emphasis is placed on achievement. Individuals must understand they are masters of their destiny. By encouraging to achieve and rewarding them when they do the school system fosters an acceptance of an "achievement" oriented ethos.
>
> Since individuals in the classroom learn to compete as equals the school system teaches children about equality of opportunity. In the competition to achieve in the classroom all students have the same basic opportunities and they learn to value competition.
>
> Though all students have the same basic opportunities, they do not perform equally and as a result there are some who achieve more. That superior

performance is rewarded is an important lesson for later life since advanced industrial societies reward meritorious efforts.

> In an advanced industrial society the work force is highly differentiated and specialized and the allocation of individuals into future occupational roles is a major social concern. By beginning the process of evaluating and training potential human resources the school system begins to screen candidates for various jobs and positions. Since not all jobs are equal in terms of their level of difficulty, required skill and training, or functional importance to society, society must develop a system of screening to ensure individuals attain a position commensurate with their skills, talents and personal attributes.

A variation on the functionalist argument is what Randall Collins refers to as the "technological function theory of education" (Collins 1979:12). According to this argument, the development of modern technology has placed new and special demands on the educational system because jobs in modern industrial society require greater and greater amounts of formal education and training. As a result of these technologically driven changes, more students are required to spend more time in the formal educational system that becomes a more and more important part of the overall social structure as society becomes increasingly complex and developed.

While the functionalist approach tends to assume that most existing social practices and institutions perform some useful or necessary function, the approach recognizes the possibility of dysfunctions emerging. It is possible that some element or component of the social system will not function properly or begin to function in a manner that is harmful to social stability and maintenance. Such a condition or process is referred to as being dysfunctional. Imagine an educational system that was not open to all members of society and thus there was no equality of opportunity. If only select members of the population had access to educational opportunities and the educational system thus served to restrict the occupational and social mobility of some members of society we would refer to this as a dysfunctional system. Such is the case if the value system of the society has been "corrupted or infected" with, for example, racist ideas that systematically block entrance to the educational system by some. Such a situation can generally be remedied, the functionalist would argue, by changing the ideas, values and norms that gave rise to the dysfunctionality.

Within the functionalist or consensus approach there is a long tradition of recognizing the difference between manifest and latent functions. The manifest function of an institution or practice is the explicit or recognized function. Latent functions are unanticipated, unrecognized or unintended functions or outcomes of the operation of some institution. An example that is often cited refers to the fact that in some societies religious rituals and practices might actually perform a function quite different from that which is officially recognized. The manifest function of the funeral is to pay respect and to offer prayers and worship on behalf of a deceased while the latent function is actually to provide emotional release and signal that it is now time to end mourning and return to "normal."

The functionalist perspective recognizes the existence of individual inequalities. In complex societies not all individuals will have the same social prestige or status, the same level of material wealth or, within specific institutions, the same degree of power and authority. The explanation for these individual inequalities is based on a complex set of arguments that relates an individual's status, wealth and power to the nature of the task they perform in society. Since some tasks or jobs are more difficult, more important, and require more skill, training and education, it is necessary for society to offer differential levels of rewards in order to motivate individuals to take on these tasks. The educational system plays a central part in the preparation of individuals for a social role that is commensurate with their abilities, aptitudes, and interests. The amount of education will thus generally be strongly correlated with income level.

While this approach recognizes the existence of individual inequalities, it generally assumes that Western industrial societies have developed a political system that prevents these individual inequalities from becoming social inequalities. While individuals may have different levels of income, social prestige or status and different amounts of power, society is based on the principles of egalitarianism when it comes to political or social power. Without reviewing the intricacies of the argument, the assumption is that the basic structures and processes of Western liberal democratic states offer all individuals, regardless of their individual income, status or power positions within an particular institution, an opportunity to participate in the political process through the selection of those who operate the policy (elections) and to influence those individuals through actions such as lobbying.

The functionalist perspective explicitly accepts that within particular institutions, such as the university, there are by necessity some positions which are more important, more difficult and which require the incumbent to have higher levels of skill, training and education. These positions carry with them socially sanctioned rewards in the form of higher income levels, greater social status and prestige and greater power in the form of authority. Not all positions within the university are equal in terms of what the incumbent is required and expected to do or in terms of the rewards received.

It is commonly accepted among thinkers adopting this approach that modern industrial society has become complex, highly structured, and bureaucratic in its basic mode of organization. The educational system is no exception, and thus one will tend to find that most components of the educational system, including the university sector, have developed this mode of formal organization. As such, these institutions will have quite rigid organizational characteristics with established sets of rules, regulations, procedures and hierarchical structures of authority. Within the functionalist literature there is a tendency to accept this as inevitable, especially given the overall complexity of society (Shepard 1990:275).

6.2 Conflict Approach

The major alternate paradigm or theoretical approach that has been important in the analysis of the educational system is located within what we will call the conflict perspective. Prior to discussing how this particular approach addresses the issue of the educational system and the university we will briefly outline its essential tenets.

Those adopting the conflict perspective generally operate from within a materialist approach. Stated simply, this means they assume that before you can have an on-going stable human society you must first solve the basic human problem of physical survival; that is, there must be material production and distribution. Put more starkly, before there can be religion, education, politics, culture, art, music or even a family, there must be material production and distribution. How material production and distribution are organized will be a primary influence shaping the structures of the entire society and all its institutions. The materialist social analysis thus always begins with an examination of how material production and distribution are organized and structured.

When conflict theorists have engaged in an analysis of the material basis of Western capitalist society they have tended to conclude that it is a class-based society. Classes within this analytical tradition are understood in terms of different structural positions within the productive processes. Income derives from market position assets held and brought to the market. Those in possession of capital come to the market with distinctive structural advantages and are able, by virtue of their ownership position, to claim a much larger share of the society's economic surplus than those coming to the market with only their labour to sell.

Associated with the different class positions, conflict theorists argue, are differential relationships of power. It is not just that some classes enjoy higher levels of income and as a result greater life chances, they also hold more power. Those with capital are in a position to make fundamental decisions about the economic direction of society. It is the owners of the economic institutions who decide if jobs are to be created or lost, if plants are to expand or contract. Economic power, this perspective holds, is directly connected to the class structure. In addition, conflict theorists tend to argue that where there are relations of power there is domination. Those who make the fundamental decisions concerning economic activity, employment and such comprise the core of a dominant class.

As was noted above, the functionalist approach views institutions largely in terms of the functions they perform for society as a whole. Conflict theory also tends to view institutions in terms of the functions they perform, but there is a radical difference in how these social functions are understood, as it is assumed that institutions function in the interests of the dominant class rather than society as a whole. While both perspectives assume institutions perform functions, they provide radically different answers to the question "In whose interests?" Prior to specifically addressing the issue of education, a further brief comment on the issue of power is required.

Functionalists view power within institutions as legitimate authority with differential levels necessary for the functioning of the institution and as a reward. From the perspective of the conflict theorists, because power is inherent to the class relations which are at the core of capitalist society, power relations permeate all aspects of society. This is nowhere more apparent than in the functioning of the state. Though there are numerous differences among conflict theorists about precisely how it occurs, there is agreement that the state in liberal democratic society is far from democratic and not always liberal. The common assumption is that, in the long run at least, the state in capitalist society tends to operate in the interests of the economically dominant class. Some have argued that the state's major functions relate to facilitating profitable capital accumulation, legitimizing the system and providing coercive support of the system if it is ever threatened.

The very name applied to this approach, the conflict perspective, suggests one last characteristic worthy of note. Given the fact that those adopting this perspective assume that relations of class domination are inherent in capitalist society, it is not difficult to understand why they also assume that conflict is inherent. Where there is a dominant class they would argue, there will be by definition a subordinate class. Where there are relations of domination and subordination, there is the potential for conflict. Since conflict may threaten the system, and with it the privileged position of the dominant class, that class will attempt to alleviate and deflect conflict. It has been argued that ideological control or manipulation is among the strategies which the ruling class adopts in its efforts to prevent or control conflict. Used in this context, ideological control refers to efforts to promulgate various belief, value and normative systems which justify and legitimate the *status quo*. In addition, beliefs and values that internally divide subordinate classes and groupings are useful in retaining control. The tolerance of, and even promotion of, racist and sexist ideas might be a case of beliefs that serve to divide various members of subordinate classes and lessen the chance of broadly based oppositional politics.

A central concept employed by those operating within the conflict tradition is contradiction. Although this term has been subject to seemingly endless philosophical and theoretical discussion, a simple definition will be sufficient here. Contradictions are those tensions and dynamics which stem from the very structure and logic of a system or structure. An example might be the notion of equality within the context of a class-based society. There is, this perspective would hold, a fundamental contradiction between a system that is based on the ideals of equality and on a set of market relations that ensures the perpetuation of systemic inequality.

When applied to the educational system, the conflict approach has tended to examine the ways in which the school system serves the interests of the dominant class. A classic statement of the conflict approach to education is Samuel Bowes and Herbert Gintis' *Schooling in Capitalist America* (1976). In this volume Bowes and Gintis focus on the ideological role of the school system, arguing that it operates as a powerful agent of socialization, instilling in students a set of beliefs, values and attitudes that systematically fosters the continuation of the system. Students are methodically taught a variety of values ranging from valuing competition to submitting to authority and observing punctuality. In addition to the formal curriculum, which is essential in terms of providing a work force for the employment by the dominant class in a technological era, the entire "hidden curriculum" molds the personalities of future workers in an appropriate manner.

The fact that the educational system is organized along bureaucratic lines means it is more like the hierarchical world in which students will subsequently be employed. A literate student who accepts hierarchical organizations and their accompanying relations of authority, values competition, and who is individualistic, aggressive and competitive is indeed well suited to meet the needs of the capitalist labour market.

6.3 Alternate views of the University

If we now apply these alternate views to the specific role, function, structures and operation of the university we will come up with different interpretations and explanations of its structures and operations.

6.3.1 Functionalist / Consensus Approach

The university is seen as one of the final steps in the educational system, completing the long preparation of the student for her or his role in society. By the time a student graduates from university she or he will have encountered the basic stock of knowledge that represents the core values of the culture. The student may or may not leave the university with specific employment-oriented skills and knowledge; however, it is expected that he or she is educated. An essential function of the university is the transmission of the central values, knowledge base and intellectual traditions of the society.

The consensus approach will maintain that the university is more than a teaching institution. In addition to transmitting knowledge, the university is the site of scholarly activity and research—knowledge production. The research activity that is carried on at the university may be applied in its orientation; however, there is a much greater chance that it is pure. University research in the natural sciences, the social sciences and humanities and the fine arts tends to be governed by an abiding commitment to uncover and discover the truth.

As a complex institution, the university will be governed by the same principles and logic that operate in society at large. There will be, by necessity, relationships of authority. There will be an internal structure of unequal reward allocation, with an individual's level of income, status and authority determined by the socially recognized rewards appropriate for that position.

Those in important positions which carry greater responsibilities and pressures and which require additional specific skills and training will receive income, status and authority that is commensurate with their position.

6.3.2 Conflict Approach

Individuals analyzing the university, its roles, structures and operation from the conflict perspective will tend to see quite a different set of structures and processes. The university, they will argue, exhibits and manifests all of the contradictions inherent in a class-structured society. While the ideals of the liberal university—open, free, courageous and open to critical inquiry and instruction—will be deemed laudable, the argument that will be presented suggests that these are seldom realized. The university might be seen as formally and officially advocating one set of important values, while in reality operating as a typical hierarchical bureaucratic formal organization. The key challenge for the university is to overcome the limitations of the past and to seek to truly operationalize the unrealized ideals of a Western university.

Teaching at the university, this more radical approach might suggest, should be innovative and critical. Rather than merely presenting the society's accumulated stocks of knowledge, the university should facilitate a critical and constant reevaluation of that knowledge. The educated person should be the critic, constantly reexamining and reevaluating all aspects of her being.

To the extent that universities have become hierarchical bureaucracies, they will have to change their modes of organization and operation in order to realize the values that they purport to uphold. Efforts must be undertaken to make the university a model of a social institution which is broadly democratic and open to the participation of all its components. Rather than mirroring the hierarchical structures of a class society, the university should be the site of open and participatory democratic politics. If the radical ideals of participatory democracy are to be realized anywhere in a class society, it is within the university that they have the greatest chance.

While the entire educational system may be seen as functioning to produce and reproduce the class structures of society, the university can break this mold. The ideals of academic freedom must be truly realized and the university should use the "space" provided in its historical position to maintain and encourage critical, innovative and even radical thought while avoiding becoming just another institution in the service of the dominant class (Bowes and Gintis 1976 :Ch. 10).

Among the most important developments in critical thought in recent years has been the rise of feminist theory. As Rosemary Tong (1989) makes clear there are a number of different streams of feminist thought. Despite the significant differences, most feminists would argue that much social science theorizing has been fundamentally flawed because is has emanated from, to borrow Mary O'Brien's term, "male stream thought" (O'Brien 1981:5, 62). Nowhere, some have argued, is this more apparent than in the literature on the university which has tended to ignore the role of the university in the perpetuation of sexist and patriarchal social structures. In the last decade a growing literature has addressed this issue.

Among the central issues raised by those influenced by feminist thought is the participation of women in Canadian universities. We have noted that participation rates, especially in undergraduate programmes, have risen, though graduate education is still dominated by men. In terms of university teaching, males still dominate. Between 1976/77 and 1986/87 there was a 36 per cent increase in the number of women faculty; however in terms of proportions this only meant an increase of 14.4 per cent to 17.6. The other side of the coin is obvious; in 1986/87, 82.4 per cent of university faculty were males. Partly because of the recent entrance of many women into the academy, we find women concentrated in the lower end of the rankings. In 1886/87 only 6.4 per cent of full professors were women as compared to 16.5 and 29.4 per cent for associate professors and assistant professors respectively. In the category of "other", referring to lecturers, special appointments, term appointments, *etc.* women were 41.7 per cent (*Trends* :82).

Without doubt, the reasons for this situation are complex and defy simple explanation; nevertheless, feminist thinkers have pointed out that the existing analytical approaches, such as those described above, are incapable of adequately dealing with what they would see as systemic and systematic discrimination against women. Some might even refer to the situation women face in the university as part of the larger process of the subordination and oppression of women (Barett 1980). Feminists are calling for alternate modes of theorizing society and the role of the educational system in structuring unequal relations based on sex and gender. What is required, this argument holds, is a radically new more of thinking about society and all its institutions and practices.

7. Summary and Conclusions

The next chapter examines the impact on individuals and institutions, and social implications of the transformations brought on by the computerization process. The chapters which follow take up and discuss in detail a number of specific issues relating to the computerization of Canadian universities, particularly issues in university teaching, research and the administrative functions; future trends in computer technology are also dealt with.

The discussions that follow make it clear that if we are to understand these processes we need to understand how the university fits into and relates to the larger social structures. In addition, the analyses which these subsequent chapters present illustrate the need to be aware of the different theoretical perspectives employed by people to understand the university. In this chapter we have presented some of the historical processes that produced the current structures that characterize the university system in Canada. We also reviewed two of the major theoretical approaches that have been employed in understanding and interpreting the role of the university in society. Since many of the issues we address remain controversial and subject to debate and disagreement, it is hoped that these introductory comments will serve to clarify the bases of the disagreements.

References

Academic Review Task Force. *From Reflection to Renewal: Report of the Academic Review Task Force.* Regina: University of Regina, Oct. 1988.

Adelman, C.G. and L.L. Lee (ed.) *The University Game*. Toronto: Anansi, 1968

Atkinson C. and E.T. Meleska. *The Story of Education*. Philadelphia: Chilton Books, 1956

Audet, Louis-Philippe. "Attempts to Develop a School System for Lower Canada: 1760-1840". In Donald Wilson, Robert Stamp and Louis-Philippe Audet (ed.) *Canadian Education: A History*. Scarborough: Prentice Hall, 1970.

Axelrod, P. *Scholars and Dollars: Politics, Economics and the Universities of Ontario 1945-1980*. Toronto: University of Toronto Press, 1982.

Barrett, Michele. *Women's Oppression Today*. London: Verso, 1980.

Bercuson, D.J., R. Bothwell, and J.L. Granatstein. *The Great Brain Robbery*. Toronto: McClelland and Stewart, 1984.

Bowes, S. and H. Gintis. *Schooling in Capitalist America*. New York: Basic Books, 1976.

Boyd, W. *The History of Western Education.* London: A and C Black Limited, 1928.

Brown. J.D. *The Liberal University*. New York: McGraw-Hill, 1969.

Burton, A. *The Horn and the Beanstock.* Toronto: Holt, Rinehart and Winston, 1972.

Canadian Education Association. *An Overview of Canadian Education*. Toronto: Canadian Education Association, 1984.

Carnoy, M. *Schooling in Capitalist America*.New York: David McKay Company 1972.

Chapman, J.W. *The Western University on Trial*. Berkeley: University of California Press, 1983.

Collins, Randall. *The Credential Society*. New York: Academic Press, 1979.

Coole, Diana. *Women in Political Theory*. Hartfordshire: Harvester Wheatsheaf, 1988.

Department of Secretary of State of Canada. *Profile of Higher Education in Canada*. Ottawa: Ministry of Supply and Services, 1991.

Duchemin, L.A. *The Challenge to Our Universities*. Sackville: Mount Saint Allison Publication, 1958.

Gamble, A. *An Introduction to Modern Social and Political Thought*. London: Macmillan Press, 1981.

Gorovitz, S. (ed.). *Freedom and Order in the University*. Cleveland: The Press of Western Reserve University, 1967.

Habermas, J. "The Idea of the University: Learning Processes". In S.W. Nicholsen (ed.) *The New Conservatism* . Cambridge: MIT Press, 1989.

Hamilton, William. "Society and Schools in Nova Scotia". In Donald Wilson, Robert Stamp and Louis-Philippe Audet (ed.), *Canadian Education: A History*. Scarborough: Prentice Hall, 1970.

Haralambos, M. *Sociology: Themes and Perspectives.* London: Bell and Hyman, 1985.

Harris, R. *A History of Higher Education in Canada 1663-1960.* Toronto: University of Toronto Press, 1976.

Hofstader, R. *Academic Freedom in the Age of the College.* New York: Columbia University Press, 1955.

Irvine, R. "Newman Revisited: the Ideal of a University." *New Zealand Journal of Educational Studies* 23.1 (1988) 3-14.

Lam, Y.L. (ed.). *Canadian Public Education System.* Calgary: Detselig Enterprises, 1990.

Livingstone, D. *Social Crisis and Schooling.* Toronto: Garamound, 1985.

Marcuse, H. *Reason and Revolution.* New York: Oxford University Press, 1941.

Metzer, W.P. *Academic Freedom in the Age of the University.* New York: Columbia University Press, 1955.

Mifflen, F.J and S.C. Mifflen (ed.). *The Sociology of Education.* Calgary: Detselig Enterprises, 1982.

Millett, J.D. *The Academic Community.* New York: McGraw-Hill Book Company, 1962.

Millett, J.D. *Conflict in Higher Education.* San Francisco: Jossey-Bass Publications, 1984.

Mulhern, J. *A History of Education.* New York: The Ronald Press, 1959.

Murphey, R. *Sociological Theories of Education.* Toronto: McGraw Hill Ryerson, 1979.

O'Brien, Mary. *The Politics of Reproduction.* Boston: Routledge and Kegan Paul, 1981.

Phillips, C.E. *The Development of Education in Canada.* Toronto: W.J. Gage and Company, 1957.

Pitsula, J. *An Act of Faith.* Regina: Canadian Plains Research Center, 1988.

Prentice, A. *The School Promoters.* Toronto: McClelland and Stewart, 1977.

Raleigh, Walter. *The Meaning of the University.* Freeport: Books for Libraries Press Inc., 1911.

Riddell, W.A. *The First Decade.* Regina: University of Regina, 1974.

Ross, M.R. *The University: The Autonomy of Academe.* New York: McGraw-Hill, 1976.

Sheeham, N. "Indoctrination: Moral Education in the Early Prairie School". In D. Jones, A. Sheeham and M. Stamp (ed.), *Shaping the Schools of the Canadian West.* Calgary: Detselig Enterprises, 1979.

Shepard, Jon. M. *Sociology.* St. Paul: West Publishing Company, 1990.

Tong, Rosemarie. *Feminist Thought.* Boulder: Westview Press, 1989.

Trends: The Canadian University in Profile. Ottawa: Association of Universities and Colleges of Canada, 1990.

Watts, R.L. "The Challenges and Opportunities Facing Post-Secondary Education in Canada". In *The Forum Papers.* Halifax: Institute for Research on Public Policy, 1987.

Wexler, P. *Social Analysis of Education.* London: Routledge and Kegan Paul, 1987.

Wilson, J.D., R.S. Stamp and L.P. Audet (ed.). *Canadian Education: A History.* Scarborough: Prentice Hall, 1970.

CHAPTER 2

THE PROCESS OF COMPUTERIZATION AT THE UNIVERSITY

How should a university decision-maker approach computerization? In this report we assume that the decision to computerize has been made. We waive the question of whether or not to computerize at all (although in some circumstances that may be a valid question—resources put elsewhere could, in some places, be better utilized). Our question is how to make computerization effective. Therefore decision-makers need to be able to anticipate potential consequences.

We also assume a situation of managed (or at least semi-managed) change. That is, we assume that the university will follow a plan in its process of computerization. Today's situation is complex and careful planning is necessary to avoid inefficiency and the waste of scarce resources. The purpose of this design model is to permit university decision-makers elsewhere to comprehend and learn from the North American experience. To do this one must understand the process of change involved in university computerization.

Unfortunately, there are many misconceptions about computers. Advertising hype, the claims of enthusiasts, and their own misunderstandings have given many people unrealistic expectations as to what computers can do. To dispel these misconceptions we have to look at the way people speak about computers.

The language we use shapes and defines issues and problems. Two metaphors are often used to describe the relationship between technology and society, in general, and the process of computerization, in particular. The first of these, "social impact," is a metaphor of collision. Technology is described as hitting or penetrating society. As usually used, this metaphor implies that technology is the active agent of change and that people passively respond. Implicit in "social impact" is technological determinism. Technology is seen as the driving force in society, or as one prominent writer put it, "technological change induces or 'motors' social change" (Mesthene 1970:26). Technology is in the driver's seat. All one needs to do, it is often assumed, is to purchase the right computer system and the hoped-for benefits will automatically follow.

In the past ten years another metaphor has appeared, a "seamless web" of the technical and the social (Bijker, Hughes & Pinch 1987). In this view, technology and society are not seen as separate entities in collision but as one sociotechnical system. Most of those who use this metaphor emphasize the scientist, the engineer, or the administrator as a decision-maker who actively builds networks tying together various technical and social elements. According to this way of thinking, the university decision-maker must weave together technical components with people's needs and interests, enlisting both into the plan for computerization.

What difference does this make to the university decision-maker contemplating plans for computerization? This chapter will begin with an examination of the concepts of "social impact" and "seamless web," and then look at selected issues and problems in the process of computerization itself.

1. Social Impact or Seamless Web?

1.1 The Ogburn Legacy

The relationship between society and technology has been one of the central questions in sociology since it arose out of the 19th century industrial revolution. Marxism, in particular, has focused on the role technology plays in society. In North America, however, the person who was the most influential in this discourse was the American sociologist William Fielding Ogburn (1886-1959). Ogburn and his associates (known as the "Ogburn School") flourished from the late 1920's to the late 1950's but their way of thinking continues today.

A functionalist (see Chapter 1), Ogburn entrenched the metaphor "social impact" in North American discourse. His main idea became known as "cultural lag theory." Its central thesis was that technology induces changes into society more rapidly than the culture and other institutions can adjust, creating a "lag." The Ogburn School made four arguments to support this idea.

First, they argued that technology causes social change. As Ogburn put it: "In order of time, the invention comes first and the changes in society follow, and secondly . . . these changes frequently require time before they develop into real readjustments to the demands of the invention" (1946:5). In saying "demands of the invention," Ogburn implied that there is a certain "logic" inherent in how a machine is used. Technology may be employed in a number of ways, but each choice involves *inevitable* consequences. "Man may," he argued, "exercise a relative freedom in choosing how to use an invention, but if he uses it at all, it will entail its own social effect of which he is necessarily the servant" (1946:10). All this implies a mechanical conception of cause and effect. Technology is the active agent, the "cause," and it interacts with people in a linear, often unidirectional, manner. The language used by this approach reflects this. The connection between technological innovation and what happens in society is compared variously to "the links in a chain" (Ogburn 1957:22), or "the play on the billiard table" (Ogburn 1957:20). A technical innovation is seen as having a direct or primary impact, which is usually the function it was intended to perform. Rippling out from this direct impact are a series of derivative, or secondary, effects which may in turn cause further derivative, or tertiary, effects, and so on (see Figure 1). Thus the causal relationship may become quite complex as one moves to more distant or higher order consequences. In other words, to speak of "social impact" is to speak in the language of technological determinism.

Figure 1

Social Impact Model

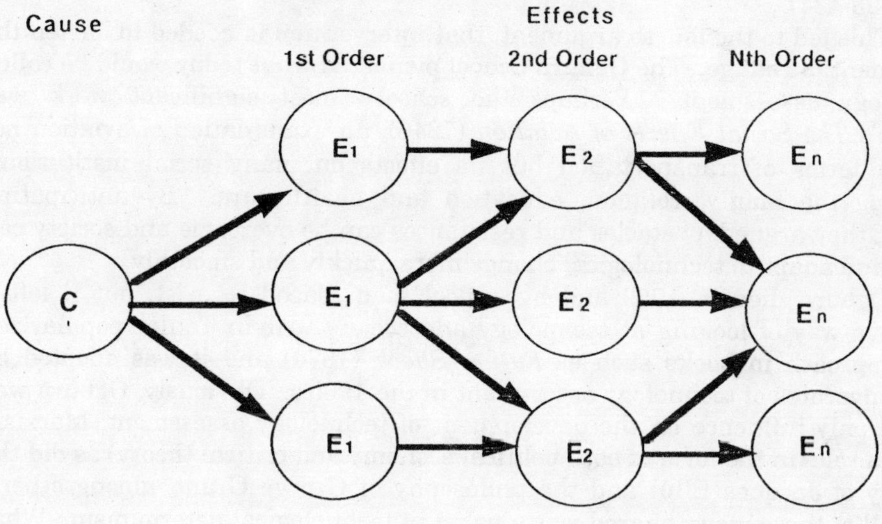

The second argument is that the pace of change is accelerating. Ogburn claimed that societies are "an accumulation of learned ways of behaving" (1964:24). He put great emphasis on the state of the art as a determining factor in the pace of invention. An invention, he said, was the product of a combination of various existing elements. As material culture accumulates, there are more elements to be combined and the rate of invention increases. The state of the art of material culture thus acts in a way analogous to compound interest: "As the amount of interest paid an investor is a function of the size of the capital he has invested, so the number of inventions is a function of the size of the cultural base, that is, the number of existing elements in the culture" (Ogburn 1964:25). As a society develops, its material culture accumulates, the state of the art expands, the rate of technological innovation increases, and the velocity of social change accelerates. As a result, the pace of accumulation in the material culture accelerates even further, beginning the cycle again.

Third, the Ogburn School argued that since technology causes social change, and the pace of change is accelerating, a lag appears between technical innovation and cultural adjustment. As Ogburn put it: "Where one part of culture changes first, through some discovery or invention, and occasions changes in some part of culture dependent upon it, there frequently is a delay in the changes occasioned in the dependent part of the culture" (1950:201). The reason for the lag was seen in the "obstacles" or "resistances" to technological innovation. These obstacles could be economic, psychological, or social (Nimkoff 1957:56-71). The consequences of cultural lag were seen as potentially disastrous. As Hornell Hart said, "If technology inevitably develops faster than social science, then the problems of social control will become ever more huge, while the means of control will progress far less rapidly than the need" (1957:433-434).

This led to the fourth argument, that intervention is needed to hasten the adjustment to change. The Ogburn School pioneered what today would be called technology assessment. Perhaps the school's most significant work was Ogburn's *The Social Effects of Aviation* (1946), an examination of aviation not only in terms of transportation but its effects on many social institutions, including the family, religion, education and health care. By anticipating change, they argued, obstacles and resistances can be overcome and society can adjust and adapt to technological change more quickly and smoothly.

Ogburn died in 1959 and his school soon ceased to exist, but it left a pervasive way of looking at technology and society. Alvin Toffler popularized their approach in books such as *Future Shock* (1970) and it was adopted by many advocates of technology assessment in the 1960's. Obviously, Ogburn was not the only influence on the development of technology assessment: Marxism played a role (in the form of both political economy and critical theory) as did the theology of Jacques Ellul and the philosophy of George Grant, among others. What all of these views shared was a belief in technological determinism. What changed in the sixties was a growing suspicion, doubt, and fear of technology. "Technology is out of control" became a common theme, a theme which is still prominently featured in titles such as *FastForward and Out of Control: How Technology is Changing Your Life* (Menzies 1989). Technology assessment gained impetus, then, not only for policy advisers concerned about long range planning but with many political groups as well, especially the growing environmental movement. As technology assessment became institutionalized in the 1970's it was divided into two components or subdisciplines, environmental impact assessment and social impact assessment, the titles of which reflected the pervasive understanding of the relationship between technology and change. Ogburn's work may be neglected today, but his legacy continues in the way in which both critics and champions speak about technology and society.

1.2 Contemporary Approaches

In the 1980's the social impact metaphor came under increasing criticism. A new generation of sociologists of science and technology appeared who challenged the Ogburn legacy. If technological determinism were correct, these theorists argue, the task of computerization would be relatively easy. Once an assessment revealed what the impacts of computers would be, it would simply be a matter of allocating resources and waiting for the anticipated benefits. Instead, they argue, experience reveals that the process is far more complex. They give a couple of reasons for this.

When analyzing policy alternatives, administrators need to anticipate their potential consequences. Believers in technological determinism claim that they can make the job easier. If, as Ogburn assumed, technology is the controlling factor, and if it produces "impacts" in the same manner as a billiard ball or chain reaction, then accurate forecasts of future results are simply a process of employing a sufficiently sophisticated predictive methodology. The problem, charge the critics, is that this approach has not been able to deliver the goods (Dublin 1989). In spite of well developed quantitative *and* qualitative methods, a standard reference work on technology assessment is forced to admit that "methodological sophistication contributes little to the accuracy of forecasts" (Porter *et al.* 1980:112). Simple extrapolations or judgement calls are as accurate as the most complex models and simulations. They add: "Basic core assumptions, not derivable from methodology, are the major determinants of forecast accuracy. When the core assumptions are valid, the choice of method is either obvious or secondary. When they are wrong, methodology can make little difference" (Porter *et al.* 1980:112). The implication is that *values* rather than *method* are the key to "prediction."

The various methodologies for prediction rely upon extrapolations of present trends or simulation of the current system. As soon as something unanticipated enters the picture, these sorts of projections will be thrown off. This problem, claim the critics, is inherent in predictive methodology. Either the forecast is based solely on current data and trends, and therefore cannot encompass anything new, or assumptions about changes are introduced into the model by the researchers. But if that is done, the whole exercise is only as good as those assumptions. Similarly, as soon as recommendations are made they become part of the information upon which people base their decisions. Whatever inferences and extrapolations are made, whatever trends discerned, they are liable to change simply because people now know about them. Forecasting, the critics charge, therefore becomes an exercise in self-fulfilling or self-defeating prophecy. A good guess made by a person with experience and common sense is as likely to be accurate as the most complicated methodology. What matters is not method but the responsibility of recommendations. Decision-makers should not be in the business of "predicting" the future but participating in creating it.

But, they add, trying to predict the "impact" of technology is not the only way to speak of the relationship between the technical and the social. Like any technology, computers are more than machinery. They form part of what Arnold Pacey (1983:6) calls "technology practice," a human activity involving technical aspects (machines and the knowledge and skills of how to make and operate them), organizational aspects (the organizational structures and economics of using them), and cultural aspects (the goals, norms, beliefs, and values surrounding the machines and their use). All three of these aspects are interwoven, influencing and shaping each other (see Figure 2). According to this scheme, cultural and organizational aspects shape the technical as much as the limits and capabilities of the machines affect the organizations and people who use them. Technical changes bring with them assumptions of interpersonal change, and also changes to the social organization of higher education. Computers mean changes to communication, work habits, and the distribution of resources (Kiesler and Sproull 1987:28). Discussion of university computerization must therefore address all three aspects of technology practice. Indeed, all three are so closely bound together that the recent literature (Bijker, Hughes, & Pinch 1987) uses the term "seamless web" to describe their interaction.

Figure 2
Technology Practice

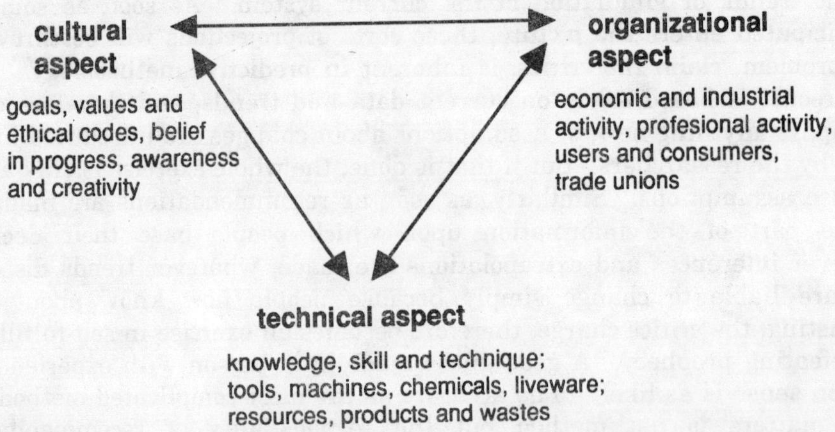

adapted from: Pacey (1983: 6)

Several theories have developed which use the metaphor "seamless web." Two of the most important are the Social Construction of Technology (SCOT) associated with Wiebe Bijker and Trevor Pinch and the actor-network theory of Michael Callon and Bruno Latour.

The central idea of SCOT is that the nature of technology is decided by a network of interested parties. A network of participants and sponsors determines what will be invented, what is important about a given technology, how it will be marketed or distributed, how it should be evaluated, and how it might be improved. This analysis results in a model which sees the relationship between the technical and the social as a web of interactions and conflicts as each group, in pursuing its interests, seeks to define the technology. Structuring the network's interactions is a "technological frame." According to Bijker:

> A technological frame is composed of, to start with, the concepts and techniques employed by a community in its problem solving. . . . Problem solving should be read as a broad concept, encompassing within it the recognition of what counts as a problem as well as the strategies available for solving the problems and the requirements a solution has to meet. This makes a technological frame into a combination of current theories, tacit knowledge, specialized testing procedures, goals, and handling and using practice. (1987:168)

This frame surrounds technology, defines it, and gives it meaning. Bijker emphasizes that the frame is interactional: "Frames are located *between* actors, not *in* actors or *above* actors" (1987:172).

Figure 3 shows how SCOT works. Connected to any artifact are a number of social groups, who may be inventors, developers, sponsors, or users. Each group will have one or more problems *vis-a-vis* the technology and each problem may have several solutions, some of which may involve additional artifacts. Note that some groups will share the same problem, several problems may have the same solution, and one artifact may be involved in several solutions. Analysis may begin at any point in the network. So, to take a very simple example, university professors are users of personal computers. Some have a problem. Their computers can generate beautiful graphics which they would like to use in the classroom, but which they have no means of displaying to their students. There are several possible solutions, such as physically moving the computer into the classroom or printing the graphics and making slides for an overhead projector. Another solution involves using an additional artifact, a recently developed large screen projection system. How computer graphics come to be used in the classroom is thus a complex web of interactions involving not only computers and professors, but the marketers of projection systems, university administrators controlling finances, and perhaps the developers of rival technologies to the projection system, such as LCD pallets for overhead projectors, or software firms offering custom slide development.

Figure 3

Social Construction of Technology

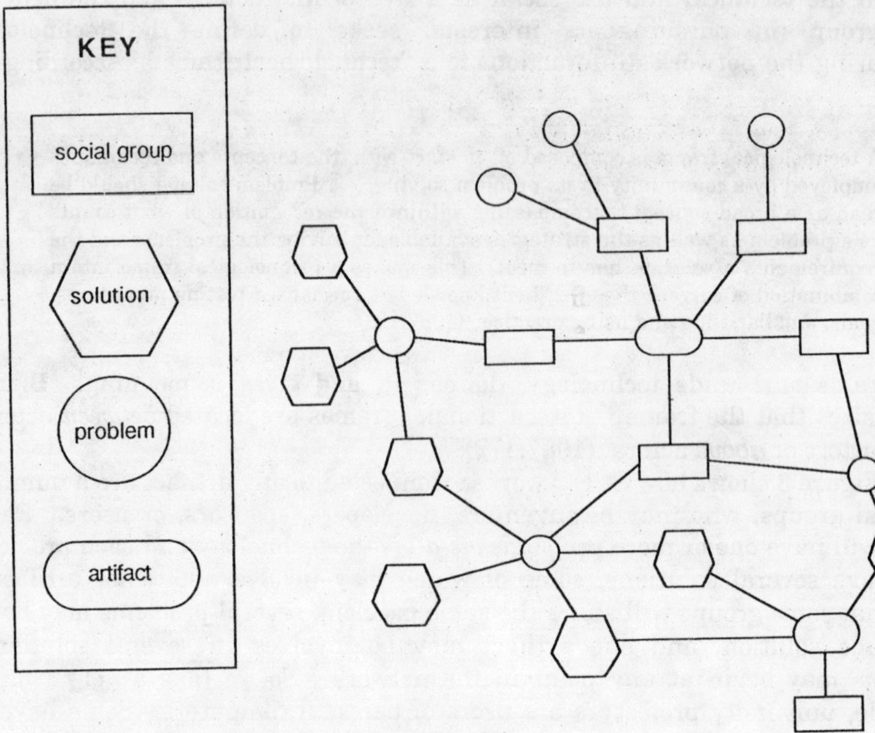

adapted from: Pinch & Bijker (1987: 37)

Closely related to SCOT is actor-network theory. Callon and Latour also see technology as a network, but unlike Bijker and Pinch they do not give the social a privileged position. "Nature" is as much a part of the network as are people. Thus, in an example used by Latour (1987), the attempt by the research team at Data General to develop the Eclipse MV/8000 computer involved a network of not only their company's marketing and finance departments and the rival Digital Equipment Corporation and its VAX 11/780, but also a balky debugging programme and uncertain PAL microchips. So to Callon and Latour, a network builder is a "heterogeneous engineer," that is, an actor (especially an inventor, scientist, or administrator) who weaves together a network of people and technical components. As Callon puts it:

> The actor network is reducible neither to an actor alone nor to a network. Like networks it is composed of a series of heterogeneous elements, animate and inanimate, that have been linked to one another for a certain period of time. . . . But the actor network . . . should not be confused with a network linking in some predictable fashion elements that are perfectly well defined and stable, for the entities it is composed of, whether natural or social, could at any moment redefine their identity and mutual relationships in some new way and bring new elements into the network. An actor network is simultaneously an actor whose activity is networking heterogeneous elements and a network that is able to redefine and transform what it is made of. (1987:93)

Networks are thus unstable, and network building is largely an ability to control resources and enlist allies. In other words, sociotechnical systems (these authors do not speak separately of technology and society) are developed out of heterogeneous elements, including theories, machines, and people; therefore, struggles over technology are seen as efforts by proponents of different networks to force their own constructions on others. Or as Latour put it, scientific and technological controversies are "made by someone building a network over someone else who stands in the way" (1987:259).

To both of these theories, then, computerization is not a matter of installing some machines and waiting for their impact; it is more like building a network. The decision-maker is confronted with diverse groups and individuals within the university, each having their own problems and interests in regards to computerization, and each will have different technical requirements. All are likely to press their claim on university resources, and offer conflicting solutions for the same problem. There may be political and moral conflicts as well (Pinch & Bijker 1987:35ff). The decision-maker must "translate" (Latour 1987) all these technical requirements, interests, and conflicts into the university's plan for computerization. That is, each of the people involved must come to see her or his own needs as being met by the technology which the university is able to provide (technically and financially). Only when the university decision-maker has woven together various technical components with people's needs and interests, enlisting both into the plan for computerization, will computers be effectively integrated into the university.

Thus the differences between the metaphors "social impact" and "seamless web" are substantial and significant. Each encapsulates a different way of thinking about the relationship between technology and society and each implies a different approach to the process of computerization. To speak of "social impact" is to regard society as a passive object and technology as the determining force. Technology is described in words implying its autonomy—technology is the cause; it has effects upon society; it is a motor force. The language does not impute actor status for society; that is, technology, not society, is described as the agent of change. To speak of "seamless web" implies that society is an active network of interests, conflicts, and resources which shapes technology as much as technology shapes it. Emphasis is placed upon people as actors, while technology is more often seen as a resource, something which aids (or hinders) their actions. Both theories stress the aspect of control in technology. With "social impact," technology is either "in control" or "out of control"; with "seamless web," technology is a "means of control." For the theories around "social impact," the main question is prediction. Once a technology is chosen, how can we anticipate the cascade of effects it will bring, either to ameliorate the undesirable consequences or to hasten adjustment to the beneficial ones? For the theories using "seamless web," the main question is power, understood as the means by which people control resources and recruit allies in building networks to achieve their interests.

Disputes between those who use these different metaphors are sharp, and in several ways are an extension of the theoretical antagonisms described in Chapter 1. The members of the Ogburn School were functionalists, and most of those who share their legacy accept the assumptions of the consensus approach. The relationship between the conflict approach as described in Chapter 1 and the group of "seamless web" theories described here is ambiguous, and they differ in a number of important ways. But both assume society is conflictual and see power as a central issue (albeit they may conceptualize power differently). As we begin examination of the process of computerization in the university, we have to keep the controversies between these approaches in mind. This chapter will usually describe the process of computerization as building a network, but when necessary both conflict and consensual approaches will be recounted, particularly where they lead to sharply differing analyses.

2. The Process of Computerization

2.1 Dimensions of the Task

Computerization is not an easy task. There is no simple formula or "one right way" to go about computerization. It is a long process of consultation and negotiation, made particularly difficult by two problems. First, if we look at it as building a network, university computerization should not be seen as a predictable process involving stable and well-defined entities (Callon 1987:93). Computer technology changes rapidly, as do people's needs and perceptions of their needs. A machine or software package which would have satisfied a department last year may not be as acceptable if this year's newest release is seen to have greater capacity. A group which previously showed little interest in (or even resistance to) computers may begin demanding resources if they start to perceive a technical solution to *their* problems. Meeting one group's needs may create demands for equity from those who feel that resources are shared unfairly. Economic restraints may mean that some planned-for technology is out of reach, or shifting prices may create a "windfall" if more (in numbers or capacity) can be purchased than was expected. Government regulations may require changes to computer systems in order to provide information or comply with tax or labour laws. The network will be constantly shifting as both its technical components and people's needs and perceptions change.

The second problem is, somewhat ironically, resistance to change. Universities are like most large organizations in having a high degree of inertia. The institution's system of control is built upon hierarchies of power and prestige which resist change (Lewis 1982:1207). At the same time, universities are ideologically committed to innovation and "new ideas." This creates a paradox. Donald Schon, in a groundbreaking study of innovation in large organizations, described this paradox in terms fully applicable to today's universities:

> Resistance to change is not only normal but in some ways even desirable. An organization totally devoid of resistance to change would fly apart at the seams. It *must* be ambivalent about radical technical innovation. It *must* both seek it out and resist it. Because of commitments to existing technology and to forms of social organization associated with it, management *must* act against the eager acceptance of new technical ideas, even good ones. Otherwise, the technical organization would be perpetually and fruitlessly shifting gears. (1963:82)

There are many sources of this resistance. Some people are suspicious of any innovation. Others fear that new procedures or technology will threaten their efficiency, or create new and unwanted burdens. Those with an emotional commitment to a particular machine or system may resist alternatives. Others may have a "buy anything but . . ." attitude. And in the university, with its rhetoric of innovation, people with doubts about computerization (especially those who are not tenured faculty) may be reluctant to express their dissatisfaction directly or openly. If there is a group disposition to be "modern," "up-to-date," or "progressive," few may be willing to be branded "Luddite" or "too negative." Schon warned that "official assumptions, masking what is often legitimate resistance to change, drive that resistance underground. . . . Once underground, this resistance to change goes out of control. . . . Underground resistance paves the way for disguised defences against change" (1963:83). When this happens the situation becomes extremely difficult and the whole process of computerization could be put into jeopardy. In finding the right balance, then, the decision-maker must recognize the legitimacy of resistance as much as the imperative to change.

The university decision-maker contemplating computerization is thus in a demanding situation. Trying to computerize "from the top" has a distressingly small probability of success. It is one thing to decree that an institution will computerize. It is quite another to get people to use the technology effectively and efficiently. Classrooms and storage closets across North America are full of expensive but unused or underutilized educational technology. If the decision-maker acquiesces to every request in an attempt to computerize "from the bottom," the network will come apart in a maze of conflicting technical standards, incompatible equipment, and broken budgets.

The question, then, is where to begin building the network. If the aim is to enlist the people within the university into the plan for computerization, decision-makers must first ask three questions. First, what are the attitudes towards computers within the institution? Those with favourable attitudes towards computers are potential sources of support, negative attitudes are signs of doubt, fears, or resistance and a source of conflict. Second, who within the university is pushing for computerization? Are there individuals with enough enthusiasm, technical skills, and political savvy to help carry the computerization plan? And third, what value commitments and value conflicts are involved? Like attitudes, value commitments may indicate acceptance of or resistance to computerization, but while attitudes are ephemeral and may quickly change, values are often deeply and tenaciously held. We will see what can be learned from the Canadian experience for each of these questions.

2.2 Attitudes Towards Computerization

Attitudes towards computers are of considerable importance to the computerization process. If there is no enthusiasm for the computer, then the changes taking place within the university could be viewed as adversity instead of prosperity. Negative attitudes signal possible resistance. While there has been considerable research into the effects of computerization upon student attitudes and performance (eg. Clarke & Chambers 1989; Lips & Temple 1990; Malaney & Thurman 1989; Miura 1987; Temple & Lips 1989), relatively little has been published on other members of the university. In our baseline survey, a thirty-question, 5-point Likert scale was used to determine attitudes (see Table 1; Appendix I). The questions can be grouped into four categories: pedagogy, administration, equity, and social concerns. We found that within Canadian universities there are few significant differences in attitudes between groups surveyed. Overall, there is a positive feeling about computers within the university which cuts across all groups (see Table 2). There are differences, however, in the level of positive attitudes among the subjects.

The most important differences in attitudes are between administrators and faculty. Administrators display significantly more positive attitudes towards computerization than do faculty members, especially with regards to pedagogical change (see Figure 4). Differences on questions of administrative computing, equity issues, and social concerns about computers are less pronounced (see Table 3). Administrators are more willing to agree that the computer could be beneficial to the teaching process, believing that computers could lay the foundation for primary and secondary education, individualize instruction, motivate students, increase creativity, and help weaker students. The more senior the administrator, the wider the gap with the faculty becomes. Two questions are particularly indicative of this split. Over 46% of academic vice-presidents strongly agree that "computers can help to achieve quality of learning"; only 14% of faculty do (see Figure 5). Only 7.7% of academic vice

Table 1

Attitude Survey Questionnaire

Please rate the following statements by circling the number that represents the response closest to your opinion.

1 = strongly disagree 2 = disagree 3 = undecided 4 = agree 5 = strongly agree

1.	Computers help to increase productivity in the educational process.	1 2 3 4 5
2.	Computers can help to achieve a higher quality of learning.	1 2 3 4 5
3.	Computers can help to individualize instruction to better meet the needs of particular students.	1 2 3 4 5
4.	Computers help to lay the foundation of primary and secondary education.	1 2 3 4 5
5.	Computers help to motivate students.	1 2 3 4 5
6.	Computers can prevent social isolation.	1 2 3 4 5
7.	Computers can help weaker students.	1 2 3 4 5
8.	Teaching with computers is too expensive and time consuming to be worth the effort.	1 2 3 4 5
9.	Computers will widen the gap between rural and urban students.	1 2 3 4 5
10.	Computers will reduce differences in the quality of universities.	1 2 3 4 5
11.	There is a lot of politics involved in the introduction of computers in higher education.	1 2 3 4 5
12.	Computerization will disproportionately benefit better funded universities.	1 2 3 4 5
13.	Computers will bring about a pedagogical revolution in higher education.	1 2 3 4 5
14.	Computers are only really useful in science and technical education.	1 2 3 4 5
15.	Computerization generally creates new jobs.	1 2 3 4 5
16.	Computers improve university administration.	1 2 3 4 5
17.	Computerization fosters fair and equitable admission to higher education.	1 2 3 4 5
18.	In education, computers are gender neutral.	1 2 3 4 5
19.	Computers adversely affect students' analytical abilities.	1 2 3 4 5
20.	Computers increase creativity.	1 2 3 4 5
21.	Computers make humans machine dependent.	1 2 3 4 5
22.	Computers widen the gap between rich and poor students.	1 2 3 4 5
23.	Computers are expensive toys.	1 2 3 4 5
24.	The introduction of computers into teaching threatens teachers.	1 2 3 4 5
25.	Computerization makes university administrators' jobs easier.	1 2 3 4 5
26.	Computers threaten workers' health.	1 2 3 4 5
27.	Studying computers will guarantee a higher paying job.	1 2 3 4 5
28.	Computers will widen the gap between men and women.	1 2 3 4 5
29.	Those with power in the university make all major decisions about computers.	1 2 3 4 5
30.	Computerization leads to the loss of jobs.	1 2 3 4 5

Table 2

Attitude Survey
Mean Scores

QUESTION	ALL FACULTY	ALL ADMIN	DEANS	ADMISSIONS	REGISTRARS	COM. CENTRE	ACADEMIC VP	ALL CANADA
# 1	3.70	4.33	4.21	4.47	4.45	3.91	4.46	3.95
# 2	3.59	4.04	3.97	3.74	4.16	3.73	4.35	3.77
# 3	3.51	3.95	4.08	3.74	3.97	3.73	4.00	3.68
# 4	2.75	2.96	3.16	2.84	2.76	2.64	3.12	2.83
# 5	3.26	3.48	3.45	3.44	3.50	3.09	3.68	3.34
# 6	2.44	2.57	2.62	2.32	2.63	2.46	2.64	2.49
# 7	3.25	3.56	3.57	3.37	3.57	3.55	3.68	3.37
#8 (-)	2.31	2.02	1.95	2.21	2.00	2.00	2.04	2.20
#9 (-)	2.59	2.55	2.40	2.79	2.52	2.46	2.69	2.58
#10	2.34	2.57	2.50	2.47	2.67	2.27	2.73	2.44
#11 (-)	3.26	3.19	3.00	2.95	3.14	3.82	3.42	3.23
#12 (-)	3.26	3.36	3.32	3.11	3.42	3.91	3.31	3.30
#13	2.66	3.27	3.05	3.17	3.40	3.27	3.50	2.91
#14 (-)	2.09	1.69	1.79	1.90	1.60	1.64	1.54	1.93
#15	3.18	3.34	3.59	3.05	3.33	3.46	3.15	3.24
#16	3.55	4.26	4.13	4.47	4.38	4.00	4.27	3.83
#17	2.64	3.03	3.05	3.26	3.00	2.82	2.96	2.79
#18	3.31	3.46	3.50	3.22	3.32	3.82	3.56	3.37
#19 (-)	2.56	2.39	2.58	2.32	2.52	2.18	2.12	2.50
#20	3.02	3.30	3.16	3.39	3.41	2.91	3.46	3.12
#21 (-)	2.83	3.11	3.21	2.79	3.21	3.09	3.08	2.94
#22 (-)	3.09	3.09	3.11	2.79	3.23	3.46	2.96	3.09
#23 (-)	2.21	2.07	1.92	1.79	2.43	2.09	2.08	2.16
#24 (-)	1.98	2.22	2.37	2.26	2.10	1.90	2.23	2.08
#25	3.48	3.70	3.74	4.11	3.63	3.18	3.65	3.58
#26 (-)	2.35	2.19	2.40	2.21	2.13	2.09	2.00	2.29
#27	2.89	2.88	2.95	2.84	2.93	2.27	3.00	2.89
#28 (-)	2.13	2.11	2.16	2.00	2.27	2.09	1.96	2.13
#29 (-)	2.88	2.95	3.08	3.00	3.07	3.09	2.54	2.92
#30 (-)	2.45	2.26	2.11	2.61	2.38	2.18	2.15	2.38
	N= 185	N= 126	N= 39	N= 19	N= 31	N= 11	N= 26	N= 310

(-) = "Disagree" means a favourable attitude towards computerization

Table 3

QUESTION	ALL FACULTY	ALL ADMIN	DEANS	ADMISSIONS	REGISTRARS	COM. CENTRE	ACADEMIC VP
PEDAGOGICAL GROUP Mean Scores							
#2	3.59	4.04	3.97	3.74	4.16	3.73	4.35
#3	3.51	3.95	4.08	3.74	3.97	3.73	4.00
#4	2.75	2.96	3.16	2.84	2.76	2.64	3.12
#5	3.26	3.48	3.45	3.44	3.50	3.09	3.68
#7	3.25	3.56	3.57	3.37	3.57	3.55	3.68
#8 (-)	2.31	2.02	1.95	2.21	2.00	2.00	2.04
#13	2.66	3.27	3.05	3.17	3.40	3.27	3.50
#14 (-)	2.09	1.69	1.79	1.90	1.60	1.64	1.54
#19 (-)	2.56	2.39	2.58	2.32	2.52	2.18	2.12
#20	3.02	3.30	3.16	3.39	3.41	2.91	3.46
#24 (-)	1.98	2.22	2.37	2.26	2.10	1.90	2.23
ADMINISTRATIVE GROUP Mean Scores							
#1	3.70	4.33	4.21	4.47	4.45	3.91	4.46
#11 (-)	3.26	3.19	3.00	2.95	3.14	3.82	3.42
#16	3.55	4.26	4.13	4.47	4.38	4.00	4.27
#25	3.48	3.70	3.74	4.11	3.63	3.18	3.65
#26 (-)	2.35	2.19	2.40	2.21	2.13	2.00	2.00
#29 (-)	2.88	2.95	3.08	3.00	3.07	3.09	2.54
EQUITY GROUP Mean Scores							
#9 (-)	2.59	2.55	2.40	2.79	2.52	2.46	2.69
#10	2.34	2.57	2.50	2.47	2.67	2.27	2.73
#12 (-)	3.26	3.36	3.32	3.11	3.42	3.91	3.31
#17	2.64	3.03	3.05	3.26	3.00	2.82	2.96
#18	3.31	3.46	3.50	3.22	3.32	3.82	3.56
#22 (-)	3.09	3.09	3.11	2.79	3.23	3.46	2.96
#28 (-)	2.13	2.11	2.16	2.00	2.27	2.09	1.96
SOCIAL CONCERNS GROUP Mean Scores							
#6	2.44	2.57	2.62	2.32	2.63	2.46	2.64
#15	3.18	3.34	3.59	3.05	3.33	3.46	3.15
#21 (-)	2.83	3.11	3.21	2.79	3.21	3.09	3.08
#27	2.89	2.88	2.95	2.84	2.93	2.27	3.00
#30 (-)	2.45	2.26	2.11	2.61	2.38	2.18	2.15

(-) = "Disagree" means a favourable attitude towards computerization

presidents disagree with the idea that "computers will bring about a pedagogical revolution in higher education" (none of them strongly) while 44% of faculty disagree or strongly disagree with the notion (see Figure 6).

Within the administrative sector of the university, there were no significant differences between the registrars, deans and student counsellors, admissions officers, computer centre directors, and academic vice-presidents. Without exception, all administrative staff are positive about the implementation of computerization. It is interesting to note, however, that academic vice-presidents differ rather sharply from everyone else on whether "those with power in the university make all major decisions about computers" (see Figure 7).

Overall, few significant differences exist among the academic staff. However, there are some faculties that disagree with the others about the role of the computer in the university, although the small number of respondents in any given category requires our generalizations to be quite tentative (see Table 4). The faculties of engineering and administration stand out as being the most positive about computers. Faculty in engineering are not as willing to say that computers will widen the gap between rich and poor students, lead to job losses, are expensive toys, are not gender neutral and are surrounded by politics. There is less of a pattern to the differences between faculty in administration and the other faculties. Faculty of administration members differ somewhat on issues of pedagogy, social concerns, administration and equity issues. For example, they are more willing to agree that computers make administration jobs easier, are gender neutral, do not lead to job losses, are not expensive toys, and lead to a higher quality of learning. The least positive are faculty in fine arts, who seem to be more reluctant to be positive about computers than all other faculty members, especially on social questions surrounding computers. Faculty in the natural sciences, the social sciences, medicine, mathematics, computer science, education, and humanities do not differ significantly in their attitudes.

Attitude surveys reveal people s opinions but tell us little about causation. Such is the case here. The strongest differences in attitudes occur between the faculty and the administrative staff. There is a strong tendency for academic vice-presidents to be the most enthusiastic of all. Yet we are left to speculate why administrators are more computer-positive than the faculty. It is perhaps due to the effects of the computer on the different types of work that administrators and faculty do. The computer potentially makes the management of the university more efficient. Both the faculty and administrative staff had positive attitudes about the administrative uses of computers. The disagreements were related to the area of pedagogical change. Indeed, it is the faculty that are more circumspect about the changes to teaching that the computer will supposedly bring. The computerization of the classroom has long been the subject of debate. There are those who see the computer as an added boon to teaching, while others are more suspicious of the computer's place within

Figure 4

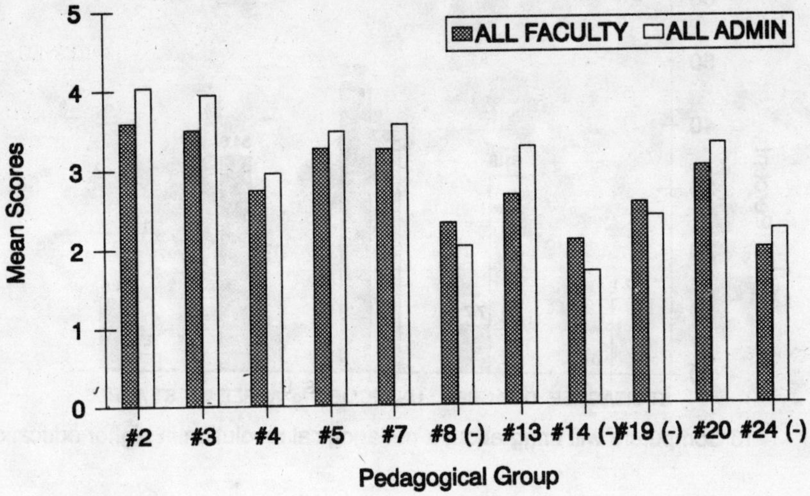

Figure 5

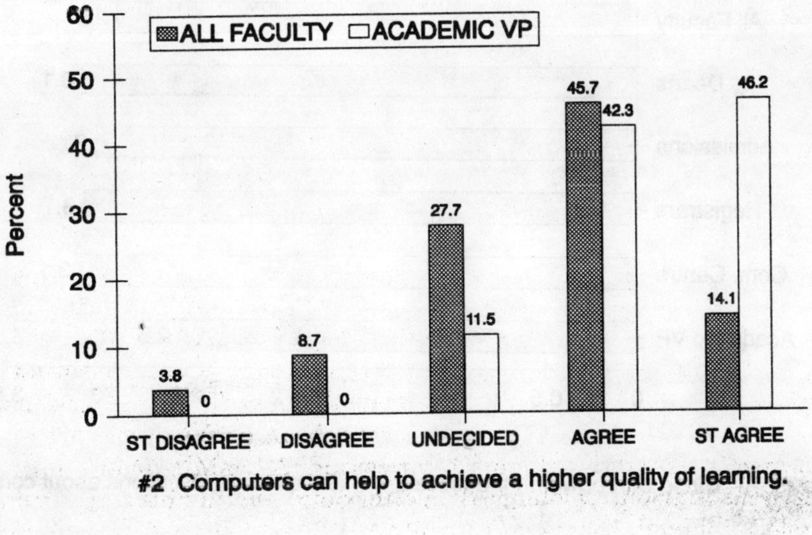

#2 Computers can help to achieve a higher quality of learning.

Figure 6

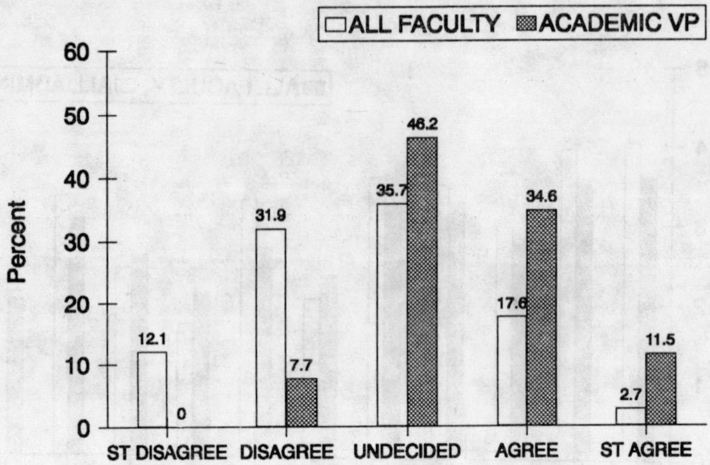

#13 Computers will bring about a pedagogical revolution in higher education.

Figure 7

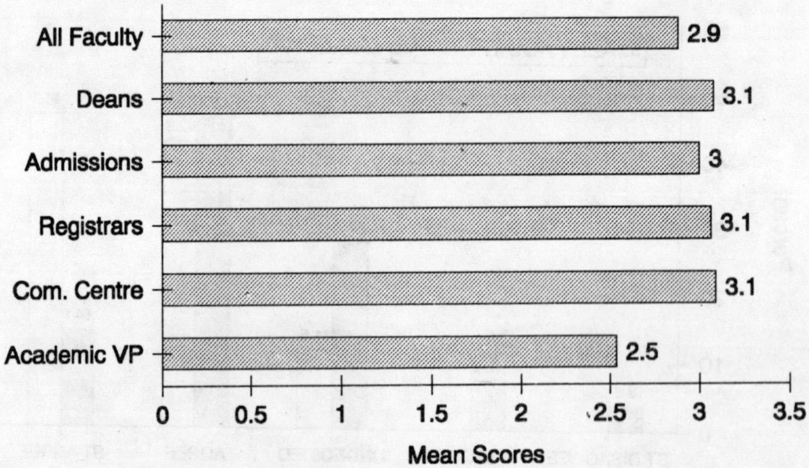

#29 (-) Those with power in the university make all major decisions about computers.

Table 4

Faculty by Unit
Mean Scores

QUESTION	ALL FAC.	FINE ARTS	HUM	SOC. SCI	NAT SCI	MATH	ADMIN	EDUC	ENG	MED
#1	3.69	3.29	4.15	3.78	3.83	3.29	3.91	4.00	3.74	3.58
#2	3.58	2.71	3.64	3.43	3.57	3.71	3.91	4.10	4.00	3.58
#3	3.49	3.14	3.50	3.25	3.65	3.14	3.73	3.80	3.47	3.54
#4	2.74	2.71	2.79	2.43	2.91	1.86	2.73	3.50	2.89	2.79
#5	3.25	3.14	3.67	2.83	3.57	3.57	3.36	3.80	3.00	3.08
#6	2.43	2.29	2.60	2.23	2.50	2.43	2.00	3.10	2.68	2.54
#7	3.24	3.29	3.64	3.22	3.14	3.29	3.00	3.80	2.95	3.33
#8 (-)	2.32	2.86	2.14	2.09	2.41	2.29	2.09	2.10	2.58	2.38
#9 (-)	2.60	2.57	2.57	2.54	2.50	2.86	3.09	2.90	2.53	2.79
#10	2.35	2.43	1.79	2.17	2.64	2.00	2.45	2.60	2.42	2.54
#11 (-)	3.25	3.14	3.14	3.74	3.00	2.86	3.27	3.80	2.79	3.42
#12 (-)	3.26	3.57	3.07	3.50	3.17	3.29	3.27	4.10	2.89	3.00
#13	2.67	2.29	2.79	2.48	2.95	1.86	2.36	3.00	2.58	3.04
#14 (-)	2.09	2.86	2.13	1.96	1.91	1.57	2.00	1.90	2.21	2.21
#15	3.17	3.57	3.14	3.04	3.17	3.14	3.45	3.10	3.26	2.96
#16	3.54	3.29	3.73	2.88	3.48	4.29	4.09	3.50	3.84	3.54
#17	2.63	2.57	2.60	2.54	2.61	2.71	2.64	2.70	2.95	2.67
#18	3.31	3.43	3.21	3.25	3.50	3.00	3.73	3.00	3.68	3.46
#19 (-)	2.57	2.71	2.71	2.63	2.59	2.86	2.64	2.56	2.47	2.50
#20	3.01	2.71	3.57	2.79	2.95	3.00	3.73	3.70	2.63	2.96
#21 (-)	2.83	3.57	3.21	2.57	2.83	2.00	2.64	2.60	2.74	2.75
#22 (-)	3.09	3.86	3.50	3.17	3.04	3.29	2.82	3.33	2.42	3.13
#23 (-)	2.22	2.29	2.43	2.17	2.04	2.50	1.36	2.20	1.94	2.46
#24 (-)	1.99	1.86	2.00	1.82	1.70	2.14	2.27	1.78	1.89	2.04
#25	3.49	3.57	3.43	3.00	3.43	4.57	4.09	3.60	3.47	3.38
#26 (-)	2.36	3.00	2.71	2.35	2.22	2.14	2.09	2.60	2.47	2.04
#27	2.90	2.00	3.00	2.78	2.96	3.57	2.73	2.60	3.16	2.88
#28 (-)	2.14	2.57	2.14	1.87	2.09	2.29	2.00	2.50	1.84	1.96
#29 (-)	2.89	2.43	2.64	3.09	2.57	3.00	2.73	3.50	2.47	2.96
#30 (-)	2.46	3.14	2.50	2.35	2.39	2.43	1.70	2.60	2.00	2.38
	N= 185	N= 7	N= 14	N= 24	N= 23	N= 7	N= 11	N= 10	N= 19	N= 24

(-)= "Disagree" means a favourable attitude towards computerization.

the educational setting. This being the case, it is evident that while responding faculty are generally positive about the impact of computers in education, they are still somewhat guarded in their enthusiasm. Administrators show no such hesitation.[1]

One should be cautious in appropriating this data. Our survey was taken after computerization had been well under way at Canadian universities for some years. The levels of support certainly reflect growing experience. The same questions asked in, say, 1980 would probably have elicited quite different responses. Our survey asked faculty if their views had changed over the last five years on the role and importance of computers (see Appendix C:C-45). Of those responding, 38.3% said yes they had changed their opinions, the largest number becoming more positive while very few became more negative. It is fair to conclude, then, that more experience with computers is likely to improve people's attitudes towards them, but current positive attitudes do not necessarily mean they have always been that way. Do not expect Canadian attitudes to be replicated in places with different degrees of experience.

Differing attitudes, then, can indicate pools of acceptance of or resistance to computerization. The university decision-maker has to identify both, enrolling those who are positive into the network, consulting and negotiating with the others to allay fears or doubts and to overcome resistance. By identifying the attitudes of the hesitant early, their concerns can be given legitimacy and they can be persuaded to participate rather than be forced into covert opposition.

2.3 The Product Champion

The second question is which people within the university are pushing for computer technology? This is a different question than finding out who has favourable attitudes. The task here is to identify those individuals, from any faculty or department, who are most enthusiastic towards computers and most active in promoting their use. These individuals may become "product champions."

Product champions are individuals whose "role is to act as internal promoter for the product" (Westrum 1991:113), enthusiasts within an institution who challenge organizational inertia to promote innovation. They tend to be individuals with technical competence, a working knowledge of the organization and its clientele, above average drive and aggressiveness, and political savvy (Fisher, Hamilton, McLaughlin & Zmud 1986:14). They play an important role in the economy, credited by studies with between 40% and 50% of all innovations in industry (Pacey 1983:128; Schon 1963). In university computerization, product champions are persons who will take the lead in introducing their department or office to computers, lobby senior administrators

---

1 There appears to be a contradiction between senior administrators' enthusiastic attitudes towards the use of computers in teaching and the limited institutional support discussed in Chapter 3.

for resources, and act as an informal consultant to their co-workers. An example from the University of Regina experience will illustrate their effectiveness.

In the early 1980's the senior administration of Luther College, one of the federated colleges of the University of Regina, had little knowledge of, or interest in, computer technology and an understandable concern with balancing the budget. In 1982 two members of the college, Mr. B, director of student services, and Professor K, both of whom owned Apple II home computers, began agitating for the college to make use of the new technology. Mr. B even brought his home machine into the office to demonstrate its abilities. The administration somewhat reluctantly agreed to purchase a dedicated word processor (a Digital DecMate I with 8" disk drive) in early 1983, and sent the faculty secretary to Calgary for training. As more people became convinced of the utility of the machine, Professor K pushed to upgrade the equipment to two newly released DecMate IIs by 1984, while Mr. B computerized the student services offices at the same time. Both men continued to lobby the senior administration for more resources for computerization and recruited others to their cause through coffee break discussions and informal consulting and assistance. Computerization at Luther College spread from these two centres—from student services through the administration offices, from the academic office through the faculty—until by 1992 all administrative offices had been computerized and 80% of the faculty had their own computers. While Luther College would have eventually begun to computerize when the university registration system was automated in late 1984, the work of these two product champions caused the process to begin eighteen months earlier and greatly accelerated its pace.

Product champions are thus one key to the success of university computerization. Indeed, Schon goes so far as to declare that "where radical innovation is concerned, the emergence of a champion is required. Given the underground resistance to change described earlier, the new idea either finds a champion *or dies*" (1963:84). They should be identified early, enlisted into the process, and encouraged by the decision-maker.[2] They can do a great deal to foster enthusiasm among their co-workers and to aid in the effective use of the technology through their eagerness to share hints on new techniques and offer assistance to novices. However, their eagerness and enthusiasm can all too often become a liability.

Product champions are by definition enthusiasts, and as such frequently do not recognize limits (Fisher, Hamilton, McLaughlin & Zmud 1986). Many become emotionally attached to a particular machine or software package, sometimes believing that "it can do anything" without paying attention to the

---

2 Although they cannot be recruited or identified beforehand. Fisher, Hamilton, McLaughlin & Zmud caution that it is "futile to attempt to identify product champions in the recruiting process as they have no distinguishing characteristics about them until moved to action" (1986:15). Nor does it seem that product champions repeat their successes very often. They promote one technology, very few make a career of being champions.

actual needs of the user. The occasionally bitter disputes between supporters of IBM and Macintosh as to which is "better" illustrate this. Those who have a strong commitment to a particular system will often feel threatened if their product is seen as one option among other options. Since they believe their choice is "the best" they think everyone should use it. This commitment can also lead them to downplay or underestimate the costs of changing existing systems. Their goal is to maximize the use of their chosen technology. So while product champions are essential to the process of computerization, the university decision-maker must also be aware of their shortcomings. They are needed in the network, but they can also be a source of problems and conflicts.

2.4 The Role of Values in Computerization

The third question is what value commitments towards technology are found in the university. This is of central importance. Values tend to be strongly held, and are a potential source of deep conflict. When values clash people are often less willing to compromise or to be persuaded to a differing opinion. This is particularly the case because value conflicts are often unacknowledged, manifesting themselves through other disputes. Complicating the question are profoundly dissimilar conceptions of values themselves. The consensus and conflict approaches discussed in Chapter 1 understand the values involved in university computerization very differently.

As was recounted in the first chapter, values are central to functionalist theory. A society is bound together by its norms and values, and the first function of education is to facilitate "social order and stability by providing the basis of a value consensus" (Haralmbos 1985:175). What is true of society as a whole is also true of the institutions which make it up—each is characterized by an underlying value consensus. This is not to say functionalists see no controversies over values, but in most cases they are over interpretation or application, not over the fundamental values themselves.

In the context of university computerization, then, functionalists would explain disputes in terms of the functional differentiation of roles rather than deep value conflict. In other words, people with different jobs or interests may have different points of view on any given issue, but that should not obscure what they share. Functionalists would point to the overwhelmingly positive attitudes towards computerization found on campus (as evidenced by our survey, above) as confirmation of consensus at a deeper level. Differences of opinion, which are to be expected in a highly differentiated organization such as the university, arise over the speed of computerization or the details of how it should be done, not over the basic process itself. The means for resolving these differences of opinion lie in the authority structure of the university itself. Those in positions of authority are there because of their knowledge and expertise and should take the lead in decision-making for the institution (although the wise administrator will consult widely). What is important are the central values of the institution. These are paramount, and throughout the computerization process must prevail over the particular interests or opinions of any individual or group.

Conflict theorists take a very different approach to values. Many do not emphasize values at all, and of those that do, most see value conflict as central, not value consensus. For all conflict theorists, what is important is the analysis of power. An investigation of values from this perspective, then, would look at the values of the most powerful groups and how they are enforced upon those with less power. In terms of computerization, one of the more interesting analyses using this approach is based on the work done by Arnold Pacey (1983).

Building upon his analysis of technology as practice (see above), Pacey sees three sets of values involved in the development and use of technology. The first are "virtuosity values." These are the values of the expert, of the product champion, and, less reputably, of the hacker, of those people who have mastered the technical aspects of computing and who are characterized by their enthusiasm for its benefits. Typically they emphasize improving performance, seeing risk as a challenge to be overcome through the technology itself (Pacey 1983:102). Often, these values can be summarized by what Cleborne Maddux called "the Everest Syndrome," the belief that "computers should be brought into educational settings simply *because they are there*" (1988:5). Virtuosity values may be encountered anywhere on campus but are strongest among the faculty, especially in science and engineering. Second, the organizational aspects of technology practice are most frequently characterized by economic values. These are the values of management and growth which emphasize productivity and the "bottom line." Enterprising rather than innovative, those holding economic values weigh costs against benefits in making decisions and allocating resources. Economic values are held most strongly at the university by the administration. Pacey's third set are user or need values. Emphasis here is placed upon maintenance and risk avoidance or prevention rather than mastery or growth (1983:102). What counts is the "use value" of the technology, that is, its ability to meet the felt needs of the person using it. Here a problem arises.

On campus, *everyone* is, of course, a potential "user" of computing. Simply using computers does not mean that everyone shares user values in Pacey's sense, however. The concept of "user" needs to be defined. Here again, different perspectives give different responses to the question "who is a user?" As shown in Chapter 1, functionalists look at the university as a highly differentiated formal organization. There are many roles, and consequently there are many kinds of users. Senior administrators use their computers differently than do secretaries. Use by science faculty is differentiated from that of humanities professors. Students use computers in a variety of ways, depending upon their programme of study. Different departments and administrative offices have different computing needs. Since there are many kinds of users, functionalists maintain, it is not meaningful to generalize about "user needs" or "user values." A conflict-oriented approach defines users by a different set of criteria. Westrum, for instance, identifies three types of users. First, "users can be people who have chosen to use a technology" (1991:216). In the university this would include senior administrators and most faculty. Second, "users can be those for whom the technology has been chosen, as is typically the case with secretaries and factory workers" (1991:216). Students would also fall into this category, to the extent that they use computers in their academic programme. Third, "users can be a client population. . . . For these users, technology is something to be reacted to, not something to operate" (1991:216). This group would include most students in regard to university administrative systems and many students in all circumstances. The difference between these groups is the amount of control they have over the technology. Conflict theorists look at the power relationships at the university and see which "users" shape and make the decisions, that is, have the power to enforce their values, and which "users" have decisions made for them.

As a practice, conflict analysis maintains, computing has been characterized by the dominance of virtuosity and economic values. This is because, in terms of its organizational aspect, all technology has a stand-point, a perspective on the nature of the work to do and how it should be done. This will embody someone's values (Kling 1991; Woolgar & Grint 1991). At the university, computer systems take the stand-point of a particular office in the hierarchy. If one takes the University of Regina as an example, the stand-point of the purchasing system is that of the accounting office. It was designed to meet the needs of the accounting office for control and ease of bookkeeping. It performs less well for those making the purchase or at shipping and receiving. The student information system operates from the stand-point of the registrar's office. The executive information system is for the president and vice-presidents rather than for deans or department heads. Which office a system reflects is an indication of power. An office or instructional system, for instance, chosen on the basis of the virtuosity values of the department head may not reflect the needs of the staff or students who have to use it. In North America, conflict theorists conclude, decisions on computerization have reflected the power structure of the universities and the values of those who make the decisions. As a consequence, user values tend to be slighted.

The dissimilarities in these approaches to understanding values are obvious. In one, there is an underlying value consensus, while those in positions of legitimate authority are required to adjudicate disputes over the interpretation and application of these shared values and maintain their paramountcy. In the other, values themselves reflect the power relations of society—the dominant values are those held by the most powerful. In the North American experience of computerization, the place where this conflict between different approaches to values has most manifested itself has been in disputes over equity and over decision-making. Has the process of computerization been equitable, that is, has everyone been treated fairly, or have certain groups been placed at a disadvantage? And who should be involved in making the decisions? Both questions turn on the issue of participation by users.

As decision-makers work to enlist the people within the university into the plan for computerization, they have to be cognizant of these questions. What are the attitudes of the people in the university towards computerization, and do these attitudes reveal potential allies or sources of resistance? Are there product champions at work, and can they be enlisted into the computerization plan? And what values are held by the people in the institution? Whichever approach to understanding values is taken, values disputes are likely to be among the most difficult to resolve and the most prone to engender resistance to the computerization plan. In order to understand the dimensions of this problem, we will have to pause and consider the place where values conflict in the computerization process is sharpest in North America, the question of user participation.

3. The Issue of User Participation

3.1 User Equity

For the past several years there has been a growing sense of crisis in North America over the inadequate number of students enrolling in science and mathematics (Alliance for Undergraduate Education 1990; Industry, Science and Technology Canada 1991; Smith 1991). The Smith Report expresses concern over the low participation rates in higher education by people from less affluent homes, native people, and people with disabilities in Canada (1991:93ff.). While women in Canada achieved parity in undergraduate enrollment for the first time in the 1980's, there is particular concern over the small number of women choosing to enter science. In spite of inducements from both government and business, the proportion of women in most sciences (biology is a notable exception) has remained static or shown little growth over the past decade (see Figure 8).

Computer science is of singular concern. Since the mid-eighties, the number of women computer science students in the United States and Canada has actually declined, both absolutely and in relation to the number of men. In 1979, women received 28.09% of bachelor's degrees in in computer science in the U. S. (*Chronicle of Higher Education* 1980:14). By 1985 this figure had risen to 36.54%, but by 1989 it had fallen to 30.73%—a decline of 5.81% (*Chronicle of Higher Education* 1987:34; 1991:28). In Canada, the same figures show a 7.5% decline, from 27.32% of bachelor's degrees in computer science in 1985 to 19.82% in 1989 (Statistics Canada, 1990; 1991). Today, fewer than one in three undergraduate computer science students are female in the United States, fewer than one in five in Canada. The situation in the graduate schools is even bleaker. Due to a high dropout rate, there is a massive "pipeline shrinkage" in all the sciences. In the United States, it currently takes 2000 grade-nine young women "entering the pipeline" to produce one woman Ph.D. in science and

Figure 8.
Women as Percent of Full-Time Undergraduate Enrollment in Canada

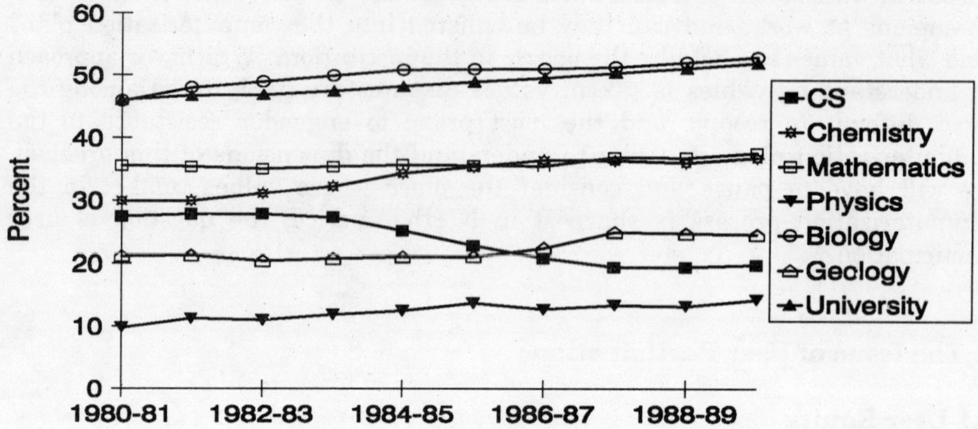

Source: Statistics Canada

engineering (Wollam 1990). In computer science the shrinkage is particularly acute. The proportion of women receiving master's degrees is declining relative to the number obtained by men, while in 1989 only 81 women received Ph.D's, a mere 15.05% (*Chronicle of Higher Education* 1991:28). In Canada in 1989, 52 women received master's degrees in computer science (16%) and only three (7%) received doctoral degrees in that field (Industry, Science and Technology Canada 1991:14).

There is little disagreement over the facts of this situation, but there is an extensive debate over why it exists and what can be done about it. All agree that there are no formal or legal barriers to participation in university computing—the problem is that insufficient numbers of women, students with disabilities, students from ethnic or racial minority groups, or less affluent students choose to enroll. Nearly everyone also agrees that much of the problem arises in the primary and secondary schools.

The university is rarely a person's first encounter with computing. Students arrive on campus with attitudes, stereotypes, and self-conceptions already formed. Shaped by their prior experiences, students' attitudes have been found to be the main factor in their decision on whether or not to study computers at the university (Clarke & Chambers 1989; Frenkel 1990). The discouragement of young women and minority students is well documented in the literature on socialization into computing, from children's earliest introduction to computers (Chen 1987), to the content of software (Frenkel 1990; Linn 1985; Pearl *et al.* 1990; Rosenthal & Demetrulias 1988; Yeloushan 1989), to computer advertising (Demetrulias and Rosenthal 1985), to computer studies textbooks and career guidance materials (Culley 1988, 1990), to the effects of the "computer culture" (Kiesler, Sproull & Eccles 1985). There are continuing problems of access to computers in many places, particularly for minority and less affluent students (Becker & Sterling 1987; Frenkel 1990; Lipkin & McCormick 1986; Urban 1986; Wessells 1990), and in the quality of the computing experience for these same groups (Boruta *et al.* 1983; Jacobs 1988; Marshall, Erickson, & Vonk 1986; McPhail 1985; Stickles 1988). To one prominent researcher of computerization in the schools, this pattern suggests:

> Two different profiles of the student-computer relationship. In one, students with greater SES [socio-economic status] advantages have more computer use, more likelihood of interacting with a computer-knowledgeable teacher, and learn an implicit message that they should control the computer rather than have it control them. In the other, less-advantaged students learn a subtle message—that the computer is in control and that their task is to respond appropriately to questions which it displays. (Collis 1985:182)

So in terms of access to computers and in the quality of their experience using them, there are considerable inequities in the pre-university experience of women, minorities, and less affluent students. This has consequences for the university in the form of negative attitudes towards computing and low enrollments.

There is little dispute over these facts. The two approaches we have described differ as to the cause and solution. Functionalists tend to see a dysfunction in the education system (see Chapter 1) and call for reform of the schools. Most of their recommendations for the university involve incentives to recruit women and minorities into the sciences. By treating everyone the same throughout their education, they aim to provide a "level playing field" which would guarantee equality of opportunity. Conflict theorists see systemic inequality as a structural problem. In particular, they emphasize the effects of systematic discrimination along racial, gender, and class lines. They come up with a rather different list of reforms, which are less concerned with equality of opportunity than with equality of results. They insist on equity and not just equality. That is, they say that fairness requires treating people differently if that is necessary to meet their needs, and that treating everyone "the same" is unfair if by doing so some people are put at a disadvantage. They also charge that simply offering incentives to recruit more computer science students is not enough—the university will have to look more broadly at how it treats computer users, especially student users.

So, while largely outside of their control, the nature and quality of prior computing experience creates problems which universities must address. There are two issues in university computing in which substantial equity questions for students have been raised: the problem of access to computers at the university and computers in university teaching.[3] We will look at each of these in turn.

3.2 University Access to Computers

The first issue with substantial equity concerns is access to computers on campus. If students are to take advantage of the opportunities which computers potentially have to offer, they must first be able to use them. The question is, do all students have computer access?

Most Canadian universities supply students with at least limited access to computers. How well students can take advantage of this varies considerably, however. Studies have shown *perceived* access to be the strongest single predictor in student computer use on campus (Malaney & Thurman 1989). Perceptions are more important than the amount of machinery available. Crowded facilities or malfunctioning equipment may provide more frustration than access. Conflict theorists charge that many students with particular needs or circumstances are put at a disadvantage. This can be seen, they say, in regards to women and low SES students, on the one hand, and students with disabilities on the other. We will look at the evidence for both cases.

The most obvious instances of inequity could arise in those schools and faculties which require students to purchase a microcomputer or which charge students user fees. A student without financial resources could be put at a disadvantage. A study of programmes which require students to purchase microcomputers found that "financing the purchase of a personal computer is a major concern to most students" (Tyagi 1984:91). Conflict theorists argue that even if the student is not excluded outright by her or his inability to pay, the necessity of curtailing expenditures elsewhere in an already limited budget, or of incurring increased debt, could place the student in an unfair disadvantage *vis-a-vis* his or her financially secure peers. Those wealthy enough to afford their own computer, they say, have a clear advantage over those who do not. Fortunately, our survey discovered that very few universities in Canada require computer purchase or charge students user fees (see Appendix C:C-23).

Providing free computer facilities does not in and of itself eliminate inequities, however. Access means little if training is unavailable. Given the widely differing experiences prior to university, little can be assumed about students' proficiency. A persistent problem reported in the literature is the frustration of the novice overwhelmed by the virtuoso display of those in the computing culture (Glynn *et al.* 1989; Kiesler, Sproull & Eccles 1985). One student's experience is typical:

---

3 Administrative equity issues are rarely raised in the literature, nor did we find substantive student equity issues in the computerization of university administrative systems, although telephone registration does create a few problems for students without ready access to a touchtone phone. Overall, the computerization of administrative systems has reduced inequities by reducing favouritism. There may be inequities in administrative systems, but we did not find that they are caused by computerization. Computerized systems may be inefficient or frustrating, but we did not find them to be unfair.

> I was on the computer and something happened. I didn't know what was going on. I saw a guy sitting over there who looked like a real hacker. So I asked him, and he got up, and he started doing all of this stuff with my account without telling me what he was doing. He started messing around, "You need this. Let's see, I'll give you this file." It's like, what are you doing? He wouldn't tell me. (Sproull, Kiesler & Zubrow 1987:190)

Relying on such informal instruction is not likely to be satisfactory. Any plan for computerization needs to consider training in computer use for novices. Conflict theorists claim that unless such instruction is frequent, convenient, and free, an advantage is given to those who have more prior experience or are able to obtain the necessary skills elsewhere.

Educational practices on campus can frequently create problems, especially in computer science. Students regularly report that their computer classes are disproportionately time-consuming (Frenkel 1990; Sproull, Kiesler & Zubrow 1987). This may combine with crowded facilities to create problems for some. One student's experience was not uncommon: "Last semester more than a couple times I got up at four o'clock [in the morning] to go to the computer room so you could get on the terminal and not be crowded out because there are so many people there" (Sproull, Kiesler & Zubrow 1987:187). Students are often required to work long hours at night and on weekends. For many women this raises concerns about security and conflicts with family obligations (Frenkel 1990; Pearl *et al.* 1990). While the problem is not unique to computer science, it is particularly acute in computing classes. Conflict theorists argue that if a woman has to reduce her working hours out of concern for her safety, or because childcare is unavailable, she is being treated unfairly, even if she is treated "the same" as male students. Here too, they say, affluence and gender translate into academic advantages.

Students with disabilities are another group with unique needs for computer access. Perhaps for no other group on campus has computer technology created more opportunities while at the same time raising new obstacles. For many, university education would not be possible without computers and computer-based communication technology. Hawkridge, Vincent & Hales describe the potential of information technology:

> It can help many disabled people to overcome barriers to time and space, and to a much greater extent it can help them to overcome barriers of communication. Since communication is at the heart of living for human beings, new information technology offers opportunities to neutralize the worst effects of many kinds of disablement and to change the lives of many individuals. (1985:vii)

Unfortunately, computer technology has not turned out to be the panacea which some habilitation and rehabilitation experts had predicted (Segal & Marciano 1988; Walpole 1987). If the economic values of the institution override the user needs of students with disabilities, conflict theorists add, the new technology itself can too easily become another obstacle.

To speak of "students with disabilities" is a misnomer. People with different disabilities have a variety of different needs (Brown *et al.* 1989; Hawkridge, Vincent & Hales 1985). For example, students with low vision need text magnification systems (ones that work with both text and graphics). Blind students require Kurzweil reading machines and computers with screen-reading systems. Modified keyboards are often required by mildly orthopedically disabled students, while those with severe disabilities need alternative input devices (sip-and-puff switches, single-switch scanning devices, voice entry, etc.). Students with tactile and kinesthetic processing disabilities need word processors with real-time spelling and grammar checkers to communicate effectively in writing. Meeting the needs of these students thus necessitates a mixture of different kinds of systems and adaptations.

Conflict theorists charge that when systems or software packages are chosen without sensitivity to the disparate needs of students with disabilities, they can become obstacles instead of opportunities. As simple a matter as a desk of the wrong height or a keyboard cord of the wrong length can mean the difference between a workstation accessible to someone in a wheelchair and one that is not. A machine or software package that *requires* a mouse is not usable by people who are visually impaired or cannot use their arms. Screen readers have great difficulty with graphical user interfaces (Brody 1989). On the other hand, a graphical user interface is the system of choice for many forms of learning disabilities (Brown *et al.* 1989). Policies which decree one system or software package to be the "university (or departmental) standard" thus immediately create problems for anyone who is not able to use that particular machine or package. As computers spread from the science lab to other disciplines, this difficulty will grow. For example, a physically disabled student who could excel in, say, languages may now find herself obstructed by language lab computers which lack suitable input devices.

But, conflict theorists continue, the greatest problems students with disabilities have are not with the technical aspects of computing but with the organizational and cultural aspects. Money is a great concern. Technology for people with disabilities is very expensive since it is not being mass-produced as it is for consumer electronics (Brody 1989). Off-campus funding is available for some students (from foundations, the Canadian National Institute for the Blind, social services, etc.) but budget-strapped universities have not committed adequate funds of their own. Training is another difficulty. When available at all, university-run training programmes usually focus on one package on one type of machine and front-load instruction (ie. everything is taught in a few short sessions). This does not meet the needs of students with disabilities, particularly those with learning difficulties, who require specialized instruction (Collins & Price 1987). Very few Canadian universities have a high-tech centre for adapted technology (Brown *et al.* 1989). For universities to treat students with disabilities equitably, conflict theorists claim, they will have to provide much more in terms of training, maintenance, and support.

Thus in the case of students with disabilities, say those influenced by the conflict approach, as with women and poor students, university policies decided on the basis of economic values frequently fail to meet user needs. Simply opening a computer facility for student use is not enough to provide equitable access to computers.

3.3 Computers in University Teaching

It is in teaching that computers perhaps offer the greatest opportunities to students. The decade of the eighties saw computers move out of the science labs as "computer literacy" came to be seen as an increasingly useful skill in the social sciences and humanities. But do all students benefit equally, or, as the conflict approach claims, are some groups once again placed at a disadvantage?

The evidence is ambivalent. On one hand are the analyses of the effectiveness of computerized instruction (which we will review in Chapter 3). While results are still equivocal, some forms of computerized instruction initially appear to be effective, particularly at the university level. Few differences between groups are found when measuring performance or ability. On the other hand, as we have already seen, there are considerable differences between groups in choosing their course of study. In particular, most women avoid computer science.

The problem does not appear to lie in the technical aspects of computer technology but in its organizational and cultural aspects. Sherry Turkle describes the possibilities and opportunities which computers can proffer in the right environment:

> When people are put in computer-rich environments, supported by flexible and powerful programming languages, and encouraged to use the computer as an expressive material, they respond in a diversity of styles. In such environments, the computer, like other powerful media including paints, pencils and words, becomes a screen for the projection of differences. Unlike stereotypes of a machine with which there is only one way of relating, the computer can be a partner in a great diversity of relationships. (1988:57)

Unfortunately, all too often this potential is unfulfilled. Conflict theorists charge that the way computing is organized on campus and the culture surrounding it reinforce the stereotypes to which Turkle refers.

The most serious equity issue, they continue, arises out of the prevalent doctrine that there is only one best way to do computing. In some of the social sciences this inflexibility extends to one statistical package, which is taken as the "standard" for the discipline. These "standards," they say, do not reflect a consensus, as functionalists would have it, but instead are often fashioned by a discipline's "authoritative knowledge." Authoritative knowledge is defined as "that knowledge taken to be legitimate, consequential, official, worthy of discussion and useful for justifying actions by people engaged in accomplishing a given task" (Suchman and Jordan 1989:153). It is a social construction of reality of particular power because it governs discourse. It determines what are the appropriate ways to think and argue and act. It is similar in many ways to what Bijker described, in a different context, as a "technological frame" (see above). But while authoritative knowledge may dominate a discipline's discourse, Suchman and Jordan maintain, it is not the only way that people think.

A number of studies postulate a dichotomy between a masculine authoritative knowledge and the knowledge of women (Brecher 1989; Fowler and Murray 1987; Greenbaum 1987; Keller 1985; Turkle 1984; Verne 1986). Others argue that Native Canadians also have a different cognitive style (Heffron 1984; Kaulbeck 1984). Perhaps the deepest investigation of this as it relates to computers was done by Turkle and Papert (1990).

In a study of how students actually go about programming computers, Turkle and Papert found two cognitive styles. The first is the formal approach which emphasizes structure, abstract manipulation of symbols, hierarchy, and planning. It dominates the computer culture and forms its authoritative knowledge. It is also a form of knowledge strongly associated with men. In opposition to this is a style they call "bricolage." The bricoleur is more concrete and tactile than abstract, more intimately involved than distant and objective:

> The bricoleur resembles the painter who stands back between brushstrokes, looks at the canvas, and only after this contemplation, decides what to do next. For planners, mistakes are missteps; for bricoleurs they are the essence of a navigation by mid-course corrections. For planners, a program is an instrument for premeditated control; bricoleurs have goals, but set out to realize them in the spirit of a collaborative venture with the machine. For planners, getting a program to work is like "saying one's piece"; for bricoleurs it is more like a conversation than a monologue. In cooking, this would be the style of those who do not follow recipes and instead make a series of decisions according to taste. While hierarchy and abstraction are valued by the structured programmers' planner's aesthetic, bricoleur programmers prefer negotiation and rearrangement of their materials. (Turkle and Papert 1990:136)

Most (but by no means all) bricoleurs are female. These two cognitive styles are thus gender-linked but not gender-determined. Some men are alienated from the authoritative style of the computer culture while many women work well within it (1990:150).

As different as these two cognitive styles may be, Turkle and Papert emphasize that *both* produce excellent results. Computers, with their capabilities in music, text, graphics, and sound can accommodate a variety of cognitive styles. Icons and graphical user interfaces are particularly amenable to bricoleurs.

The problem, they maintain, is that "although the computer as an expressive medium supports epistemological pluralism, the computer culture often does not" (1990:132). Because authoritative knowledge claims to be the only right way, bricoleurs are often caught in a conflict. Many women and some minority students are thus trapped between the social definition of their work (embodied in the authoritative knowledge) and their cognitive style. Most deal with this conflict by withdrawing, forcing themselves to conform, or "faking it." For many students with disabilities, conflict theorists add, insistence upon the authoritative knowledge as the only way to approach the technology creates new obstacles. These theorists conclude that the virtuosity and economic values dominating university computing place students with different cognitive styles at a disadvantage. The insistence on treating all students "the same" is unfair to those whose user needs are different.

3.4 Recommendations For Incorporating Users

So, in part due to the effects of students' computing experience prior to university, the issues of access to computers at the university and in the way computers are used in university teaching have created considerable conflict for North American universities. Underlying these issues is the question of values. According to functionalists, there may be dysfunctions in the primary and secondary schools which account for the negative attitudes held by some students and which lead them to avoid computing. While these attitudes need to be addressed, the university must first of all maintain its core values, chief of which is equality of opportunity for *all* students. Conflict theorists charge that the dominant values of the computer culture have tended to exclude or put at a disadvantage women, racial and ethnic minorities, students with disabilities, and poor students. The design and implementation of computer systems, facilities, and instruction need to incorporate the values of the actual users, they add, rather than impose the economic values of the organization or the virtuosity values of someone in the hierarchy.

The question for university decision-makers dealing with computerization, then, is how can this conflict be handled? Should user values be incorporated into the plan? If so, how? The literature is replete with recommendations, but unlike the analyses we have been examining, they do not break down simply into consensus or conflict approaches. There is a much broader spectrum of responses. We will look at the recommendations pertaining to women in some detail, remembering that the advocates for other groups present their own lists (e.g. Brown *et al.* 1989, for recommendations to include people with disabilities).

For some, a commitment to equality of opportunity does not preclude providing incentives to recruit more women into science and engineering, including computer science. Industry, Science and Technology Canada, for instance, has instituted an $80 million, five-year Canada Scholarships Program to award $2,000/year scholarships to students in science and engineering. At least 50% of first-year scholarships are awarded to women (Industry, Science and Technology Canada 1991:29). Several large businesses contribute to this programme, in particular NOVA Corporation, which is providing $24,000 in special awards for women. The Smith Report also urges programmes to establish equality of opportunity, particularly reforms in the secondary school curriculum and efforts to promote more women faculty and administrators (Smith 1991:140-141).

Others go beyond incentives to look in more detail at university practices. One of the most complete and thorough sets of recommendations regarding women and computing is to be found in "Becoming a Computer Scientist: A Report by the ACM Committee on the Status of Women in Computer Science" (Pearl *et al.* 1990). The authors make seventeen recommendations for change:

- Ensure equal access to computers for young girls and boys and develop educational software appealing to both.

- Establish programs to encourage high school girls to continue with math and science—for example, science fairs, scouting programs, and conferences in which women speak about their careers in science and engineering.

- Develop programs to pair undergraduate women with women graduate students or faculty members who serve as role models providing encouragement and advice.

- Provide women with opportunities for successful professional experiences such as involvement in research projects beginning as early as the undergraduate years.

- Establish programs that make women computer scientists visible to undergraduates and graduate students—for example, invite women to campus to give talks or to serve as visiting faculty members (eg. the NSF's Visiting Professorships for Women).

- Encourage men as well as women to serve as mentors for younger women in the field.

- Establish more reentry programs that enable women who have stopped their scientific training prematurely to retrain as computer scientists.

- Develop and enforce safety procedures on campus. Provide safe access at all hours to public terminal areas, well-lit routes from offices to parking lots and services to escort those walking on campus after dark.

- Award small grants to female professors for the purchase of terminals or workstations, printers, and modems for home use for safety reasons.

- Educate all computer science faculty about self-esteem issues that women computer scientists face.

- Increase awareness of and sensitivity to the use of a variety of communication styles, especially less aggressive styles.

- Increase awareness of subtle discrimination and its effects.

- Develop effective grievance policies to deal with overt discrimination and sexual harassment. Implement studies of existing policies to determine what makes certain policies effective.

- Investigate ways of changing the pattern of academic careers and tenure decisions to make them more compatible with childrearing demands.

- Provide affordable quality childcare.

- Expand parental leave policies to allow both fathers and mothers to participate actively in the rearing of small children.

- Maintain lists of qualified women computer scientists to increase participation of women in influential positions such as program committees, editorial boards, or policy boards. (1990:55)

This report stands out in its recognition of the "seamless web" of the technical and the social, particularly in arguing that the integration of women into computing at the university requires that the social integration of females must be taken into account. The authors see their recommendations on security, subtle and overt discrimination and harassment, childcare, and parental leave as essential. Of particular importance is the recognition of the problems created for women (and many men) by the academic career path and tenure decisions. People with family responsibilities who do not have a "helpmate-in-the-background" (1990:53) are at a severe disadvantage and frequently find their academic careers stalled or terminated. Caring for small children is simply incompatible with the research and publication schedule demanded by most universities. The report calls for changes in the "tenure clock" and suggests that "it is even possible that . . . the entire tenure process is incompatible with the demands of a dual-career society" (1990:54). All of these recommendations are necessary, they say, even though many are not specific to computer science.

Others argue that these recommendations do not go far enough. They are limited, say some feminists, by both their underlying assumptions and by their analysis of the causes of gender differences in computing. Griffiths, for instance, dismisses these kinds of recommendations as "predicated on the supposition that a little tinkering with surface features will make a lot of difference" (1988:150). In particular, the question of power is not addressed. For instance, several of the ACM recommendations speak of "educating" and "increasing awareness and sensitivity." The assumptions made here are that, first, there is a lack of awareness of the issues on the part of university faculty and administrators and, second, increasing awareness will solve the problem. But, some feminist critics ask, is this credible? The problem, they charge, is not lack of awareness but the unwillingness to change on the part of those who have power. Demands for equality are not enough; a fundamental change is needed. These reformers seek to emancipate computer technology from its appropriation by men. The recommendations they make include, among other things, segregated classes for female students so that the women could not be intimidated by men (Giffiths 1988; Wollam 1990). The aim is not to "beat the boys at their own game," say Perry and Greber, "but instead is one that turns the game on its side and changes the rules" (1990:98). Unless the androcentric nature of the computer culture is addressed, they conclude, remediations, however meritorious in and of themselves, will not be very likely to effect change.

The literature thus gives university decision-makers a plenitude of advice on how to incorporate more women into computing. The recommendations for less affluent students, racial and ethnic minorities, and students with disabilities cover an equally broad range. The point is for university decision-makers to listen to and involve the users at their own institution. One way to meet user needs is to incorporate the participation of users into campus decision-making. But this raises another issue, one which is equally controversial.

3.5 User Participation in Decision-making

There is one additional consideration. University decision-makers considering a plan for computerization will also have to contemplate changes in decision-making itself. Computers are unique in that they permit a quantum increase in the amount of information available to every level of the organization. The ability to plan, control, and develop alternatives shifts with the information (Meyrowitz 1985:62ff.). This creates opportunities, and also hazards. Once again, what these are depends upon one's perspective.

For functionalists, potential efficiencies gained by this decentralization of information are balanced by a potential loss of authority. Many are concerned, in particular, that should the decision-making process become too open the university system itself could suffer. This could happen if people who lack expertise, or in some cases even sufficient background knowledge, become involved in deciding technical and policy questions. They point to the resistances which already occur when people's emotions influence their judgement on technology. Furthermore, as was described in Chapter 1, the university decision-making process is complex. Faculty and administrators are already involved in many consultative committees (see Chapter 3). To open this consultative process to every category of user would invite chaos, at worst, and at a minimum would lead to the politicalization of university decision-making.

Conflict theorists see things differently. University decision-making is already political, they charge. The only question is whose interests are being served. For them, user participation is essential if computers are to fulfill their potential. As Arnold Pacey comments:

> The user sphere of technology is nearly always neglected or under-emphasized in professional research. The most ironic aspect of the many technological projects that fail because of a lack of any real understanding or dialogue between professionals and people is that the failure is often blamed on the people. They are said to lack willingness to change, and sometimes sociologists are brought in to study the cultural blockages or vested interests that are assumed to be opposed to progress. Yet the real problem is often with the technologist, who has never sat down with people to discover what their lives are about and what they want and need. (1983:150)

Effective computerization, to conflict theorists, means that the decision-making process must include dialogue with *all* categories of users. And as Pacey concludes, "to engage in a genuinely open dialogue is inevitably to share power over the final decision" (1983:157).

We conclude that an effective process of computerization requires that user needs be addressed. This is not to say that user values should simply replace virtuosity or economic ones. University decision-makers must pay close attention to *all three* value sets in building the computerization network. Building a network requires consultation and negotiation. Once again, it is balance and judgement which are required.

4. Implementing The Plan

4.1 Allocating Resources

The necessity for judgement and balance in building the computerization network has been a recurring theme in this chapter. Perhaps in no place is it more required, or more difficult to achieve, than in allocating resources.

Compounding the inherently political problem of how to divide the resource "pie" is the absence of a generally accepted methodology by which to establish distribution. Cost-benefit analysis does not work well in this context, due in large part to the lack of an agreed upon frame of reference (Bellah *et al.* 1991; Lowrance 1985). A major study of computerization at Carnegie-Mellon University in the United States looked at this kind of measurement problem and concluded:

> When "technology optimists" talk about the effects of computers, they frequently ask about productivity improvement. Unfortunately, measuring productivity is no simple matter. Should we measure efficiency in student learning by counting the number of instructors who can be dismissed? Should we try measuring the proportion of time instructors have for research? Productivity is an abstract and value-laden idea. We did not feel prepared to say that something learned in 15 minutes is more efficient than something learned in 1.5 hours. On the other hand we can find out how people actually use computers and then let the reader decide if these uses are productive. (Kiesler & Sproull 1987:41-42)

We concur. There is no calculus or decision-making matrix which can replace experience, which is why some of the chapters of this report place emphasis upon the historical development of computing at Canadian universities.

Although Canadian universities are affluent by world standards, their experience in resource allocation may still prove instructive. Few Canadian universities shared in the prosperity of the 1980's, and the economic downturn of the 1990's has intensified a difficult financial situation. Computerization at most universities has taken place in a context characterized by cutbacks and restraint. This has greatly intensified the disputes we have been discussing, as there simply have not been enough resources to meet everyone s needs. As computerization has gained momentum over the past decade, needs and demands for computing services have escalated as well. This has led to a shifting pattern in resource allocation.

The first computers at North American universities were primarily dedicated to military-oriented research in the sciences and engineering (Flamm, 1988; see Chapter 4). By the 1960's advances in the technology brought wider use, especially in administration. These computers were still very large and expensive mainframes which required a highly centralized organization (see Chapter 5). The late 1970's and early 1980's saw the rapid development of microprocessor technology and concurrently a proliferation of uses. Resource allocation began to shift increasingly towards administrative uses, that is, as the computing "pie" grew larger, administration took a progressively larger share. This trend continues. As we will see in Chapter 3, pedagogical uses have lagged behind, relative to administration and research. Today, the widespread availability of relatively low-cost microcomputers is transforming university computing again. Several trends in resource allocation have emerged.

The first trend, as will be detailed in Chapter 5, is a massive decentralization of computing on campus. Computer centres are still expanding, of course, but the number of microcomputers on desks and in offices and labs all over campus means that central computer facilities are taking a decreasing share of resources. Few faculty or offices are dependent upon the central facility for their day to day computing needs. The proliferation of microcomputers has meant a rapid expansion in the number and types of applications used. This has brought computing into new areas, but also creates problems for training and maintenance (see below). Decentralization also means that there is a great deal of unused computer capacity on campus. Not everyone uses a computer for every activity, but if there is a computer on nearly every desk it will not be used when its "owner" is doing something else. One of the benefits of decentralization is that it allows departments to rely upon their own resources in accomplishing tasks, but frequently this is achieved by duplicating effort or neglecting common problems. As Weisband and Siegel conclude, "As long as computation implies large common problems, then decentralization of purchasing and services wastes resources. But where local experts can handle the work, centralization wastes talent" (1987:61). As will be more fully discussed in Chapter 5, finding the right balance among organizational structures and the functions they perform is a major question in the process of computerization.

The allocation of resources at Canadian universities is incredibly complex. Computerization has to a great extent been achieved, in a time of fiscal restraint, by moving a large number of relatively small amounts of money here and there in various budgets. The purchase of microcomputers and associated technology has meant that expenditures have not gone elsewhere. One aspect of this is what some have called "jobless growth" (Cordell 1985). For example, prior to computerization faculty turned their typing over to a secretary. With personal computers, most faculty find that they now prepare their own papers, examinations, and correspondence without the assistance of a secretary. Consequently, as enrollments increased and the workload of the university expanded, "productivity" was maintained without hiring additional personnel proportionate to the increase in work. To be more concrete, in 1980 Luther College at the University of Regina had an enrollment of approximately 250 students and an academic office staff of 1.5 people. By 1992 enrollment had soared to over 800 students but the academic office staff had increased to only two. Without computerization, many more people would have had to be hired to do the same amount of work.

The problem of resources allocation, then, is one of finding the most effective way to build the computerization network. Four elements will form the building blocks of the network. First, but not necessarily the most important, is the computer technology itself. Today there is a wide range of hardware and software to choose from, a diversity which is likely to increase (see Chapter 6). What is important is to choose technology which is appropriate for the real needs of the university. This leads to the second element—money. As we will see in Chapter 5, computer prices are falling relative to capacity, which confirms Flamm's earlier finding that, "in real terms, [computer prices have] fallen, on average, more than 20 percent each year over the last three decades and may even have exceeded 25 percent (that is, relative to some average price for all goods and services produced in the economy)" (1988:1). Prices may be falling, but implementing a well-thought-out plan will still require major financial resources. Since monies spent on computerization will not be available for other expenditures, network building requires that decision-makers convince their faculties and departments to forego other possible resources, especially, in the Canadian experience, additional personnel. The third element is space. Whether a university adopts a centralized or decentralized approach to computing, the machines require special treatment. In particular, they must be protected from extremes in temperature and humidity, dust, power surges, theft, and vandalism. This means not only the allocation of suitable space, but the costs of air conditioning, a reliable electrical supply, and security that must accompany it. The final and most crucial element is people. The success or failure of university computerization depends upon the quality of the people who make and execute the plan. We have already discussed the importance of product champions to the network, but they should not be expected to carry the plan. Unless there is active commitment from senior people to computerization, the plan will fail. Leadership is needed to adjudicate between rival interests and champions, to make sure user needs are addressed, to prevent "empire building," and to ensure the good of the whole university is advanced. The task is to find people who are both skilled managers and who know computing. People who are good programmers may lack knowledge of the larger context. A competent administrator without computing skills may not realize that computing cannot be managed just like any other department. What is needed are people who have been cross-trained, that is, people who know both computers and the operations of the university.

4.2 Training And Maintenance

Another recurring theme in this report is the importance of training. The significance of training cannot be over-emphasized. Unless computer users have been adequately trained they will be inefficient, at best, and their full potential will not be realized.

As will be discussed in Chapters 3 and 5, training can take several forms. Formal training classes are widely used in Canada, offered either by software vendors, the university itself, or by private, off-campus computer schools. Most of these extend over several days and provide instruction in the use of a particular software package. University decision-makers need to build these classes into the computerization plan. If the choice is to rely on non-university training, provision must be made to provide personnel with release time and monies to cover fees and related costs. University-run classes should be frequent (particularly if staff turnover is high), with priority given to those software packages (word processing, spreadsheets, databases, etc.) which are most widely used.

Informal training has been an important part of the Canadian experience of computerization. We have already discussed the role product champions play in providing informal instruction and advice. This will undoubtedly continue, but it is no substitute for a formal training programme. Additionally, there is a virtual "oral tradition" growing around computer use. Many people have trouble remembering the many details learned in a training class, particularly for functions not used frequently. Computer manuals have a reputation for being difficult to understand, so many people turn to other workers or colleagues for advice. Informal training frequently is what makes computerization "work," but it also can lead to inefficiencies as a champion or even an only somewhat more knowledgeable co-worker may find him- or herself spending a great deal of time acting as a *de facto* instructor.

The plan must also pay attention to the type of training provided. As will be discussed in Chapter 3, computer literacy classes may be useful for novices but are of relatively little value in teaching most people how to effectively use software. Differences between applications are usually sufficiently great that what is learned for one package will be of marginal utility for another. Training therefore needs to be discipline (or office) specific, concentrating on the software actually used at the university.

A final concern is maintenance. As Chapter 5 discusses, maintenance should be a major consideration in choosing hardware and needs to be built into the plan from the beginning. A system which is difficult or expensive to maintain is no bargain, no matter what the initial price. Various approaches have been tried in Canada, service contracts with the vendor or developing in-house expertise are the most common. Decentralization of computing has created difficulties for maintenance. As the number of systems and applications proliferate the task of maintaining them all grows more difficult even as the likelihood of incompatibilities increases. Many universities try to solve the problem by limiting the types of machines and applications for which support will be provided (see Chapter 5).

5. Conclusions

To help achieve the greatest benefit in the computerization process, we conclude the following:

1. There are several ways of speaking about computerization. One which is particularly useful speaks of the process of computerization as building a network. University decision-makers must weave together various technical components with people's needs and interests, enlisting both into the plan for computerization.
2. There is no simple formula or "one right way" to go about computerization. It is a long process of consultation and negotiation, made particularly difficult, on the one hand, by unpredictability and rapid change in the elements (both technical and human) that make up the network, and, on the other hand, by inertia and resistance to change within the organization. Balance and judgement are required.
3. In order to enlist people into the network, decision-makers must first ask three questions: What are people's attitudes toward computers within the institution? Are there product champions which can be mobilized for support? And what value commitments are involved? Enrolling product champions is crucial to the success of the computerization plan. Value conflicts are likely to be particularly difficult to deal with.
4. An effective process of computerization requires that user needs be addressed. User values should not simply replace virtuosity or economic ones. Rather, university decision-makers must pay attention to all three value sets in building the computerization network. This necessitates the participation of users in decisions regarding computerization.
5. The problem of resources allocation is not one of simple cost-benefit analysis in the economic sense, but one of finding the most effective way to build the computerization network. Four elements will form the building blocks of the network—people, technology, money, and space. The most crucial element is people. The success or failure of university computerization depends upon the quality of the people who make and execute the plan.
6. The significance of training cannot be over-emphasized. Unless computer users have been adequately trained they will be inefficient and unhappy, and their full potential will not be realized. Training needs to be more

than formal instruction. Informal training and consultation done by product champions and other co-workers is essential and should be rewarded.

References

Alliance for Undergraduate Education. *The Freshman Year in Science and Engineering.* Washington: The National Science Foundation, 1990.

Becker, H. J. and C. W. Sterling. "Equity in School Computer Use: National Data and Neglected Considerations." *Journal of Educational Computing Research,* 3.3 (1987), 289-311.

Bellah R. *et al. The Good Society*. New York: Alfred A. Knopf, 1991.

Bijker, W., T. Hughes, and T. Pinch (ed.). *The Social Construction of Technological Systems*. Cambridge, Mass.: The MIT Press, 1987.

Bijker, W. "The Social Construction of Bakelite: Toward a Theory of Invention." In Bijker, W., T. Hughes and T. Pinch (ed.), 1987, 159-187.

Bortua, M. *et. al.* [The Computer Use Study Group]. "Computers In Schools: Stratifier or Equalizer." *The Quarterly Newsletter of the Laboratory of Comparative Human Cognition* 5.3 (1983), 51-55.

Brecher, D. "Gender and Learning: Do Women Learn Differently?" In K. Tijdens *et al.* (ed.) *Women, Work and Computerization: Forming New Alliances.* Amsterdam: North-Holland, 1989, 207-210.

Brody, H. "The Great Equalizer." *PC/Computing* 1989, July, 83-93.

Brown, C. *et al. Computer Access in Higher Education for Students with Disabilities: A Practical Guide to the Selection and Use of Adapted Computer Technology, 2nd edition*. U.S. Department of Education, 1989.

Callon, M. "Society in the Making: The Study of Technology as a Tool for Sociological Analysis." In Bijker, W., T. Hughes and T. Pinch (ed.), 1987, 83-103.

Chen, M. "Gender Differences in Adolescents' Uses of and Attitudes Toward Computers." In McLauglin, M. (ed.) *Communications Yearbook 10.* Beverly Hills: Sage Publishing, 1987, 200-216.

Chronicle of Higher Education. 21.13 (1980) 17 Nov.

Chronicle of Higher Education. 33.44 (1987), 15 July.

Chronicle of Higher Education. 38.1 (1991), 28 Aug.

Clarke, V. and S. Chambers. "Gender-Based Factors in Computing Enrollments and Achievement: Evidence from a Study of Tertiary Students." *Journal of Educational Computing* 5.4 (1989), 409-429.

Collins, T. and L. Price. "Microcomputers and the Learning Disabled College Writer." *Collegiate Microcomputer* 5.1 (1987), 41-44.

Collis, B. "Reflections on Inequalities in Computer Education: Do the Rich Get Richer?" *Education and Computing* 1.3 (1985), 179-186.

Cordell, A. *The Uneasy Eighties.* Science Council of Canada. Ottawa: Minister of Supply and Services, 1985.

Culley, L. "Girls, Boys and Computers." *Educational Studies*, 14.1 (1988), 3-8.

— "Option Choice and Careers Guidance: Gender and Computing in Secondary Schools." *Western European Education* 21.4 (1990), 41-53.

Demetrulias, D. and N. Rosenthal. "Discrimination Against Females and Minorities in Microcomputer Advertising." *Computers and the Social Sciences* 1 (1985), 91-95.

Dublin, M. *FutureHype: The Tyranny of Prophecy*. Markham, Ont.: Viking, 1989.

Fischer, W. *et al.* "The Elusive Product Champion." *Research Management* May-June (1986), 13-16.

Flamm, K. *Creating the Computer*. Washington, D.C.: The Brookings Institution, 1988.

Fowler, C. J. H. and D. Murray. "Gender and Cognitive Style Differences at the Human-Computer Interface." In Bullinger and Shackel (ed.), *Human-Computer Interaction_INTERACT'87*. Amsterdam: North-Holland, 709-714.

Frenkel, K. "Women and Computing." *Communications of the ACM* 33.11 (1990), 36-46.

Glynn, S. *et al.* "Computer Environments for Managing Writers' Thinking Processes. In Britton, B. and S. Glynn (ed.). *Computer Writing Environments: Theory, Research and Design.* Hillsdale, N.J.: Lawrence Erlbaum Associates, Publishers, 1989.

Greenbaum, J. *The Head and the Heart*. Aarhus (Denmark): Aarhus University, Department for Information and Media Science, 1987.

Griffiths, M. "Strong Feelings About Computers." *Women's Studies International Forum* 11.2 (1988), 145-154.

Haralmos, M. *Sociology: Themes and Perspectives*. London: Bell and Hyman, Ltd., 1985.

Hart, H. "The Hypotheses of Cultural Lag." In Allen, Francis *et al.* (ed.), *Technology and Social Change*. New York: Appleton-Century-Crofts, 1957, 417-434.

Hawkridge, D., T. Vincent, and G. Hales. *New Information Technology in the Education of Disabled Children and Adults.* London: Croom Helm, 1985.

Heffron, K. "Native Children Interface with Computers." *Canadian Journal of Native Education* 11.3 (1984), 15-26.

Industry Science and Technology Canada. *Women in Science and Engineering, Vol. I: Universities*. Ottawa, 1991.

Jacobs, J. "Social Implications of Computers: Ethical and Equity Issues." *ACM SIGCUE Outlook* 20.1 (1988), 100-114.

Kaulback, B. "Styles of Learning Among Native Children: A Review of the Research." *Canadian Journal of Native Education* 11.3 (1984), 27ff.

Keisler, S. and L. Sproull (ed.). *Computing and Change on Campus.* Cambridge: Cambridge University Press, 1987.

Keisler, S., L. Sproull, and J. Eccles. "Pool Halls, Chips and War'Games: Women in the Culture of Computing." *Psychology of Women Today* 9 (1985), Dec., 451-462.

Keller, E. F. *Reflections on Gender and Science*. New Haven and London: Yale University Press, 1985.

Kling, R. "Computerization and Social Transformations." *Science, Technology and Human Values* 16.3 (1991), 342-367.

Latour, B. *Science in Action*. Cambridge, Mass.: Harvard University Press, 1987.

Lewis, J. "Technology, Enterprize, and American Economic Growth." *Science* 215 (1982), 5 Mar., 1204-1211.

Linn, M. "Fostering Equitable Consequences from Computer Learning Environments." *Sex Roles* 13.3/4 (1985), 229-240.

Lipkin, J. and L. McCormick. "Sex Bias at the Computer Terminal—How Schools Program Girls." *The Monitor* 1986, Jan.-Feb., 14-17.

Lips, H. and L. Temple. "Majoring in Computer Science: Causal Models for Women and Men." *Research in Higher Education* 31.1 (1990), 99-113.

Lowrance, W. *Modern Science and Human Values*. New York: Oxford University Press, 1985.

Maddux, C. "Preface." In Roblyer, M., W. Castine and F. King (ed.), *Assessing the Impact of Computer-Based Instruction: A Review of Recent Research.* New York: The Hawthorn Press, 1988, 1-10.

Malaney, G. and Q. Thurman. "Key Factors in the Use and Frequency of Use of Microcomputers by College Students." *Journal of Educational Technology Systems* 18.2 (1989), 151-160.

Marshall, J. P., F. Erickson, and J. Vonk. "Access Equity of Computer Instruction in High Schools." *Free Inquiry in Creative Sociology* 14.2 (1986), 129-131.

McPhail, I. "Computer Inequities in School Uses of Microcomputers: Policy Implications." *Journal of Negro Education* 54.1 (1985), 3-13.

Menzies, H. *FastForward and Out of Control: How Technology is Changing Your Life.* Toronto: Macmillan of Canada, 1989..

Mesthene, E. *Technological Change: Its Impact on Man and Society*. Cambridge, Mass.: Harvard University Press, 1970.

Meyrowitz, J. *No Sense of Place: The Impact of Electronic Media on Social Behavior.* Oxford: Oxford University Press, 1985.

Miura, I. "The Relationship of Computer Self-Efficacy Expectations to Computer Interest and Course Enrollment in College." *Sex Roles* 16.5/6 (1987), 303-311.

Nimkoff, M. "Obstacles to Innovation." In Allen, F. *et al.* (ed.), *Technology and Social Change*. New York: Appleton-Century-Crofts, 1957, 56-71.

Ogburn, W. *The Social Effects of Aviation*. Boston: Houghton Mifflin Company, 1946.

Social Change. New York: The Viking Press, 1950 (1st ed. 1922).

"How Technology Causes Social Change." In Allen, F. *et al.* (ed.), *Technology and Social Change*. New York: Appleton-Century-Crofts, 1957, 12-26.

On Culture and Social Change. Duncan, O. (ed.) Chicago: University of Chicago Press, 1964.

Pacey, A. *The Culture of Technology.* Cambridge, Massachusetts: MIT Press, 1983.

Pearl, A. *et al.* "Becoming a Computer Scientist." *Communications of the ACM* 33.11 (1990), 48-57.

Perry, R. and L. Greber. "Women and Computers: An Introduction." *Signs: Journal of Women in Culture and Society* 16.11 (1990), 74-101.

Pinch, T. and W. Bijker. "The Social Construction of Facts and Artifacts: Or How the Sociology of Science and the Sociology of Technology Might enefit Each Other." In Bijker, W., T. Hughes, T. and T. Pinch (ed.), 1987, 17-50.

Porter, A. *et al. A Guidebook for Technology Assessment and Impact Analysis.* New York: North-Holland, 1980.

Rosenthal, N. R. and D. M. Demetrulias. "Assessing Gender Bias in Computer Software." *Computers in the Schools* 5.1/2 (1988), 153-163.

Schon, D. "Champions for Radical New Inventions." *Harvard Business Review* 1963, Mar.-Apr., 77-86.

Segal, G. and V. Marciano. "Issues of Equivalent Access to Computer Technology for the Disabled Student in the Classroom." *SIGCUE Outlook* 20.1 (1988), 131-140.

Smith, S. *Report of the Commission of Inquiry on Canadian University Education* [the Smith Report]. Ottawa: Association of Universities and Colleges of Canada, 1991.

Sproull, L., S. Kiesler, and D. Zubrow. "Encountering an Alien Culture." In Kiesler, S. and L. Sproull (ed.), 1987, 173-194.

Statistics Canada. *Education in Canada: A Statistical Review for 1984-85.* Ottawa: Minister of Supply and Services, 1986.

Statistics Canada. *Education in Canada: A Statistical Review for 1988-89.* Ottawa: Minister of Supply and Services, 1990.

Statistics Canada. *Education in Canada: A Statistical Review for 1989-90* Ottawa: Minister of Supply and Services, 1991.

Stickles, M. "Girls, Minorities and Low-Income Students: Are They Getting Computer Time?" *PTA Today* 13.6 (1988), 10-11.

Suchman, L. and B. Jordan. "Computerization and Women's Knowledge." In K. Tijdens *et al.* (ed.), *Women, Work and Computerization: Forming New Alliances.* Amsterdam: North-Holland, 1989, 153-159.

Temple, L. and H. Lips. "Gender Differences and Similarities in Attitudes Towards Computers." *Computers in Human Behavior* 5 (1989), 215-226.

Toffler, A. *Future Shock.* New York: Random House, 1970.

Turkle, S. *The Second Self: Computers and the Human Spirit.* New York: Simon and Schuster, 1984.

— "Computational Reticence: Why Women Fear the Intimate Machine." In Kramarae, C. (ed.), *Technology and Women's Voices.* London: Routledge and Kegan Paul, 1988, 41-61.

Turkle, S. and S. Papert. "Epistemological Pluralism: Styles and Voices Within the Computer Culture." *Signs: Journal of Women in Culture and Science* 16.11 (1990), 128-157.

Tyagi, P. "Student Reaction: Mandatory Use of Microcomputers in Business Education." *Journal of Business Education* 1984, Nov., 89-92.

Urban, C. *Inequities in Computer Education Due to Gender, Race and Socioeconomic Status.* Indiana University: Exit Project, 1986.

Verne, G. "Women's Challenge to Computer Science and Technology." In M. Dahms *et al.* (ed.), *Women Challenge Technology. European Conference On Women, Natural Sciences and Technology.* Elsinore (Denmark): University of Aalborg, Centertrykkeriet, 1986, 261-267.

Walpole, P. "Computers, Wheelchairs and One Reality." *Computers in Education* 4.9 (1987), 10-12.

Wessells, M. *Computer, Self, and Society.* Englewood Cliffs, N.J.: Prentice Hall, 1990.

Westrum, R. *Technologies and Society: The Shaping of People and Things.* Belmont, Calif.: Wadswoth, 1991.

Weisband, S. and J. Siegel. "The Computers Are Coming!" In Kiesler, S. and L. Sproull (ed.), 1987, 43-69.

Wollam, J. "The Advantage of Same-Sex Programs." *The Gifted Child Today* 13.2 (1990), 22-24.

Woolgar, S. and K. Grint. "Computers and the Transformation of Social Analysis." *Science, Technology and Human Values* 16.3 (1991), 368-378.

Yeloushan, K. "Social Barriers Hindering Successful Entry of Females into Technology-Oriented Fields." *Educational Technology* 29.11 (1989), 44-46.

CHAPTER 3

COMPUTERS IN TEACHING

1. Computers in Teaching: Past and Present

1.1 The Canadian and American Experience

1.1.1 Introduction

While few people nowadays would question the decision to computerize such administrative functions as student registration or payroll in post-secondary institutions, and virtually no one would dispute the tremendous impact of computers on research, there are widely divergent opinions among academics with respect to the use of computers in teaching (*cf.* Chapter 2, 2.2). There are computer enthusiasts who argue, often in a rather naive fashion reminiscent of the exaggerated claims made for other instructional technology, such as language laboratories (Underwood 1989:71), that computing will revolutionize post-secondary education.[1] There are some academics (the so-called "product champions", *cf.* 2.2.2) who are experimenting with instructional uses of computers, assuming that "affordable interactive technologies can add value to the curriculum" (Graves 1989:1). Yet another group of academics opposes instructional computing, believing for example that the use of machines might dehumanize the instructional process, eliminate teachers in the long run[2] or have detrimental effects on students' health (Hirvela 1988:310).

The attitude of the majority of academics towards instructional computing would appear to be characterized by various degrees of indifference and indecision.[3] This attitude may appear somewhat surprising, given that computers have been for many years "a major stimulus for eliciting work and thought about teaching methods and the processes by which human beings learn" (Bok 1985:37), in particular through recent developments in cognitive psychology and artificial intelligence. However, a striking feature of post-secondary institutions in North America (and probably elsewhere as well) is

---

[1] According to our baseline survey, 2.7% of the faculty respondents agreed strongly and 17.5% agreed with the statement that computers will bring about a pedagogical revolution in higher education (see Figure 6 in Chapter 2 for further details).

[2] See Tables 2, 3 and 4 in Chapter 2 for the responses to statement # 24 in our attitude survey. See also Appendix I.

[3] A number of factors which may explain this attitude will be discussed later in this chapter. According to our baseline survey, 27.7% of respondents are undecided as to whether computers can help to achieve a higher quality of learning, while 35.7% are undecided as to whether computers will bring about a pedagogical revolution in higher education (*cf.* Figures 5 and 6 in Chapter 2).

the

> lack of systematic effort to understand the ways in which students learn. Faculties rarely spend time thinking collectively about the educational process. When they do, they almost always discuss *what* students should read and study rather than *how* students learn and how they might be helped to learn more effectively (Bok 1985:37).

While this is, regrettably, an accurate assessment of the situation, it is also true that extensive research on instructional computing in post-secondary education has been published in recent years. In fact, there has been an "explosion" of research in this field, as demonstrated by the existence of many specialized journals, the increasing frequency of well-attended workshops and conferences on instructional computing, and the publication of many books and extensive bibliographies.

There are indeed good reasons for investigating the potential of instructional computing at post-secondary institutions. "Academe's traditional tentativeness in matters of curriculum revision and innovation" (Graves 1989:1) notwithstanding, it is simply no longer possible for academics to ignore the role of computers in society at large (*cf.* Chapter 1). It is of particular significance in this respect that students are entering the university with increasing familiarity with computers and that new demands are being placed on universities, especially in programmes which are oriented towards job training (*cf.* 1.2.3.1).

1.1.2 Terminology

Given the frequent use of jargon in the discussion of instructional computing, a few comments on terminology are in order. Various terms, usually in the form of acronyms, are used to refer to instructional computing in general. They reflect different approaches to the instructional process. While the terms Computer-Assisted/Aided Instruction (CAI), Computer-Based Instruction (CBI), and Computer-Managed Instruction (CMI) emphasize the role of the teacher, terms such as Computer-Assisted Learning (CAL) and Computer-Based Learning (CBL) stress the role of the learner. In this chapter, the term CAI, probably the most commonly encountered in the literature, will be used. It is broadly defined here to include all varieties of instructional computing, not in the restrictive sense used by some authors to refer to a "programmed learning approach in which specific educational objectives are achieved through step-by-step instruction" (Simonson & Thompson 1990:122; for a discussion of these terms, *cf.* also Morrison, Ross & O'Dell 1991:188; Hannafin & Peck 1988:3ff). In addition, a range of more specific terms related to particular disciplines or tasks, such as Computer-Assisted Distance Education (CADE), Computer-Assisted Language Learning (CALL) and Computer-Assisted Language Acquisition (CALA), will be used here.

1.1.3 Types of Instructional Computing

There are many varieties of instructional computing. Computers may serve, first of all, to prepare lecture materials with the help of appropriate software, e.g. for data analysis, complex calculations, graphics, word processing, and visual presentation (for the perceived impact of these uses, *cf.* Appendix C:C-13, Table 6.4). The material may be delivered to students either in a more traditional form (hand-out, overhead) or with an "electronic blackboard" (*cf.* 1.2.3.3). Secondly, a course component in which use of the computer is made to illustrate selected material may be integrated into lectures (*cf.* 1.2.3.1). More frequently, computer lab sessions are added on to courses otherwise taught in the traditional lecture format, to give all students an opportunity for hands-on learning. Instructional computing also includes various types of out-of-class use of computers by students either on- or off-campus, such as for drill and practice, data analysis, access to expert systems, simulation and modelling (*cf.* Appendix C:C-5).

1.2 The University of Regina Experience

1.2.1 Comparison with other Canadian/North American Universities

According to our baseline survey on academic computing, research in the use of computers for teaching purposes is presently not a major undertaking in Canadian universities (*cf.* Appendix C:C-4). A report recently submitted by the Commission of Inquiry on Canadian University Education has found that CAI with its "promise of individualized, self-paced learning through the development of advanced software" has had very little impact on Canadian universities (Smith 1991:50). As noted in the survey on innovations in teaching in Canadian universities undertaken in preparation of the Smith Report, it is difficult to assess with precision the extent of innovation in Canadian university programmes and classrooms: "There are certainly many exciting new initiatives, but these have to be interpreted in the light of prevailing educational practice. Other (and incomplete) evidence suggests that teaching approaches in Canadian universities are predominantly traditional, and rely heavily on lectures and formal examinations" (Knapper 1991:XVII).[4]

This general characterization also applies to the situation at the University of Regina. The vast majority of courses are taught in the traditional lecture format, although a number of faculty have demonstrated considerable commitment to instructional computing (*cf.* below), in spite of insufficient institutional support (*cf.* 2.2.3) and little recognition (*cf.* 2.6.2). It should be mentioned here that a report submitted by the Academic Review Task Force to the University of Regina specifically recommended "that faculty members be

---

[4] A forthcoming report on creative applications of information technology in North American post-secondary institutions ("The Joe Wyatt Challenge—101 Success Stories of Information Technologies in Higher Education") mentions only three Canadian projects; *cf.* Careless (1992:5).

encouraged and given assistance to become more familiar with, and to make appropriate use of computers and other technological developments" (1988:67).

1.2.2 Use of Computers in Off-campus Classes[5]

Like many other Canadian institutions, the University of Regina has attempted for a number of years to address the "challenge of teaching students remote from the campus" by experimenting with "technological and pedagogical innovations" (Knapper 1991:XI). According to our baseline survey on academic computing, the most widespread use of computers for distance education in Canadian universities appears to be in Administration, Education and Medicine (*cf.* Appendix C:C-5). While many institutions still rely mainly upon very traditional media, in particular print,[6] University of Regina professors, teaching off-campus classes, make use of facilities at Audiovisual Services (AV) which are especially designed for distance education and equipped with appropriate technology, including a computer which may be used by instructors to demonstrate selected lecture material. Instructors lecture in the AV classroom to students registered on-site and may be reached over the telephone by off-campus students during the lectures.

Courses are delivered to nearly seventy sites in the province of Saskatchewan through the Saskatchewan Communications Network (SCN). This distance education programme, offering first and second year credit courses, is funded by the provincial government. Decisions about course offerings are made by a committee with representatives from the University of Regina, the University of Saskatchewan, SIAST (Saskatchewan Institute of Applied Sciences and Technology) and the regional colleges.

Presently, in-class use of computers occurs in only one of the three courses offered through the University of Regina, the introductory computer science class (for a discussion of the rationale for in-class use of the computer in CS courses, *cf.* 1.2.3.1) However, the Language Institute of the University of Regina is presently considering establishing a distance education degree programme in French which would include a CALL component. The instructor who has been coordinating off-campus teaching of French through SCN is being granted release time to carry out research on the pedagogical and technological planning of this new programme.[7]

---

[5] Interview Wilhelm (1992); interview Maguire (1992); memorandum Wilhelm (1992).

[6] *Cf.* Knapper (1991:XI) and Figure 1. For a report on a new experiment in electronic teaching, the "Electrohome Classroom/Guelph Waterloo Education Link System", which allows graduate students at both institutions to attend the same lectures in Chemistry and Physics, see Eberlee (1992).

[7] Other Canadian universities are considering offering 24-hour access to language instruction both to off- and on-campus students (Deakin 1991).

1.2.3 Use of Computers in On-campus Classes

This section is not intended to give a comprehensive overview of past and present instructional computing activities at the University of Regina, but rather to illustrate its major aspects, such as the in- and out-of-class use of commercially available software for teaching in Administration, Chemistry, Computer Science, Engineering, Geography, Sociology/Social Studies, the on-site development of CALL software for Cree and German as well as the use of computers for the preparation of class materials. These activities at the University of Regina must be seen in the general context of instructional computing in Canadian universities, which is analyzed in sections III, IV and V of Appendix C. Figures 1 to 6 summarize the results of the survey with respect to the various types of in- and out-of class use of computers, class size, the computer systems used as well as evaluation and student response. Survey results concerning the use of computers for the preparation of class materials are illustrated by Figure 7.

Figure 1. In-Class Use of Computers

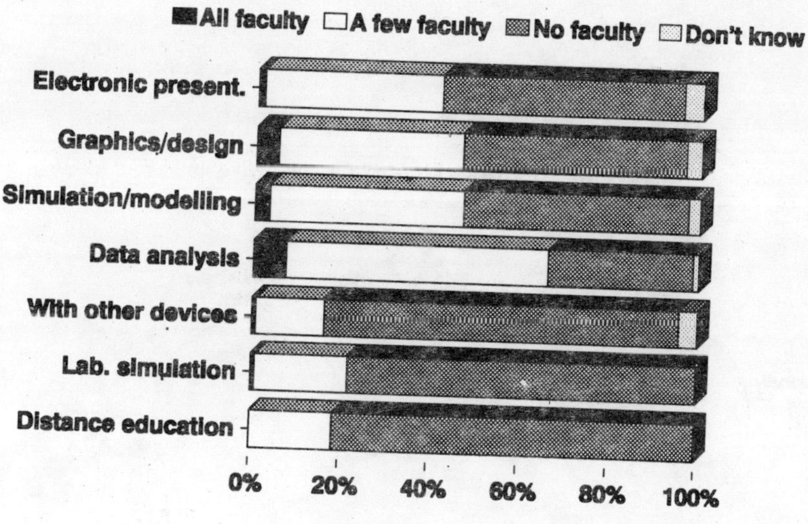

Figure 2. In-Class Use of Computers

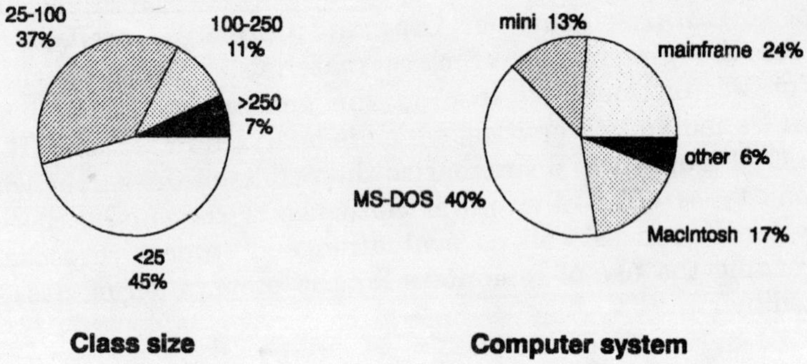

Commercially available software makes up about 75% of all software used

Figure 3. In-Class Use of Computers

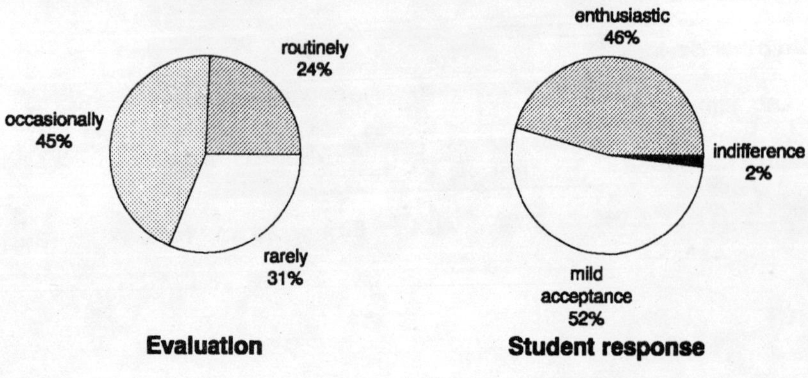

Figure 4. Out-Of-Class Use of Computers

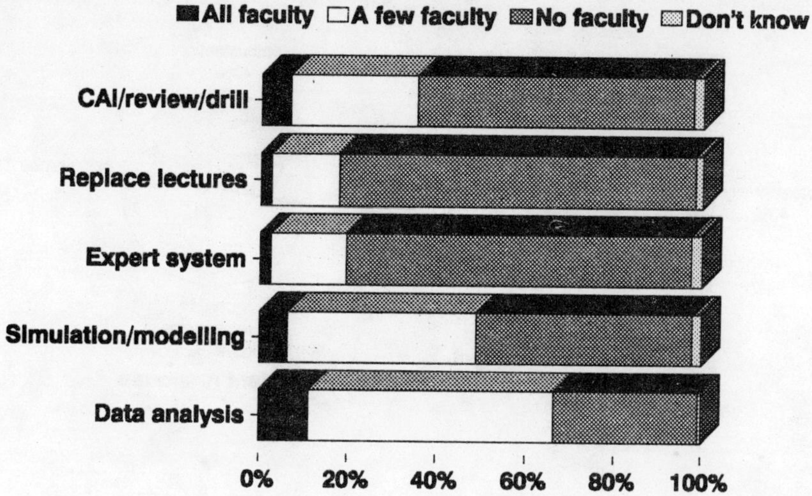

Figure 5. Out-Of-Class Use of Computers

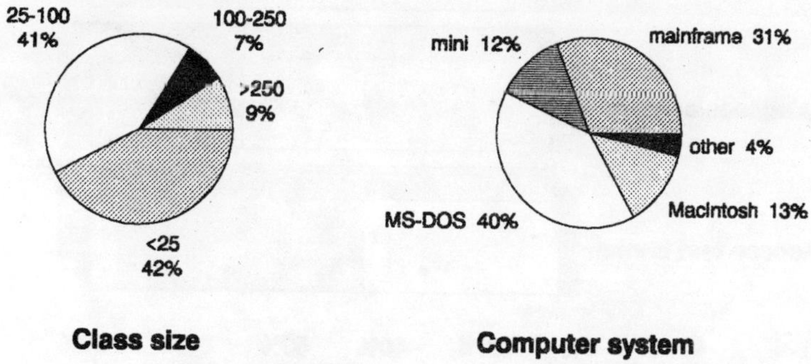

Commercially available software makes up about 75% of all software used

Figure 6. Out-Of-Class Use of Computers

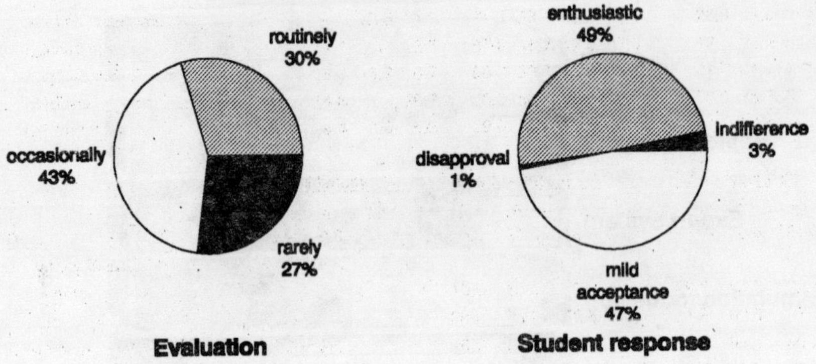

Figure 7. Computer Use For Class Material Preparation

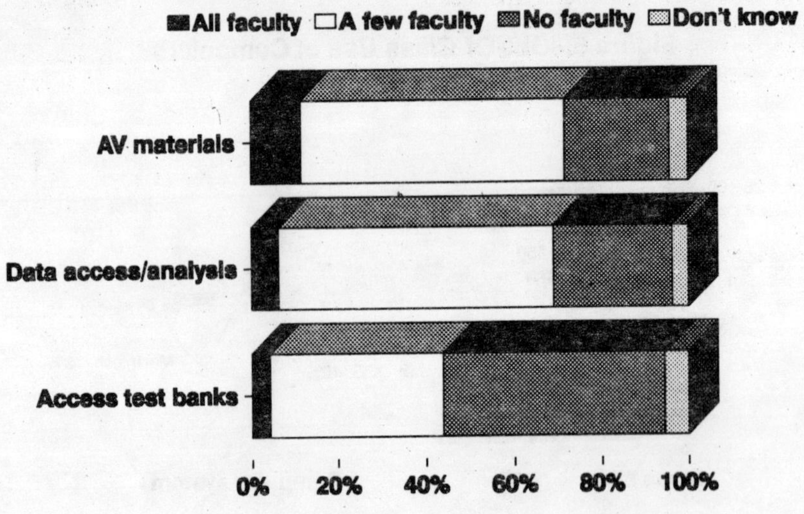

1.2.3.1 Use of Commercially Developed Software in Selected Disciplines

Administration[8]

Since Fall 1988, a compulsory non-credit course has been offered by the Faculty of Administration to bring students in their first semester to the level of computer literacy required for courses in Administration. While students majoring in Administration are also required to take the introductory computer science course, this non-credit course was established to teach discipline-specific applications of word processing and spreadsheet packages. The decision to use Microsoft Word (and not Word Perfect, more commonly used outside of the university) was primarily based on the fact that the university provides technical support for Microsoft Word only. After experimenting with the database package dBase, the package Quattro-Pro was selected to introduce the students to both spreadsheet and limited database applications. Students receive a total of 20 hours instruction in a microcomputer lab, which is also accessible to students outside of class times. Instruction in the lab sessions is based on a locally produced manual. Student performance is measured only through assignments to be completed in each session, and grades are assigned as Pass/Fail. The course provides flexibility with respect to attendance as students who are already familiar with word processing and spreadsheets may leave the lab sessions after completing their assignment.

According to our informant, most students are satisfied with the basic design of the course although some feel that credit should be given for the course and others question the selection of the packages. The need for this course is anticipated to be a transient one as familiarity with computers among first year students will most likely continue to increase.

Support for faculty members who are exploring the use of computers in teaching is available from the programme coordinator of this course. However, only a few instructors are presently using software (spreadsheet packages) in their classes.

Chemistry[9]

Unlike some other North American universities (see Jones & Smith 1989 for a report on the experience at the University of Illinois at Urbana-Champaign), the University of Regina has not given much support to CAI research and development in Chemistry. Although ten out of thirteen faculty members in the Department use computers, (purchased mainly through grants, research contracts, accountable allowance funds or personal resources), few of them are interested in instructional computing, and the use of computers is virtually limited to research and/or preparation of materials for in-class use, in

---

[8] Interview Sollars (1992).

[9] Interview Chandler (1992).

particular for graphics and calculations.

To this date, little use has been made of computers to address instructional problems specific to Chemistry (Jones & Smith 1989:28), either through drills, quizzes or fully developed interactive video lessons, although some instructors have experimented with using the computer for simulations. The lack of adequate lab facilities and the inadequacy of commercially available instructional software[10] for Chemistry appear to be the main reasons for the low level of involvement in instructional computing.

Experience with commercially available software for teaching Chemistry has shown that there is some potential for CAI in Chemistry, based in particular on the computer's infinite "patience", the possibility to repeat drills as frequently as needed, and to do complex calculations, graphics and graphic manipulation. However, many of the packages were found to be either trivial or too limited in scope. Another limitation is hardware; one of the packages tested for instance, the Beaker "expert systems" for Organic Chemistry, may be used only with Macintosh computers. Of the faculty teaching Chemistry, none has engaged in on-site software development.

A computer lab facility for senior undergraduate students in Chemistry and Biochemistry has been planned by a research team and may be available to students in Fall 1992. The lab will be equipped with three computers (provided by the Faculty of Science), a laser printer (provided by the Department) and sophisticated software for graphics and calculations as well as molecular simulations (acquired through a grant from a major US software company). It is planned to make the lab accessible twenty-four hours a day to students working on class assignments and/or term projects. Since computer literacy can be assumed for the vast majority of the students taking upper-level Chemistry classes, teaching in the lab will focus on familiarizing students with the use of the software. The research team is also investigating how the new computer lab component is to be integrated with the course content of those senior undergraduate classes which will make use of the new facility. As well, a new class on computer modelling for fourth year students is being developed. It is anticipated that this course will include regular in-class use of computers. Finally, it should be noted that as in other areas at the University of Regina (see below), there has been little institutional support with respect to computer training for faculty and lab instructors in Chemistry. Informal help and advice on hardware and software are provided by product champions (*cf.* 2.2.2).

Computer Science[11]

Of fourteen full-time faculty members in the department, only three have experimented with CAI in various courses (CS 102, Introduction to Computers;

---

10 This appears to be generally a major concern for instructors in Canadian universities; *cf.* 2.4.1.

11 Interview Maguire (1992).

CS 230, Software Productivity Tools; CS 300, Elements of Computer Hardware and Software; CS 372, Advanced Systems Analysis and Design, and CS 405, Principles of Computer Graphics). These instructors have found that graphically oriented tasks are best demonstrated through in-class use of computers as opposed to using the blackboard, overhead transparencies or slides. For example, when introducing students to software for Macintosh computers, in-class illustration allowing for visualization of icon movements appears to be an obvious pedagogical choice. In the introductory course, there is also some in-class use of the computer for text-oriented tasks, in particular to demonstrate the various steps involved in programming.

It may seem surprising that the use of computers and commercially available software in Computer Science classes offered at the University of Regina has not been more extensive, and that of the faculty teaching Computer Science, none has engaged in on-site development of instructional software. The informant mentioned a number of factors which may explain the limited involvement of faculty in CAI. First of all, adequate facilities are lacking: only two classrooms are wired, but have no fixed equipment; the computer and display technology have to be set up by the instructor for every in-class use. Moreover, in-class use of computers requires more preparation time than the traditional lecture format. This may well be the major factor preventing more faculty involvement.

Furthermore, it is felt that there is little support from the university administration for faculty to engage in instructional computing activities. Another factor is the assumption that the computer labs scheduled in addition to the lectures provide sufficient and appropriate demonstration of hardware and software. This may in fact not always be the case as lab sessions, held by lab instructors, are not necessarily closely coordinated with the course content presented by the main instructor in the lectures (except for the introductory course). Finally, as a result of a strong emphasis on research within the Faculty of Science and a restrictive definition of research (research in instructional computing is not considered to be "appropriate" research; *cf.* 2.6.2), incentives for faculty to focus on the quality of teaching by exploring the potential pedagogical benefits of CAI are virtually non-existent.

In spite of the lack of adequate facilities and the greater amount of preparation time, those instructors who have made use of computers in their classes to illustrate specific course content when appropriate for pedagogical reasons, consider this to be a worthwhile endeavour, and informal student feedback has generally been positive.

Engineering[12]

In 1990, the conventional drafting lab was replaced by a computerized facility, the Computer-Aided Engineering Center (CAEC), designed to function

---

[12] Interview Waldal (1992); *cf.* also Waldal (1991).

both as a microcomputer lab with 25 workstations and an instructor's console, and as a 50-seat video lecture theater.[13] When planning the lab, the decision was made not to install a large-screen projection system. It was felt that the dark environment required for this technology would not be suitable for the particular pedagogical situation (need to record notes, manual drafting; Waldal 1991:74). More importantly, large-screen projection systems do not allow for two-way communication between students and instructors. The system adopted for the CAEC does not limit interaction to the instructor transmitting information to the class, but enables students to give feedback through their monitors. With a special control unit, instructors can, however, lock out the students' keyboards whenever they want the class to concentrate on the information displayed on each monitor.

In addition to allowing for interaction, the new facility has a number of technological features which enable instructors to experiment with innovative teaching techniques. For instance, a two-camera system and a special-effects generator allow students to work on one task while the instructor sets up the next example. Also, the split-screen capability of the effects generator makes it possible for instructors to demonstrate different problem-solving methods simultaneously (Waldal 1991:73).

The CAEC is now regularly used for all undergraduate courses with a computer component in the Electronic Information Systems Engineering, the Industrial Systems Engineering and the Regional Environmental Systems Engineering programmes. One of these courses is EN 100 (Engineering Graphics), in which drafting concepts were previously taught in lectures and instructors had to rely on subsequent lab sessions to check whether students had actually understood the material. These concepts are now illustrated by the instructor while lecturing in the CAEC (Waldal 1991:73). There has been so much demand for the facility that its use now has to be priorized, with larger classes getting priority.

The CAEC is also used for the Professional Training Development Programme, a result of the cooperation between the Faculty of Engineering and two software companies, Generation 5 Technology (Regina) and Autodesk Inc. (Sausalito, Calif.). In exchange for the free use of industry standard CAD software in undergraduate teaching, the Faculty of Engineering runs intensive professional training sessions for this software in the CAEC (1 week/month). This programme also supports the teaching function in another way, by covering the costs for lab maintenance, estimated at $ 15,000 per year.

Students, faculty and professionals have responded very positively to the new teaching and learning environment. The ratings for the facility in course evaluations by students have been consistently high. Because of this positive response and of the high demand, the Faculty of Engineering is in the process of planning two new facilities of this kind, one for the Regional Environmental

[13] A detailed description of the technology is given in Waldal (1991).

Systems Engineering Programme (for which funding is being sought from the University) and one for the Professional Training Development Programme (for which outside funding is being secured).

Geography[14]

As a result of the initiative of two junior faculty members, strongly oriented towards computer use because of their exposure to computers in graduate school, the situation has changed considerably since 1982 when there was not a single computer in the Department of Geography. There are now twenty computers, most of which were purchased by the Department. Its seven full-time faculty members each have a computer at their disposal; three now use the computer regularly in their teaching. The Department has established a committee to deal with instructional and research computing in Geography.

In the early 1980's, when microcomputers became widely available, cartography was computerized on a large scale. In order to reflect this change in the field, computers have been used extensively since 1987 for teaching in two senior undergraduate courses in Geography (GEOG 405, Advanced Spatial Analysis, and GEOG 407, Computer-Assisted Cartography). Occasional use of computers is made in other classes as well to illustrate particular issues, such as constructing a topographic map both manually and with the computer, or to present statistical data through demographic diagrams in GEOG 340 (Population Geography).

In 1986, the Department of Geography submitted a proposal for a GIS (Geographic Information System) computer lab with 10 workstations to the Faculty of Arts and the Faculty of Graduate Studies and Research. The proposal, which emphasized the great potential of GIS both for teaching and research in Geography, was accepted by the university administration. The funding came mainly from the Faculty of Arts as opportunities for increased enrolment in Geography were recognized. The GIS lab is now being used primarily for research as another lab facility, the Electronic Learning Centre, has since become available for teaching purposes.

The number of students majoring in Geography has increased sharply since the GIS lab was installed. The demand for GEOG 405, a required class for Geography majors, offered at least once a year, regularly exceeds the number of spaces available. The normal enrolment limit is 20 in order to have no more than two students per workstation in the lab. With one hour of lecture and three hours in the lab, there is a strong emphasis on "hands-on" learning. In addition to the GIS software, which includes modules for producing maps, analyzing data, digitizing maps, outputting maps, and managing map data (e.g. storing, searching, and recombining data), students learn to use statistics packages as well.

GEOG 407, an optional class offered every second year, also has a high

---

[14] Interview Sauchyn (1992).

enrollment and is taught in a format similar to GEOG 405. In this course, students are introduced to computer-assisted cartography, using GIS modules as well as other specialized packages. It is worth mentioning that the instructor of GEOG 407 has taken the initiative to familiarize himself with computer technology and the software available for computer-assisted cartography, over an extended period of time normally designated for research. Classes in computer-assisted cartography and advanced spatial analysis are also offered at the graduate level (GEOG 805 and 807, taught concurrently with GEOG 405 and 407, with additional assignments for graduate students).

Although there has been no formal evaluation of the use of computers in teaching Geography, informal feedback from students, who perceive direct benefits in terms of the job market, has generally been positive.

While some faculty, supported by outside grants and/or contracts, have engaged in on-site development of software for research purposes, the use of software in teaching has been confined to commercially developed software. The faculty involved in instructional computing have found the various commercially developed packages used to be fully adequate for teaching Geography. It should be noted that this is highly sophisticated software which could only be purchased because vendors granted substantial educational discounts to the institution. For instance, ARC/INFO, one of the major GIS packages, was acquired at one third of the regular price, and the annual maintenance fee of $25,000 was waived. This is not an uncommon practice as corporations seek to attract future customers among students. Vendors have also supported the teaching function by supplying free educational materials, such as literature on the packages.

With the exception of support from Computing Services (e.g. for repair and maintenance of equipment, advice on use of mainframes, availability of some PC-based software), and the original funding for the GIS lab, there has been no internal support for instructional computing in Geography. Understaffing has been a serious problem for several years; there is only one half-time lab technician to assist faculty with computing activities for teaching and research and to supervise the GIS lab. As a consequence, undergraduate students have only limited access to the lab outside of class times. The informant perceives lack of support personnel and of incentives for faculty to devote time to instructional computing to be the major factors preventing a wider use of computer technology in the classroom.

GIS software has also been heavily used for research by two faculty members who have received substantial outside grants since 1987. This has entailed major benefits for the teaching side, as these research funds have allowed the replacement of obsolete equipment in the computer lab, and the hiring of a significant number of students as research assistants, thus contributing to their education.

Sociology/Social Studies[15]

In North America, statistics in the Social Sciences have been strongly linked with computing for many years. The decision to train all students in introductory statistics classes to use the computer for statistical calculations was made in 1975. The package SPSS was adopted for these courses primarily because of its capacity to handle large amounts of survey data and because it was already being used by a research unit on campus, Sample Survey and Data Bank Unit (*cf.* Chapter 4, 1.2). The computer lab sessions (1 hour/week), presently held in the Electronic Learning Centre, are integrated with the lectures. After an initial familiarization with the use of the terminals, students are assigned problem sets. In addition to the instructor, student assistants and SPSS experts from Sample Survey provide support for the lab component of the class.

Spending a considerable amount of the time normally designated for research, the main instructor has produced manuals for the computing component of this course. The preparation and organization of the lab sessions also requires a significant time commitment throughout the semester. The instructor perceives this, however, to be a worthwhile commitment as he feels teaching statistics using SPSS is more effective than the traditional lecture format. Based on his partly negative experience using the IBM mainframe and terminals for his classes (he found the hardware not very convenient to use for teaching), he has participated in an initiative of the Department to submit a proposal for a microcomputer lab, which was recently approved by the Faculty of Arts. The new facility will serve students in the Social Sciences and should be available in 1993.

Computers are also used in two other classes, Social Studies 203 and SOC 306. The first class is a course on research methods in which students do a mini-survey and write a research report using computer manipulated data from questionnaires. Students not familiar with SPSS may work with computer printouts supplied by Sample Survey; there is no compulsory hands-on computing in this course. In SOC 306, students spend one hour per week in the lab, using SPSS and Minitab for assigned problem sets.

There has been no formal evaluation of instructional computing in the Department of Sociology/Social Studies. Informal feedback from students is mixed and tends to be more positive for those who go beyond the introductory statistics course.

One instructor also uses the computer to analyse census data when preparing lectures for SOC 206 (Social Stratification). More generally, there appears to be a vast potential, which is not being exploited at the present time, for the use of computer-manipulated data to prepare for classes in Sociology/Social Studies. This may be attributed to a number of factors. First of all, it is felt that faculty development opportunities, both for training in the use

15 Interviews Knuttila and Gingrich (1992).

of computers and for discipline-specific packages such as SPSS, are lacking. Secondly, there appears to be no encouragement or initiative from senior administrators with respect to CAI. Faculty wishing to explore the use of computers for teaching and/or research have to rely on the few colleagues who have become computer experts by personal initiative. Thirdly, there is a perception among faculty that there are no incentives to engage in instructional computing activities. For instance, one informant felt that the manuals he wrote for the computer component of the statistics course should have been given the same weight for promotion as published research. Presently, out of ten faculty members in the department, only two are strongly committed to the use of computers for teaching.

1.2.3.2 On-site Development of Instructional Software[16]

As a consequence of insufficient availability of instructional material for the American Indian languages taught at one of the University of Regina's federated colleges, the Saskatchewan Indian Federated College (SIFC), an instructor specializing in Linguistics was asked a few years ago to develop CALL materials for Cree. While he did not receive institutional support, he was successful in securing some external funding from the Canadian government, which allowed him to purchase the hardware and software required for this project. After experimenting with various types of computers and different authoring systems[17], he found Macintosh and Hypercard to be most suitable for his particular objectives. Assuming that second language acquisition is most effective when interactive learning occurs, he set out to develop adventure games, also referred to as "interactive fiction," for Cree, (Klokeid & Ratt 1989), in cooperation with several Cree language instructors. As well, he initiated the development of interactive fiction prototypes for Spanish, English as a second language, French and German. The final outcome of the project is to be a collection of interactive fiction programmes, conceived as supplementary material for the Cree language course sequence from the beginners' to the advanced level and designed primarily for individual use, both in- and out-of-class. At this point, however, only a few adventure games for Cree have been completed and tested by students. While the material has not been formally evaluated by students, the feedback obtained informally from students and language instructors has been positive.

Although the instructor who initiated and supervised the material development did not keep track of the time spent, he pointed out that the development work represented a major time commitment which was not recognized or rewarded by the college's administration (e.g. by granting release time). The major barriers to completing the project were felt to be lack of time

---

16 Interviews Klokeid and Rubrecht (1991).

17 Authoring systems are packages designed to help instructors create their own CAI materials without having to do any programming.

and lack of incentives for colleagues as well as students to become and remain involved with the project.

The motivation for engaging in on-site development of CALL programmes for German was quite different, as a fairly wide selection of commercial software is available for university-level courses in German. The primary impetus was, then, to investigate whether the use of computers might improve the quality of teaching German as a second language. After experimenting with a dozen off-the shelf programmes for beginners, not associated with textbooks, it was found that while some of the computer lessons were of high quality, students did not respond well to and benefit significantly from the use of these materials because they were not course-integrated. As a consequence, one of the instructors in the Department of Germanic and Slavic Studies decided to explore the possibility of on-site development of fully course-integrated computer lessons, hypothesizing that an integrated CALL course component would best respond to the variety of students' individual learning strategies. He opted to develop materials with CALLGEN, an authoring system developed at the University of Calgary and specifically designed for CALL applications.

As was the case with Cree, institutional support was not available. Only outside funding, obtained through various sources for a five year period, allowed the instructor to carry out his development project with the help of support personnel. Numerous volunteers also contributed to the material development in various ways (Rubrecht 1990 for a description of the "Waskesiu Project"). While the total funding received in the five year period (1986-1991) was $40,000, the estimated overall project value for this period is $70,000. This figure does not include, however, a price-tag for the approximately 4,000 volunteer hours which were contributed by faculty, support personnel, and other participants.

As a result of the Waskesiu Project, more than one hundred CALL and CALA lessons for German are now available. Many are regularly used in language classes for beginners at the University of Regina (GER 100 and GER 101). These lessons are continuously reviewed, updated and improved, taking into account student feedback obtained informally, through direct observation and through questionnaires. They may be used either on-campus in the Electronic Learning Centre, or off-campus by all students registered in these classes and are also available as shareware to German language instructors at other Canadian institutions.

The director of this CALL development project firmly believes that this has been a worthwhile undertaking, given the positive student response and the greater flexibility in language learning and acquisition options with respect to time and location. However, he also points to the lack of funding for sustained programme development and research and to the limited technical support within the institution. These two factors have held up the progress of the project by at least two years and have prevented a concerted effort to provide computer-based language materials for the intermediate level. These major barriers have only been overcome with a great deal of determination and the dedication of both volunteers and project co-workers.

1.2.3.3 Other In-class Use of Computers: the "Electronic Blackboard" as an Example

The results of the baseline survey on academic computing in Canadian universities indicate that computers have been used only moderately by instructors for electronic presentation of course material (*cf.* Figure 1 in section 1.2.3). The most widespread use is in Education (88% of respondents), Administration, Engineering and Medicine (*cf.* Appendix C:C-4). Before a decision can be made with respect to the implementation of the electronic blackboard, *i.e.* of microcomputer-based presentational technology in the classroom (Stahl & Johnson 1990:2), its effectiveness needs to be assessed.

However, researchers attempting to evaluate innovative teaching methods are confronted with a number of methodological problems, owing to the current state of research on the effectiveness of instruction in general: "The goals are generally in dispute, the methodology still quite primitive, the relevant variables numerous and hard to disentangle. Because of these difficulties, the results are often intuitively suspect or simply inconclusive" (Bok 1985:37). Not only is there little "firm evidence" for the success of innovative teaching methods such as electronic presentation, but "evidence for the learning outcomes from traditional educational approaches is equally lacking" (Knapper 1991:XV).

As part of the research carried out for the Design Model, an experiment was conducted in three sections of SOC 100 (Introduction to Sociology), taught by different instructors, with the objective of evaluating the use of the electronic blackboard. Selected lecture material was presented with the electronic blackboard in two sections for one week while the material was presented to students in the third section in the traditional lecture format. It was hypothesized that the use of the electronic blackboard would have a negative impact on faculty productivity, due to the increased preparation time, but result in a better quality of learning (Stahl & Johnson 1990:2). The authors of this study found that faculty productivity declined sharply since "for a moderately experienced user with research complete and all materials at hand, it took five times as long to prepare an illustrated lecture as the same material presented normally" (Stahl & Johnson 1990:9).

The authors of the study were surprised with the strongly negative response in the detailed questionnaires given to students in order to determine whether the quality of learning was enhanced by the use of the electronic blackboard. Only student satisfaction was measured, not student performance (Stahl & Johnson 1990:4). To elicit further responses, a random sample of students was also interviewed. However, the outcome was influenced by major uncontrolled factors, in particular the personality and teaching style of the instructors, and student expectations (Stahl & Johnson 1990:24). A major problem for students appeared to be the "divided attention and distraction which the electronic blackboard produced in the classroom" (Stahl & Johnson 1990:25).

Again, the novelty of the situation, in this case for both instructor and students, is likely to have affected the outcome.

It is difficult, then, to draw any general conclusions from experiments like this. As well, one should keep in mind that software and hardware continue to improve at a very rapid pace (*cf.* Chapter 6). There have been major improvements of both presentational software and projection technology since the study was carried out, and results from a repeat experiment using the latest technology might be quite different.

Experiments in other North American universities have resulted in a far more positive assessment of the electronic blackboard. For instance, after teaching English composition for several semesters using a computer, a projection unit, and word-processing software, the instructor concluded that this was a "highly productive way to use classroom time in teaching students various strategies and styles possible in writing and ways to revise their work successfully" (quoted in Hazen & Parker 1989:380).

The use of the electronic blackboard may indeed be more appropriate for this type of task than for the display of information. With respect to the large amount of time initially required for CAI development, including electronic presentation of class materials, some authors have also stressed the potential for substantial reduction of preparation time in the long run, if the material is reused (adapted and revised if necessary) in subsequent semesters (Rubrecht 1990:54). At any rate, considerably more research will have to be carried out before the use of the electronic blackboard with respect to both quality of learning and faculty productivity can be adequately assessed.

1.2.4 Other Uses of Computers Related to the Teaching Function

A number of faculty members make use of specific software, e.g. spreadsheets to keep class records or bibliography programmes to generate course-related bibliographies for their students. Many have access to SIS (Student Information System, *cf.* Chapter 5). For faculty involved in instructional computing and/or distance education, it is possible to access the most recent information in these fields through various networks (e.g. EDTECH; *cf.* Chapter 5). It is also worth mentioning that some units of the University of Regina require instructors to have their teaching evaluated by students through questionnaires and that the analysis of student responses is computerized to a large extent.

2. Major Issues

In this section, we will address a number of issues which we consider to be particularly significant with respect to the use of computers for teaching. These include a discussion of methodological problems associated with assessing the effects of instructional computing; of the degree of computer literacy required or desirable for students, faculty, and administrators; of resources; of options for the use of instructional software ("build" *vs.* "buy"); of administrative issues such as planning and policy-making for instructional computing activities; and of the impact of decisions made by governments and corporations on instructional computing.

2.1 Effects of Instructional Computing

As noted above, a number of methodological problems are associated with the assessment of instructional computing. In fact, it is difficult to assess the effectiveness of any media used in teaching with any great precision. This is the case for both traditional media, such as textbooks, and technology-based media (Graves 1989:428).

At the present time, there are some practical limitations associated with the evaluation of the impact of instructional software. There are simply not enough high quality university-level packages available to instructors who are willing to experiment with and evaluate educational software (*cf.* 2.4.1 and 2.4.3). In other words, a broader range of high quality packages for various disciplines is needed before the effects of instructional computing in universities can be adequately assessed. Presently, "the issue of effectiveness has some of the qualities of a cart-and-horse dilemma" (Graves 1989:428). Still, this issue is a legitimate concern which must be addressed, as instructional computing activities not only represent a major time commitment from faculty and support staff, but require considerable funding as well (Wilson & Badger 1989:350).

In the existing literature on the effectiveness of instructional computing, there is a tendency to present positive results. Instructors who have used high quality commercial software suitable for their teaching or have developed their own courseware frequently report a positive outcome of their experiments in instructional computing. However, these reports often include some words of caution. A typical example of this is a study undertaken by a research team at the University of Illinois at Urbana-Champaign to assess the effects of CAI in various disciplines. Several projects were evaluated on the basis of comparative studies of student test groups as well as attitude surveys conducted among students. While the authors of the study reported that "the results of these evaluations are encouraging and suggest that microcomputers are having a positive effect on both the cognitive and affective aspects of teaching and learning", they also noted that these findings are "not conclusive" (Wilson & Badger 1989:352).

2.2 Computer Literacy

In this section, the issue of computer literacy (also referred to as computer competence) will be discussed as it relates to the various categories of "players" involved in instructional computing: students and faculty, of course, but also administrators as "decision-makers" (*cf.* Chapter 2). As we will see, it may be desirable to define computer literacy more comprehensively in order to address ethical and social issues involved in the computerization of universities.

2.2.1 Students

As mentioned earlier in this chapter, an increasing number of students are entering post-secondary institutions with some computer familiarity. However, for a transition period, universities are still faced with the task of providing basic training for students without prior computing experience. Depending on the discipline, this basic training may include an introduction to one or more packages for word processing, spreadsheets, databases and graphics (*cf.* the Administration computing course described in 1.2.3.1). Some students, such as mature students, may not have keyboarding skills when entering the university. Twenty-nine percent of the academics who responded to our baseline survey indicated that computer training of students was a major constraint to instructional uses of computers, particularly in Education, Administration and Medicine (*cf.* Appendix C:C-10).

The extended debate about the nature of computer literacy in recent publications demonstrates that there is no clear consensus among academics on this issue (Knapper & Cropley 1991:153f; Simonson & Thompson 1990:131-134; Rosenberg 1991). What is the nature of the computer training university students should receive? The answer to this question will vary among institutions and disciplines. Faculty in the various disciplines will make different pedagogical decisions with respect to the degree of computer competence required from their students.[18] Ideally, the various degree programmes should include some discipline-specific computer training. Some North American institutions have established a range of discipline-specific introductory computer courses, offered through the department of Computer Science (Tannenbaum & Rahn 1985).

The degree of computer literacy required from students varies considerably within the different disciplines. For instance, students need only keyboarding skills to work with CALL lessons, while other packages used in teaching, particularly older ones, may require a higher degree of computer competence.

There are different approaches towards defining computer literacy. For some, the term simply refers to the ability to use a computer correctly and does not include programming expertise. Others argue that effective use of computers presupposes programming skills:

> A computer literate person should have a rudimentary understanding of the architecture of a simple computer and knowledge of introductory programming language and of techniques for developing programming solutions. In addition, this person should understand the principles involved in design and implementation of certain important types of software, such as word processors,

---

[18] It should be noted that some North American universities (or areas within these) require students to have their own computers (*cf.* Appendix C:C-2).

operating systems, spreadsheets, databases, and computer graphics (Computer Science Curriculum for the Year 2000, 1990).

A third position defines computer literacy more comprehensively to include an understanding of basic programming principles, of present and potential computer applications, of general concepts of computers as systems and "a positive, anxiety-free attitude about computers and computer technology" (Simonson & Thompson 1990:131).

The recent discussion among academics subscribing to the EDTECH network suggests that computer literacy in the university context needs to be defined as discipline-related. Of the definitions discussed, the following may serve as a guideline for the above mentioned decision-making process, as it proposes to give a comprehensive meaning to computer literacy:

1. Knowledge and skill in operating a computer using . . . programmes as determined by each discipline's requirements.
2. Knowledge of various ethical and social issues . . . relating to computer use.
3. Knowledge and skills in computer programming using a high level language as deemed appropriate or not by each discipline's requirements.
4. A functional level of knowledge for the use of computers as an aid to problem solving, and roles of computers as a source of problems as deemed appropriate by each discipline . (Duckett 1992).

2.2.2 Faculty

Faculty hold widely divergent opinions with respect to instructional computing (*cf.* 1.1.1). In some instances, this divergence may lead to conflicts, particularly when "product champions" (*cf.* Chapter 2) are confronted with "computerphobes" within a department. Conflicts may then occur, particularly with respect to the career review process (Schwartz *et al.* 1989:161).

As previously noted, the majority of faculty may be described as indifferent or undecided with respect to CAI. Some resist strongly any computerization of teaching. There are several reasons for faculty resistance to computerization. First of all, they may not be aware of the potential advantages of CAI, such as the possibility to emphasize the learner's role as opposed to the instructor's.[19] Another reason may be general technophobia (Jalbert 1986:14). In order to overcome this fear with respect to CAI, which is largely "fear of unknown consequences," faculty "need to progress through the stages of awareness, interest, trial, and appraisal before either acceptance or adoption

---

[19] *Cf.* Gentry & Csete (1991:21); for a more detailed discussion of potential benefits, see also Garland (1991:254).

will take place" (Gentry 1991:7).[20] As well, when the computerization process in post-secondary institutions is determined by "top down decision-making", "psychological reactance" may occur from faculty members who feel that their autonomy is threatened (Jalbert 1986:14).

Several options are available with respect to faculty development in instructional computing. Given the leading role product champions have had in CAI research and development until now, the most obvious choice is to rely on them "to provide leadership that combines knowledge of the discipline with knowledge of computers" (Schwartz *et al.* 1989:161). This leadership is indeed essential to the novices among the faculty, because "educationally sound, widespread use of computers does not spontaneously emerge from faculty who have computers put on their desks" (Schwartz *et al.* 1989:161).

Institutions may also decide to offer faculty training programmes. In contrast to the University of Regina experience, a majority of faculty indicated in their response to our academic baseline survey that training courses are readily available in Canadian universities, particularly in large institutions (see Figure 8 below and Appendix C:C-3). However, one should not conclude from these findings that faculty development with respect to computing is no longer an issue in Canadian universities. In fact, particularly in areas such as the Humanities, which have not computerized to the same extent as others, such as the Natural Sciences, a major need clearly persists.

Figure 8. Consulting Services Available

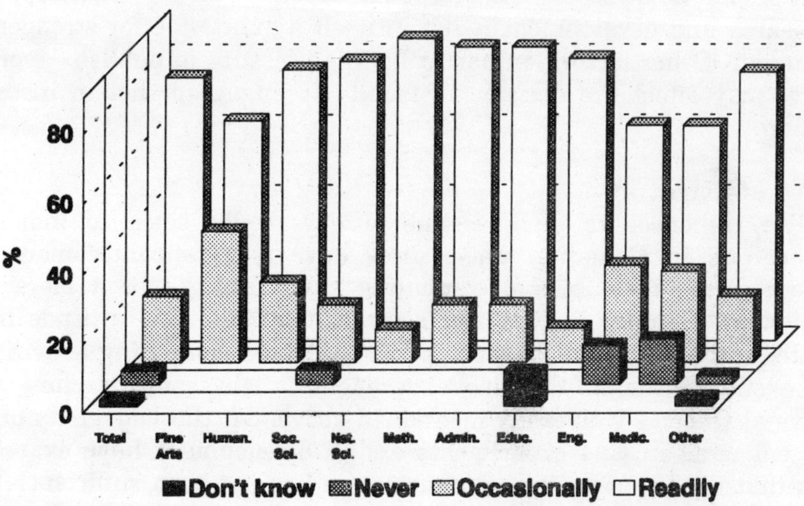

20 Gentry seems to imply here is that acceptance or adoption are the only alternatives. It should be clear, however, that rejection of instructional computing by faculty is another possible outcome.

As Schwartz *et al.* (1989:166ff) point out, faculty training has to be carefully planned if the goal is to get more academics involved in instructional computing. Faculty who are novices in this field require different institutional support than product champions; they need thorough training programmes to help them progress through the various stages of expertise. Training must go beyond "survival skills" and lead faculty to a sense of "ownership", based on an ability to set and adapt syllabi to students and instructional goals (Schwartz *et al.* 1989:169f). Furthermore, faculty development programmes should be tailored to the particular needs arising in a given institution, and planned as an ongoing activity, embedded in institutional routine (Schwartz *et al.* 1989:171). In some institutions, these training programmes for instructional computing are part of an overall plan to familiarize faculty in a given area of the university with computing. An example of this is the Humanities Computing Project at Duke University which provides faculty with training in and support for both instructional and research computing (Gillette 1986).

Information on CAI as well as individual or group training to instructors and teaching assistants (a sometimes neglected group with respect to training) may also be provided through central facilities, such as the Instructional Development Centres established by some Canadian universities, among which are the University of Waterloo and, more recently, Queen's University. One of the mandates of these teaching resource centres is to familiarize instructors with innovative teaching methods, including CAI (*University Affairs*, April 1992, p. 9; see also Donald 1986).

It should be stressed, however, that adequate institutional support[21] for CAI research and development is not in itself a guarantee for stronger faculty involvement. Other factors, in particular the pressure to publish "appropriate" research, may affect the decision of faculty to engage or not in instructional computing.

2.2.3 Administrators

The responses to our baseline survey would seem to indicate that administrators in Canadian universities have a significantly more positive attitude towards instructional computing than faculty (for a more detailed discussion, *cf.* Chapter 2, 2.2). In some institutions, this attitude has been translated into substantial support for instructional computing activities, as in the case of the Guelph/Waterloo experiment in electronic teaching and the initiative at Queen's University mentioned above. At the University of Regina, faculty engaging in CAI experiments and/or development have expressed the opinion that the support from administrators has not been sufficient. There is indeed a strong perception among faculty that instructional computing

---

[21] Until wider training is available to faculty, institutions may continue to rely on "product champions" and decide to recognize their contribution.

initiatives have generally not been encouraged by administrators, and that the institution has not provided faculty with sufficient financial resources, support staff and technical support for these activities (*cf.* 1.2.3.1). A major concern appears to be the low degree of recognition for CAI research and development in career assessment by the university's administration (for further discussion, *cf.* 2.6.2).

2.3 Availability of Resources

As previously noted, University of Regina faculty who are contemplating experimenting or have engaged in instructional computing generally perceive resources to be insufficient. The data from our baseline survey would seem to support this view (*cf.* Appendix C:C-10). As many as 70% of the respondents felt that the cost associated with academic computing is a major constraint, while 40% indicated that lack of space is a major constraint. Computer or terminal availability was perceived as a major constraint by 42% of the respondents (as many as 59% in the Sciences).

Typically, where computer lab facilities are made available for instructional use, there is a rapid increase in demand, resulting in the need to establish priorities regarding access to these facilities (*cf.* the experience at the University of Regina described in 1.2.3.1). This raises questions with respect to the decision-making process within universities; for example, what are the criteria for deciding which areas should be given priority for access to existing computer lab facilities for teaching or which areas have the greatest need for additional facilities?[22]

2.4 Use of Instructional Software: "Build" *vs.*"buy"

Whether for on-campus courses or for distance education, for in- or out-of-class use, academics engaging in instructional computing are faced with the basic decision as to whether they should use commercially available software ("buy") or develop their own ("build"). At the present time, a number of problems are associated with both options.

2.4.1 "Buy"

According to our survey on academic computing, this option has been chosen by most instructors; about 75% of all software used for teaching in Canadian universities is commercially available (*cf.* Figures 2 and 4 and Appendix C:C-4).

In some disciplines, instructors may be able to find commercial software which is adequate for their teaching. As reported in 1.2, this was the case for some courses in particular disciplines at the University of Regina (Engineering, Geography, Sociology/Social Studies). However, several respondents indicated

---

[22] The decision-making process in general and equity issues in particular are discussed in detail in Chapter 2.

that commercially produced instructional software was unavailable for their discipline (Cree), found to be of poor quality (Chemistry), or could not be integrated with course content (German). It is interesting in this context that as many as 41% of the respondents to our baseline survey perceived inadequacy of software to be a major constraint (*cf.* Appendix C:C-10).

Commercially available software may be inadequate for different reasons. First of all, some of the existing software, designed for older computers, such as the Commodore 64 or the Apple II, does not take advantage of recent technological advances. Generally, poor quality, both of content and design, is the most obvious problem (*cf.* 1.2.3.1); it is frequently addressed in the literature dealing with software evaluation (*cf.* the references in Kaltz *et al.* 1990; Woloshyn and Kaltz 1991). For instance, some programmes are so poorly designed that they are difficult to use and frustrating for both students and instructors. Given the trend towards a stronger emphasis on ease of use of both hardware and software (Gentry & Csete 1991:29), one might expect problems of this nature will gradually become less frequent (*cf.* Chapter 6).

Instructors who have evaluated and rated particular packages as being of good quality may nevertheless find these to be inadequate for their particular needs if integration with other course materials, such as textbooks, cannot be accomplished (*cf.* 1.2.3.2). Ideally, the use of instructional software should be fully integrated with course content. North American publishers of university-level textbooks have realized that the development of textbook-related instructional software represents a vast commercial potential; many are now beginning to develop textbook-related CAI materials ("courseware") on a larger scale.

2.4.2 "Build": On-site Development of Instructional Software

As we have seen in 1.2.3.2, there may be different reasons for faculty to engage in on-site CAI research and development. Other than authoring systems, or in addition to these, instructors may use a wide range of software, such as spreadsheets, data base, graphics and word processing packages, to develop their own CAI materials, depending on their discipline. Some may choose to create fully course-integrated programmes for in-class use, others may opt to develop supplementary CAI lessons for out-of-class use, for instance to enable students to review and further practice selected course material. Another important aspect of in-house CAI development is the preparation of computer-based tests and examinations, with partially or totally computerized grading.

For faculty contemplating developing their own instructional software, it is essential to cooperate closely with colleagues in other institutions, and every effort should be made to avoid duplication. However, as Gentry and Csete (1991:26) note, there seems to be a "predilection" of educational technologists and other educators to do precisely that, so that "the trend of continually reinventing the wheel is likely to continue."

Prior to engaging in on-site CAI development, instructors should therefore carefully investigate whether instructional software which might be suitable for their purposes or adaptable to their particular needs exists, either commercially available or developed in other institutions. Apparently, this first step, as obvious as it may seem, has often been neglected. As a consequence, there has been considerable duplication in some disciplines, for instance in the area of CALL research and development (Kaltz 1991).

Faculty considering developing CAI materials should also determine whether appropriate resources are available at their institution (*cf.* 2.3). In particular, they may require technical support as well as advice with respect to software design.

While some product champions may have expertise not only in their own discipline and in computing but in instructional design as well, a team effort is normally required to develop high quality CAI material. Ideally, such a team would consist of one or more instructors from a given discipline, a specialist in instructional design and a computer specialist (Perkey 1986; Sanders & Sanders 1989). Some authors have argued that it might be helpful to include students as well, since students may have valuable input from their perspective as end users of CAI (Rubrecht 1990).

Cost and time factors must also be considered. As Garland (1991:257) points out, "while development and capital cost may be higher for technology-based instruction, it may yield substantial delivery savings over the volume and life of the training." The need to carry out a cost-benefit analysis before engaging in on-site development of CAI materials is frequently overlooked (Gentry & Csete 1991:22f). Such an analysis would determine whether the initial high cost might be partially offset in the long run, by substantial reduction of time spent by faculty on grading tests and examinations for instance, or by faculty time savings when a course component previously delivered through contact hours is replaced by out-of-class use of these materials. With respect to the development of CALL lessons for German courses at the University of Regina, Rubrecht (1990:54) argues that "cost-recovery in terms of freed-up contact hours and savings in time previously spent on homework correction which now can be applied to classroom preparation is possible in less than two years."

Another important issue, to be discussed in more detail in 2.6.3, is copyright. Faculty who have developed their own instructional software may choose to have it protected by copyright and distributed commercially or to make it available, for a nominal fee, as shareware to other institutions.

In summary, these are the lessons to be learned from the "realities of software development" in North American universities (Galloway 1989:229):

1. Developing high quality instructional software is a difficult and extremely time-consuming task.
2. Faculty engaging in on-site development of software often start out with unrealistic goals and may then experience frustration due to limited resources, lack of time and technological constraints.
3. While some excellent instructional software has been developed by faculty, many CAI programmes developed on-site have major flaws. For instance, they may not have been adequately tested and debugged, or they may not be user-friendly or sufficiently documented (Galloway 1989:230). As mentioned above, careful planning with respect to resources and to software design are therefore essential if the outcome is to be high-quality software.

2.4.3 Evaluation of Instructional Software

As previously discussed, the assessment of effectiveness of any technology-based instruction is an extremely complex issue fraught with a number of methodological problems. These problems seem to be particularly pervasive in comparative studies attempting to demonstrate the superiority of innovative teaching methods such as CAI over traditional methods (Geis 1984). Whatever might be the outcome of future research in this area, many instructors are currently experimenting with using the computer for teaching or considering doing so, and particularly the novices in this group need guidance from specialists *now* with respect to the evaluation of instructional software.

While both theoretical issues pertaining to the evaluation of instructional software and the more practical matter of developing evaluation guidelines have been discussed at length in numerous publications, this is still an ongoing and at times confusing debate, particularly when authors fail to distinguish clearly between the various phases of software evaluation (Kaltz 1991).

It is indeed important to differentiate between "pre-implementation," "formative" and "summative" evaluation of instructional software.[23] The pre-implementation step involves examining a given programme, in order to determine whether it is suitable or adaptable for a specific teaching situation. The term "formative evaluation" refers to the assessment of the programme as it is being implemented. "Summative evaluation" is the assessment of the programme after its completion (Murray & Murray 1984:15). Different problems, of which only a few can be discussed here, are associated with each of these stages.

One problem with respect to the first stage is that instructors, except possibly some product champions, need far better guidance for the selection of both commercially developed software and shareware developed at other institutions. The literature on CALL software evaluation, for instance, contains a wealth of checklists and questionnaires, but these are often poorly designed

[23] See also Demaizière (1986:512ff).

and unsystematic. In particular, criteria are frequently not ranked, important criteria are omitted, and some of the criteria proposed are vague or subjective (Kaltz 1991). Moreover, instructors engaging in software evaluation will find that generic checklists or questionnaires are in many ways inappropriate for use in their discipline. While some criteria used in evaluative instruments apply to any instructional software (questions with respect to hardware requirements, for instance), it is essential to develop discipline-specific sets of criteria, taking into account the particular teaching needs of a given discipline.

The primary subset should include criteria derived from the specificity of CAI as a new medium, which will allow for an evaluation of the software design. In the case of CALL software for instance, instructors need to find out how the programme handles branching, error anticipation, answer processing, and record-keeping, and to what extent it is interactive.

User-based criteria might form a second subset, including learner-oriented and teacher-oriented criteria. From the learner's perspective, some important criteria are user options, ease of use and, in the affective domain, the extent to which programmes are motivating or allow for creativity. Teacher-based criteria address issues such as progression within the programme or the overall pedagogical approach.

Language-based criteria constitute a third subset, dealing with questions such as the linguistic level of the intended user, the linguistic and cultural content of the programme (e.g. is it accurate, and free of racial and other stereotypes?), and the relative importance given to the various language skills. The last subset of criteria concerns the delivery of the programme, e.g. hardware requirements (Kaltz 1991).

Software reviews published in specialized journals may contain useful information for the pre-implementation phase. However, input from other sources is essential. Instructors should also seek advice locally, from specialists in Teaching Resource Centers where available, or from colleagues at other institutions who have experimented with instructional software. Existing networks, such as the EDTECH E-mail network, the Canadian CCALLNET and the clearinghouse recently established by the Division of Instructional Technology at the University of Colorado at Denver, will facilitate contacts with instructors throughout Canada and the United States. The objective of the clearinghouse is to review and distribute instructional software and to make recommendations for revisions.

Based on the information gathered, instructors should then determine through a comprehensive evaluation, taking into account discipline-specific criteria, whether the software under consideration is adequate for the particular teaching situation. When pre-evaluating software, instructors would benefit greatly from sharing and comparing evaluations with other colleagues. It is therefore recommended that the evaluation format for instructional software be standardized within each discipline (Kaltz 1991).

With respect to summative evaluation, it is interesting to note that only 24% of the respondents to our baseline survey on academic computing indicated that evaluation of in-class use of software by students has been carried out routinely at their institution (45% occasionally; 31% rarely; *cf.* Figure 3). Student response to CAI appears to have been quite positive; as many as 46% were described as being "enthusiastic" about in-class use of software, while the response of 52% was characterized as "mild acceptance", with 2% of the students being "indifferent" (*cf.* Figure 3 and Appendix C:C-4). The findings for both evaluation of and student response to out-of-class use of software are quite similar (*cf.* Figure 6 and Appendix C:C-4). While the responses to our baseline survey would seem to indicate a trend towards overall favourable student reactions to instructional computing in Canadian universities, thereby confirming positive reports in the literature on CAI, the preliminary nature of these findings must be stressed.

2.5 Other Uses of Computers Related to the Teaching Function

As illustrated by the University of Regina experience and the findings of our baseline survey, instructional computing is not limited to in- or out-of-class use of CAI programmes. Faculty also increasingly rely on computers to prepare course materials, both for presentation in the traditional lecture format and for AV presentation (e.g. overhead transparencies; electronic blackboard). Depending on the discipline, they may make use of a variety of programmes, such as expert systems, simulation/modelling and graphics packages, spreadsheet, word processing and bibliography programmes, or software for data analysis.[24]

2.6 Administrative Issues Related to Instructional Computing

2.6.1 Infrastructure and Planning

In North America, post-secondary institutions have organized the infrastructure required to support instructional computing in various ways. Some have opted for a highly centralized computing environment. This is the case at the University of Regina, where a central facility, Computing Services, supports the different types of computing activities undertaken by faculty, staff and graduate students.[25] Others, such as the University of Illinois at Urbana-Champaign, have moved in the opposite direction, establishing a highly decentralized computing environment (Graves 1989:205f). After personal computers became widely available, some institutions decided to complement the existing centralized environment by adopting a distributed approach.

At Dartmouth College for instance, the decision was made to provide some of the support for instructional computing in a distributed fashion. In addition to the existing support through a computing centre, "divisional computing

---

[24] *Cf.* the section on "potential educational uses of computation" in Balkovich, Lerman & Parmelee (1985:1215ff).

[25] However, Computing Services does not directly support undergraduate students, who are advised to seek assistance from lab instructors.

centres" were created for the Social Sciences and the Humanities. The primary mandate of the divisional centres is to assist faculty with instructional and research computing. This includes assistance to faculty with obtaining funding for initiatives in instructional computing. The response from faculty has been very positive. In particular, novices in computing among faculty who had previously refrained from approaching the computer specialists at the central facility for support felt more confident seeking advice from the divisional centres, directed by academics with computing expertise and a background in teaching and research. As a result, instructional computing activities have increased considerably at Dartmouth (Levine, Byrne & Wolford 1989:247f).

As part of an overall plan for computerization ("Computer Intensive University Programme"), Drake University has adopted a comprehensive plan to encourage and support instructional computing. Computer training and advice are offered to instructors through a Faculty Resource Center. At this centre, faculty also have access to a library containing a variety of public domain software and shareware as well as commercial software donated by vendors. In addition, a series of faculty development grants was established, providing faculty with salary supplements to develop projects for subsequent use in teaching, or with grants to purchase hardware or software for their instructional computing activities. Not surprisingly, the programme was well received by faculty (Lutz, Cheney & Staunton 1989:258f).[26]

As well, some institutions, such as Stanford University, Brown University and Iona College, have established leadership at the senior administration level for computing, by creating a new position of Vice-President for Computing and Information Services, whose responsibilities include the coordination of instructional computing (as one component of computing activities on campus), and overseeing the development of instructional software (Lougee & Carter 1989:70; Turner 1986:14; Halaris & Sloan 1989:278f).

In many institutions, the administrative infrastructure for planning and coordinating instructional computing includes advisory committees at the university, faculty or departmental level. The University of Regina has established an Advisory Committee on Research and Instructional Computing, a University Policy Committee, a Faculty of Arts Computing Advisory Committee, and the previously mentioned Research and Instructional Computing Committee of the Geography Department, to name a few.[27]

---

26 *Cf.* also the report on a similar planned effort at Iona College, where instructional computing was promoted through a combination of faculty enrichment grants, advancement incentives and computing support services (Halaris & Sloan 1989:273).

27 For a comprehensive analysis of the administrative infrastructure for computing, including the function of committees with respect to instructional computing, *cf.* Chapter 5. Infrastructure with respect to potential priority conflicts between instructional, research and administrative computing is discussed in Chapter 4, section 3.2.

2.6.2 Institutional Reward Structure

Faculty engaging in instructional computing frequently feel that these activities are not adequately rewarded by their institution, if at all. The University of Regina experience (*cf.* 1.2.3.1) is not an unusual case in this respect. In fact, it has often been argued that institutions committed to supporting instructional computing need to establish a reward structure for CAI research and development (Schwartz *et al.* 1989:184, 191; Lutz, Cheney & Staunton 1989:264f; Hazen & Parker 1989:375; Gerhold 1989:418f; Graves 1989:429f).

As noted above, on-site development of instructional software is extremely time-consuming (*cf.* 2.4.2). Integrating existing software into the curriculum (possibly including adapting the programme to the particular needs) also requires a significant time commitment from instructors. In institutions where these activities are not valued, faculty members who engage in instructional computing may be at risk, particularly with respect to tenure and promotion decisions. On the other hand, "given the number of competing forces that pull at faculty—forces such as teaching, research, advising, committee service, and consulting—a faculty member must perceive that some benefit will accrue as a result of choosing to invest time in a major curriculum development activity" (Lutz, Cheney & Staunton 1989:264). The absence of institutional policies rewarding CAI research and development, in conjunction with the emphasis on "appropriate" research in the presently prevailing incentive structure, may well have prevented increased use of instructional computing on many campuses (Gerhold 1989:418).

Institutions committed to supporting instructional computing may offer different incentives to faculty. Examples include the previously mentioned release time, salary supplements, and grants for hardware and software purchase. More importantly, the existing performance review sytem needs to be adjusted so that these activities may be taken into account for decisions regarding promotion, tenure and merit increases (Schwartz *et al.* 1989:191). In addition, it has been suggested that a "secondary reward structure" be implemented, recognizing faculty who have developed instructional software by providing a continual upgrading of their hardware (Gerhold 1989:419).

2.6.3 Copyright Policy

In institutions committed to supporting faculty who develop instructional software for subsequent commercial distribution, a policy is required in order to regulate software ownership and to clarify the issue of royalties (Wilson & Badger 1989:363; Gerhold 1989:419). Existing policies usually stipulate that copyright for software is to be held jointly by the author and the university (Lougee & Carter 1989:71 with respect to Stanford University). Regarding the sharing of royalties, Western Washington University, for instance, has established the following policy for software developed by faculty using the university's resources (space, hardware, and time). Faculty will receive the first

$500 of royalties for software they have developed on campus. In the $501 to $100,000 range, the division is 75% to the author, and 25% to the university. Royalties over $100,000 are split equally between the two parties.[28]

2.7 Effect of Decisions Made Outside the University

2.7.1 Government (Federal and Provincial)

Although education in Canada, including post-secondary education, is the responsibility of the provinces, decisions made at the federal level do have considerable impact on teaching at Canadian universities, either directly or indirectly. Canadian universities receive operating grants from the provincial governments, but these grants are largely funded by transfer payments from the federal government (*cf.* also Chapter 2, section 3.4 and Chapter 4, section 3.6.1).

The "Open and Distance Learning Materials Development Program," established several years ago by the Secretary of State, illustrates how decisions made at the federal level may have a direct impact on instructional computing in Canadian post-secondary institutions. This programme offers operating grants to instructors who submit projects for developing materials targeted for open learning and distance education, which use various delivery techniques, including computer programmes. One of the requirements of the programme is that these instructional materials must be related to the historical, cultural, economic, social, intellectual, and political life of Canada.[29]

Provincial governments may also decide to give direct support to instructional computing at the university level. The funding by the government of Saskatchewan for the SCN distance education programme previously mentioned (*cf.* 1.2.2) is an example of this.

As well, it must be noted that decisions made at the provincial level with respect to computer literacy programmes in the primary and secondary school system are bound to have a significant impact on the evolution of instructional computing in post-secondary institutions. As noted in section 2.2.1, students are entering the university with various degrees of computer competence, and any changes at the primary and secondary level will require adjustments at the post-secondary level.[30]

2.7.2 Corporate Policy

A number of corporations have been supporting instructional computing at Canadian and American universities, by donating hardware and software or granting substantial discounts, by waiving maintenance fees, or by supplying

---

[28] "Unfortunately, no one has yet reached the 50 percent range", as Gerhold (1989:420) notes.

[29] See Newsletter published by the Office of Graduate Studies and Research, University of Regina, 7,1, p.10.

[30] *Cf.* Graves (1989:2) with respect to problems of "articulation" between the school system and higher education.

technical support to software development projects.

As noted above (*cf.* 1.2.3.1), instructional computing activities at the University of Regina have received considerable support from various vendors. A project undertaken at the University of Toronto, with support from IBM Canada, aimed at exploring new teaching and learning methods in complex mathematics as well as enhancing the computer skills of students in mathematics and management, is another recent example. IBM Canada will be contributing equipment, software and technical support to this project (*University Affairs*, November 1991, p. 16).

By participating in the cooperative work/study programmes offered by many Canadian universities[31], numerous hardware and software corporations, and other companies have been contributing to the education of a large number of students with respect to computing.

In the United States, corporate support of instructional computing at post-secondary institutions has been significant as well. For instance, a total of nineteen universities have formed partnerships with the Academic Information Systems division of IBM in the Advanced Educational Projects (AEP) programme. In this programme, IBM supported projects in instructional computing through donations of hardware and software, while the universities covered other expenses (Jones & Smith 1989:27).

With assistance from the Digital Equipment Corporation, IBM, and other corporate sponsors, a major research project was undertaken at the Massachusetts Institute of Technology to explore the potential instructional uses of advanced computer technology (Balkovich, Lerman & Parmelee 1985; Morgenstern 1986). To give another example, IBM and Apple Computer Inc. have been contributing to EDUCOM activities as "Corporate Leadership Sponsors" (Graves ed. 1989). This has included support of the EDUCOM/NCRIPTAL awards, given annually to faculty who have developed high-quality instructional software, and of the publication of an in-depth study on instructional computing in American universities and colleges (Graves ed. 1989).[32]

3. Future Trends in Instructional Computing

First of all, it should be noted that the present underfunding of many post-secondary institutions in North America is likely to have a significant detrimental

---

31 At the University of Regina, for instance, undergraduate, pre-professional work experience is available to students of Administration, Engineering, Chemistry, Computer Science, Mathematics and Physics. Students admitted to these programmes spend alternate semesters off campus, engaged in paid employment that closely follows and enhances their academic studies.

32 This study gives numerous other examples of corporate support for instructional computing in American post-secondary institutions.

effect on the future of instructional computing. Over the next few years, few institutions will be in a position to satisfy the increasing demand for instructional computing from students and faculty. Budgetary constraints will likely prevent institutions from adding to existing computer lab facilities to the extent desired, from hiring more support staff or running faculty training programmes on a large scale, to name a few examples.

Predicting future trends, generally a risky undertaking, is especially difficult with respect to instructional computing. Budgetary considerations are one factor, the rapidly changing technology is another. The future of instructional computing in post-secondary institutions will also be affected by the evolution of computing in the school system, by increased pressure on universities from the society, and particularly the business sector, to expand instructional computing and adjust it to new demands, or by changing attitudes of faculty or influx of younger faculty. In institutions with a strong commitment to the use of computers in teaching, which translates into appropriate support of faculty, including adequate technical support, faculty training programmes and a reward structure recognizing instructional computing, the number of faculty engaging in such activities may well increase significantly.[33]

Advances in computer technology have had and will continue to have an impact on instructional computing. This is especially true of the shift from mainframe to microcomputer use for applications in teaching.[34] Of the technology trends frequently discussed in the recent literature dealing with instructional computing[35], the potential transformation of CAI into ICAI (where *I* stands for *Intelligent*) as a result of new developments in Artificial Intelligence[36] and the increased attention given to multimedia/ hypermedia applications for teaching[37] are particularly significant.

The trend towards increased use of computers in off-campus courses, reflecting changes in the student population (higher percentage of older and part-time students), might well continue (Gentry & Csete 1991:29; Holloway & Ohler 1991:259ff). It also seems reasonable to anticipate that students will

---

[33] In addition to an increase in number, Hazen & Parker also predict increasing "sophistication" of faculty engaging in instructional computing at their institution, the University of North Carolina at Chapel Hill (1989:398).

[34] For an analysis of this shift from mainframe to microcomputer instructional computing, based on the experience at the University of North Carolina at Chapel Hill, *cf.* Hazen & Parker (1989:367ff).

[35] *Cf.* in particular Anglin ed. (1991), Graves ed. (1989), Hannafin & Peck (1989), and Simonson & Thompson (1990).

[36] *Cf.* for instance the large number of entries dealing with AI and ICALI (Intelligent Computer-Assisted Language Instruction) in our bibliography on CALL (Kaltz *et al.* 1990).

[37] *Cf.* for instance Mitterer 1989; see also Morrison *et al.* (1991:191) and Chapter 6.

increasingly use computers in self-learning situations, with AI-enhanced instructional systems emphasizing learner control (Gentry & Csete 1991:30; Morrison *et al.* 1991:189).

4. Concluding Remarks

This chapter has discussed the various possible instructional uses of computers to develop a model guiding the process of computerizing universities. In this context, it is essential to keep in mind that no technology is value-free. In North America (and elsewhere), instructional computing activities at all levels of education have evolved within a particular framework of values (*cf.* Chapters 1 and 2) and have been influenced strongly by developments in the corporate sector. It is not intended here to offer any "prepackaged solutions to the educational problems of other countries" (Romiszowski 1991:250); decisions made and solutions adopted in the North American context may be entirely inappropriate elsewhere.

However, some general conclusions may be drawn from the North American experience with instructional computing, summarizing and complementing the arguments presented earlier in this chapter:

1. Given the current state of research, any assessment of the effectiveness of instructional computing must be considered as tentative.
2. Institutions should not opt for computer use in teaching assuming that this is a way of reducing the overall cost of instruction (Wilson & Badger 1989:362).
3. If the decision is made to "infuse computing into the curriculum," individual faculty members, departments, institutions, corporations, and governments will all have to cooperate (Graves 1989:426).
4. Overall planning and coordination of instructional computing activities within a given institution are essential and may best be implemented at the senior administration level, for instance by establishing a new position of Vice-President for Computing and Information Services.
5. A discipline-specific approach towards computer training, both for students and instructors, may be appropriate in the university context.
6. Given that institutions will likely not be able to provide all resources desired by faculty for training as well as research and development in instructional computing, it may be necessary to rely increasingly on product champions, both for formal computer training and for informal support and advice.
7. The presently prevailing institutional reward structure needs to be adjusted in order to recognize faculty achievements in instructional computing, particularly those of product champions.
8. Given the current emphasis on research, it may be advisable in the interim

for institutions promoting tools for instructional computing to concentrate on packages such as simulation and modelling programmes or presentation software, which faculty can use both in their research and their teaching (Hazen & Parker 1989:401; see also Chapter 4, 2.2).

9. Commercially available software should only be used for teaching after a thorough evaluation, based on discipline-specific criteria.
10. On-site development of instructional software requires careful planning in terms of resources (faculty and support staff time; equipment) and software design. To develop high quality software, a team approach is recommended. Institutions should recognize the interdisciplinary nature of instructional computing, by encouraging and supporting interdisciplinary development projects or workshops for faculty (Graves 1989:431).
11. Instructors across the disciplines will need some understanding of computers, enabling them to make well-informed decisions about instructional computing in their field. This does not imply, however, that all faculty members need to become "sophisticated users of technology-based materials and technological tools in all aspects of their professional lives," as suggested by some CAI advocates (Garrett *et al.* 1989:138).

Bibliography

1. References

Academic Review Task Force. *From Reflection to Renewal: Report of the Academic Review Task Force*. Regina: University of Regina, Oct. 1988.

Anglin, Gary J. (ed.). *Instructional Technology: Past, Present, and Future.* Englewood; Libraries Unlimited, 1991.

Balkovich, Edward, Steven Lerman, and Richard P. Parmelee. "Computing in Higher Education: The Athena Experience." *Communications of the ACM* 28.11 (1985), 1214-1224.

Bok, Derek. "Looking into Education's High-tech Future." *Harvard Magazine* May-June (1985), 29-38.

Careless, James. "High-tech Success Stories." *University Affairs*, March 1992, p. 5.

Center for Computing in the Humanities (ed.). *Computers and the Humanities: Today's Research, Tomorrow's Teaching*. (Conference Pre-Prints). Toronto: University of Toronto, 1986.

Demaizière, Françoise. *Enseignement assisté par ordinateur*. Paris: Ophrys, 1986.

Donald, Janet G. "Teaching and Learning in Higher Education in Canada: Changes over the Last Decade." *The Canadian Journal of Higher Education* 16.3 (1986), 77-84.

Eberlee, John. "The Electronic Classroom: A New Reality." *University Affairs*, March 1992, pp. 3-4.

Galloway, Gordon L. "Cornell University: An Institutional Perspective on Using Information Technologies to Add Value to Teaching and Learning." In Graves (ed.), 1989, 213-233.

Garland, Keith P. "Diffusion and Adoption of Instructional Technology." In Anglin (ed.), 1991, 253-258.

Garrett, Nina, Frank Dominguez, and James Noblitt. "Computers in Foreign Language Teaching and Research: A "New Humanism"." In Graves (ed.), 1989, 101-139.

Geis, George L. "Comparing Instructional Methods: Some Basic Research Problems." *The Canadian Journal of Higher Education* 14.2 (1984), 91-98.

Gentry, Cass G. "Educational Technology: A Question of Meaning." In Anglin (ed.), 1991, 1-10.

Gentry, Cass G. and Josephine Csete. "Educational Technology in the 1990s." In Anglin (ed.), 1991, 20-33.

Gerhold, George. "Western Washington University: Instructional Computing." In Graves (ed.), 1989, 407-421.

Gillette, Jeffrey William. "Humanities, Computing at Duke University: The Past, the Present, the Future." In Center for Computing in the

Humanities (ed.), 1986, 11-15.

Graves, William H. (ed.). *Computing Across the Curriculum: Academic Perspectives*. McKinney, Texas: Academic Computing Publications, 1989.

Halaris, Antony S. and Lynda W. Sloan. "Iona College: Instructional Computing from the Institutional Perspective." In Graves (ed.), 1989, 271-291.

Hannafin, Michael J. and Kyle L. Peck. *The Design, Development, and Evaluation of Educational Software*. New York: Macmillan Publishing, 1988.

Hazen, Margret and Anne Parker. "The University of North Carolina at Chapel Hill: Instructional Computing." In Graves (ed.), 1989, 365-404.

Higgins, John. "A Reply to Alan Hirvela's Reply." *System* 17.1 (1989), 67-70.

---. "Response to 'Hirvela's Article 'Marshall McLuhan and the Case against CAI'." *System* 16.3 (1988), 313-317.

Hirvela, Alan. "The Case Against CAI: A Reply to John Higgins." *System* 17.1 (1989), 61-65.

---. "Marshall McLuhan and the Case Against CAI." *System* 16.3 (1988), 299-311.

Holloway, Robert E. and Jason Ohler. "Distance Education in the Next Decade." In Anglin (ed.), 1991, 259-266.

Jalbert, Norine Lau. "Computer Literacy and the Forgotten Professor." Paper presented at the Annual Meeting of the American Educational Research Association, San Francisco, April 16-20, 1986.

Jones, Loretta L. and Stanley G. Smith. "Case Study: Exploring Chemistry." In Graves (ed.), 1989, 27-33.

Kaltz, Barbara et al. *Computer-Assisted Language Learning (CALL) in Postsecondary Education: An Annotated Bibliography*. Regina: University of Regina, 1990.

Kaltz, Barbara. "On Developing a Set of Criteria for the Evaluation of CALL/CALA Software." Paper presented at the Regional Conference "Computer-Assisted Second Language Learning and Acquisition: The Next Generation", University of Alberta, Edmonton, May 2-4, 1991.

Katz, Larry and Chari Keet (ed.). *Innovations in Laser and Optical Disc Technology*. Calgary: Alberta Laserdisc Committee, 1990.

Klokeid, Terry J. and Solomon Ratt. "Using Computer Adventures to Teach Cree." In William Cowan (ed.). *Proceedings of the Twentieth Algonquian Conference*. Ottawa: Carleton University, 1989.

Knapper, Christopher. "Foreword." *Enquête sur les innovations récentes en matière d'enseignement dans les universités canadiennes*. Ottawa: Commission of Inquiry on Canadian University Education, 1991. xi-xix. Rapport de Recherche #4.

Knapper, Christopher and Arthur J. Cropley. *Lifelong Learning and Higher Education*. London: Kogan Page, 1991.

Lane, Eric T. "Developing Standing Waves." In Graves (ed.), 1989, 51-66.

Levine, Lawrence M., Thomas E. Byrne, and George L. Wolford. "Dartmouth College: The Evolution of Instructional Computing - An Academic

Perspective." In Graves (ed.), 1989, 235-253.

Lougee, Carolyn Chappell and Michael P. Carter. "A Historical Simulation of the France of Louis XIV." In Graves (ed.), 1989, 69-79.

Lutz, Robert W., Michael R. Cheney, and Lawrence P. Staunton. "Drake University: Instructional Computing - An Academic Perspective." In Graves (ed.), 1989, 255-268.

Mathurin, Creutzer (en collaboration avec Edite Noivo et Teeya Blatt). *Enquête sur les innovations récentes en matière d'enseignement dans les universités canadiennes.* Ottawa: Commission of Inquiry on Canadian University Education, 1991. 1- 178. Rapport de Recherche #4.

McHenry, Hugh and Stan Franklin. "Microcomputer In-service Training for University Faculty and Staff: A Case Report." *Collegiate Microcomputer* IV.2 (1986), 173-178.

Mitterer, John. "Hypermedia and Education: Just Another Pretty Medium?" *Technology and Learning* 3.1 (1989), 6-8.

Moeller, Joseph J. Jr. "Stevens Institute of Technology: Integrating Information Technology into the Curriculum." In Graves (ed.), 1989, 321-336.

Morgenstern, Douglas. "Simulation, Interactive Fiction and Language Learning: Aspects of the MIT Project." *Bulletin de l'ACLA* 8.2 (1986), 23-33.

Morrison, Gary R., Steven M. Ross, and Jacqueline K. O'Dell. "Applications of Research to the Design of Computer-Based Instruction." In Anglin (ed.), 1991, 188-194.

Murray, David R. and Mary G. Murray. "A Comprehensive Evaluation Model for Computer-Based Education." *NALLD Journal* 19.1 (1984), 14-22.

Perkey, M. Nadine. "The effect of a machine-rich environment on courseware development: The process and the product." *Behavior Research Methods, Instruments, & Computers* 18.2 (1986), 196-204.

Romiszowski, Alexander J. "Applications of Educational Technology: The International Perspective." In Anglin (ed.), 1991, 244-252.

Rosenberg, R. L. "Debunking Computer Literacy." *Technology Review* January (1991), 58-65.

Rubrecht, Werner H. "How to Get Into CALL on a Shoestring Budget - And With the Help of Friends." In Mary Louise Craven, Roberta Sinyor, and Dana Paramskas (ed.). *CALL: Papers and Reports.* Athelstan, Calif.: Athelstan Publications, 1990, 51-55.

Rudman, Joseph. "Teaching Computers and the Humanities Courses: A Survey." *Computers and the Humanities* 21 (1987), 235-243.

Sanders, Alton F. and Ruth H. Sanders. "Syntactic Parsing: A Survey." *Computers and the Humanities* 23 (1989), 13-30.

Schcolnik, Miriam and Harriet Rubin. "The Computer Lesson As An Integrated Element in the Academic EFL Reading Curriculum." *CALICO Journal* 8.3 (1991), 81-92.

Schwartz, Helen J. et al. "Computers in Writing Instruction: Blueprint for Progress." In Graves (ed.), 1989, 141-203.

Simonson, Michael and Ann Thompson. *Educational Computing Foundations.* Columbus: Merrill Publishing, 1990.

Smith, Stuart L. (commissioner). *Report: Commission of Inquiry on Canadian University Education.* Ottawa: Association of Universities and Colleges of Canada, 1991.

Stahl, William A. and Brian Johnson. *Evaluating the Electronic Blackboard.* Technical Paper #1. Regina: University of Regina, 1990.

Tannenbaum, Robert S. and B. J. Rahn. "Computer Literacy for Undergraduate Humanities and Social Sciences Majors." *Collegiate Microcomputer* III.2 (1985), 169-178.

Turner, Judith Axler. "Campus-Written Software May Herald New Chapter in Computer Revolution." *Chronicle of Higher Education* July (1986), 14-15.

Underwood, John. "On the Edge: Intelligent CALL in the 1990s." *Computers and the Humanities* 23 (1989), 71-84.

University Affairs, November 1991, p. 16.

University Affairs, April 1992, p. 9.

Waldal, Kelly A. "New CAE Facility Offers Industry Training and Insights." *T.H.E. Journal* March (1991), 72-74.

Wilson, Richard F. and George F. Badger. "The University of Illinois at Urbana-Champaign: Computing and Instructional Innovation." In Graves (ed.) 1989, 339-363.

Woloshyn, Gayle and Barbara Kaltz. "Computer-Assisted Language Learning (CALL) in Postsecondary Education: An Annotated Bibliography. Addendum." *CCALLNET* 5.2 (1991).

2. INTERVIEWS

Chandler (1992). Dr. David Chandler, Department of Chemistry, University of Regina.

Gingrich (1992). Dr. Paul Gingrich, Department of Sociology and Social Studies, University of Regina.

Klokeid (1991). Dr. Terry Klokeid, Department of Indian Languages, Literatures and Linguistics, Saskatchewan Indian Federated College, University of Regina.

Knuttila (1992). Dr. Murray Knuttila, Chair, Department of Sociology and Social Studies, University of Regina.

Maguire (1992). Dr. Brien R. Maguire, Department of Computer Science, University of Regina.

Rubrecht (1991). Dr. Werner H. Rubrecht, Department of Germanic and Slavic Studies, University of Regina.

Sauchyn (1992). Dr. David Sauchyn, Department of Geography, University of Regina.

Sollars (1992). Ms. Joanne Sollars, Programme Administrator, Faculty of

Administration, University of Regina.
Waldal (1992). Mr. Kelly Waldal, Faculty of Engineering, University of Regina.
Wilhelm (1992). Dr. Bernard Wilhelm, Department of French, University of Regina.

3. OTHER SOURCES

"Computer-Based and CAL Materials Development." *Newsletter* 7.1, 1992, p. 9 (Office of Graduate Studies and Research, University of Regina).
Computer Science Curriculum for the Year 2000 (1990).
Deakin, Annick (University of Western Ontario). Electronic mail *EDTECH*, 17 Sept. 1991.
Duckett, George (Ohio State University). "Computer Literacy Survey: Part One". Electronic mail *EDTECH* , 19 Mar. 1992.
—. "Computer Literacy Survey: Part Two." Electronic mail *EDTECH*, 19 Mar. 1992.
—. "Computer Literacy Survey: Part Three." Electronic mail *EDTECH*, 19 Mar. 1992.
Wilhelm, Bernard (University of Regina). *Memorandum*, 1992.

CHAPTER 4

COMPUTERS IN RESEARCH

1. Historical Perspective

1.1 The American/Canadian Experience

Universities and digital electronic computers have had a close and mutually beneficial relationship for over fifty years. Not only has much of the pioneering and fundamental developmental work in hardware, software and network technology been carried out in universities, they have also been major users of computing facilities. Elsewhere, we will discuss how universities in North America have used computing for administrative and pedagogical purposes. In this chapter we survey research utilization.

The history of research computing at North American universities reveals that, aside from mathematicians, computer scientists and computer engineers, the earliest users of the developing computer technology were natural scientists and engineers, particularly those who needed the enhanced calculational and numerical analysis facilities that electronic computers afforded. While, as we will see, computers are now used widely by most academic units within universities, scientists have continued to be major users particularly of large mainframes, supercomputers and more powerful workstations. In a recent interview with *DATAMATION*, J. Presper Eckert, the coinventor of ENIAC and UNIVAC I[1], when asked whether computerization spurred creativity in individuals, replied, "certainly in the scientific area, because it allows you to tackle problems you couldn't tackle before. Instead of spending all your time grinding away at a desk with pencil and paper, you have more of your time to be thinking about the results and less time doing the dog work" (Brousell 1991). FORTRAN, introduced as a programming language in 1957, is still the preferred language of scientific programmers even though newer languages exist; so vast is the array of programs originally written in FORTRAN and still in use, there is little motivation for change.

During the 1960's and 1970's programmed control and data collection became greatly simplified as batch methods using punched cards and tape gave way to on-line methods and magnetic media storage. The computers themselves became smaller and far more reliable as the result of improvements made in electronics, particularly in solid-state technology. As computers became easier to use and commercial software appeared, many people involved in social

---

[1] ENIAC was the first large-scale North American digital computer and UNIVAC I was the first commercially available computer. The US. Census Bureau purchased a UNIVAC I in 1951.

research requiring manipulation and analysis of vast amounts of data came to realize the advantage of using digital computers. Social Sciences, Schools of Business (or Commerce or Administration) and Education have become significant users of computing power as part of their scholarly activity.

Other academic areas, particularly the Arts and Humanities, are more recent converts to using computers in research, primarily as the result of the widespread availability and use of microcomputers. A study among Humanities faculty members at the University of Illinois (Jacobson and Weller 1987-1988) showed that for over 70% familiarity with computers meant awareness only of microcomputers and, of those, 77% used computers for word processing; the other major uses (*vide infra*) were supported by 20% or less of the respondents.

In spite of the growing use of microcomputers in research by academics, regardless of discipline or area, there has remained a perceived need at universities for large computing facilities including supercomputers. In the United States, the National Science Foundation (NSF) took the initiative in providing $300,000,000 over five years to create and maintain five super computing centers (National Centers for Advanced Scientific Research) at universities—Princeton, Cornell, Illinois, California at San Diego and Pittsburgh/Carnegie-Mellon (Roskies 1987:15; Lee 1989:38)[2]. The Cornell facility, for example, supports more than 1700 researchers from 115 academic institutions in 40 states; it is a truly national resource available for solving problems not amenable to solution or as easily solved by other computing facilities (Lee 1989:39). In Canada there is only one super computing centre, the Ontario Center for Large Scale Computation at the University of Toronto (George 1990:9)[3].

The increased use of computers generally, and in research specifically, can be attributed to several important factors:

1. Hardware and software have become more sophisticated but, at the same time, easier to use or more user-friendly;

2. High level programming languages and specialized software are readily available;

3. There is a constantly improving price/performance ratio[4]. Estimates suggest that a 25% price/performance decrease in real dollars occurred every year between 1957 and 1978 with greater gains since (Runyan 1991:34);

---

[2] At the time of writing there are only four of the original centers remaining.

[3] While the report of the ad hoc Committee on Research Computation lists only one supercomputer in Canada, the Cray XMP at the University of Toronto, other Universities have large computers that might be considered to be supercomputers. The University of Calgary, for example, has a Control Data Corporation Cyber 205 supercomputer.

[4] Price/performance ratio is the initial cost of a computer normalized for speed, capacity and all-round computing power. Early computers were very expensive but had relatively little computing power by today's standards.

4. There has been an increase in available computational power. The accepted increase is an order of magnitude a decade or a factor of 10,000 since 1950 (George 1990:14). A $3000 microcomputer sitting on an academic's desk can provide her with more computing power and greater flexibility, to say nothing of ease of use, than a far more expensive mainframe of only a few years ago.

1.2 The University of Regina Experience

The University of Regina is a relatively new institution; its predecessor, the University of Saskatchewan, Regina Campus, came into existence in the early 1960's. At that time, an IBM 1620 was the University computer. Subsequently, the mainframes used have included an IBM 1130 (1966), an IBM 360/40 (1969), a XEROX/Honeywell Sigma 9 (1973), a VAX 750 (1984), a VAX 785 (1985), a VAX 8600 (1985), an IBM 4381 (1985), a VAX 6310 (1988) and two VAX 6320's (1989). One of the VAX 6320's and the IBM 4281 are still used for academic research purposes[5].

Following the general North American trend, most of the early users of the mainframe computer(s) at the University of Regina were scientists with need for analysis of large amounts of data—X-ray crystallographers, nuclear physicists and spectroscopists. During the early to mid 1970's these groups obtained dedicated PDP 8, PDP 11, Nicolet, Wang or other mini and desktop computers to control instruments and to handle some of their data collection and analysis. In 1969, researchers in the Social Sciences' Sample Survey and Data Bank Unit converted to using the mainframe computer to carry out contract social surveys and the attendant data analysis. The Sample Survey Unit has been a major user of mainframe computing facilities and commercial statistical analysis software such as SPSS ever since.

During the 1980's others began to take advantage of computing. These included researchers in Economics, Psychology and Social Work who needed statistical analysis of large amounts of data and manipulation of sophisticated models. The association of the Physics Department with TRIUMF (the Canadian meson factory and intermediate energy particle research facility in Vancouver) added new demands on the University's computing and networking facilities; much of the experimental work was carried out in Vancouver but the data were "carried" to Regina for analysis. The Regina nuclear physics group has recently purchased a VAX workstation which has been added to the University's VAX cluster. Other researchers in Physics and Mathematics use a SUN workstation with several attached desktop units, while a PRIME 9755 computer has been dedicated to research in Engineering and to GIS research in Geography using the software package ARC/INFO (graphics, mapping and analysis of such variables as land use).

---

[5] *Cf.* Appendix A. The second VAX 6320 is devoted to administrative computing.

The campus communication network was completed in 1989 when switches were installed on the College Avenue Campus and in Campion College (the latter to integrate the two largest Federated Colleges). Its growth, from a system in the early 1970's designed to provide members of the Computer Science Department access to the mainframe computer and the Department's PDP-11/20 microcomputer, to a campus-wide network with in excess of 1200 connections, mirrors the overall increase in computing at the University of Regina. In 1985 the University became part of the NetNorth (Bitnet) network and in 1991 part of CA*net, the Canadian research network.

During 1989 the University Library began the major task of computerizing its catalogue system, integrating it with those of Government libraries in the City, and making access possible to students and staff from terminals throughout the Library, and from remote locations such as faculty offices.

2. The Present Situation

2.1 The Baseline Survey Results

In 1989, as part of this project, an academic computing questionnaire was sent to a stratified sample of 957 academics at 13 Canadian universities (see Appendix C for details). The questionnaire, also shown in Appendix C, was designed to obtain information about the extent of and attitudes toward computer use in teaching and research. Appendix C also contains a detailed presentation of some of the data as well as a summary of the responses received. In this chapter we will discuss only those aspects of the replies to the questionnaire that relate to scholarly activity while bearing in mind that, in some cases, the small sample sizes may call into question the results' reliability.

As Figure 1 shows, 45% of the respondents are provided with no-direct-cost access to a mainframe computer. Availability of a minicomputer/workstation (29% overall) is most likely in Administration/Business/Commerce (58%), Mathematics and Engineering. Shared microcomputers are most prevalent in the Fine Arts (50%), Humanities, Education and Medicine. While overall about 11% are provided with microcomputers by their academic units, the percentages are considerably less in the Humanities, Social Sciences and Natural Sciences (0-4%), and are much higher in areas such as Administration (33%), Mathematics and Medicine.

It is extremely interesting that nearly three quarters of all faculty have a microcomputer for their own use, some more than one. The numbers are slightly lower in small universities (67%) and significantly lower in Mathematics (57%) and Engineering. The Social Sciences (85%), Natural Sciences, Administration, Education and the Humanities are slightly more likely to have faculty with their own micros. Figure 2 illustrates the composite picture of the sources of personal microcomputers for academic use. Faculty in small universities are much more likely to have their computers purchased by the academic unit or university (50%) and much less likely to have purchased them using a grant or contract (10%). Approximately 40% of academics in the Fine Arts, Humanities and Social Sciences who have computers have purchased their own; those in the Engineering (75%), Mathematics and the Sciences have been more likely to use grants or contracts while those in Administration and Education have had the greatest luck in having their microcomputers provided by the academic unit (50%). Seventeen percent in Administration shared the cost of their computer with the university or academic unit.

Figure 1. Availability of Computing Resources

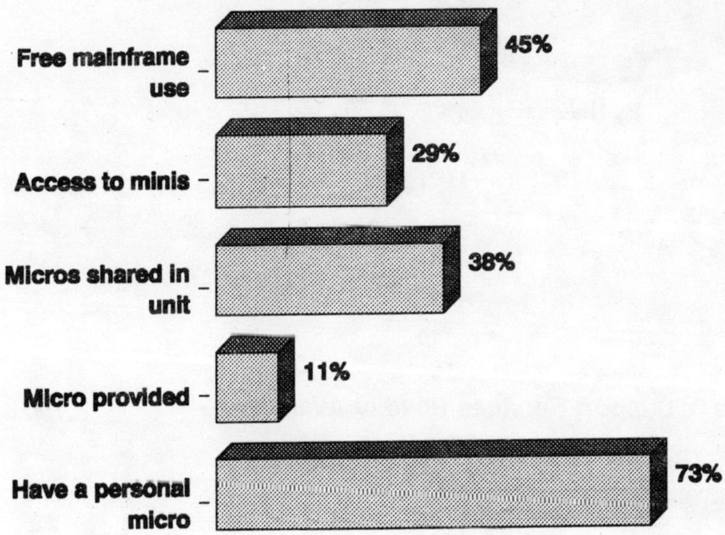

Fifty eight percent and 75% of the respondents indicated that computer training courses and consulting services, respectively, are readily available (Figure 3). Large universities are most likely to provide training courses (72%) and consulting services (86%); small universities are least likely (38 and 56%). The Sciences (86%), Mathematics, Administration, Education and the Social Sciences appear to have greater access to consulting services, in particular, than in other academic units. Fine Arts, Medicine and Engineering have the poorest access.

Figure 2. How Microcomputer Was Purchased

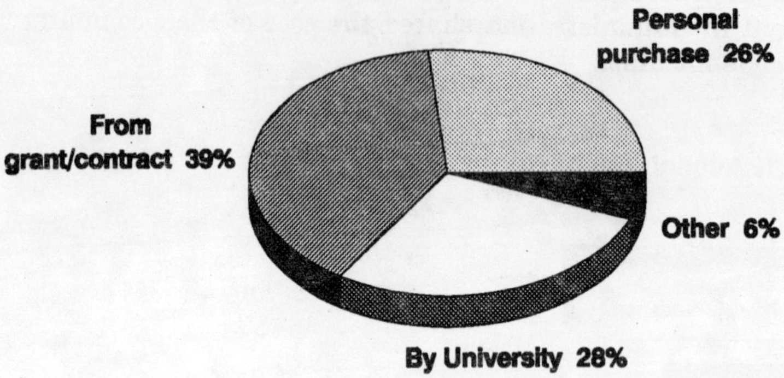

Figure 3. Support Services Readily Available

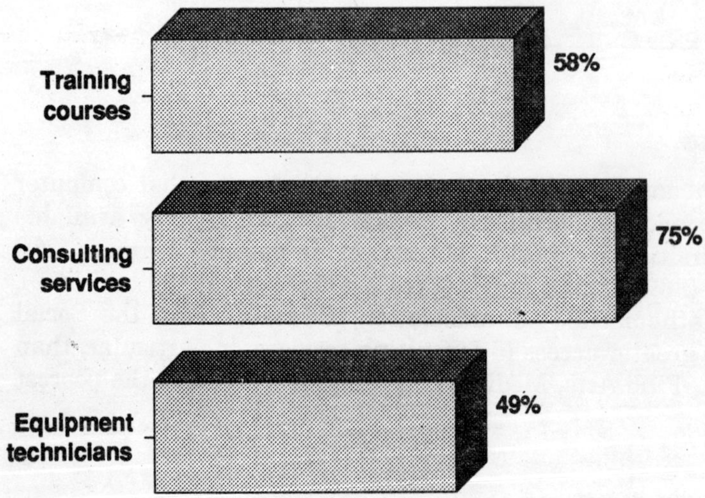

Figure 4 shows that 88% of those responding to the questionnaire indicated that their library has a computerized catalogue system. Libraries of the large universities are more likely to be computerized (93%) while those of small universities are much less likely to be (33%). However, a third of the respondents from small universities noted that computerization was coming. Social Science (69%), Medical, Fine Arts and Humanities libraries are least likely to be computerized; Mathematics (up to 100%), Engineering, Natural Sciences and Education libraries are most computerized.

Figure 4. Computerized Library Catalogue System

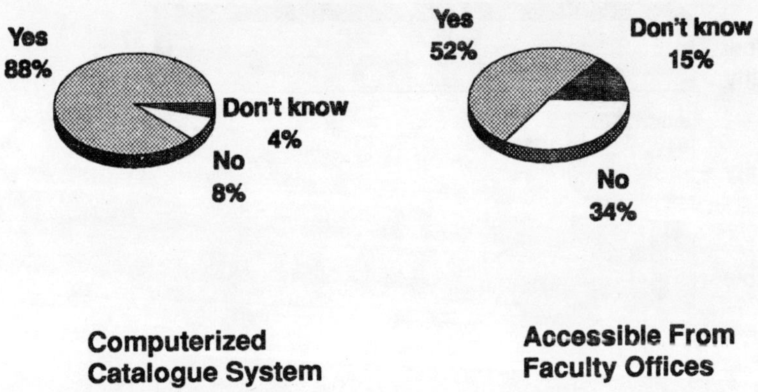

Computerized bibliographical, informational or library databases are most prevalent in Medicine, Education, the Sciences, Humanities and Engineering. They are not so readily available in Administration and Mathematics. Large Universities are much more likely to provide computerized access to databases.

Large universities provide a greater opportunity of accessing library indexes (or other library resources) from faculty offices (61%) than medium-sized universities; there is very little access in small universities (11%). By discipline, access is greatest in Education (78%), the Sciences, Engineering, the Fine Arts and the Social Sciences; it is least in Medicine (13%).

Only about 12% indicated that no faculty use electronic mail for local or national/international communication although, in most areas, use is limited to a few faculty (Figure 5). The small universities have a larger percentage (25%) not using E-mail. For medium-sized universities and large universities the corresponding percentages are 18-20% and 6-7% respectively. The reported use of electronic communication is greatest in Education (up to 100%), Engineering and Administration. It is least used in Medicine (up to 30% don't use it in any form) and the Fine Arts.

Figure 5. Electronic Mail Use

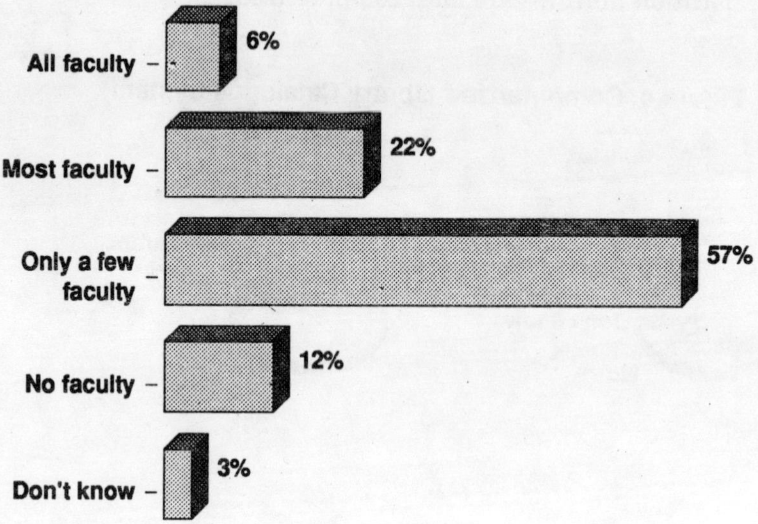

Seventy seven percent of the respondents are convinced that faculty are doing substantially more manuscript preparation as the result of the widespread availability of word processors (Figure 6). This feeling is most widely held in Administration (92%), the Sciences, Engineering and the Social Sciences. It seems to be less prevalent in Medicine (58%) and Education. Interestingly, a significant number of faculty, especially in Education (30%), Medicine and the Humanities, are not certain whether academics are doing more of their own manuscript preparation.

Figure 7 illustrates the perceived major constraints on academic computing. The results, while more detailed, are similar to those reported among the Humanities faculty at the University of Illinois (Jacobson and Weller 1987-1988:84,92). Cost is seen as a constraint by 70% of the respondents, particularly those in the Sciences (91%), Education, Mathematics, Administration and Engineering. The Humanities (54%), Social Sciences, Medicine and those 60 or older seem to be less concerned with cost. Space is a

Figure 6. Has Word Processing Increased Faculty Manuscript Preparation?

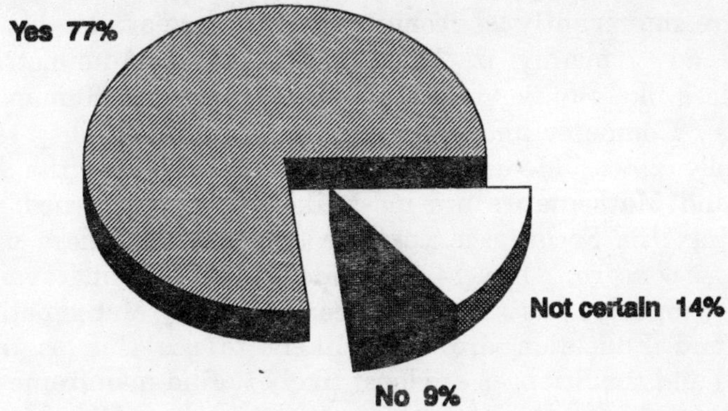

Figure 7. Major Constraints On Computer Use

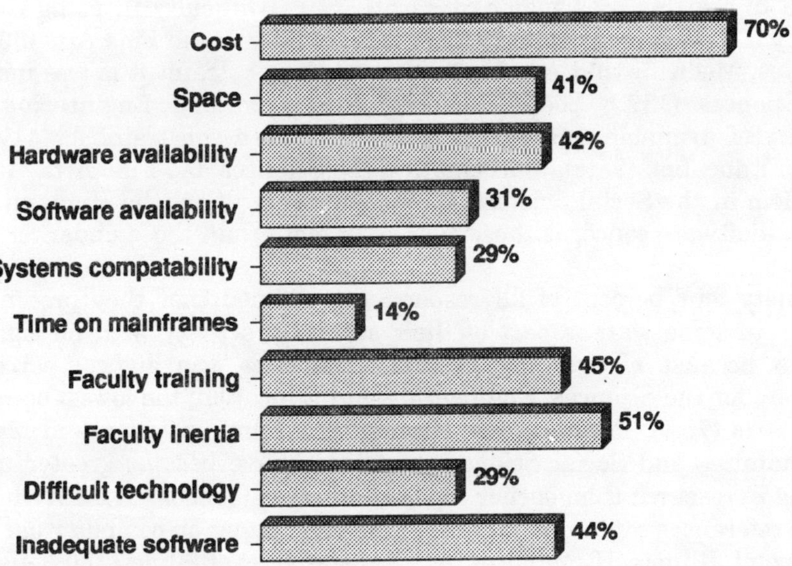

major constraint for 41% overall, highest in Administration (64%), the Sciences, Mathematics and Engineering, lowest in the Fine Arts (29%) and Education. Computer or terminal availability is a major constraint for 42% with the greatest concern in the Sciences (59%), Education, Humanities, Social Sciences, Mathematics and Administration. Faculty in Fine Arts (17%), Engineering and those under 40 are significantly less concerned. Software availability is seen as a constraint by 31%, mainly in Mathematics (50%), Administration and Medicine. It is less likely to be viewed as a problem in the Humanities (23%) and the Sciences. Computer and operating system compatibility represent a constraint for only 29%. Medicine (44%), the Humanities, the Fine Arts, Administration and Mathematics are most likely to be concerned; Education (11%), Engineering, the Social Sciences, the Sciences and those under forty expressed the least concern. Only 14% consider capacity of and available time on mainframe computers as a major constraint. Mathematics (33%), Administration and Education are more likely to see this as a problem. Engineering (6%) and the Sciences are least likely to find mainframe capacity a constraint. Training of faculty is a major constraint for 45%, particularly in Administration (73%), Medicine and Education, but less so in Mathematics (14%), the Sciences, Engineering, the Fine Arts and the Social Sciences. In a 1987 report from the University of Illinois, 60% of Humanities faculty there considered lack of training an obstacle to increased computer use (Jacobson and Weller 1987-1988). Faculty inertia is a major constraint for 52%. The areas most likely to view inertia as a problem are Education (78%), Fine Arts, the Social Sciences and Administration. Only in Mathematics is there little likelihood to see this as a major concern (17%). Difficulty in using computer technology is a major constraint by only 29%, mainly in the Fine Arts (50%), the Humanities, Medicine and Administration. As a constraint it is less important in the Sciences (18%), Social Sciences, Education and Engineering. The inadequacy of available software is reported to be a constraint for 41%, most notably in Education (78%), Mathematics, the Sciences and Fine Arts. It is less of a problem in the Social Sciences (23%), Administration, the Humanities and Medicine. Software concerns those over sixty more than those under forty (55% to 32%).

Ninety four percent of all respondents claimed that they presently use computers in some way as part of their scholarly activity with no significant differences because of age. As Figure 8 indicates, the highest percentages (100%) were for the Sciences, Engineering and Education; the lowest occurred in the Fine Arts (75%), Mathematics, Humanities, Administration and Medicine. The Humanities and Social Sciences appear to have become greater users of computing in research than earlier reports indicated (Jacobson and Weller 1987-1988 and references contained therein). The 1987 paper on computer use among University of Illinois Humanities faculty stated that almost 80% used the computer more than twice a week or daily. Of the computers used by Canadian academics for research, microcomputers comprise 63%, mainframes 21%,

Figure 8. Computer Use In Scholarly Activity

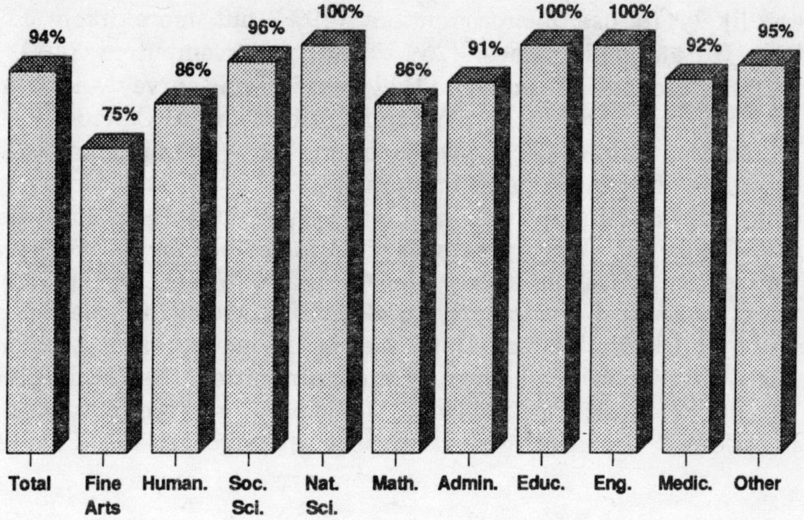

Figure 9. Research Computers

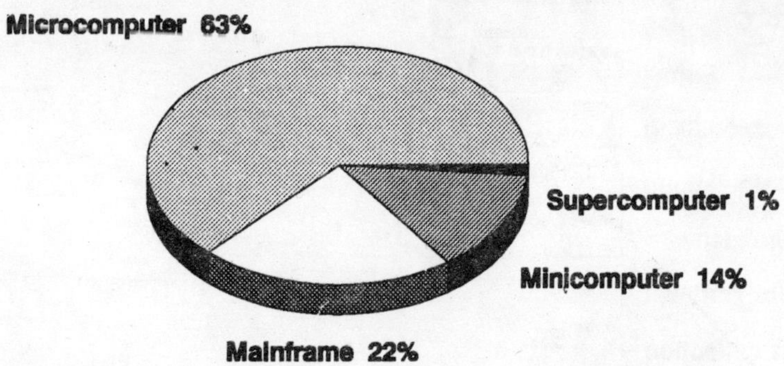

minicomputers/workstations 15% and supercomputers 2% (Figure 9 gives percentages representing total use as many respondents indicated that they make use of more than one type of computer). Respondents in Administration indicated utilization of microcomputers only. Engineering and Science respondents are less likely than the average to use microcomputers but are more likely to use larger computers (all the use of supercomputers occurred in the Sciences). While Education, the Humanities and the Social Sciences use minicomputers less than the average, Medicine uses them more. Faculty under 40 seem less likely to use microcomputers (49%) but more likely to use minicomputers (21%), mainframes (26%) and supercomputers (4%). A distribution of computer usage similar to that found in our survey was obtained from a survey carried out among academic scientists in Canada (George 1990:10-13): microcomputers (79%), workstations (28%), mainframes (32%), minisupercomputers (4%) and supercomputers (4%).

The major uses of computers for research by the survey's respondents are summarized in Figure 10. Word processing is a major use for all faculty as it was in the University of Illinois survey (Jacobson and Weller 1987-1988:93-5). Data analysis is important particularly in Education, Medicine, the Sciences, Social Sciences and Administration. Database operations represent a major use in the Fine Arts, Education, Medicine and the Humanities. Use of graphics is important in the Sciences, Engineering, Medicine, the Fine Arts and the Humanities. E-mail is used more than the average in the Fine Arts,

Figure 10. Uses Of Computers In Research

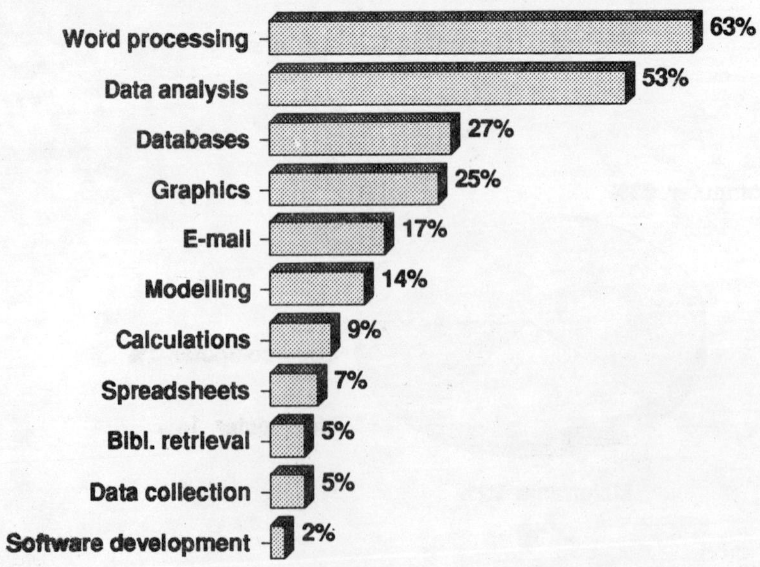

Mathematics, the Social Sciences, Humanities and Education. Modelling is most important for the Sciences and Engineering; numeric calculations most

important for Mathematics and Engineering; use of spreadsheets most important in Administration and Engineering.

There is a general feeling that research use of large mainframe computers will decrease, with an concomitant increase in the use of workstations and microcomputers (Figure 11). Administration, Education, Engineering and the Humanities are most likely to predict decreased use in mainframe computers; the Social Sciences, Medicine, Mathematics and the Sciences are less likely to do so. Engineering and the Sciences foresee the greatest increase in research use of workstations while Administration, Social Sciences, Education and the Humanities see the least. Faculty under forty predicted a greater use of workstations than their older colleagues.

Although there are area differences, overall, Canadian academics view the greatest impact of computers to be in word processing, communications, information access, visual presentations, data storage and manipulation, simulation and complex calculations, in that order. Sixty three percent believe that within five years all faculty will have a microcomputer in their offices. Fifty seven percent think that all faculty will be able to access the library from their offices and 50% are convinced that all faculty will use electronic mail within the same time period.

Figure 11. Future Computer Use For Research

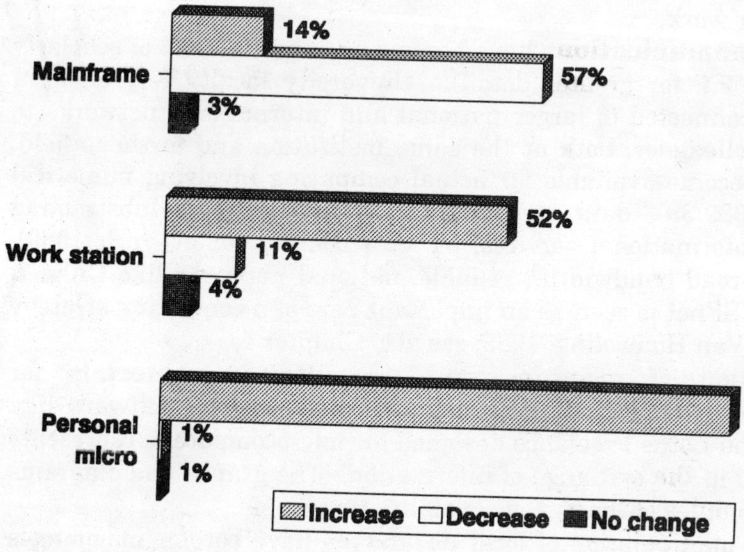

2.2 Computers and Research/Scholarly Activity

The survey makes it clear that the uses of computers in scholarly activity are many and varied. Some are specific to a particular academic area or even to a single research problem. Others have wider utilization. This section comments in broad terms on some of those uses that have been identified as being more common.

Word processing was identified in the survey as the most common and, in some cases, the only use of computers by scholars. The word processor has all but replaced the typewriter for preparation of papers, manuscripts, books *etc.* Some of the modern word processing software packages such as Microsoft Word, WordPerfect, WordStar and Ami provide features that rival desktop publishing software, with an ease of use that almost anyone with some training can master; in most cases, the incorporation of graphs and pictures (scanned or drawn) presents little problem. Word processors and complementary software usually provide tools that allow the writer to check spelling, grammar and style and to have access to a built-in thesaurus. Many publishers of scholarly journals and monographs now require a print or camera-ready manuscript rather than using older type setting procedures. Scholars using a language other than English (or French in Canada), especially one with a non-Latin-based script, or mathematical and scientific symbols, have rather special needs that are only now being met by commercial text processors. It is becoming easier to prepare manuscripts using these languages and symbols especially when computers are coupled to laser printers. There are also sophisticated microcomputer programs, like Finale, that allow music composers and arrangers to prepare commercial-quality scores of their work.

Electronic communications have become an essential part of scholarly activity (see section 3.5 for greater detail). University faculty rely on local computer networks connected to larger national and international networks to communicate with colleagues, both at the same institution and further afield. Remote computers become available for actual computing involving numerical calculations (Lee 1989:39), data transfer, access to databases (abstracting services, libraries, informational services, bulletin boards) *etc.* (Lynch 1989). The availability of broad bandwidth[6], reliable, national networks like CA*net, Bitnet, NREN and NSFnet is seen as an important part of a computing strategy (George 1990:30-41; Van Houweling, 1989; see also Chapter 5).

The preparation of **graphics and presentation materials** for publication, conference delivery or seminars using commercial software like Harvard Graphics and Lotus Freelance designed for microcomputers, represents a powerful tool to aid in the exchange of information. The graphs and diagrams in this report are examples of the sort of capability that exists.

Access to and manipulation of local **databases** have become major tools in the hands of scholars in all disciplines. Commercial databases like Oracle

---

[6]Capable of high speed data transfer. Bandwidth is a measure of transfer speed.

and Ingres, designed initially to run on large computers, or dBase, FoxBase, Paradox and specially written ones running on microcomputers, allow a researcher to store information and then analyze it in a variety of useful ways. There are also hypermedia programs that combine graphics with text in databases that can be searched interactively and non-linearly[7]. More sophisticated databases, often residing on remote large computers acting as servers, that can be linked to graphic displays are available commercially for areas as diverse as Geography (mapping) and Molecular Biology (gene mapping or protein structure and dynamics).

Data management and analysis also provide researchers with the opportunity to use a different variety of powerful tools like SPSS and SAS. Information is coded and stored in the computer so that it may be extracted and analyzed, multi-variant statistical analysis carried out and, in some cases, a graphical presentation prepared. Often the data to be analyzed are obtained from government or similar sources as the result of surveys like a national census.

Data collection is easily automated by interfacing computers, often dedicated to the purpose, to other pieces of equipment. The computers can then be used to carry out data analysis on the stored information. The high speed and large storage capacity of modern computers have increased the speed of event logging and have improved data sampling.

Time-consuming **numerical calculations** are often a necessary part of engineering and scientific research. With sufficient computation, it is possible to make measurements in the same way as they can be made in the laboratory. In addition, a computational model is often better in that experiments can be simulated that cannot be performed, and systems "observed" that could not be "observed" in any other way. Sometimes the calculations can be carried out only through the use of the largest, fastest computers. When such a computer is not available at the researcher's home institution, communication through a network makes its access possible.

Model design and assessment are areas of research requiring computers capable of carrying out untold calculations rapidly. In fact, accurate modelling in areas such as meteorology, nuclear physics, drug design, astrophysics and molecular genetics, to name only a few, requires computers currently considered to be supercomputers (Roskies 1987:15-18; Lee 1989:32; George 1990:14-25; Miller 1988; Hut and Sussman 1987). Simulation and modelling are areas where the techniques and language of artificial intelligence (AI) are being successfully employed (Miller and Walker 1988:3).

Equipment control, **robotics** and **intelligent control** are also areas where artificial intelligence research is important (Prince 1986:16; Miller and

---

[7] The user can influence the flow of information by using the keyboard or a pointing device such as a mouse to indicate choices. One piece of information can be "linked" to other items in much the same way as a concordance or encyclopedia has linked terms.

Walker 1988:1-2, 6-7); a computer that "learns" can be useful as a laboratory assistant and technician or as an "advisor".

Textual analysis and the use of large **computer concordances** represent a special case of database application in the Humanities and Fine Arts, particularly useful for analyzing literature, papers and letters. Specific words or phrases can be searched for rapidly, or stylistic comparisons of various written works can be made. Artificial intelligence (AI) techniques can also be useful to literary researchers (Cercone and Murchison 1986).

Interactive computer graphics, especially making use of dedicated graphics workstations with high resolution display, is an area of increasing importance particularly in Engineering, scientific and geographic research where visualization is vital. While graphics research can be an area of interest in its own right, more important is its application in modelling and in computer assisted design (CAD).

Expert/information systems have also become important areas of research using the latest in AI techniques (Prince 1986:4-8; Miller and Walker 1988) coupled with large databases. Medical and computer research are areas that are ideally suited to expert systems; a properly programmed computer can be utilized so as to take advantage of its speed, patience and reliability to analyze large quantities of experimental data intelligently, noting patterns, suggesting theories and models to account for them, and even proposing new relationships.

Computing **hardware** and **software development** can also be areas of research for academics.

3. Major Issues

3.1 Hardware

Perhaps most crucial for a researcher is the question of the type of computer to be used. For many, if not most, modern microcomputers can handle their needs—word processing, database management, graphics *etc.* As this chapter is being written, the cost of MS-DOS (or OS/2) microcomputers using Intel 80386 or 80486 processors, or even top-of-the-line Macintosh computers, has reached the point where their purchase is possible for most academics, and the choice of manufacturer is almost endless. For those requiring more powerful workstations for computational and graphics work, there are also a number of minicomputers available at attractive prices.

Although smaller computer systems are becoming increasingly powerful, all indications point to the continuing need for large computers by researchers whose calculations, modelling and data analysis require speed and/or storage capabilities simply not available with smaller computers. While there are a number of North American mainframe vendors, the academic market is dominated by two. For the past several decades, scientific and some other academic computing has been permeated by a "VAX mentality"; the only computing worth doing was that done on a computer manufactured by Digital Equipment Company (DEC). A spectrum of choices is available to those looking for computing devices that could be classified as "super." This spectrum includes: supercomputers of the Cray Y-MP class (with as many as 16 processors and a peak performance of 1 GFLOP per processor)[8]; minisupercomputers; super workstations; massively parallel computers (hundreds of microprocessors connected together); multiprocessor mainframes and superminicomputers (Bell and Miranker 1990). A somewhat facetious definition of a supercomputer is "the most powerful general-purpose scientific computer that is at least an order of magnitude below current needs" (Roskies 1987:14). As many authors point out (Roskies 1987; Lee 1989; George 1990; Miller 1988), there are problems whose numerical solutions are readily obtained and visualized in real time only with very large, multiprocessor, vector computers. While these are extremely expensive[9], and are likely to be used by only a small fraction of the research community, it is argued by many that a technologically advanced country must have at least some available for academic research and training of students; their efficient use requires that students must know special programming techniques and how to overcome some unique technical problems.

A large University must be able to provide a range of computing options—large mainframe, workstations, and microcomputers. Groups of Universities and, perhaps, governmental and other research institutions could cooperate in providing and maintaining a supercomputing facility.

A majority of computer scientists, and others using a multitude of computers, have suggested that an ideal situation is for all types of computers to be able to share a common operating system; when that is so, commercial and locally written programs could be used, in theory, on any computer with little change. While this open-system approach is probably some way off, hardware vendors are moving in that direction with a suggestion that UNIX will become the universal operating system; UNIX appears to be the only presently existing operating system flexible enough to port to practically any platform, including computers with reduced instruction set (RISC) and complex instruction set (CISC) processors. At the present time, a number of the largest software companies do have products that run, with little difference, on a number of different computers. In the realm of microcomputers, the long-standing incompatibility of Intel 80XXX and Motorola 6XXXX-based systems has been a source of frustration. Our survey indicated that, for teaching purposes, MS-DOS micros were used between 2.5 and 3 times more frequently than Macintosh

---

[8] A GFLOP is 1 billion floating-point operations per second, roughly six thousand times faster than a VAX 11/780.

[9] A Cray Y-MP supercomputer can cost as much as $24,000,000. Operational and associated costs can be in the range of $200,000 to $400,000 a month, and lease time charges can be as much as $10,000 per central processing unit hour (Abbott 1991).

computers and there is no reason to believe that the ratio is any different when the computers are used for research.

For the researcher who uses microcomputers, a decision also has to be made on the configuration, particularly the number and nature of storage devices. At least one floppy disk drive and often two are included while a hard disk of at least 40 MB is now a necessity; with the size of modern software and employment of virtual memory techniques, a drive of much larger capacity is strongly recommended. When a large hard drive is available the problem of rapid, reliable backup and secondary storage becomes real. Many people use tapes to provide this important function. but very large amounts of data require other devices like optical disks. For operating systems or shell programs such as OS/2 and Windows 3.X that provide for multitasking, large amounts of RAM (at least 4 MB) are also necessary.

Particularly in the case of workstations and larger computers, an important question to be answered is whether the systems should all be centrally located and managed, or whether it is more desirable to distribute the devices more widely. The tendency of the first three decades of the computer era toward large central systems seems to be a thing of the past (see also Chapter 5). Some universities still maintain centralized mainframe capability and may even link minicomputers to larger machines, but there is a growing tendency for smaller academic units such as faculties, schools, research units or even departments to purchase, operate and maintain their own computers even up to the size of superminis. The additional questions of organization, maintenance and operating policies (*vide infra*) then take on even greater urgency. Large units or units with electronic technicians may, in fact, be able to provide the expertise necessary to maintain their own computers and related equipment, but a central facility to handle this function may prove to be more cost effective and reliable even in those cases.

With the large amounts of money necessary to supply adequate computing facilities for researchers, universities have to deal with how best to provide these facilities. Outright purchase of microcomputers and minicomputers is the norm. In the case of microcomputers, individuals more often provide their own through purchase from research grants, contracts, allowances or from personal funds; the university and its academic units have not typically been the main source of this funding. Minicomputers are usually purchased from research grants or special capital equipment grants provided by the university. For the larger computers and supporting equipment, the university has to decide whether it is advantageous to buy the equipment outright or to lease it. Service contracts on large mainframes and minicomputers make sound economic sense.

3.2 Local Organization, Infrastructure and Policy Matters

As mentioned earlier, computing is now less likely to involve single isolated machines than it did during its early history. The Report of the ad hoc Committee on Research Computation points out (George 1990:27):

> With the evolution of workstations and networks, the computing environments being used by many researchers to conduct their research extend far beyond whatever device happens to be on the researcher's desktop, and the costs and resources associated with supporting this broader research environment are substantial. . . . The provision of adequate infrastructure is at least as important and at least as difficult as selecting and acquiring the particular pieces of computing equipment supported by that environment, and requires dedicated funding. This is all too often ignored or underestimated.

Included in a consideration of infrastructure support should be maintenance, hardware for connecting systems to local networks, networks themselves, licensing fees, software purchase and upgrading for large systems, and administrative and support personnel (technicians, consultants, software specialists, programmers, *etc.*).

Unless there are resources in place to provide adequate assistance, computers acquired by researchers are:

> under-supported and ineffectively used. . . . Powerful workstations are sometimes left with older, less efficient operating systems . . .; equipment is sometimes left without maintenance contracts; workstations are sometimes left as stand-alone devices rather than installed in departmental or research group-based local area networks (LANs); LANs are sometimes not supported or maintained adequately or are not connected to the broader networking community . . . Possibly worst of all, scientists and engineers sometimes are forced to use their own time... to perform the functions of system managers and technicians, time that could otherwise be used to conduct productive research activity. (George 1990:28).

In its survey, the ad hoc Committee on Research Computation found that 83% of the respondents needed some consultation and assistance from on-campus sources in using computer hardware and software while 47% needed assistance from off-campus sources (George 1990:12-13).

How such computing infrastructure support is to be provided is very much an issue. The survey noted above (George 1990:13) indicated that the average respondent spent $16,000 on direct computing activities. Sometimes, granting agencies such as NSERC in Canada and NSF in the United States provide grants specially to meet these costs or include infrastructure support within grants for computing equipment. These grants, however, tend to be limited to purchase of mini to large scale computer systems (the supercomputing centers in the United States are an example). Departments, faculties, schools or universities must include computing infrastructure as part of their ongoing operating expenses. In some cases users are billed directly for services or researchers are "taxed" on grants and contracts to help support computing overhead. Although these practices are presently not widespread, they will undoubtedly increase in frequency as universities find their resources inadequate to meet all the demands placed on them.

Even when some formal, overall organization exists to handle computing policies at the local academic or university level, a number of questions have to be posed and answered: How is the organization to be arranged and managed? To whom is it responsible? How will priority conflicts for resources between users and among academic teaching, research and administrative computing be adjudicated? How will users have input into the decision-making process when there are questions of what hardware and software is to be purchased? How will resources be divided among personnel and equipment demands? It is not our intention to answer these questions but rather to emphasize that well-informed decisions must be based on previously established criteria in each particular case.

3.3 Software

No computing system, however sophisticated, is of much benefit to the researcher without appropriate and usable software being available. When it comes to common productivity tools for microcomputers and workstations—word processors, general purpose databases, spreadsheets, numerical analysis and statistical analysis packages, presentation software, graphics programs, language compilers and interpreters and so forth—commercial software is readily available throughout North America, often at marked educational discounts for academics. Even for larger computers, a wide variety of commercial software and compilers exists. Upgrades are common, particularly for microcomputer software that has the business community as its prime focus; unfortunately, the newer versions are invariably larger and are not always more useful. Although they are often expensive, they can be purchased at considerable savings, as upgrades, by users of earlier versions.

Specialized software, aimed at a particular problem, is almost always prepared by a user. A drawback to research software development, shared with teaching software development, especially for large programs, is the relatively insignificant recognition for career growth that normally results (see also Chapter 3, 2.6.4); books, and peer-reviewed papers or conference presentations are usually more highly regarded. Nonetheless, software development is essential for much scientific and engineering research. As mentioned earlier, the popularity of FORTRAN as a high-level language is attributable to the large numbers of programs still employed that were written using it. Some successful programs have enabled their developers to become incorporated for the purpose of marketing the software. The Gaussian XX series of molecular orbital calulation software from a group associated with Carnegie-Mellon University is a case in point; this series was originally developed by researchers in the Chemistry Department for their own use but has achieved great popularity throughout North America, Japan and Europe.

The successful application of massively-parallel supercomputers to research problems will present very special programming opportunities and needs.

3.4 Training and Consultation

As computers have become more readily accessible, easier to use and more affordable, they are no longer the preserve of highly motivated specialists. In fact, many academics view computers as a more sophisticated version of a typewriter or an electronic calculator. They have a general feeling that computers can make them more efficient and aid their scholarship in a way they might find difficult to enunciate. They object when the university fails to provide or is slow in providing the assistance they need for purchasing hardware and software, in maintaining their equipment, in training them in the use of hardware and software, and in solving whatever problems might arise. The survey mentioned in section 2.1 of this chapter clearly shows that nearly half of Canadian academics see the lack of support as a major constraint on academic computing. Much of the help readily available to them comes from colleagues, meaning that providing assistance puts an added burden on those faculty members "more in the know", hardly the most cost-effective method of providing assistance. Consideration of adequate and efficient consultation and training must be made in planning the infrastructure necessary to support research computing.

3.5 Networks

One of the fundamental imperatives in research is to communicate; we provide colleagues with the results of our work for their criticism and edification, and we learn of their work in return. Such communication can be made through verbal contact or by less immediate methods like books and journals. Modern, computer-assisted communication requires reliable networking that links computers in a local area network that might be within a Department or cover an entire university. LANs are then connected as the nodes in wider area networks including a region of the country (a province in the Canadian context), an entire country or several countries. Canada's CA*net, the American NSFnet and Bitnet are but three examples of the latter. Through a desktop terminal, a researcher can access a colleague elsewhere on campus or at another university. There is also the potential for obtaining information from libraries on campus and elsewhere, from abstracting services, informational databases and bulletin boards although there may be a real cost associated with the service provided (long distance telephone charges as well as a charge assessed by the service providing the information). The network also provides the option of data exchange with a remote computer or of transmitting a publication to a publisher.

The Report of the ad hoc Committee on Research Computation (George 1990:36-41) makes a number of recommendations concerning networks. Specifically, every researcher should be supplied with a microcomputer or workstation appropriate to the type of work done; each computer should be attached to a "high bandwidth" departmental and campus network; the campus networks should be interconnected through regional networks; the regional networks should be connected to each other through a national backbone. The Report estimates that a network providing minimal 56,000 bit per second (bps) bandwidth, and including operating staff, would cost the average university $75,000 per annum. That would translate to a national cost in excess of $5,000,000 annually. Regional and national bandwidths (CA*net) should quickly grow to speeds of 1.5 million bits per second (T-1). The suggested goal for 1995 is 1.5 Mbps for inter-campus links and a national backbone and international connections of at least 45 Mbps (T-3). Higher speeds will be required to support masses of high speed graphics and transmission of whole documents that significant library access would make necessary. The existence of reliable and experienced carriers in North America makes these goals feasible. NSFnet also consists of a backbone connecting the supercomputing centers and 13 regional networks to more than 400 campus networks (Van Howeling 1989:18). At the present time, the University of Regina is connected to other users in the Province by the 56 kbps Sask#net. The CA*net Toronto-Vancouver backbone, to which Sask#net is connected, is operating at 1.5 Mbps although some parts of CA*net have faster lines.

One major, and often overlooked factor, in providing the necessary network facilities, is the cost of using long distance data communications facilities. It is estimated that, in Canada, these costs are an order of magnitude greater than comparable ones in the United States (George 1990:35,37)[10].

Capital costs of instituting LANs are also significant. Although wireless LANs are becoming available and the technology will undoubtedly improve (Bunker 1991) it is likely that the medium for connecting workstations and terminals will be copper wire or the more reliable fibre optics. The estimated cost of installing an upgraded network at the University of Regina using ethernet, fibre optics and with 1684 connections is $3,000,000 (*cf.* Chapter 5).

3.6 The Effect of Decisions Made Outside the University

3.6.1 Government Policy

In a Federal system like Canada and the United States, funding for universities is, in reality, a shared responsibility even when one level of government is constitutionally responsible for education. Within Canada, operating grants are provided by the provinces although much of that money may have come in the form of transfer payments from Ottawa. The ongoing operation of the universities, including infrastructure and some limited equipment purchase for computing, is funded in this manner. Capital expenditures may be made for one-time purchases or ongoing replacement from grants arising in much the same way.

---

10 In Canada the long-distance telephone service is a monopoly with tariffs designed to underwrite part of the more expensive local telephone system.

Research is normally funded in a different manner; grants from national (mainly) and provincial granting agencies provide the bulk of such funding. Governments may make overall allocations to the granting agencies but, in North America, decisions on which researcher is funded are the result of a peer review system. In Canada, the three major Granting Councils—NSERC (Natural Sciences and Engineering Research Council), MRC (Medical Research Council) and SSHRC (Social Sciences and Humanities Research Council)—provided nearly $600,000,000 to universities in 1990-91 (Figure 12). While some of that money was provided explicitly for computing hardware and operating expenditures, the report mentioned several times earlier in this chapter recommends that NSERC do much more in providing financial and policy leadership for computing (George 1990). If even some of the Committee's recommendations were adopted by NSERC and were to be funded as the result of government policy, a major impact would be made on scientific computing. As Figure 12 indicates, government policy towards university research clearly favors the Sciences and Engineering, which are the largest users, at present, of computing facilities. Although computer needs vary with discipline and within disciplines, the Sciences and Engineering would appear to be relatively well

Figure 12. Granting Council University Research Grants Over Ten Year Period

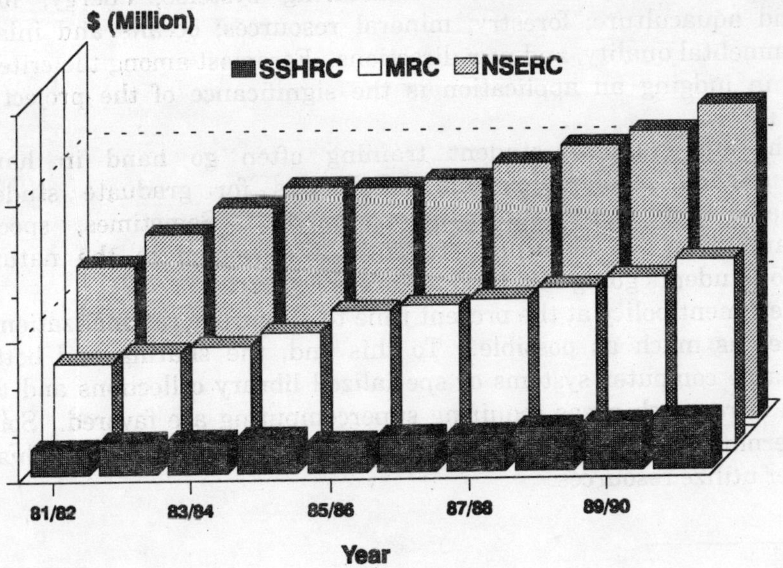

Source: NSERC Facts and Figures 1990-1991

endowed. It may well be that the obvious emphasis in the scientific area, which is made for the potential economic benefit, can encourage other areas indirectly to do more research.

Canadian government policy, as reflected in the policies of the Granting Councils, also encourages creation of Centers of Excellence[11]. If the recommendation of the Ad Hoc Committee on Research Computation were followed, NSERC would fund at least one research supercomputing facility in the Country, to be operated similarly to the four centers in the United States currently funded by NSF. Researchers throughout the country would be able to make use of the facility for those problems requiring a supercomputer, while they and their students would be able to learn the special techniques needed for this type of computing. A national supercomputing facility would make sense only if a fast and reliable network were operational (see section 3.5).

Government policy can also play a role in identifying those areas of research that are considered to be in the provincial or national interest. Unfortunately, areas which will contribute in an immediate way to economic and technological growth are "in." The short attention span of governments does not favor less practical research even though experience has taught that it often serendipitously provides the greater benefit. The Natural Sciences and Engineering Research Council has, in addition to its regular grants programme, a Strategic Grants Program for 1992 that has targeted such areas as information systems and computing technologies; biotechnology; industrial materials, products and processes; manufacturing systems; energy; food, agriculture and aquaculture; forestry; mineral resources; oceans and inland waters; environmental quality, and new directions. Foremost among the criteria to be applied in judging an application is the significance of the project to Canada.

Research and graduate student training often go hand in hand. Governments provide scholarships and fellowships for graduate student education, thereby indirectly supporting research. Sometimes, special scholarships are given for identified students, like women in the natural sciences, and for students going into targeted areas.

It is government policy at the present time to encourage rationalization of scarce resources as much as possible. To this end, the sharing and better utilization of large computer systems or specialized library collections and the rationalization of research areas requiring supercomputing are favored. Some provincial governments are even suggesting reducing the number of graduate schools to better utilize resources.

---

[11] In the Canadian context, a Center of Excellence is created in an existing faculty, school or department of a university. Extra funding is provided for equipment purchase, operation and maintenance so that there exists the potential for research that could not normally carried out. It is expected that researchers from other institutions will be provided with the opportunity to make use of the Center.

3.6.2 Corporate Policy

In Canada, less industrial research is carried out than in most other developed industrialized countries since so many companies are subsidiaries of foreign-owned corporations. As a result, the policies of businesses and industries are less likely to influence academic research than would be the case in the United States, Japan or Europe, although the bigger companies often do carry out collaborative and contracted research involving university faculty, particularly in the Sciences and Engineering. In those cases, a university's location can be an important factor; it is easier to be involved in contract research and consulting when the university is close to the business paying for that research.

University education can be driven, in part, by the demands of those employing the graduates. At the same time, methods utilized in academic disciplines are carried into the corporate world.

3.7 The Changing Nature of Research

No one would deny that computers have changed the nature of research. It might be argued that computers add to the cost of doing research particularly in those areas where more expensive computing facilities are used. If that is the case, those universities that can afford the capital outlay for computing equipment and the operating funds necessary to support the infrastructure that will provide the greatest return on computer investment, will be in a position to reap the major benefits from computerization; they would also be better able to attract and retain outstanding academics. In that way "the rich would get richer." Enhanced institutional reputations mean better students, greater ability to attract research grants and so forth.

On the other hand, the actual price/performance index of computing has been and continues decreasing; the Intel 80486-based computer sitting on a scholar's desk, purchased for just over $3000, has far more power and flexibility than a several hundred thousand dollar mainframe of only a few years ago. Except where very expensive computing systems are required, smaller and less well endowed universities should be able to maintain a faculty that can do high-quality research with a reasonable investment in computing. The survey seems to indicate that this is so since the only substantial difference size of university makes involves the probability that the library or libraries are computerized and part of the campus network.

Computers have been important in making some types of research much easier than they would otherwise have been, and in permitting research which could not have been carried out without them. All areas or disciplines have benefitted from the first of these, the potential increase in productivity. As mentioned earlier, the Sciences, Engineering and those areas requiring graphics and modelling with tremendous amounts of calculation or data handling have benefitted most from the second. For example, only now is it becoming possible to handle the complicated models necessary to adequately predict climate, to understand astrophysics and nuclear physics, to calculate molecular properties and reactions of biological molecules or to simulate human thinking, to mention only a few.

> In this new environment, researchers combine the computational power of the supercomputer with the tools of numerical simulation and scientific visualization in a way that multiplies their power. The result is no longer an increment in capacity, but rather that final increment which transforms quantity into quality. In this environment scientific insight is stretched along new dimensions (Maisel 1989).

Computers are also changing the way scholars obtain information and communicate with one another. The increasing use of networks to access library resources, of large databases resident on CD ROM disks or central computers, and of expert systems is making information easier to obtain and to use. The traditional methods, usually paper-based, are being augmented and, in some cases replaced, by faster and more reliable ones.

With a microcomputer available at home or a lap-top, portable computer, university academics can take work home or can access a larger computer through a modem thereby allowing them to do more of their research and writing away from the university. Such possibilities are changing in a profound way the nature of some scholarly activity.

Most academics have not been formally trained in the use of computer hardware or software and, even if they have, the technology is changing so rapidly that they must make a conscious effort to maintain a reasonable level of competence. Using computers in research, then, requires familiarity with the technology as well as keeping up to date in a particular scholarly area.

4. The Future

While it is impossible to accurately predict the future in all respects, there are some general observations that can be made. The price/performance ratio of computers will continue to decrease so that most researchers will be able to have very powerful computers sitting on their desks, computers that will be able to perform much, and perhaps all, of their research computing. One estimate is that a dollar will buy between 8 and 30 times more computing power over the next 10 years (Moad 1991:62). Lap-top technology will improve to such an extent that a lot of the microcomputers will be carried to and from work, as brief cases are now, to be used wherever the academic is. Mainframes, as we know them, will probably disappear. As J. Presper Eckert indicates, larger computers will most likely "consist of a hundred small computers, chips built into a box, working like a telephone exchange" (Brousell 1991:31).

It is a certainty that only a few institutions will actually possess the largest and most powerful supercomputers. Academics at other institutions will be provided access to a supercomputer as needed, usually from their own desktop terminal and using a high bandwidth network. Supercomputers will change to a more massively parallel and scalable structure. By 1995 such computers may well be capable of over a trillion floating point operations per second to simulate a wide range of physical phenomena (Bell and Miranker 1990:80). The biggest challenge that remains for massively parallel supercomputer and supermini systems is to win users over to the new software development techniques required to produce programs that exploit the full power of their independent processors (Abbott 1991:77).

There will be far-reaching improvements in such other hardware technologies as storage and display devices, and networks. As more users take advantage of the sophisticated networks, bandwidth will increase and there may even be "intelligence" added to the network applications so they can filter out what is pertinent to the user from the vast amount of information surging through huge networks (Moad 1991:63). Network carriers in the future will almost certainly be able to provide bandwidth dependent on the user's needs. There are presently modems, costing under $500 and using existing communication media, that provide data compression for increased speed and automatic error detection.

Although software advances have tended to lag well behind those in the area of hardware, there will continue to be improvements in sophistication, ease of use and power especially in areas such as graphics applications (see Chapter 6). More and more of the common software packages will run on a variety of different-sized computers. A recent article points out that a number of large-system fourth-generation languages and the databases they operate with have been designed to work with many hardware platforms and operating systems, including OS/2, MS-DOS and Windows (Lindholm 1992). While there may be an attempt to move toward operating systems such as UNIX that can be used on any platform, it is unlikely that the Macintosh graphical user interface or MS-DOS/Windows or OS/2 will disappear; there are just too many software packages making use of them and users feel comfortable with them. Computers of the near future will probably be able to understand human speech, visual images and tactile pressure as input to programs (Moad 1991:64).

The increasing power of micro- and minicomputers, along with their high quality graphics capabilities, will mean an even greater use for on-line interactive and graphical visualization. "By the mid-1990s . . . workstations might be our next-generation textbooks, where students can read text, then solve a complex problem in real time, taking advantage of three-dimensional, animated graphics" (Lee 1989:44).

As academics continue to do more preparation of their written work using sophisticated word processing software, they will increasingly find less need for secretaries, typesetters and editors. The advantages are better quality and consistent manuscripts, but at the expense of faculty members' time.

More and more university, government and private libraries are being linked by computer networks and there will be an increasing use of dedicated computers acting as "information servers." All these sources will become accessible from any institution. In spite of its inherent costs, that trend will be mean better rationalization of increasingly expensive library resources, a decreasing need for the actual books and journals, and a more efficient method of carrying out literature searches; on-line catalogue searching is far superior to the card catalog searching which it replaces. Unfortunately, it will be some time before academics have the same access to journal literature that they have, even now, to monographic literature. Journal-article abstracting and database indexing services will exist only if many institutions and companies cooperate in providing the services and sharing the costs. It is also true that the actual delivery of information in useful form, once it is located, will be a problem for some time to come, particularly until better technologies exist for handling pictures and until the large bandwidth networks become generally available.

5. Conclusions

To achieve the greatest benefit of computer use in academic research the following should occur:

1. Since scholarly activity is an important part of the mission of modern universities, wherever possible an academic who is encouraged and expected to be involved in some form of research and who wishes to make use of a computer should have access to one, most likely a microcomputer, appropriate to his or her work;
2. Criteria must be developed to assist in deciding what hardware, software and operating systems are to be purchased and supported. The number of different kinds of computers, operating systems and general-use software packages should be limited within the institution to allow for maximum compatibility and for the provision of effective hardware maintenance and assistance in software use. While individual faculty members or academic units may be free to make their own decisions outside the accepted guidelines, they should be made aware of the consequences of these decisions;
3. Each desktop computer should be attached to a departmental or campus network which, in turn, should be connected by reliable and high bandwidth media to regional and national networks;
4. The infrastructure, necessary to provide such services as maintenance of the computing hardware and network, taking responsibility for licence fees, major software purchases and upgrades, provision of support personnel and general training, should be established and maintained. Who provides these services will depend on their nature and on the size of the university. It may make sense to centralize hardware support as much as possible to minimize costs and maximize efficiency, while decentralizing software support and training. Software is generally more discipline-specific;

5. Regular training in the use of hardware and commonly used software packages should be provided by the department or university. Readily available avenues of advice on appropriate hardware and software, help with problems and frequent courses in the use of computing will overcome some academic inertia;
6. Universities need to develop database acquisition, access and support policies to make sure that the best use is made of library computerization and the growing range of database resources;
7. For most scientific and engineering problems, the largest computers are rarely the most cost-effective. Universities should provide other options such as larger minicomputers and microcomputers or even mainframes for those needing that kind of power for calculations;
8. A supercomputer may be the best resource for the very largest users with big, highly tuned parallel programs that require large memories, file capacity and so forth. However, supercomputers or minisupercomputers should be provided only on a regional or national basis. Access to a supercomputer facility can be accommodated through a network or by travel grants to allow the researcher to be physically present at the facility;
9. It would be advantageous to recognize, that as part of their assigned duties, some faculty could act as "product champions" or "facilitators" by being a resource from whom others, less knowledgeable in computing techniques, could obtain advice and informal training.

References

Abbott, Lawrence. "Supercomputers: Big Bang, Big Bucks." *DATAMATION*, 15 Feb. 1991, 73-77.

Bell C. Gordon and Glen Miranker. "Shopping for Supercomputers." *DATAMATION*, 15 Oct. 1990, 76-80.

Brousell, David R. "What Hath He Wrought." *DATAMATION*, 15 Mar. 1991, 31.

Bunker, Ted. "Wireless LANs Cut Cabling Hassles." *DATAMATION*, 15 Feb. 1991, 43-44.

Cercone, Nick and Carol Murchison. "Integrating Artificial Intelligence Into Literary Research: An Invitation To Discuss Design Specificiations". In *Conference Pre-Prints, Computers And The Humanities, ToDay's Research Tomorrow's Teaching*, (Centre for Computing in the Humanities, University of Toronto, March 1986), 160-175.

George, J. Alan (Chairman). *Report of the ad hoc Committee on Research Computation.* Ottawa: The Natural Sciences and Engineering Research Council of Canada, Sept. 1990.

Hut, Piet and Gerald Jay Sussman. "Advanced Computing for Science." *Scientific American*, Oct. 1987, 145-153.

Jacobson, Michael J. and Martha H. Weller. "A Profile of Computer Use Among the University of Illinois Humanities Faculty." *J. Educational Technology Systems* 16 (1987-88), 83-99.

Lee, Lawrence A. "Beyond Megaflops: The Cornell National Supercomputer Facility." *EDUCOM Review*, Spring 1989, 38-44.

Lindholm, Elizabeth. "The Portable 4GL?" *DATAMATION*, 1 Apr. 1992, 83-85.

Lynch, Clifford A. "Library Automation and the National Research Network." *EDUCOM Review*, Fall 1989, 21-28.

Maisel, Merry. *Computational Science: The Continuum: Science at the San Diego Supercomputer Center*, San Diego Supercomputer Center, San Diego, 1989. Quoted in J. Alan George (1990:14).

Miller, Richard K. and Terri C. Walker. "Artificial Intelligence Applications in Research and Development." *SEAI Technical Publications* (1988), 1-9.

Miller, Warren F. "Supercomputing: An Indispensible Component of Applied Research." *CNSS Papers* 15 (1988), 1-4.

Moad, Jeff. "Miles to Go." *DATAMATION*, 15 Mar. 1991, 62-65.

Prince, Mary Ellen. "Applications of Artificial Intelligence to Scientific Research." *NASA/ASEE Summer Faculty Fellowship Program*. Marshall Space Flight Center, Contract NGT 01-002-099, 1986.

Roskies, Ralph Z. "Science and Supercomputers." *EDUCOM Bulletin*, Spring 1987, 14-18.

Runyan, Linda. "A Retrospective: 40 Years on the Frontier." *DATAMATION*, 15 Mar. 1991, 34-57.

Van Houweling, Douglas E. "The National Network: A National Interest." *EDUCOM Review*, Summer 1989, 14-18.

CHAPTER 5

ADMINISTRATIVE COMPUTING

1. Historical Perspective

In North America the development of university computing was tightly coupled with the early advancements in the computing field. Some of the early pioneers and their associated institutions include (Goldstine 1972):

- J. Atanasoff — Iowa State University
- H. H. Aiken — Harvard University
- J. P. Eckert Jr. & J. Mauchly — University of Pennsylvania
- J. L. von Neumann — Princeton University
- G. M. Hopper — Harvard University

Many commercial firms' involvement with computing traces back to an association with pioneering university projects. For example, IBM participated in the work of H. H. Aiken which resulted in the MARK I (1944). Eckert and Mauchly, after ENIAC (Electronic Numerical Integrator and Computer) became operational in 1945, formed the Eckert-Mauchly Computer Corporation[1] which built UNIVAC I (Universal Automatic Computer, completed in March 1951). In the late 1970's, Bill Joy left the University of California at Berkeley to help found a new company–SUN Microsystems (Horspool 1992). In the 1980's Project Athena was initiated at the Massachusetts Institute of Technology (MIT) in association with DEC and IBM. As a result, in March 1988, the X Window System[2] Version 11, Release 2 was released (Johnson & Reichard 1990).

Nestman *et al.* (Nestman, Swinburne & Pohlmann 1980:23) report on a 1967 study by J. Caffrey and C. J. Mosmann, *Computers on Campus, A Report to the President on their Use and Management*. In this report Caffrey and Mosmann indicate that there were at most 25 universities with a computer on campus in 1955 in the United States and less than 150 in 1960. The history of computing at the University of Regina, while it does not go back to the days when universities spawned machines, is very rich (*cf.* Appendix A). Today, if we

---

[1] The Eckert-Mauchly Computer Corp. was acquired by the Rand Corporation in 1950 which merged with Sperry Gyroscope Co. in 1995 to form Sperry Rand (Goldstine 1972:326).

[2] X Window System is a registered trademark of the Massachusetts Institute of Technology.

count mainframes, minicomputers and microcomputers, the campus has around 1,200 computers[3].

The first computer was introduced onto the Regina Campus in November 1963 through the combined efforts of a private company, a federal government agency and the university itself. This machine was rapidly followed (replaced) by a second and then a third as computing quickly took hold on the campus. In early 1971, when it became time to replace this machine with yet another larger one, the institution was no longer able to fund the purchase. The result was an extended period of debate involving, initially, the university and its two campuses, then the provincial (state) government, some of its crown corporations and governmental departments. The result of this discussion was the creation in April 1973 of a new crown corporation, SaskComp, which was to provide computing to the province's other crown corporations, government departments as well as the university. Consequently, the university relied for almost a decade on a service bureau for a large portion of its computing needs. In 1984 the contract with SaskComp was terminated and the university re-established itself as its own provider of computing (*cf.* Appendix A).

Since its establishment on campus, computing has been organized in almost every conceivable format. They include:

- a combined centre;
- a combined centre managed jointly with the Department of Computer Science;
- a department of computing services with responsibility for a centrally managed staff and communication but no hardware;
- two separate centres–academic and administrative with a decentralized staff;
- a combined centre with a distributed staff.

A book, published in 1983 by Digital Press, entitled *Campus Computing Strategies* (McCredie 1983), describes computing at ten American universities. The book, resulting from a study conducted in 1981-82 by the staff at EDUCOM, endeavored to examine strategic planning in the area of information processing. Additional material related specifically to the administration of university computing is published by The Association for the Management of Information Technology in Higher Education. Their quarterly publication, *CAUSE/EFFECT*, regularly contains a section, Campus Computing Environment, which features a selected campus–*e.g.* Florida State University (Rudy 1992), Marquette University (Rudy 1991).

---

[3] Correspondence from Paul Still, October 1992.

2. A Profile of Administrative Computing

2.1 Survey of Canadian Universities

In the fall of 1989 five questionnaires were prepared in an effort to ascertain baseline information concerning administrative computing in Canadian universities. The five questionnaires which were sent out in January 1990 were:

- "Administrative Computing"–sent to Administrative Vice-Presidents at 65 colleges and universities (*cf.* Appendix D);
- "Directors–Computer Centres"–sent to the Director of the Computer Centre at a subset of 57 of the same institutions (*cf.* Appendix E);
- "Registrars"–sent to Registrars at 76 universities (*cf.* Appendix F);
- "Deans/Student Counselors"–sent to Faculty offices at 99 universities (*cf.* Appendix G);
- "University Admissions"–sent to Admissions Offices at 78 universities (*cf.* Appendix H).

2.1.1 Administrative Computing

The Administrative Computing questionnaire attempted to ascertain the development of five major administrative systems: the Payroll System, the Accounting System, the Human Resource System, the Energy Control System and the Inventory System. Replies were received from 28 institutions–43%. Information was sought regarding when each system was implemented; if it was built in-house or purchased; if it was part of an integrated system; what portions of the institution have access to the system; the time required for minor and major modifications to be completed; outstanding issues and problems with each system; and what the future plans are for each system.

2.1.1.1 Payroll System

While almost all of the institutions responding have now computerized their payroll system, by 1972 only 21% of the institutions had. Half of the systems were built in-house, and half of the systems were part of an integrated system. Access was generally restricted to the payroll office. Forty-six percent (46%) reported that they performed maintenance on the system themselves, with the remainder divided evenly between the use of contract maintenance and an arrangement whereby some of the maintenance was performed themselves and some through a contract. As most major and minor modifications did not take long to complete, this was most likely the reason why most institutions reported no change in the number of support staff.

The major concern reported by respondents (39%) was that their system was old and out-of-date. Fourteen percent (14%) expressed a desire to have their payroll system integrated with the personnel/human resource system. The third concern expressed by respondents (11%) was that the system was run by a service bureau. Eleven institutions reported that they wanted an on-line payroll system which was integrated with the personnel system and accessible by different departments. About 25% of the institutions planned to use a service bureau for payroll.

2.1.1.2 Accounting System

Forty-six percent (46%) of the respondents reported that, by 1972, they had computerized the accounting system. As with the payroll system half of the institutions reported having built their accounting system. However, 71% (or 21% more than with payroll) reported that the accounting system was part of an integrated system. Access to the accounting system was considerably different from the payroll system, with half of the institutions reporting that faculty and departmental offices had direct access. The majority of institutions (57%) maintained the system themselves, with only 18% relying solely on contract maintenance and 25% on a combination of contract and in-house maintenance. It was reported that a minor modification took less than a month to be effected at 61% of the institutions, and from one to three months in another 21% of the cases. The range of time required to effect a major modification ranged from fewer than 4 months to 18 months.

Accounting systems did not meet the functional requirements of the institution in 32% of the cases. Thirty-two percent (32%) of the respondents reported plans to develop a new on-line system, and 18% indicated that they planned to upgrade their current system.

2.1.1.3 Human Resource System

When compared to payroll and accounting, the computerization of the personnel (human resource) office has been relatively slow with only 18% of the institutions reporting the installation of a human resource system by 1972 and 25% reporting that they do not yet have a computerized system. While half of the institutions reported that the human resource system was integrated with another system, only 39% reported they had built their own system. Twenty-five (25%) of the institutions reported that departmental offices had direct access to the human resource system. About 43% of the respondents indicated that minor modifications were completed in less than a month. The time span for major modifications varied from fewer than 4 to 24 months. Possibly due to the relatively late introduction of this system, institutions reported that they were increasing their support staff.

In 21% of the cases, respondents indicated that the system did not meet their functional requirements, and 32% wanted to have the human resource system integrated with their payroll system.

2.1.1.4 Energy Control System

Computerization of the energy control function commenced only after 1974. At the time of the survey 32% of the institutions had not given this function a priority sufficient to have it computerized. Of those that had such systems, almost half had been built in-house.

2.1.1.5 Inventory Control System

The first reported computerization of an inventory control system was in 1972, and 57% of the respondents indicated in 1990 that they did not have such a system installed. The vast majority of these systems were built and maintained in-house. It is rather strange that the results indicate that faculty and departmental offices are not normally given direct access to the system, but it was frequently reported that they had their own computerized inventory control system.

2.1.1.6 Summary

As we anticipated, almost all institutions reported that they had implemented an accounting and a payroll system. The degree of dissatisfaction expressed with currently installed systems was surprising. In the case of the payroll system 39% reported that their system was out of date. For the accounting system 32% reported that it did not meet the functional requirements of their institution. With the human resource system 21% reported that it did not meet the functional requirements of their institution. One cause for this dissatisfaction might be the time between major upgrades or replacement of existing systems and another could be the growing sophistication of the users as time passes.

2.1.2 Directors–Computer Centres

The questionnaire sent to the Directors of Computer Centres attempted to obtain information concerning computing budgets, the development of computing, the present computing environment, and planning and organizational structure. As with all questionnaires, an attitude survey was attached.

The results obtained must be viewed with some skepticism, for only 11 of the 57 institutions responded to the questionnaire (2 large, 3 medium and 6 small). Actually 12 institutions returned the questionnaire but 1 was essentially blank. Instead of a summary of results, some of the highlights are presented below:

a) Approximately three quarters of the institutions indicated that their computer centre provided service for microcomputer maintenance on campus;
b) Lack of budget was reported as being the biggest problem with respect to the implementation of current plans;
c) No institution responded in the affirmative to the question: "Do you separate the computer centre into an academic centre and an administrative centre?";

d) Almost three quarters of the institutions reported that they used the services of contract programming personnel.

2.1.3 Student Related Administrative Applications

The particular academic structures and traditions of Canadian universities provide considerable flexibility in terms of student program and course offerings. In many programs, especially in arts and science faculties, students have the option of choosing from a wide variety of options and electives in order to meet some of their degree requirements. While these programs offer students an opportunity to develop programs with both depth and breadth, they create certain administrative problems. As a part of the baseline survey, information was gathered on how computing and computers are utilized in the student-related academic and administrative operations.

2.1.3.1 Admissions

A total of 78 instruments were sent to Registrars and 36, representing 46%, were returned. According to this data, computers have become an important part of the admission process in Canada. At 74% of those universities responding, the student's previous educational records are entered into the computer system. Such information typically includes high-school grades, transfer credits, previously attended schools, as well as basic demographic data and addresses.

2.1.3.2 Counseling

Given the flexibility of many programs in terms of courses and requirements, data was collected on the role of computers in assisting the student counseling process. While only 35% of those responding indicated that first-year students were required to see a counselor, 58% of sophomores through seniors saw counselors. About 60% of these counselors had a wide range of information on the student available via their computers. Such information included high school grades, university classes and grades, basic demographics, visa information, addresses and phone numbers.

2.1.3.3 Registration

At the time of the survey, 23 of 29 institutions reporting had computerized their registration systems. When asked how computer-based technology had changed student registration, respondents provided a variety of mostly positive assessments with the most common being it has made the process faster, improved the availability and accuracy of the data, made checking student files easier, and as well provided better service. Perhaps the most significant development was the adoption of telephone registration systems.

Of the 44 respondents, only 11 indicated that their university currently utilized an automated telephone or "touch tone" registration system. None of the small universities have a telephone registration system. Three respondents indicated that the telephone registration system had been implemented in 1987, 6 indicated implementation in 1988 and 2 indicated implementation in 1989.

The reasons cited for adopting a telephone registration system were varied and included: more accurate data, efficient for administrators, reduced labour required, faster service for all, convenient for students, more class time available, fairer to all students, avoidance of arena-style registration, easier planning, efficient fee collection and flexibility. The large universities provided for 30 of the 38 responses which might indicate that they have had their systems in place longer and have had more time to assess the adoption of the telephone registration systems. The medium-sized universities with telephone registration systems indicated that convenience, efficiency and accuracy were the three main reasons for adopting the telephone registration systems. Two of the institutions that indicated that they had telephone registration systems in place did not cite any advantages/benefits of the system.

All eleven institutions with telephone registration did cite specific problems that they had hoped to overcome with the adoption of a telephone registration system. Six respondents indicated that they hoped to overcome student line-ups during registration. Four respondents cited that the old system of registration was too slow and five indicated that their old registration systems were too time-consuming. A further three respondents indicated that much time was spent on registration. Three respondents also indicated that their old registration system did not provide for early availability of enrollment data. Other problems cited as reasons for adopting the telephone registration system were that the old system of registration was too confusing, lacked control over class changes, provided inaccurate data, resulted in students registering without prerequisites, involved obsolete equipment, and led to students manipulating the registration process.

For both large- and medium-sized universities, speed, accuracy and availability of information appear to be the major problems that they hoped to overcome with the implementation of a telephone registration system. Student-related problems (*i.e.* system manipulation and registration without prerequisites) were experienced at the large universities.

Efficiency and availability of information were cited as the major advantages of the telephone registration system. Time-saving was also considered to be an advantage of the system with respondents indicating that time is saved by all parties involved–students, administrators and faculty.

As in the questions relating to the problems/benefits and advantages/disadvantages of a telephone registration system, the large universities seem to have a better knowledge of the system. However, the majority of responses came from the large universities.

The impersonal nature of a telephone registration system as well as physical and technical limitations are seen as the primary disadvantages of the system. Some respondents indicated that their systems were incapable of accommodating special needs, while others indicated that the need to have access to a touch-tone telephone is a disadvantage since not all students have such access.

When starting up the telephone registration systems, respondents indicated that they encountered several problems, including: unfamiliarity with the system, a lack of phone lines, telephone and line failures. Resistance to change by particular academic units was cited as a problem, as well as long distance phone costs. Other problems cited included student manipulation of the system, changing work patterns, earlier preparation of schedules and user training. Only one respondent indicated that there were no major problems.

Five of the eleven institutions with telephone registration systems indicated that students have the option of not using the system. At the remaining six institutions, there is no option.

Of the 33 universities not currently using a telephone registration system, 13 indicated that they are planning to implement the system within the next three years. Two institutions indicated that they were not certain as to plans for implementing telephone registration. Of the 13 who plan to implement telephone registration, six were planning to do so in 1990 and three in 1991.

Among the reasons cited for moving to this type of registration system were convenience for students; a reduction in line-ups during the registration process; other universities using the system; lack of personnel to continue old system; current system too complicated; technology now available; less work for faculty; reduced staff, administration and student frustration; enrollment growth; efficiency and speed.

Of the eight institutions that gave reasons for not implementing the telephone registration system, four cited the cost and four cited that their present system was adequate for their needs. Two institutions indicated that their enrollment was too small to merit a telephone registration system. It is interesting to note that the University of Toronto does not have a telephone registration system and cites cost as the reason. Cost was a factor cited by one of the large universities and two of the medium-sized ones. As well, two large and two medium-sized universities indicated that their present systems were adequate.

2.1.3.4 Student Record Maintenance

An additional function that has been widely computerized is student records. Of the 44 institutions participating in the survey, 35 indicated that the master or main files of a student's academic record are kept on the university mainframe computer. Twenty-two of the 44 respondents indicated that the records are kept in the registrar's office which would indicate that several institutions utilize both the computer and hard-copy records. Ten institutions indicated that records are kept in the faculty offices.

In the vast majority of cases (33 or 75.0%), student records are not shared with other computer systems outside the central computer system. Nine respondents indicated that these records are shared.

As well, 33 respondents indicated that paper copies (non-computer based) of a student's records are kept.

2.1.3.5 Summary

Computer use varies widely from institution to institution. The most common application areas for computers are: the automated creation of computer accounts for students in class (20 or 57.1%) and the preparation of electronic class lists (26 or 74.3%). Plans for computerization in the areas of electronic submission of grades are indicated by six (or 17.1%) of the institutions.

The level of computerization and the types of hardware and software used by the various institutions is indicative of the changing face of computerization. At 31 of the 35 institutions participating in this survey, computers are used in the admissions process with 26 of the 31 using a mainframe (74.3%) for hardware and 28 of the 31 using developed software (80.0%).

Student registration is computerized at 30 of the 35 institutions with 24 of the 30 using a mainframe (68.6%) and 27 of the 30 using developed software (77.1%).

Telephone registration is in place at only 10 of the institutions with nine using a mainframe and seven using developed software.

Exam scheduling is computerized at 20 of the 35 institutions (57.1%) with all 20 using mainframe hardware and 15 using developed software.

Time-tabling is computerized at 14 of the 35 institutions (40.0%) with 13 using a mainframe and 11 using developed software.

Classroom allocation is computerized at 14 of the 35 institutions (40.0%) with 12 using a mainframe and seven using developed software.

Student records are computerized at 30 of the 35 institutions (85.7%) with 26 using a mainframe and 24 using developed software.

2.2 Literature Survey

Two publications provide a good overview of university computing. In 1986, CAUSE (College and University Systems Exchange), a Professional Association for Computing and Information Technology in Higher Education, published its second profile on Administrative Information Systems (AIS) (Thomas & van Hoesen 1986), covering the period 1980 through 1985. The first had covered the period through 1980. The 1985 profile was based upon responses to a questionnaire returned by over 450 member institutions of higher education in Canada and the United States.

The survey determined that in 1985 approximately 65% of the responding institutions had a combined academic/administrative computing organizational structure, with the remaining 35% having separate centres for academic and administrative computing. This represented a 4% decrease in the number of combined centres between 1980 and 1985. However, large institutions reported more combined centres in 1985, and medium to large institutions reported no change.

In general, in the five-year period from 1980 to 1985, administrative information system staff size decreased. However, during the same period the number of individuals involved in systems development increased by approximately 7%, while the number of operational staff members decreased by about 6%. In addition there was a trend to having more of the development staff working with end-users.

Below is the average distribution of AIS staff by job function. The only really large discrepancy between the average across all institutions and those of particular institutions occurred in the management and development categories at small institutions, where the small institutions reported that they had 19% of the AIS staff employed as managers and only 32% in the development area. This discrepancy can be largely explained by the fact that managers, at small institutions, are also involved in development and the total number of individuals involved with AIS at these institutions is small:

- 12% Management
- 45% Development (Analyst/Programmer)
- 6% Systems Programming
- 28% Operations
- 9% Clerical

The majority of institutions (70%) reported that they spent more than 1% but less than 4% of their operational budget on computing; 26% reported spending less than 1%; and only 4% spent 4% or more. The report issued a caution regarding these figures as it is difficult to apportion costs between academic and administrative computing and a complication has resulted from the trend towards purchasing hardware instead of leasing it. This change requires the institution to estimate the number of years it will be keeping the hardware–the time over which the equipment is to be amortized.

In general, between 1980 and 1985, budgets for AIS increased but not as rapidly as the overall institutional budget. In 1980 only 5% reported their AIS budget as being less than 1% of the institution's budget, whereas in 1985 26% of the institutions reported that their AIS budget was now less than 1% of the institution's budget. The distribution of the average budget also changed over the five-year period. Below is the percentage breakdown of the computing budget in 1980, and in 1985, subdivided into 5 categories:

	1980	1985
Staff	53%	57%
Hardware	28%	23%
Software	3%	6%

Communications	2%	3%
Other	14%	10%

The survey indicated that the market share of hardware vendors was: IBM 37%, DEC 27%, Hewlett-Packard 7%, Prime 7%, with the remainder each having less than 7%. During the five-year period both DEC and Prime significantly increased their campus administrative computing installed base, Hewlett-Packard reported some increase in their market share, and IBM's share remained constant.

Attempting to determine the types and numbers of administrative systems installed, the survey listed 157 individual administrative applications (functions) divided amongst 11 major categories. Below is a list of the 11 categories in decreasing order of the number of applications systems implemented per category:

1. Admissions and Records Applications
2. Financial Management
3. Planning Management & Institutional Research
4. Faculty/Staff/Student Services
5. General Administrative Services
6. Logistics and Related Services
7. Auxiliary Services
8. Library Applications
9. Physical Plant Operation
10. Computing Installations Management
11. Hospital Applications

Appendix J contains a list of all of the 157 applications and the number of institutions, from the 452 surveyed, which have implemented each.

The number of applications implemented per institution increased between 1980 and 1985 and there was a significant shift from batch to on-line processing (Noyes 1987). The 1985 survey identified a total of approximately 28,000 administrative applications implemented at the 452 institutions responding. The results indicate that the average campus had implemented 62 applications out of the total of 157 unique applications reported. This represented a 17% increase in the number of applications per campus over the five years, and a significant shift away from batch systems–70% to 35%. Below is a breakdown of the applications by mode of implementation on the average campus in 1980 and 1985:

Mode	1980	1985
Batch	36	22
On-line	10	25
Combined	6	9
Total	51	62

The results of another survey are reported by Charles H. Warlick (Hawkins 1989, chapter 15). The information reported is based upon data collected for the *1989 Directory of Computing Facilities in Higher Education* (Warlick 1989). In 1989, 1,420 American post-secondary institutions participated in the survey which primarily focused on academic computing–research and instruction–as opposed to administrative computing which was the above survey's focus.

The survey report has placed the 1,420 institutions into groupings based upon the characteristics of the institution. The groupings are developed from a classification done by the Carnegie Foundation for the Advancement of Teaching in 1987 (Carnegie 1987), which attempted to measure the institution's primary focus and its quality–for example, is its primary focus on research, or is it on providing a four-year liberal arts education? Table 1 is derived from a table in Hawkins (1989:320) and presents the 1,420 institutions by classification group along with information on whether the institution is publicly or privately funded, and information on the structure of computing on campus (separate centre, a combined center, or no central facility for computing). It should be noted that totals do not always add up to 1,420 in this table as well as in the other survey-based material which follows:

Table 1

Category	Total Sample	Public	Private	Separate Centres	Combined Centre	No Central Facility
Research Univ.	89	24	65	39	49	1
Doctorate Univ.	84	29	55	22	61	1
Comprehensive Univ.	370	166	204	121	233	8
Liberal Arts Univ.	194	278	16	130	128	21
Two-Year College	484	69	415	149	249	49
Prof. School	99	76	23	30	36	14
Totals	1,420	642	778	491	756	94

The survey reports that the average and median percentage of the institutions' budgets spent on computing facilities are 2.9% and 2.7% respectively, based upon a sample size of 494. In computing these values "the budget of the combined centre or the sum of the budgets of the two separate facilities for each institution is used..." (Hawkins 1989:321). The highest average and median percentage expenditure arose at institutions classified as Doctorate I (3.6% and 3.5%–sample size 27), with the lowest occurring at institutions classified as Liberal Arts II (2.0% and 1.7%–sample size 43). In general, publicly funded institutions spent more of their budget on computing than private institutions did–3.3% and 3.0% vs. 2.3% and 2.1% from sample sizes of 307 and 180.

The overall average and median expenditure per student is $178.00 and $138.00 (sample size 703). The highest average ($356.00–sample size 40) occurs at institutions classified as Research I and the highest median ($327.00–sample size 49) occurs at Liberal Arts I institutions. It should be noted that all these institutions are privately funded. The low average and median expenditure per student ($99.00 and $79.00–sample size 202) occur at Two-Year Colleges.

The survey breaks down the average budget expenditure into six categories where the previous study divided it among five. From the 1,037 institutions responding to the survey (out of 1,420), the percentage breakdown of the average budget into the six categories is:

	1988/89
Staff	44%
Hardware	27%
Software	11%
Communications	3%
Supplies	10%
Other	5%

The survey further noted that between 1983/84 and 1988/89 operations and programming staff each showed a decline of 4%, whereas user service staff increased by 6%.

The rapid growth of computing in universities is shown in the following table from a paper by Russell (Russell 1980). The table presents an estimate of the expenditure on computing at universities in the United States in three fiscal years, in percent and millions of dollars. In addition, the annual expenditure is subdivided by type into the three main areas–instructional computing, research computing and administrative computing.

	1966-67		1969-70		1976-77	
	%	$	%	$	%	$
Instructional	30	66	30	142	27	268
Research	40	88	32	151	22	218
Administrative	30	66	34	161	45	446
Other	-	-	4	19	6	59
Total	100	220	100	473	100	991

3. Major Issues

3.1 Organizational Structure

The niche into which computing fits in the overall organizational structure of a university has undergone many changes over the years. Some of these have been brought about by technological change while others have been brought about by the priority given to administrative computing by the institution. The changes are not limited to the North American experience. Edgar Frackmann in his paper presented to the 1989 CAUSE National Conference "describes the state of the administrative and management computing in German universities, the planning process for re-integration and the expected future developments regarding the opportunities and limitations of re-integration" (Frackmann 1990). He further categorizes the time since 1970 into three eras:

a) 1970-1983 – the Big System Era;
b) 1984-1989 – the Decentralization Era;
c) 1989- – the Reintegration Era.

Jane Ryland (Hawkins 1989, chapter 1) similarly categorizes the eras as:

a) through the late 1960's–the ADP Era;
b) late 1960's-late 1970's–The Integration Era;
c) late 1970's-1980's–The Individual Computing Era.

In the ADP (Automated Data Processing) Era, the manager of data processing reported to the Vice-President Administrative or the chief financial or accounting officer, who in turn set the priorities for systems development. Individual systems were typically self-contained and little thought was given to the need for system interaction–integration. For example, if the processing of a student application by the student information system required a name and address file, and the accounting office billing system application also had the need of a student name and address file, each application would create and maintain their own separate versions of this file.

The major expense during this period was the computer itself. One consequence of this was that data-processing staff, in an effort to reduce run-time costs, usually exceeded the budget for developing a system and did not meet the implementation deadline–for in their attempt to minimize run-time costs they employed complex coding techniques that they had not yet mastered. In addition, because of the cost of hardware, Grosch's Law[4] (James 1986; Freeman & York 1991) had a significant effect on acquisition decisions in this era as well as the next.

During the Integration Era (Big System Era), personnel from the user departments started to become more involved in the design of their systems. As demonstrated by the debate between the two campuses of the University of Saskatchewan and the creation of SaskComp (*cf.* Appendix A), acquisitions and

---

[4] Herbert Grosch postulated that computing power increased as the square of the cost–for twice the price you obtained four times the computing power.

organizational decisions were driven by Grosch's Law. Punched cards gave way tc terminals, and the title of database manager appeared as the concept of data sharing started to take hold (Steingraber & Kunkel 1982). Integration was initiated when institutions started, for example, to keep one name and address file and to share it between several applications.

The Individual Computing Era saw the movement of the minicomputer from the research and teaching laboratory, where it had appeared much earlier, into administrative computing. This movement was soon joined by the microcomputer, which broke Grosch's Law. The introduction of the microcomputer, with its associated increased involvement of the user in the system design and implementation phase, resulted in the introduction of the term "End-User computing" (Blackmun, Hunter & Parker 1987; Tumolo & Saltzberg 1987). Other terms such as "Decentralized Computing" (Moldovan & Gleason 1987; Ernst 1987; Gardner & Schwob 1990), "Information Resource Management" (Sherron 1987; Gloster 1987), "Client/Server" (Freeman & York 1991), and "Outsourcing" (Van Brassel 1992; Careless 1992) started to appear. These terms reflected a fundamental change in focus. There no longer was a single point of applications development and delivery–there were now many. Consequently, institutions must put in place a management structure which will insure that from the various alternative technologies available (mainframes, micros, networks, file servers) only those that satisfy their information needs at minimum cost will be employed (Thompson & Wright 1986). This objective must be tempered as follows:

> An alternative is satisfactory if: (1) there exists a set of criteria that describes minimally satisfactory alternatives, and (2) the alternative in question meets or exceeds all these criteria. Most human decision-making, whether individual or organizational, is concerned with discovery and selection of satisfactory alternatives; only in exceptional cases is it concerned with the discovery and selection of optimal alternatives. To optimize requires processes several orders of magnitude more complex than those required to satisfice. An example is the difference between searching a haystack to find the sharpest needle in it and searching the haystack to find a needle sharp enough to sew with (March & Simon. 1958;140-141).

The development of a strategic plan (Hawkins 1989, chapter 6) and the establishment of priorities are essential to the evolution of campus computing, for without such a plan individuals or possibly groups of individuals will develop their own plan. Without the aid of such a planning process some will satisfy their own information processing needs with the aid of technology, some will employ inappropriate technology, while others will turn away from technology, possibly out of fear, likely out of ignorance. The net result undoubtedly will be sub-optimal from the institution's perspective.

The form of strategic planning and the organizational structure under which computing operates are inextricably linked. The organizational structure (King 1983; Bateman & Barnes 1980; Heterick 1981; Blunt & Hazboun 1983;

McGhee 1983; Plourde 1986) of university computing can be categorized into two formats, each of which has several alternatives:

a) Separate units. In this form there are separate units responsible for academic computing and administrative computing. Variances on this revolve around whom the units report to in the organization. One variance would see academic computing reporting ultimately to the Vice-President Academic and administrative computing reporting ultimately to the Vice-President Administration. Another would see them both reporting to one Vice-President, usually the Vice-President Academic.
b) Combined unit. In this form there is only one organization charged with the responsibility for computing, and the Director of this unit reports ultimately to one of the Vice-Presidents, usually the Vice-President Academic.

Robert Blackmun (Blackmun 1991) reports that the trend through the mid-1980's was from separate units to a combined organizational structure for university computing. It should be noted that the merging of the two units involves the combining of two staff groups each with its own value set and well-established culture. But, individual units do not achieve any economies of scale from the perspective of either hardware, software or staff (support, operations, professional or management).

The cultural value set difference between academic and administrative computing is an extension of the differences in values between a computer science department and a computer centre (*cf.* Appendix A). Where the members of the academic centre view themselves as aligned with the faculty and thereby involved in the dissemination of information through experimentation, the latter want to control access on a need-to-know basis.

Another issue associated with integration/centralization is responsiveness. Care must be taken to ensure that as the organization grows it does not become too inward looking, forgetting that its reason for existence is to service its outside customers.

Blackmun goes on to say that the trend since the mid-1980's has been to a modified version of the combined unit organizational structure in which the profile of computing is raised by having it managed by a member of the university's senior management. That individual, with vice-presidential rank, has been referred to in the literature as the chief information officer (CIO) or computing czar (Plice 1988; Ernst 1987; Sherron 1987; Blackmun 1991; Fleit 1986; Penrod, Dolence & Douglas 1990). Where previously there had been a tendency for the medium to large institution to use the separate organizational structure and the small to medium to use the combined, Blackmun reports that since 1985 all sizes of institutions have moved to the CIO model. Some of the reasons for this change include:

a) the degree of penetration of computing into the academic enterprise. The library was affected early through the use of computing to replace the card catalog. Today it uses CD-ROM and computer networks to provide its users with access to databases and other forms of information. Tomorrow it likely will be using these networks to gain access to electronic journals. The preparation of classroom materials and tests has used computing for some time. Venturesome instructors are bringing their machines into the classroom. With the new high-speed networks being developed, they will further come to rely on computing for the presentation of materials. Further, the development of computer networks has blurred the line of responsibility for communications on campus. Previously, the responsibility for communications, the telephone system, was in the hands of physical plant;

b) senior management must be aware of the issues involved, and must provide support and commitment (Emery 1985);

c) there is a need for senior-level attention to the balance between and the integration of end-user and centrally run systems;

d) long term strategic planning;

e) the management of information technology requires the attention of an individual who understands the needs of all of the constituent groups on campus.

The responsibility for developing a strategic plan (Arns & Curran 1983; Robinson 1981; Lukesh 1986) for campus computing can be left to the individual in charge of computing. That individual can subsequently call on user groups' advice, and can employ needs studies in an effort to determine accurately the requirements of the various constituent users. However, this process requires a defined structure or it is likely to fall into disuse during good times only to be revived during periods of trouble. Tumolo and Saltzberg (Tumolo & Saltzberg 1987) and Vaught (Hawkins 1989, chapter 7) put forward the concept of a steering committee. This parallels a structure which has been implemented at the University of Regina since it re-combined academic and administrative computing into a single entity–the Department of Computing Services, in 1983.

The official organization chart for computing at the University of Regina is given in Figure 1.

A policy committee (steering committee) (Richards, Whitelaw & Pryor 1990) was created in an attempt to ensure that policy questions always take into account the question of their global impact on the institution–all units as well as the functions of each: teaching, research, and administration. Figure 2 places the policy committee in the organizational structure of the institution. The actual organization structure with the introduction of the policy committee differs considerably from the official organizational chart. It is flatter, tending towards the CIO model without actually having officially adopted it.

Figure 1. Official Organization Structure

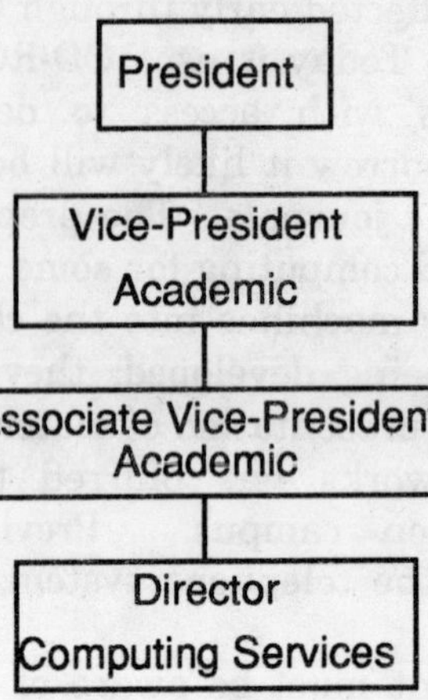

Figure 2. Actual Organization Structure

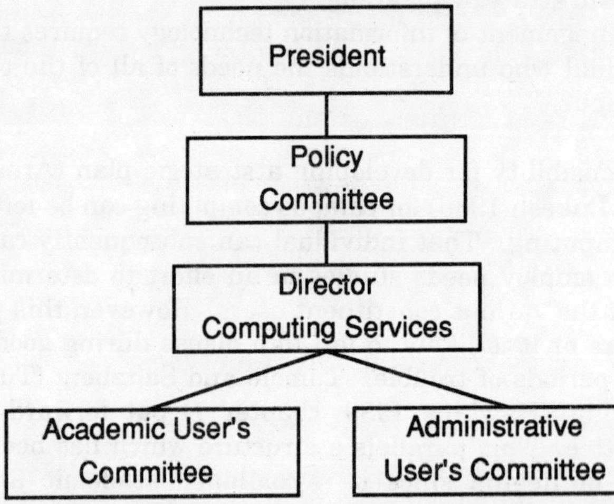

Using an analogy from business, in the structure outlined in Figure 2, the president can be assumed to be the single shareholder of the computing enterprise on campus. The president, in turn, has appointed a board of directors to provide direction to the chief executive officer–the Director, Computing Services/Chief Information Officer. With this structure, approval of the budget, of policy questions and planning proposals is given, as it would be in a commercial firm, after debate by the board. The membership of the Policy Committee is made up of senior individuals drawn from both the academic and administrative sides of the institution. In the case of the University of Regina the membership is:

- Associate Vice-President Academic–Chair
- Vice-President Administrative Services
- Associate Vice-President Research
- Associate Vice-President Facilities
- Dean of Science
- Head, Computer Science Department
- Director, University Services
- Chair of the Academic Users Committee
- Director, Computing Services

Two user committees exist to aid the Director, Computing Services, when putting together the budget, formulating a new policy question or updating the strategic plan. The Academic Users Committee is composed of individuals who are nominated to represent the various faculties on campus and are elected by the Academic Council. There is one member of the committee who does not represent a faculty, but rather a department–the Head of the Department of Computer Science. This person is ex officio to obtain the individual's expertise as well as to insure that the Department is fully aware of and has input into the planning regarding computing on campus. The Administrative Users Committee is not an elected body. It is composed of the heads of administrative units on campus (or their designates) that are involved with computing.

Both of these committees advise the Director with respect to their needs concerning software, the level of service being provided and new requirements, and provide reactions to the Director's proposals.

A policy issue which must be addressed at some point is the question of whether or not to implement a charging policy (Hawkins 1989, chapter 13; Biedenweg & Gardner 1990; Roberson 1987) for the use of computing resources. Below is a list of some of the points which must be addressed when this issue is debated:

1. The academic will put forward the argument that computing should be free just as service from the library is;
2. The administrator will put forward the argument that a scarce resource must be controlled and a charging policy will provide such a control mechanism;
3. Researchers receive funds to purchase required computing as part of grants and contracts. A charging policy is required to capture these funds;
4. How do you provide research computing to faculty members who do not have any external support for their research activities?
5. Do you charge students for computing? If so, do you provide funds for each individual student or for a whole class? If you assign money to

individual students, what do you do when one student runs out of funds before the class is over while others have funds remaining in their computing accounts for the same class? What is to be done with the computing funds allocated to a student who drops out of the class?

6. Do you charge your chemistry student for using the centrifuge or the history student for borrowing a book from the library?
7. Do rates vary with the time of day?
8. If you charge for computing, budgets must be established in the user departments in order to pay for computing. Is the user free to spend his computer budget in any fashion he chooses or does the central computing facility have a monopoly?
9. How frequently are rates for computing adjusted?
10. What happens if computing rates give rise to a deficit or a surplus?
11. What units do you charge for–central processor time, memory utilization, disk usage, tape mounts, lines printed, terminal connect time, consulting time, installation of a terminal line?

When discussing the issue of charging policies with Dr. S. Conte[5] in the spring of 1970, he summed up our conversation with the statement–"Whatever you do, keep it simple".

3.2 Staff

As with the implementation of a computing system in business or government, the implementation of an administrative application in a university is significantly affected by the quality of the staff performing the implementation and by how much thought has been given to the effect that the system will have on existing staff and procedures. A paper by C. F. Gibson and R. L. Nolan (Gibson & Nolan 1974), expanded by Nolan (Nolan 1979), analyzes the problems associated with electronic data processing (EDP) management by looking at how data processing departments grow and how they fit into an organization's structure at various stages in that growth. From their observations, they postulated that there were four distinct stages in the development of an EDP department:

- Initialization
- Expansion
- Formalization
- Maturity

Further, they contend that an organization must pass through each of the four stages. That is to say, it is necessary to solve the problems associated with each

[5] Dr. Conte held the positions of Professor of Computer Science, Head of Computer Science and Director, Computer Center, during his career at Purdue University.

stage if one is going to pass into the next stage "without a crisis and if the growth of the resource is going to be managed to yield maximum benefit" (Gibson & Nolan 1974) to the organization.

At stage 1, Initialization, there is no strategic plan for computing and it is likely that computing has developed in a single department (unit) by the members of that unit. These individuals will view the results of their efforts with a considerable degree of ownership. Therefore, when the time comes to develop a more structured approach to computerization, conflict may erupt as ownership may need to be moved; this conflict may lead to managerial turnover at worst, and to lingering hostility at best.

A significant staff problem is the perception of individuals as to how computerization might affect them. Unfortunately, most organizations, particularly during stage 1, only give lip-service to this problem. The best policy is to provide all employees with the most up-to-date and accurate information possible. Undoubtedly, fear and rumors are bound to develop with respect to the loss of jobs and the changes that are going to take place in the work place. "Management can make no bigger mistake than to falsely reassure all concerned that the computer will not change their work or that it will mean no less work for everyone. Such comfort blankets lead to credibility gaps that are notoriously hard to close" (Gibson & Nolan 1974).

Resistance of the community (whether faculty or staff) to new administrative systems, often seen as a transfer of work load from a central agency, can usually be traced to one or more of the following reasons. There was a lack of involvement in the decision making process at a sufficiently early date. The objectives and benefits of the system were not sufficiently well explained. There was not enough attention paid to training before and after installation

During stage 2, Expansion, there will develop a need to select middle management personnel for computing. Where possible, middle management personnel should be obtained from within. This provides a career path for those capable of balancing organizational needs with professional and technical interests. It also fosters the integration of computing with the other service units on campus.

With the development of on-line interactive systems, one has to ask who the user of a system really is. When only batch processing systems were available, it was clear that the student information system was the Registrar's Office system, for the only direct contact with this system was through the Registrar's Office or the Computer Centre. Now with on-line and distributed systems, the personnel in the Registrar's Office are no longer the only direct users of the system; indeed, they may not even compose the majority of users.

Frequently, institutions have not fully recognized the operational significance of a change in systems and have left the responsibility for the selection of a new system to the current user department or unit. When this is done, it is not uncommon to find, after the new system is installed, that while it solved the old problems of the previous "owner", it has created a number of new and possibly more severe problems in other areas of the campus, because insufficient consideration was given to the new users. When an organization is planning such a change in systems, it is essential that steps be taken to ensure that all affected user groups are consulted during the planning stage, to ensure that the needs of all personnel who will be affected by the new system have been taken into account. For example, do the new users have enough time in the daily work schedule to assume the new duties that are being thrust upon them by the system change, do they have the required equipment and are they sufficiently trained?

In addition to the fear associated with the possible loss of one's job through computerization, there is the fear of loss of prestige (power). Typically the individual doing the design or implementation of a computer system is younger than the manager (and staff) of the unit which is being computerized. The introduction of computing is therefore likely to induce stress in the manager en several accounts. First, the manager is confronted with a younger employee who possesses a skill set which is new and foreign. Secondly, this younger individual is likely to take the lead in the computerization of the manager's unit. Finally, when computerization is complete the manager may, perhaps correctly, perceive that her role in the organization has been diminished by the introduction of the new system.

The role of the campus' computer centre is that of a service unit. While the service that this unit provides may indeed be essential, it is not the primary good that the institution is delivering–the primary good is education. The members of the computer centre must always remember that their role is to provide service to the other units on campus.

There are a number of methods that can be used to distribute and manage the personnel and resources required to provide computing (Klingenstein & Devine 1985). On one extreme there is the decentralized model, where there is no central facility charged with the responsibility for computing–equipment or personnel. In this case all computing is done by personnel hired by the user departments, some of whom can be termed end-users because their main responsibility is not computing (section 3.4). The other extreme is the centralized model where all the resources needed to provide the organization with computing are assigned to a single central unit.

There is a third option which has been given the label "dispersed" computing. In this option there is a central organization which controls all computing resources, including staff. However, in the dispersed model these resources are distributed, as required, throughout the campus. This gives the central organization the ability to develop and easily implement unified policies in respect to computing, and at the same time makes the user departments stakeholders as equipment and more importantly the computing professionals associated with their systems reside and work in their departments. Further, this structure provides for backup for employees and a formal mechanism for technical staff to feel they have a peer group and a career path, even when they are the only member assigned to a particular user department, for they are still a member of the central organization. Clark (Clark 1992) notes that "dispersion was much more common than decentralization, although decentralization was observed."

3.3 Hardware

As noted in section 3.1, university computing has passed through what was labeled as the Big System Era (Frackmann 1990) where the choice of hardware, and indirectly systems design, was governed by Grosch's Law. Today we find ourselves in a situation where there is a great deal of choice, including supercomputers, mainframes, minicomputers, microcomputers, complex instruction set computers (CISC) and reduced instruction set computers (RISC) (Patterson 1985). At the same time, as Emery put it, the cost of hardware is tending to zero (Emery 1985). This statement is indeed true when one considers the computing power that can be purchased today as opposed to just a few years ago. The microcomputer of today, be it an Intel based 80486 or a Motorola 68040, can be purchased for under $4,000.00 with 8MB of main memory and 150MB of disk storage. This compares to a $17,000.00 monthly lease in 1972 for an IBM 360/40 with 128KB of main memory and 60MB of disk storage. Further, the microcomputer is capable of giving the user just under 10 MIPS of computing power, while the 360/40 was rated in the fractional MIPS range. However, given the number of individual units which are purchased, the institution must pay a great deal of attention to the question of hardware acquisition, because today a campus will likely have more total computing power available on individual desks than there is available in the central computing facility, due to the penetration/proliferation of microcomputers and workstations.

The situation at the University of Regina, in this rich environment, is typical. The institution has installed CISC mainframes from two vendors (IBM 4381 and 2 DEC 6320's), RISC based superminicomputers (2 MIPS R120's 1 MIPS RC3330 and 2 IBM RS/6000's), a significant number of minicomputers (older PDP-11's and LSI-11's), workstations (Digital, SUN, Silicon Graphics), approximately 1,200 microcomputers (IBM, IBM compatible and Macintosh) and a large number of terminals. The Campus has a switched campus-wide terminal network connecting 1,226 terminals and microcomputers to computers across campus and a 50 Kilobit connection to CA*net which links its users to computing at other institutions in Canada and ultimately to other computer networks worldwide. The campus network will be replaced over the summer of 1992, in cooperation with Digital Equipment Corporation, by a new 100 Megabit backbone network and 10 Megabit Ethernet connection to each office laboratory and classroom on campus (*cf.* Appendix A).

Without these networks faculty members, administrators and students could not access the library "card" catalog from their office. Networks also permit faculty to exchange papers and correspond with colleagues around the world by electronic mail (E-mail) (Updegrove, Muffo & Dunn 1990). Faculty communicate with students from their class, and can access immediately the student information system, to check a student's record or class availability when counseling.

In addition to their use for communicating with a particular individual or system, these networks can be used as a means of seeking answers to questions by posting queries to discussion groups on the network. The term "product champion" has been used in describing individuals willing to work with new technologies and introduce new approaches to their colleagues. The world-wide Internet (LaQuey 1990) is an excellent tool for communicating with product champions. There are hundreds of special interest groups and discussion groups active on the Internet every day. For example, the EDTECH (educational technology) discussion list has over eight thousand members. Electronic mail queries such as "Is product XYZ available?" or "has anyone tried using XYZ?" will be answered in hours. Raising an interesting question, issue or problem in a discussion group mailing can result in a lively electronic panel interchange for days to weeks.

A similar resource or tool for surveying the user community is the use of a conferencing software system rather than simple electronic mail. E-mail is excellent for distributing a message to the user community rapidly. However, if you want to allow the user community to debate significant issues, you require a conferencing system (*e.g.* CoSys–Guelph University), allowing users to join the thread of an ongoing debate and contribute their views

One can make some statements and assumptions concerning technology. First, there is a great range of choice in hardware. Second, the price per unit of computing will continue to decrease. Third, there are proprietary and open operating systems. There are a number of proprietary operating systems, each tied to a line of equipment from a particular vendor. There is not a lot of choice from which to select an open system. UNIX, is, however, available in various forms for a fairly wide variety of computers–platforms. Fourth, some software tools and application packages are available for various machines and different operating systems. Fifth, there are a number of network technologies–Ethernet, Token Ring. Sixth, as our survey of Computer Centre Directors indicated (*cf.* Appendix E), there will not be enough money available to permit an institution to implement all of the technology required to meet all of the demand for systems (Heterick 1991).

Freeman and York (Freeman & York 1991) describe a new architecture, the client/server architecture (Ricciuti 1991), which is the new paradigm for providing computing to users: "The client/server model is an architecture for the kind of multi-vendor, networked information system environment that promises to become broadly accepted in the 1990's" (Freeman & York 1991:15). This model will permit institutions to make choices from the wide array of alternatives available and to implement systems on a combination of platforms in such a fashion expenditures are minimized while functionality is maximized.

Using current technology, systems are likely to have been built or acquired to run on top of proprietary operating systems, on hardware from one or more vendors. One extreme situation would occur when an institution had acquired all of its systems from a single vendor and was running them on a single computer system. Another scenario would have the institution acquiring its systems from several vendors but running them on a single computer system. In this situation, the user will be required to build interfaces to integrate the application systems that need to be integrated. Finally, there is the other extreme where systems are acquired from separate vendors and each system runs on a different computer system. The task of integration in this case is more difficult because there are two levels of interfacing required–one between the application packages and one between the proprietary operating systems. Hence, there is an inverse relationship between choice and integration which is likely to affect functionality and cost of systems, for the degree of integration is likely to be reduced as the degree of choice is increased.

The client/server model of system implementation (and integration) divides each application into two components–the request or client task and the performer or server task. The object of this model is to permit each function to be performed at the most cost-effective point in the system (computer network). With the increase in cheap cycles available on the user's desk through a microcomputer, this means moving away from central mainframes towards the user's workstation.

Applying the terminology of this model to an existing single vendor on-line applications system being accessed through a dumb terminal, the client is the terminal and the server is the single machine on which the application runs. However, a client/server implementation provides the option to the systems designer to divide an application into a number of subtasks and to have each of these performed at the most effective point in the computing system. This means that work is likely to be performed on various machines between the user's workstation (micro) and the system(s) on which the applications' data are stored. For this to be effective there is a requirement that the serving of the client's request by the various components in the client/server system network be transparent to the user. Hence, if this is to be achieved by using a number of machines (servers) which make up a network, openness (a standard) is a necessity or the system implementor will be required to build a new interface each time a machine is added to the network. Only as open system standards are developed and implemented will applications designers be able to achieve interoperability across heterogeneous platforms.

Figures 3 and 4 are adaptations of a figure presented in a paper by Freeman and York (Freeman & York 1991:18). Figure 3 describes a traditional on-line system.

Figure 4 shows various versions of the client/server model as more and more work is shifted to the client. While the diagram in Figure 4 divides the request into three tasks, each of these tasks may be further subdivided for execution into different subtasks.

Figure 3. Traditional On-line System

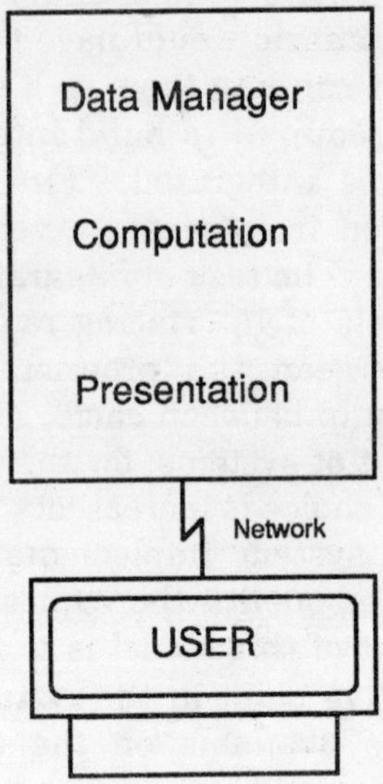

A word of caution is required. As has been the case in the past, hardware has advanced more quickly than the tools and methodologies required to employ it. The hardware available today will easily support the client/server model but all of the software tools are not yet available. Further, the openness required to develop all of the necessary tools requires the development of standards and subsequent compliance with these standards. Standards sometimes have the effect of impeding innovation. Finally, there is a problem associated with maintenance–support and staff training are complicated and costs are likely to be increased by the introduction of multi-vendors. These concerns have to be addressed when institutions consider moving to the client/server model for systems development.

An excellent reference to the acquisition of computer-related goods and services is the book *Computer-Related Acquisition*–(Naginey, King, Kroculick, Lias & Mayne 1984), published by the Association for the Management of Information Technology in Higher Education. It discusses topics such as *A Three-Step Approach to Computer-Related Acquisition* (Chapter 1), *Acquisition as a Subset of the Development Process* (Chapter 2), *One Vendor's View of the Acquisition Process* (Chapter 3), *Avoiding Oversights in the Computer Acquisition Process* (Chapter 4) and includes an appendix entitled a *System Guidelines Manual on Electronic Data Processing.*

Figure 4. Client/Server System

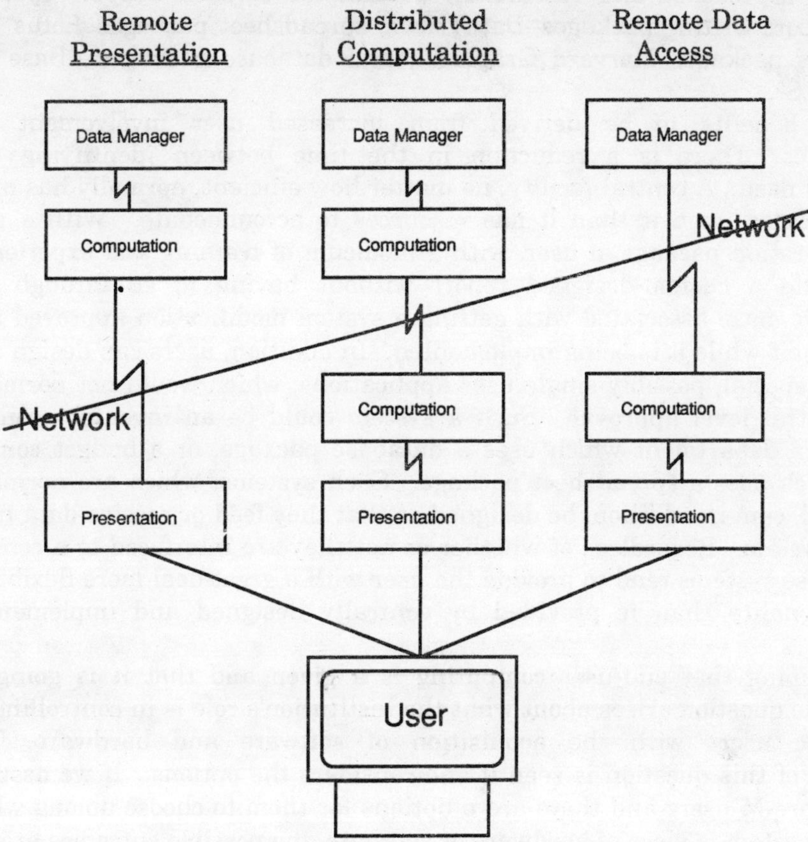

3.4 End-User Computing

In the short period since the first computer appeared on a university campus, the distance between the end-user and the computer has been reduced considerably. Punch boards have long since been replaced by "user friendly" software packages; cards by terminals or work stations; and single-user batch systems by multi-user systems or local-area networks. All of these technological advances have contributed to getting the user more and more directly involved in computing–users no longer need to be dependent on the computing professional and the central department of computing services (computing centre).

While the majority of users still employ a system developed by someone else to access information or enter data, there is a growing number of systems (packages) which allow users to participate directly in the programming and systems design/implementation process. These are in addition to the numerous systems that faculty members have become accustomed to using in support of their roles as teacher and researcher. Examples of such support systems include: report writing packages–DataTrieve, spreadsheet packages–Lotus 1-2-3[6], graphics packages–Harvard Graphics[7], and database packages–dBase IV[8] and INGRES[9].

The benefits to be derived from increased user involvement are considerable. There is a reduction in the time between identifying and satisfying a need. A central facility, no matter how efficient, normally has more demands placed upon it than it has resources to accommodate. With a new report generation package, a user, with a modicum of training and experience, can generate a custom-designed report without having to go through the bureaucratic maze associated with getting a system modification approved and having to wait while it is being implemented. In addition, users can design and implement special, possibly single user applications, which would not normally receive central level approval. Such a system could be an inventory control system for a department which uses a database package, or a budget control system which uses a spreadsheet package. Such systems, which are normally micro based, can, in addition, be designed so that they feed or receive data from a central system. Regardless of whether or not they are interfaced to a central system, these systems tend to provide the user with a great deal more flexibility and functionality than is provided by centrally designed and implemented systems.

Assuming that end-user computing is a given and that it is going to increase, the question arises about what the institution's role is in controlling or guiding the users with the acquisition of software and hardware. The importance of this question is seen if one considers the options. If we assume that there are M users and there are n options for them to choose among when selecting a system–a piece of hardware or software–the possible outcomes are:

a) M different systems
b) n different systems, where $1 < n < M$
c) 1 system

If there are fewer options than users, option a) disappears but option b) still exists and n can, indeed, be very large. Assuming option b), with n being large, how does the institution insure that service is available to its users? On the other hand, if we assume option c) is operable, it is highly likely that the

---

6 1-2-3 is a registered trademark of Lotus Development Corporation.

7 Harvard Graphics is a registered trademark of Software Publishing Company.

8 dBase IV is a registered trademark of Borland International.

9 INGRES is a registered trademark of ASK Computer Systems Incorporated.

institution has imposed its guidance. The question then is whether or how the users can be assured that they are obtaining the best value for the money.

In the case that each user is free to select whatever hardware or software he wishes, unless the user is completely independent and self-sufficient, it is likely that he will at some time experience a problem which will require the assistance of another part of the institution–likely the central computing department. When this "problem" occurs, it is highly probable that there will be no one available within the institution with the expertise (training) necessary to economically provide a solution. In the extreme, there may not be anyone available in the local or immediately surrounding community either.

In the case that there is no choice, it is likely that the system which has been chosen will not fit some needs. Further, there is a tendency not to change the preferred system as technology changes because experience has been gained with it and the user group has already been trained in its use.

In the distributed model, the role of the computer center in providing the user group with both leadership and service can be seen through the example of the acquisition of a word processing package. If the computer center does not provide the required leadership each area on campus could conceivably buy a unique package and we are into the worst case situation noted above. However, if the center were to provide leadership by putting a package on the approved list or getting a site license (which would reduce the cost to each individual user), users would likely follow the lead of the center and acquire the approved/recommended piece of software (hardware).

This leadership role by itself is not sufficient to prevent each subgroup from pursuing its own agenda with respect to hardware and software acquisitions. If the center does not provide the necessary service all will likely be lost, for the users will quickly detect that their needs are not being satisfied and will go to the supplier who will commit to meeting these needs. Some of the services that need to be provided include: training, consulting and maintenance.

The policy implemented at the University of Regina was based upon a policy developed in the mid 1980's by the University of Saskatchewan's Associate Vice-President Information Services, Dr. R. Kavanagh. It attempts to find a balance between the two extremes–free choice and no choice. Each year the Department of Computing Services reviews its list of approved products, deleting some and adding other new products. Items on the list include: microcomputers, workstations, peripherals such as printers, and software packages for microcomputer use–word processing, spreadsheet applications and terminal emulation. Users who purchase products from the approved list are assured technical support from the Department of Computing Services in the form of hardware maintenance, software consulting and training programs. Users who do not purchase products from the list are not given this guarantee and may find themselves unable to get any support.

When selecting or deleting items from the list some of the parameters which must be considered are:

a) the technological level and the cost of the product. Old products must be deleted from the list as new and superior ones become available. Sometimes an item which is a functional duplicate of an existing product is added to the list without removing the existing approved product. This is done in an attempt to encourage users to migrate to the new product;
b) the level of institutional usage. If a product has gained a significant degree of acceptance as defined by users on campus choosing it themselves, it should likely be added to the list. If a product is still widely used and is on the list, its deletion from the list will not eliminate the need to support the product for a few additional years.

While the choice of a software package can have significant ramifications, the biggest concern is with respect to the choice of hardware–microcomputers. This is due to the need for maintenance (Fiekbe, Brusk & Sanders 1990) and the incompatibilities that have, from time to time, appeared with vendor defined "compatible" systems. The user's and the institution's concern with maintenance stems from the following:

- the cheapest system may not be the easiest (cheapest) to maintain;
- unknown systems are difficult to maintain;
- mail-order systems may require mail-order maintenance.

The incompatibility of systems frequently is not recognized until an addition is made to the system. The University of Saskatchewan reported a situation which developed when one of their departments attempted to link onto the campus network some non-approved microcomputers which they had purchased. The machines, it turned out, after extensive investigation, were incompatible with the interface board which was on the approved list. The saving that the department initially achieved by purchasing non-approved systems turned out to be completely nullified by the cost of the investigation and modifications required to get the machines attached to the network.

The University of Regina, in addition to placing products from different manufacturers on the approved list, has signed a dealership agreement with some of these manufacturers. When an approved machine of a type not covered by a dealership arrangement is purchased, the user deals with a retailer initially and the Department of Computing Services for maintenance after the warranty period. In the other two cases, the user deals only with the Department of Computing Services–acquisition and maintenance.

In the fall of 1991, the Department of Computing Services started to assemble its own machines in response to market pressures. Even with the dealership arrangements, the price of approved machines was considerably higher than that offered by small retailers and a number of large mail-order suppliers. In an effort to provide users with an approved price and performance alternative, Computing Services started to fabricate its own line of machines–

the Cougar. Maintenance and compatibility are assured as Computing Services has been involved completely in the machine, from the selection of components to assembly.

3.5 Software

It is extremely difficult to decide which is the most profitable applications package to implement next (Evancoe 1984; Neiheisel 1981). However, one must remember that the relative cost of software versus hardware is increasing. Boehm (Boehm 1979; Boehm 1981) claimed that in 1955 hardware costs were 7 times that of software, but he estimated that thirty years later their positions would be reversed with software costs exceeding hardware by 9 to 1. In section 2.2 and Appendix J a listing is given of eleven categories of administrative systems along with the various applications identified as having been implemented in a 1985 survey (Thomas & van Hoesen 1986). The classification and the listing of the individual applications give an indication of how the 452 responding institutions have assigned their priorities with respect to administrative information systems development.

Table 2 below lists the 11 categories, the number of unique applications in each category, the total number of individual applications implemented in each category at all institutions, the average number of applications implemented at an institution and the percentage of all applications implemented by category. In total 157 unique applications were identified and the 452 reporting institutions had implemented a total of 28,233 applications. Thus an average institution had implemented 62 of the 157 applications.

As Table 2 indicates, applications in the category of Admissions and Records Applications Analysis (Student Information Systems) are by far the most widely implemented with 30% of all implemented applications coming from this area. Further, 6 of the applications from this category have been implemented at over 90% of the 452 institutions responding to the survey. They are:

• Student Registration	442	98%
• Enrollment Reporting	433	96%
• Course Drop & Add	442	96%
• Enrollment Statistics	442	96%
• Term Grade Reporting	430	95%
• Undergraduate Admissions	427	94%

The only other category with an application implemented at over 90% of the institutions is Financial Management Application Analysis where the General Fund Ledger Application has been implemented at 412 of the 452 institutions–91%. (Appendix J gives a complete listing of all of the applications and their categories ordered by the number of institutions which have implemented each of the applications.)

Table 2

Application	Number Unique Applications	Total Number Implemented	Average Number Implemented	%
Admissions & Records	28	8600	19.3	30%
Financial	22	5783	12.8	20%
Planning & Inst. Res.	19	3159	7.0	11%
Fac./Staff/Stud. Ser.	13	2619	5.8	9%
Gen. Admin. Ser.	13	2276	5.0	8%
Logistics & Rel. Scr.	12	1575	3.5	6%
Auxiliary Ser.	8	1260	2.8	4%
Library Applications	7	749	1.7	3%
Comp. Install. Man.	6	653	1.4	2%
Hospital App.	16	394	0.9	1%
Total	157	28233	62.5	100%

When the decision has been made to implement an application, the question arises whether to build the application in-house or to acquire it from a vendor–build versus buy. The experience of the University of Regina may provide a little insight (*cf.* Appendix A). When computing was first introduced onto the campus almost all of the packages were developed in-house. During the rationalization period of the early 1970's the two campuses of the University of Saskatchewan jointly acquired a financial package from the University of Toronto. Next, the Regina Campus started to process its Library applications off campus, using a library system at the University of Toronto. The campus had to spend a great deal of effort converting the remaining applications when the Sigma 9 was installed, replacing the IBM 360/40. Finally, when the SaskComp agreement was terminated and the Sigma 9, which had been re-acquired from SaskComp, was removed from service the University purchased new administrative systems from a vendor. It is currently pursuing the implementation of some new and replacement applications by the use of a fourth generation package–INGRES. It is too early to fully assess the effectiveness of the activity. The trend, however, is clear. There has been a significant shift towards the purchase of administrative applications systems from vendors instead of building them in-house.

At the beginning of this section we noted the inversion which has occurred between hardware and software costs over the years. This must be factored into the decision of whether software should be purchased from a vendor or created in-house by your own employees–the build versus buy question. Canadian experience indicates that over the years there has been a trend towards purchasing more and more software from vendors as the cost of labor has increased. While there are reasons to build some software in-house, the reasons for doing this must be extremely well justified in terms of cost. The argument that we are unique and therefore must build the application in-house is not sufficient. The experience with the cooperation in the acquisition of a financial package between the University of Regina and the University of Saskatchewan, UNIFACTS, was positive and would suggest that where possible such cooperative ventures should be investigated and pursued when mutually beneficial.

What has been said above with respect to the build versus buy policy of software acquisition should be viewed in terms of local context with respect to labor costs. Whichever avenue is adopted, it should be cost justified and reviewed with each new proposal to insure that the justification is still sound.

The requirement for systems maintenance is never ending. It is simply interrupted by the installation of a new system. According to Dr. Grace M. Hopper[10] maintenance for a time after the installation of a new system does remove problems (bugs) from the system. However, as time passes maintenance eventually starts to introduce new bugs in its attempt to fix old problems–the system eventually becomes unstable.

The problem of maintenance is further complicated by the fact that most professional computing staff members find maintenance to be an unrewarding task. Hence it is normally assigned to newly hired staff members, thereby leaving the creative tasks to the more senior members.

Other maintenance problems arise when the institution acquires an applications package. It is common for the vendor to offer, for a fee, maintenance and the distribution of updates–new versions (releases) of the applications package. It is also common for the vendor to organize periodic meetings of their clients, where maintenance issues and new features which are being considered for possible incorporation in a new release are discussed.

The question of maintenance of application packages acquired from vendors is further complicated by the fact that employees generally consider their institution and their method of operation to be unique. This uniqueness manifests itself in a desire expressed by the members of the user department to make local modifications to the acquired package. This desire is reinforced by the members of the computing staff because as noted above they prefer to create rather than to maintain.

The question that must be answered is, therefore, whether to purchase maintenance and upgrades from the vendor and install them when they become available or to permit local modifications to be made to an acquired package. If the first option is adopted, one is following a course similar to the one pursued when acquiring a proprietary operating system for a piece of hardware. Maintenance costs are predictable from the outset and, as the package is updated, one will be able to install the new release. If the second option is followed, and local modifications are permitted, it is unlikely that maintenance

---

[10] Talk given at the University of Regina on November 5, 1974.

costs can be predicted. As more and more of the local modifications are made, the ability to incorporate these modifications into a new release when it is distributed by the vendor decreases as time passes. Eventually, as the number of these modifications grows, the user's version of the system moves farther and farther away from the specifications of the original system. Therefore, ultimately two distinct systems are created–the vendor's and the institution's.

The process described above of modifying an acquired piece of software locally may be a valid path to pursue. The acquired system is then being used as a basis for development. If this is the case, it must be a planned activity, and not one which the institution starts to pursue by happenstance.

3.6 Externally Purchased Computing Services

As indicated in section 2.1.2, one of the most difficult problems to solve with respect to computing is related to finance. This is complicated by the fact that the demand for computing is not constant. While the demand for administrative computing is more predictable than that for research and instructional computing, it is nevertheless variable.

The demands for research and instructional computing are even more volatile because they are determined almost completely by individual choice. For example, an individual researcher may have very heavy demands for a time, then go back into the laboratory to obtain new data or analyze the output obtained from the current set of computer runs. Similarly, individual instructors may vary the assignments they give, vary the due dates or even change the class requirements for computing.

In the case of administrative systems one knows the periods when high or low demands are placed on the computing resources. The payroll system, for example, is not as large a consumer of computing just after payday, as it is just prior.

In an attempt to cope with this variability in demand, universities tend to acquire computing capacity which will satisfy the peak load. It may be more fiscally responsible to acquire internal capacity for something considerably less than the peak load and purchase the difference elsewhere, when it is required.

While the scenario presented above was very true in the Big System Era, it is not as significant a problem today. It is, however, applicable in some situations in today's decentralized, multi-vendor environment. One example of this is the acquisition of capacity for large research applications (Chapter 4 Section 3.1).

As indicated in the history of computing at the University of Regina (*cf.* Appendix A), by far the biggest advantage that the University achieved through its association with SaskComp was the ability to acquire capacity for its research users at very nominal cost–capacity of a magnitude that the campus could never have afforded otherwise.

Today there is another new word appearing in the computing lexicon–outsourcing. York University, located in Toronto, announced in March 1992

(Van Brassel 1992) that it had signed a $6.3-million contract with a Toronto firm to outsource its mainframe computing over the next five years. During this period the announced plan calls for the replacement of mainframe computer applications with ones which run on a network using PCs, workstations and servers.

Another area to be considered for outsourcing is personnel. As our survey reported (section 2.1.2), almost three quarters of the institutions responding indicated that they used the services of contract programmers. At the University of Regina, this proved to be extremely beneficial when it installed its new systems in the early 1980's in the Registrar's Office, Business Office, Payroll Office, and Personnel Office. While all of these systems were purchased, their installation required more resources than were available, and the additional personnel required were not needed after the installations were completed.

3.7 Faculty/Staff–Training

Even though the range of familiarity with respect to computing is still great, the number of individuals with little or no familiarity is rapidly declining. Table 2 in K. M. King's concluding chapter (Hawkins 1989), "Looking Back and Looking Forward", indicates that the percentage of faculty using computing has gone from 5% in 1960 to 60% in 1990. It further indicates the percentage of students using computing has increased even faster–from 5% in 1960 to 95% in 1990.

One might be tempted to conclude that, as the percentage of computer users increases, so does the general level of competency, and consequently the need for faculty and staff training is correspondingly reduced. There is indeed a direct relationship between users and computer literacy. The linkage is, however, very closely tied to the user's specific application or applications; and thus there is still a need for training when a new application is introduced.

As was determined by our survey and others (Zinck 1989), word processing is the major user application of computing. Competency with one word processing package does not necessarily transfer into competency with another. An example of this can be seen in the University of Regina experience. In the early 1980's word processing was introduced into each of the six departments in the Faculty of Science: Biology, Chemistry, Computer Science, Geology, Mathematics and Statistics, and Physics. Prior to its introduction a faculty-wide committee was assigned the task of investigating the available technology and making a recommendation for the system to be acquired. The recommendation was that each department be supplied with a Televideo microcomputer, the word processing system Palantir, and a letter quality printer. One of the objectives of this committee was to provide each department with a uniform system so that work and personnel could be interchanged freely.

Today all of the word processing systems except the system employed by Computer Science are MS-DOS[11] based systems. The Computer Science Department chose Macintosh[12] while the rest of the departments chose IBM[13] compatible equipment. Consequently, within the 6 departments in the faculty, there are 3 different word processing systems in use–WordPerfect[14] for MS-DOS, WORD for MS-DOS and WORD for the Macintosh. As a result, personnel cannot be shared nor does work flow freely between the departments–work could be transferred more frequently than it is with the aid of the conversion packages that are built into the new word processing packages.

The most troubling aspect of what has occurred is the non-interchangeability of personnel, particularly when personnel are off the job due to illness or holidays, for while individuals are competent with their particular word processing system, this skill is not readily transportable to another system. If an individual is transferred to a new location or a new employee's experience is with a different system, then training is required. The latter situation can not be avoided but the former can be minimized if the number of different word processing systems is limited.

Another example of non-transferability of skills is demonstrated by the student information system at the University of Regina. All secretarial staff in the Faculty of Science are computer users–word processing. In the early 1980's, when the current version of the student information system was installed, all members of the secretarial staff were trained in its use. However, as time passed some individuals used the system more than others, thereby increasing their proficiency, while others left the university and were replaced by new individuals who did not receive any formal training in the use of the system. As a result, while all members of the group are computer users, only some are competent in the use of the student information system.

Ideally one would like to have all individuals competent in the use of all systems. This is impossible for a number of reasons:

a) Upgrading of systems. New versions of software packages replace old versions. This is true for mainframe systems but it is increasingly true for microcomputer based systems–WORD 5.5 for MS-DOS has a new competitor from Microsoft itself, WORD 2.0 for WINDOWS[15];

---

11 MS-DOS and WORD are registered trademarks of Microsoft Corporation.

12 Macintosh is a registered trademark of Apple Computer Inc.

13 IBM is a registered trademark of International Business Machines Corporation.

14 WordPerfect is a registered trademark of WordPerfect Corporation.

15 WINDOWS is a registered trademark of Microsoft Corporation.

b) Replacement of systems. This replacement includes both hardware and software. As noted in Appendix A, the type of hardware installed in the main facility was replaced frequently–IBM, Xerox, DEC.; the time interval between major technical changes in hardware seems to be shortening. This is particularly true of the microcomputer. Take, for example, the life span of Intel's xxx86 line of microprocessor chips. The life span of a software package is also finite. Heller (Heller 1990) makes the following observation with respect to the life of a system as viewed from the perspective of a system's life cycle–"As an application ages, the real dollar cost to maintain and operate it usually increases each year. If the real dollar cost of maintaining an older system is not increasing annually, then one should examine whether or not all maintenance requests are being met on a timely basis.";
c) Staff turnover;
d) Addition of new users.

Consequently, training must be a major concern and this concern should not be limited to the introduction of a new system–training is continually required (Byrne & Kardonsky 1983). The question thus is: who is responsible for providing the required training? The options are:

a) The central computing services department;
b) The individual units themselves;
c) The product champion–the first, most experienced, user;
d) A combination of the above.

In each of the first two options, either institutional staff or outside consultants can be used to conduct the training. The third option involves an individual who, because of his own interest/expertise with a particular package, becomes the resident expert to whom others go to obtain answers to questions and guidance concerning its use. The degree of use of this option increases dramatically when one of the other two options is not available or not offered frequently enough or in the format necessary to satisfy demand.

Clearly, option one is preferable when the system involved is in general use throughout the institution. This involves centrally run systems, such as the student information system, and the accounting system as well as distributed systems, such as word processing, when a single system is employed widely in the institution.

Option two should be used for centrally run systems, such as the energy control system, which are operated only by a limited number of employees in a single department–physical plant. This option is also the preferred option when there is no uniformity with respect to the type or version of distributed systems such as word processing.

If the product champion happens to be a faculty member it is highly unlikely that the reward structure will adequately recognize his contribution.

Typically the reward system for an academic is based upon his research, teaching, public service and, in special circumstances, administration. The work of the product champion does not directly fit into one of the four criteria listed above, but his efforts may have enabled one or more of his colleagues to excel, and should thus be rewarded.

4. Conclusions

The conclusions listed below are drawn from the material presented above and the experience of the University of Regina which is outlined in Appendix A.

1. Organizationally, campus-wide computing (instructional, research and administrative) should be the responsibility of a single unit managed by a member of the university's senior management, the CIO (Chief Information Officer), an individual with vice-presidential rank. This unit is responsible for:
   - central facilities
   - support for campus-wide facilities such as networks
   - maintenance services
   - consulting services.
2. There should be a strategic plan for campus computing which is reviewed and updated yearly.
3. There should be a policy advisory committee composed of senior academics and administrators to advise the CIO regarding policy and budget matters, and revisions to the strategic plan.
4. Administrative systems should be integrated and run on hardware that does not use proprietary systems software. This will permit the development of an integrated network of on-line administrative applications which run on multi-vendor equipment following the client/server model.
5. Systems should perform as much of their tasks as close as possible to the user in order to capture the advantage of the cheap cycles available on the user's desk through a microcomputer.
6. When an administrative unit proposes a new or major modification to a system, an advisory committee should be struck consisting of users from the administrative unit and representatives from affected academic units and other administrative units. This committee should participate in the framing of system specifications. These specifications should be reviewed to ensure that they satisfy institutional needs and not just the needs of the administrative unit that is proposing the system.
7. Administrative software should be purchased.
8. Modifications to purchased software must be minimized so that updates from the vendor can be incorporated easily.

9. The services of external service bureaus should be used to handle unusual or peak demands–personnel and cycles.
10. End-user computing should be encouraged and the user should be aided by consultants from the central organization. To guide users in the selection of hardware and software, the campus-wide computing organization should prepare a list of supported hardware and software products and this list should be reviewed and updated annually. The creation of such a list will ensure that there is compatibility with existing systems and that consultants have the background necessary to provide the user with advice. Users should be cautioned that if they choose an item that is not on the approved list they are assuming total responsibility for the product.
11. Personnel from the central computing facility should be integrated into the user departments and when possible they should be given line responsibility in these departments to permit the expansion of career paths and to further cross training–and vice versa.
12. The need for training is continual. It should not be limited to the immediate post installation period.
13. The three most important application areas are:
    - Admissions & Records
    - Financial
    - Planning & Institutional Research
14. Universities should be encouraged to make alliances with organizations which will promote the development of computing.
15. The installation of a computer network and its linkage to regional, national and international networks should be given high priority.
16. A budgeting and charging policy should be implemented for administrative computing.

References

Arns, Robert C. and Fred A. Curran. "Information System Requirements for Strategic Planning and Strategy Implementation". In *The Information Resource: A Management Challenge, Proceedings of the 1982 CAUSE National Conference*. Boulder, Colorado: CAUSE, 1983, 17-28.

Bateman, Barry L. and Ben B. Barnes. "Trends in Computing Services at American Universities." *CAUSE/EFFECT* 3. 6 (1980), 20-25.

Biedenweg, Frederick M. and Catherine A. Gardner. "Administrative Computing at Stanford: What Didn't Work and What Might." In *Managing Information Technology: Facing the Issues, Proceedings of the 1989 CAUSE National Conference*. Boulder, Colorado: CAUSE, 1990, 137-145.

Blackmun, Robert R., Jeff N. Hunter, and Anne S. Parker. "User Support for Evolving Technologies in Higher Education." In *Proceedings of the 1987 CAUSE National Conference*. Boulder, Colorado: CAUSE Publications, 1987, 207-217.

Blackmun, Robert R. "Organizational Structure for Managing Information Technology." J. A. Rudy (ed.). In *The Best of CAUSE/EFFECT, 1978-1991*. 1991, 19-26.

Blunt, Charles R. and Kamal A. Hazboun. "Sharing Administrative Information Resources Through Office Systems Networks". *CAUSE/EFFECT* 6. 2 (1983), 8-13; 16-17.

Boehm, B. "Software Engineering: RTD Trends and Defense Needs". P. Wagner (ed.). In *Research Directions in Software Technology*, Cambridge, Mass.: MIT Press, 1979, 44-86.

Boehm, B. W. *Software Engineering Economics*. New York: Prentice-Hall, 1981.

Byrne, Michael M. and Stanley Kardonsky. "Preparing Administrators for Automated Information Technologies". In *The Information Resource: A Management Challenge, Proceedings of the 1982 CAUSE National Conference*. Boulder, Colorado: CAUSE, 1983, 29-43.

Careless, James. "York Transforms Computer System". *University Affairs*, May 1992, 9.

Carnegie Foundation for the Advancement of Teaching. *A Classification of Institutions of Higher Education*. Princeton, New Jersey, 1987.

Clark, Thomas D. Jr. "Corporate Systems Management: An Overview and Research Perspective." *Communications of the ACM* 35. 2 (1992), 61-75.

Emery, James C. "Managing the Planning Process for Information Technology on Campus." *ACM SIGUCCS Newsletter* 15. 4 (1985), 13-18.

Ernst, David J. "Stanford Jumps to the 90's: Distributed Programming, Promising or Premature?" In *Proceedings of the 1987 CAUSE National Conference*. Boulder, Colorado: CAUSE Publications, 1987, 141-151.

Evancoe, Donna C. "Implementation of a Small-College Administrative Computer System." *CAUSE/EFFECT* 7. 2 (1984), 18-21.

Fiekbe, Martin, Donâld Brusk, and Donald Sanders. "Office of System and Computer Services In-House Micro Computer Repair in the College Computing Environment." In *Managing Information Technology: Facing the Issues, Proceedings of the 1989 CAUSE National Conference*. Boulder, Colorado: CAUSE, 1990, 213-222.

Fleit, Linda. "Choosing a Chief Information Office: The Myth of the Computer Czar". *CAUSE/EFFECT* 9. 3 (1986), 26-30.

Frackmann, Edgar. "Administrative and Management Computing the Next Steps." In *Managing Information Technology: Facing the Issues, Proceedings of the 1989 CAUSE National Conference*. Boulder, Colorado: CAUSE, 1990, 321-334.

Freeman, Grey and Jerry York. "Client/Server Architecture Promises Radical Changes". *CAUSE/EFFECT* 14. 1 (1991), 15-22.

Gardner, Don E. and Carol S. Schwob. "Meeting the Challenges in Computer User Support." In *Managing Information Technology: Facing the Issues, Proceedings of the 1989 CAUSE National Conference*. Boulder, Colorado: CAUSE, 1990, 95-203.

Gibson, C.F. and R.L. Nolan. "Managing the Four Stages of EDP Growth." *Harvard Business Review*, January-February 1974, 76-88.

Gloster, Arthur S. II. "Establishing an Information Resource Management Organization at Cal Poly." In *Proceedings of the 1987 CAUSE National Conference*. Boulder, Colorado: CAUSE Publications, 1987, 227-238.

Goldstine, Herman H. *The Computer from Pascal to van Neumann*. Princeton, New Jersey: Princeton University Press, 1972.

Hawkins, Brian, (ed.). *On Gravitating and Managing Information Resources on Campus*. Academic Computing Publication, Inc., 1989.

Heller, Donald E. "Strategic Applications Enhancement: Revitalizing and Aging System", *CAUSE,* Summer 1990, 41-49.

Heterick, Robert C. "Administrative Support Services." *CAUSE/EFFECT* 4. 6 (1981), 28-32.

Heterick, Robert C. Jr. "Academic Sacred Cows and Exponential Growth." *CAUSE/EFFECT* 14. 1 (1991).

Horspool, R. Nigel. *The Berkeley UNIX Environment*, 2nd ed. Toronto: Prentice-Hall Canada Inc., 1992.

James, E.B. "Small is Beautiful: The Next Ten Years In University Computing." *ACM SIGUCCS Newsletter* 16. 3 (1986), 8-16.

Johnson, E. F. and K. Reichard. *Advanced X Windows Applications Programming: The Basics and Beyond!* Portland, Oregon: Management Information Sources, Inc., 1990.

King, John Leslie. "Centralized versus Decentralized Computing: Organizational Considerations and Management Options." *ACM Computing Surveys* 15. 4 (1983), 319-349.

Klingenstein, Kenneth and Gary D. Devine. "Distributed Computing: Options in the Eighties." *CAUSE/EFFECT* 8. 3 (1985), 4-9.

LaQuey, Tracy L.. (ed.). *The User's Directory of Computer Networks*. Bedford, Massachusetts: Digital Press, 1990.

Lukesh, Susan. "Planning for Computing in Higher Education." *CAUSE/EFFECT* 9. 5 (1986), 9-11.

March, James G. and Herbert A. Simon. *Organizations*. New York: John Wiley & Sons, Inc., 1958.

McCredie, John W. (ed.). *Campus Computing Strategies*. Bedford, Massachusetts: Digital Press, 1983.

McGhee, Charlotte Davis. "The Fourth Generation of University Administrative Data Processing: THE BRANDEIS SOLUTION." In *The Information Resource: A Management Challenge, Proceedings of the 1982 CAUSE National Conference*. Boulder, Colorado: CAUSE, 1983, 201-210.

Moldovan, John C. and William M. Gleason. "Long-Range Strategic Planning in a Decentralized Administrative Information Systems Environment-Phase II: Structure, Content and Implementation of the Plan." In *Proceedings of the 1987 CAUSE National Conference*. Boulder, Colorado: CAUSE Publications, 1987, 77-87.

Naginey, Charles H., Ronald E. King, Joseph A. Kroculick, Edward J. Lias and Glenn W. Mayne (CAUSE RFP Committee). *Computer-Related Acquisition*, Boulder, Colorado: CAUSE Publications 1984.

Neiheisel, Steven R. "A Comprehensive Study of Administrative Computing at Leading Institutions of Higher Education." *CAUSE/EFFECT* 4. 4 (1981), 18-25.

Nestman, Chadwick H., Bruce R. Swinburne, and John T. Pohlmann. "A View of Administrative Computing Centers in Higher Education." *CAUSE/EFFECT* 3. 2 (1980), 22-27.

Nolan, R.L. "Managing the Crisis in Data Processing.". *Harvard Business Review*, March-April (1979), 115-126.

Noyes, Jeffrey W. "Hidden Impacts of On-Line Systems." In *Proceedings of the 1987 CAUSE National Conference*. Boulder, Colorado: CAUSE Publications, 1987, 53-63.

Patterson, David A. "Reduced Instruction Set Computers." *Communications of the ACM* 28. 1 (1985), 8-21.

Penrod, James I., Michael G. Dolence, and Judith V. Douglas. "The Chief Information Office in Higher Education." *CAUSE Professional Paper Series #4*, 1990.

Plice, Samuel J. "Academic and Administrative Computing: Are They Really Merging?" In *Proceedings of the 1988 CAUSE National Conference*. 1988, 133-141.

Plourde, Paul J. "Computing Trends and Strategies." *CAUSE/EFFECT* 9. 3 (1986), 23-25.

Ricciuti, Mike. "A CASE for Client/Server." *DATAMATION* 37, 17 (1991), 28-30.

Richards, Michael, D. Chandler Whitelaw, and Glen Pryor. "Implementing a Campus Computing Plan." In *Managing Information Technology: Facing the Issues, Proceedings of the 1989 CAUSE National Conference*. Boulder, Colorado: CAUSE Publications, 1990, 53-59.

Roberson, Robert E. "Making It Happen Without Appropriation." In *Proceedings of the 1987 CAUSE National Conference*. Boulder, Colorado: CAUSE Publications, 1987, 111-122.

Robinson, Robert J. "Computers and Systems for Higher Education in the 1980's: Options and Opportunities." *CAUSE/EFFECT* 4, 5 (1981), 4-9.

Rudy, Julia. "Campus Computing Environment: Marquette University." *CAUSE/EFFECT* 14. 4 (1991), 30-32.

Rudy, Julia. "Campus Computing Environment: Florida State University." *CAUSE/EFFECT* 15. 1 (1992), 26-29.

Russell, Robert E. "Information Systems in Higher Education: Perspective for the Eighties." P. C. Skarulis and C. R. Thomas (ed.). In *Productivity - A Key to Survival in the 1980's, Proceedings of the 1980 CAUSE National Conference*. Boulder, Colorado: CAUSE, 1980, 39-45.

Sherron, Gene T. "Organizing to Manage Information Resources". In *Proceedings of the 1987 CAUSE National Conference*. Boulder, Colorado: CAUSE Publications, 1987, 185-195.

Steingraber, Jack K. and Douglas F. Kunkel. "An Integrated University Online/Data Base System: A Reality." *CAUSE/EFFECT* 5. 3 (1982), 8-13; 24.

Thomas, Charles R. and Dana S. van Hoesen. *Administrative Information Systems: The 1985 Profile and Five-Year Trends*. Boulder, Colorado: CAUSE Publications, 1986.

Thompson, K.W. and Tana Neff Wright. "The Electronic Campus of the Future." *CAUSE/EFFECT* 9. 2 (1986), 26-30.

Tumolo, Paul and Steven Saltzberg. "How Do You Support a Campus-Wide Office Automation System and End User Services?" In *Proceedings of the 1987 CAUSE National Conference*. Boulder, Colorado: CAUSE Publications, 1987, 275-284.

Updegrove, Daniel A., John A. Muffo, and John A. Dunn, Jr. "Electronic Mail and Networks: New Tools for University Administrators." *CAUSE/EFFECT* 13. 1 (1990), 41-47.

Van Brassel, Carolyn. "York University to Spend $6.3 Million on Outsourcing." *COMPUTING CANADA*, March 2, 1992, p. 2.

Warlick, Charles H. (ed.). *1989 Directory of Computing Facilities in Higher Education*. Austin, Texas: University of Texas at Austin Computation Center and Seminars on Academic Computing, 1989.

Zinck, R. Ann. "Loan-a-Mac. A Successful Computer Literacy Program for Faculty." In *Managing Information Technology: Facing the Issues, Proceedings of the 1989 CAUSE National Conference*. Boulder, Colorado: CAUSE, 1990, 410-408.

[illegible] Proceedings of the [illegible] National Computer Conference [illegible] (1984) [illegible]

[illegible] Proceedings of the 1984 [illegible] Symposium [illegible] Publication [illegible]

Robinson, [illegible] Organizations. [illegible]

Rudy, Julia. [illegible] CAUSE/EFFECT [illegible] (1981) 30-32.

Rudy, Julia. [illegible] Environment. [illegible] CAUSE/EFFECT [illegible]

Russell, Robert [illegible] in Higher Education. [illegible] In Proceedings of the [illegible] Conference [illegible]

Sherron, Gene T. [illegible] CAUSE/EFFECT [illegible] Publication [illegible]

Simpson, Jack [illegible] CAUSE/EFFECT [illegible]

Thomas, Charles R. and Lena [illegible] Profile [illegible] Publication [illegible]

Thompson, R.W. [illegible] CAUSE/EFFECT [illegible]

Thrasher, [illegible] Office Automation [illegible] Proceedings of the 1987 CAUSE [illegible] Publication [illegible]

Updegrove, [illegible] and Networks. [illegible] CAUSE/EFFECT [illegible]

Van Brunt, [illegible] COMPUTING [illegible]

Wasileski, [illegible] Computer [illegible] In Proceedings [illegible] National Conference [illegible] CAUSE, 1980, [illegible]

CHAPTER 6

TECHNOLOGY TRENDS

1. Introduction

Gibson and Nolan describe four stages that business organizations go through in incorporating and managing computer technology (Gibson and Nolan 1974:76; Nolan 1979:115; for a further discussion of administrative practices and stages in growth, *cf.* Chapter 5, 3.2). An organization's increased expenditures as new technology is absorbed follow an S-shaped budget curve. The S-curve is driven either by hardware or software innovations. Gibson and Nolan try to advise managers how to cope with these innovations. The repetitive nature of these stages is especially interesting in that it appears possible to recognize progress through the same stages approximately every five years. As Gibson and Nolan comment: "One thing certain is that computer technology advancements are continuing at an unrelenting pace. More S-shaped curves are inevitable" (1974:88). This five year cycle coincides with the 4.5 year cycle of major machine upgrades in manufacturers' mainframe computers, the type of machines used in the organizations studied by Gibson and Nolan.

Technological innovations are more rapid and more chaotic in the microcomputer market. As a result, it is necessary for decision-makers and managers of technology in universities to be aware of current and historical trends. The reoccurring nature of an organization's reaction to innovation noted by Nolan indicates that planners may be able to anticipate and guide their own organization through its reaction to significant new technologies. The key issue is not just to be able to assess how new technology will improve existing applications or solve current problems, but to appreciate that the new technology will result in new, often unforeseen, applications. These new applications will bring their own problems and stresses to the art of managing a university.

The purpose of this chapter is to recall recent technology trends mentioned in the earlier chapters and to provide additional information on pertinent innovative technology that will be available this decade. Certain developments, such as larger memories and faster processors, are a constant in that these are long standing trends and planners are quite confident, though not necessarily always accurate, in estimating the rate and effect of such changes over a five to ten year span. Other technologies, such as pen interface portable computers, voice recognition and hypermedia, are more perplexing and simultaneously more interesting. Thus, this chapter speculates somewhat, not so much about the technology itself, but about the applications that may arise from the technology. As projections move further into the future, it becomes more difficult to imagine the form the technology will take. Hence, the discussions concentrate on developments expected within this decade.

1.1 The University of Regina Experience

The type of computer technology used at the University of Regina has been described in the chapters on teaching, research and administrative structure. These chapters reveal the degree to which technology is used and, through a series of case studies, the associated benefits and problems that have been observed.

As described in Chapter 5, the University of Regina has a centralized Department of Computing Services which operates a decentralized system of public-access computer facilities based on modestly configured MS-DOS microcomputers, mainly Intel 80286 or 8086 processors. More advanced microcomputers are found in facilities operated by individual departments and units. Advanced workstations, usually RISC-based, are also located in such departmental facilities and are primarily identified with individual research projects. Consistent with the survey results presented in Chapter 3, only isolated use is made of computer technology in the classroom and the use of technology in teaching is growing modestly. Recent innovations in technology, such as optical storage and hypermedia, are not widely used and are not yet being promoted by the Computing Services Department. The use of such technology remains in the hands of the "product champions" described in Chapter 3. One exception is the Fibre Distributed Data Interface (FDDI) network being installed to connect over sixteen hundred machines across campus. A second exception is a recent decision that sees Computing Services assembling and selling its own line of high-end "Cougar" microcomputers to faculty and staff and, through the University Bookstore, to students.

Thus, in addition to its service role in providing for public-access microcomputers, the centralized computing organization tends to deal with high-priced technological innovation that affects the university community at large. The installation of a campus local area network is one such example. The cost of a campus network exceeds the resources, as well as the mandate, of an individual or department unit. Thus, as technology, initially adopted by individuals or by department units, is seen to be of potential value to the larger university community, the centralized computing organization plays a role in reducing the cost of the technology or distributing it to the wider university community. These roles augment the service function. Product champions often do not come from the central computing organization, but rather from the departments and units across the institution. The central computing organization should look to adopt technology that has been demonstrated and developed by product champions and pass it on to the rest of the institution. This transition may or may not give rise to conflict as the focus of attention, expertise and control moves away from the product champion.

2. Hardware Trends

The major factor in computer innovation is the rapid rate of change in the amount of processing power available to the computer user. This rapid and seemingly continuous increase in computing speeds and simultaneous enhancements in storage and memory technologies is a trademark of the computer industry. However, in the 1980's, the widespread use of microcomputers brought computing power and changes in computer technology directly to .the user's desktop. Previously, minicomputer and mainframe computing was provided by a central or departmental agency. Unless the user was actively involved in the planning or purchasing of such machines, technology shifts appeared to occur only when the departmental or central facility was upgraded. Now many of the decisions to purchase technology reside with individual users. Because of the small size and diversity of most microcomputer manufacturers, microcomputer technology moves to the market more rapidly than is the case in the mainframe and minicomputer market sectors. Individuals faced with new responsibilities for purchasing are increasingly aware that the equipment they will purchase or recommend will be obsolete almost before it can be delivered.

Awareness of the rapid change in technology can affect the decision-making process in several ways. Users may in fact delay purchases, realizing that limited budgets will purchase more speed, storage or other capabilities in the near future. Users will also be more personally involved in, or identified with, the outcome of their decisions and recommendations. Indeed, they may be quite defensive in the face of later criticism, especially with respect to comments alluding to the obsolete nature of the "old" equipment and the better models and configurations that were just announced. After all, they knew this would happen. However, decisions will eventually have to be made, equipment purchased and used, and, of course, the equipment begins to "age." Yet one can, and perhaps must, plan for obsolescence as a tradeoff for purchasing equipment now. Part of that planning process will be to extend the useful life span of the computer purchase. University budget realities and the extended working lifetime of modern electronic circuits encourage the application of older technology to less demanding roles as the equipment ages. However, the question now arises as to how the individual who made the original decision to purchase can participate in a more global strategy for moving older equipment to other roles throughout the institution. Thus, in addition to a basic familiarity with the technology and trends, decision-makers need to understand and prepare policies to cover issues such as maintenance, upgrading and reuse or reallocation of technology.

2.1 Dramatic CPU Power Increases

The microcomputers which so dominate computing at universities today can be traced to the introduction of large scale integration (LSI) technology that allowed manufacturers to produce the first single chip microprocessors. Intel introduced the first commercial four-bit microprocessor, the 4004, in late 1970 under contract to Busicom, a Japanese calculator manufacturer (Augarten 1984:236). "Four-bit" refers to the length of the data field that the microprocessor uses in its basic operations. For example, a four-bit processor is capable of adding two four-bit values in one add operation. The 4004 microprocessor chip contained 2250 transistors. Intel's latest microprocessor, the 80486, contains 1,180,000 transistors. While the 4004 microprocessor was too limited to be practical as the basis for a stand-alone microcomputer system, Intel quickly followed the 4004 with the 8008 in April, 1972, and the 8080 in 1974. These were both eight-bit processors, powerful enough to lead to the first sales of microcomputers. For several years Intel was the sole supplier of microprocessors and this early lead eventually made Intel one of the world's largest suppliers of integrated circuits.

The first microcomputers were sold to hobbyists in kit form. Jonathan Titus, a doctoral student in chemistry, built a machine he called the Mark 8 using the Intel 8008 and the machine was featured in the July 1974 issue of *Radio-Electronics*. Ten thousand people purchased the instruction booklet that detailed how to build the Mark 8. *Popular Electronics* published an article on the Intel 8080-based Altair 8800, available in kit form from Micro Instrumentation and Telemetry Systems (MITS). The Altair did not come with any software. William Gates and Paul Allen contracted with MITS to write a BASIC interpreter for the machine. The microcomputer industry was underway. The early era of microcomputers saw Zilog introduce the Z80 and later the Z8000, Mostek the 6502 (used in the Apple II), and Motorola the 6800 and later the 68000.

In 1981, International Business Machines (IBM) introduced the IBM PC with an Intel 8088 microprocessor. The 8088 was a sixteen-bit processor and memory sizes on a well equipped system had jumped to 256 kilobytes from the 4K-64K (K representing a kilobyte) of the earlier eight-bit processors. The operating system for the IBM PC was developed by Microsoft. IBM sold the operating system under the name PC-DOS while Microsoft sold the same system as MS-DOS. Microsoft was able to license the operating system to manufacturers developing machines which were compatible with the IBM PC. These manufacturers produced machines that eventually outsold IBM in the marketplace because of better performance or lower pricing. Competition for market share was oriented towards machine performance rather than towards application software or a proprietary (available from only one vendor) operating system. The popular software packages could be used on any vendor's hardware. This contrasted with the situation a few years earlier when, for example, the first spreadsheet package, VisiCalc, was available only on the Apple II computer. Availability of applications software, warranty and service concerns and many other issues still influenced decisions to purchase from various manufacturers. However, the stage was set for manufacturers to compete on hardware performance versus price when PC-DOS/MS-DOS became a generic system.

2.1.1 The Intel 80486 and Its Successors

The processing power limit of the Intel 8088 microprocessor used in the IBM PC was quickly reached by processor-intensive and memory-demanding packages such as Lotus 1-2-3 and other electronic spreadsheets, as well as by database products like dBase III, which also strained the capabilities of the storage and file transfer limits of the PC. Hardware improvements appeared rapidly to overcome these limitations. Intel introduced the 8087 math coprocessor in 1980 to be added to the PC to relieve the 8088 processor of floating-point calculations[1]. The PC XT model, introduced in 1983, extended the storage capability of the PC by offering a hard disk. In 1985, the PC AT provided a bigger and faster hard disk as well as the pseudo 32-bit 80286 microprocessor with its ability to use 16 megabytes of memory. While the original DOS (PC-DOS and MS-DOS) implementation limited usable memory to 640 kilobytes, the operating system evolved along with these hardware changes, allowing for larger disk drives and providing support for memory above 640K. In 1987, Intel introduced the 80386, a true 32 bit microprocessor with circuitry to manage memory amongst several programs residing concurrently in the system's memory. The 80386 microprocessor was supplanted, in 1989, by the 80486 as Intel's high-end offering. This microprocessor provides an integral floating-point processor, eliminating the need for a separate math coprocessor. Current processor speeds range up to 50MHz, although 25MHz and 33MHz configurations are more common.

The next processor in this sequence, Intel's iAPX 86 family, is the 80586 which will be released in early 1993. This processor will have more on-chip cache memory than the 80486 and will therefore be able to deliver a higher MIPS (millions of instructions executed per second) rating than the 80486. It is expected to have a higher clock speed than the 80486's maximum 50 MHz.

2.1.2 RISC Technology

The Intel microprocessors, as most processor designs until the 1980s, followed the pattern of increasingly more complex processors with more sophisticated instruction sets for each new processor. Such processors are examples of complex instruction set computers (CISC). CISC processors include high-level instructions in hardware in order to improve the performance of programs written in high-level languages. CISC is possible due to increasing sizes of integrated circuit dies and corresponding increases in the number of transistors that can be placed on a die. The trend is illustrated in Figure 1 for

---

[1] A floating-point number is a fraction multiplied by a power of two, ten or some number. Floating-point numbers are used extensively in mathematical and scientific calculations and the speed of a machine in such calculations is a measure of its ability to perform scientific calculations.

both memory and processor devices. Advances in integrated circuit fabrication technology provided computer designers with more space to put more devices on a chip and they decided to utilize it by implementing more complex instructions in the processor's microcode.

Figure 1

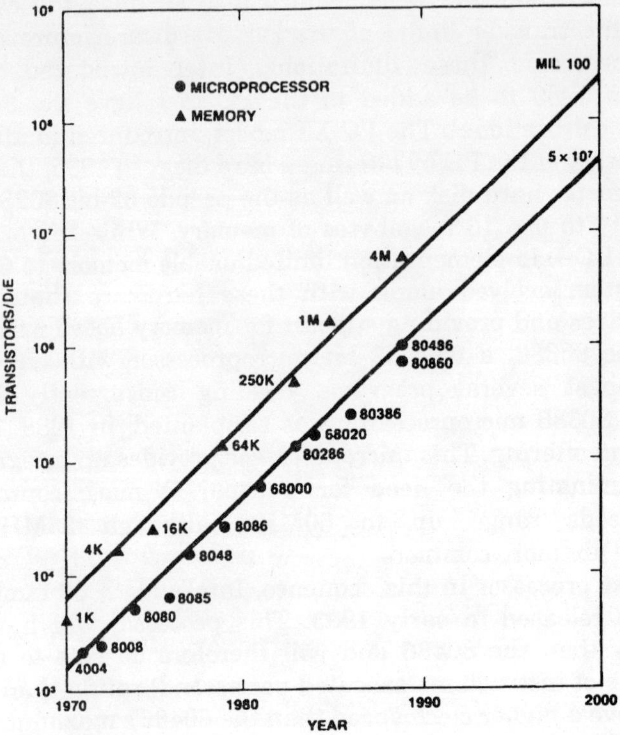

Transistor Density/Die for Memory and Processor Chips (Gelsinger 1991:100)

However, performance did not improve in accordance with improvements in technology. The assumption that language compiler designers would be able to reduce the number of machine instructions used for each high-level language instruction was incorrect. In reality, the code generated by compilers is such that only 20% of the processor's instruction set is executed 80% of the time. Additionally, because of the complexity of CISC instructions, it became necessary to increase the processor's cycle time, which offset the higher clock speeds permitted by the improved chip fabrication techniques. Analysis of this situation and of the actual code being generated by compilers led John Cocke and his colleagues at the IBM Yorktown Research Center to conclude that substantially increased performance could be attained by implementing only the basic simple set of instructions that are executed 80% of the time. The instruction set was made completely uniform: each instruction had the same format, size and execution time to facilitate pipelining of instruction execution. The instructions were also hard coded in the chip rather than being emulated by microcode to improve speed. This approach to processor design was called reduced instruction set computer or RISC technology.

Since the advent of RISC technology, the processing speed of RISC processors has increased by a factor of about 1.5 to two per year. The first RISC processor, the IBM 801 developed by John Cocke in 1980 (Gazis 1991:63), did not become a commercial product. Subsequently, David Patterson at the University of California at Berkeley developed Sun's SPARC processor and John Hennessy at Stanford University developed the Mips processor (Poole 1992:57). Both RISC designs have had excellent commercial success. The Mips processor family is used as the central processor in machines manufactured by Mips, Silicon Graphics and Digital Equipment Corporation while the SPARC chip is used primarily by Sun Microsystems. Sun and the smaller companies that use its technology have formed the SPARC Consortium while those companies committed to the Mips architecture have formed an organization called ACE (Advanced Computing Environment). The ACE group is committed to the EISA (Extended Industry Standard Architecture) for the PC compatible machines and to the Mips architecture for the UNIX workstation and file server market. The companies in these two organizations are attempting to increase their market share while promoting software and hardware standards.

Digital Equipment Corporation, a member of ACE and a major supplier in the RISC-based workstation market, has recently released the Alpha processor. It has a 64-bit architecture optimized for speed and engineered to support the UNIX operating system and Digital's own proprietary VMS operating system. The first Alpha processor, the 21064AA, operates at 150 MHz. Demonstrated at 200 MHz, it is currently the fastest RISC processor. However, systems based on this technology are not yet available in volume. Other vendors, particularly IBM, Sun and Hewlett Packard, can be expected to match these speeds soon.

RISC-based workstations offer excellent CPU price/performance ratios. The availability of such technology from vendors with a history of selling to the university marketplace has enabled university departments to address their research computing needs independently of the central computing department. While such workstations across campus have reduced pressure on the central organization to purchase systems capable of satisfying the often localized but high CPU demands of researchers, they have further contributed to the decentralization of computing and decision-making related to computing. Most of the RISC-based workstations use the UNIX operating system, a system unfamiliar to most centralized support staff accustomed to IBM and Digital computers. This again increases the gap between departments using workstations and the central organization since programmers are not easily moved between the user areas and the central facility.

2.1.3 Workstation Projections for 1995-2000

Future workstations will be based on 64-bit microprocessors like the Mips R4000, Digital's Alpha architecture, the recently announced Mips R5000 and 64-bit implementations of Sun's SPARC processor. A 64-bit processor provides memory addressing on the order of terabytes (10^{12}). This capability will be required for multimedia applications and for the next generation storage technologies such as large optical storage devices, wafer-scale RAM discs and optical memory technology. The most significant workstation trend this decade will be the closing of the gap between workstations and microcomputers. Current top-end microcomputers use Intel 80486 microprocessors operating at 50MHz. Burger and Holton extrapolate from recent chip technologies to the year 2000 and predict top-end machines will use 64-bit microprocessors with forty million transistors, operating at 250MHz (1992:142). These systems will have a four megabyte memory cache, photo realistic graphics and image processing capabilities, a flat screen display with four million pixels and 24 bits per pixel for colour. Machines will execute at 2 BIPS (billions of instructions per second), have two gigabytes of memory and one hundred gigabytes of disk storage. This immense computing and storage capability will allow researchers to perform computations on their desktop that currently require access to supercomputers.

2.1.4 Other Microprocessor Technology

Advancements in very large scale integration (VLSI) will bring products like special-purpose chips, systolic arrays and neural-network chips into the microcomputer and workstation arena. The Next computer already includes a special purpose digital signal processor (DSP) chip for high-quality audio and video applications. The standard resolution of today's computer screen is 640 by 480 points or pixels with eight bits of colour information stored for each pixel. High-end microcomputers are beginning to use screens with approximately 1000 by 1000 pixels, necessitating video memories of one megabyte or more. Multimedia applications already require 24 bits per pixel for better colour representation. Specialized microprocessors to handle the processing of all this graphical data will become commonplace. These high-resolution images will need to be stored and retrieved utilizing data compression techniques. The multimedia microcomputer of the year 2000 will contain numerous coprocessors to handle the demands imposed by high-quality audio and video applications.

2.1.5 Supercomputers

The need for researchers to have access to supercomputers for certain problems was explained in section 4.1 of Chapter 4. Achieving and maintaining supercomputer performance requires continuing improvements in processor fabrication, cooling technology and architectural enhancements like pipelining and vector processing. Another alternative is parallel processing. For some applications, parallelism does not provide as much benefit as one would expect. When multiple processors are used to run multiple programs concurrently, the overhead involved in managing this concurrency can ultimately lead to a point of diminishing returns where adding processors reduces performance rather than increasing it. However, applications that have massive data parallelism can benefit greatly if a very large number of processors are used. These are called SIMD (Single Instruction Multiple Data) machines. The data is loaded into the processors and a single instruction stream is broadcast to all the processors. This technology is expected to dominate the next generation of supercomputers.

A massively parallel architecture is implemented in models of the Connection Machine (CM) from Thinking Machines Inc. This design permits as many as 65,535 processors spread over four modules of 16,384 processors each. Several Connection Machines with one or more modules are in operation today. The title of "world's most powerful computer" is claimed regularly by CM models, seemingly in competition with the Intel Touchstone Delta System at the California Institute of Technology (Myers 1991:96). The CM-200 is capable of 9.03 Gflops (*cf.* Chapter 4, 3.1). This is slightly better than the previously claimed record of 8.6 Gflops by the Touchstone machine, which, in turn, had been better than the record set by the CM-2 at 5.2 Gflops. The immense power of the Touchstone machine was equated to giving each of the 2,500 students and faculty at Caltech a processor with 250,000 transistors, 3.4 megabytes of memory and 36 megabytes of disk storage. Of course, this configuration is paltry compared to the microcomputer these same students and faculty could purchase at the university bookstore.

The real significance of such development and these claims is the approach used in building the machines. The Connection Machine uses a very simple proprietary microprocessor as its processing element. Intel uses a much more powerful microprocessor, the i860, which contains approximately one million transistors, comparable to the Intel 80486. The Touchstone has 528 of these, each with sixteen megabytes of memory, delivering peak speeds of 31.7 Gflops and 17,000 MIPS. Intel has announced the i860 XP, which will have 2.5 million transistors and be twice the speed of the i860. Intel is aiming at a machine with 2,048 of these processors delivering 150 Gflops and 100,000 MIPS. Microprocessors that can be mass produced in these designs will reduce costs and allow manufacturers to upgrade machines by upgrading the microprocessor. This is much simpler than designing a complete new computer system based on a new processor design.

Interestingly, redundancy of inexpensive components is the same approach being used by Patterson, a key RISC developer, in RAID (redundant array of inexpensive disks) development (Poole 1992:58). That is, the economies involved in using mass produced processors or disk drives outweigh the disadvantages to be gained from developing specialized or high performance devices. The goal in supercomputer development is not to deliver a supercomputer to the desktop within the decade but to combine the massive parallelism approach with low cost mass production economics to deliver systems capable, for example, of eliminating delays in data compression of real-time, full-motion video.

2.2 Memory Technology

While most microcomputers are using one megabit chips, four megabit chips are readily available today, albeit at a higher price. Advertisements in the June, 1992, issue of *BYTE* magazine offered a megabyte of memory with one megabit chips for $38 to $45 (US), depending on speed, and four megabytes with four megabit chips for $190. By 1995 sixteen megabit chips will be available and sixty-four megabit chips will certainly be available in quantity before the year 2000.

2.2.1 Wafer-scale Memory

In the fabrication of integrated circuits, the wafer onto which the circuits are etched is divided into individual circuits or chips. The individual circuits are tested and typical yields are from 20% to 50%. Only 20% to 50% of the chips on a wafer are usable. If it were possible to improve the fabrication process, the individual circuits could be much larger, the goal being to use the complete wafer. Since memory circuits contain repetitive components, efforts are underway to increase the amount of the wafer used in memory production, to build what is called wafer-scale memory. Using fault tolerant software techniques, Anamartic Inc. of San Jose, California has built a wafer-scale memory which gives yields of 80% instead of 20%. The technique they employ is to keep a map of all the usable blocks of 32 kilobit tiles on the wafer and map out the 32 kilobit tiles containing faults instead of discarding the entire chip block. Each chip block contains additional control logic to do the mapping (Herriot 1990:37).

These wafers have been used to manufacture 160 megabyte solid-state disk subsystems called the "Wafer Stack" where each wafer contains 20 megabytes of dynamic RAM. Access time varies with the location of the accessed memory element on the wafer. The average access time is 200 microseconds. The overall system bandwidth is a minimum of 2.5 megabytes per second and can be improved by accessing wafers in parallel. This type of memory technology is appropriate to multimedia applications where it would replace disk storage rather than main memory.

2.2.2 Optical Memory

At the University of California at San Diego, a project is underway to build a three dimensional optical random access storage device which will have storage capacity of up to a terabyte and access times as low as one microsecond (Stein 1992:168). The material used is a block of transparent styrene doped with a light sensitive chemical. When two orthogonal beams of polarized, monochromatic, coherent light (laser) coincide, a bit is recorded at the point of intersection of the beams. Miniature laser sources that can be focused to 1 micrometer offer a potential recording density one thousand times greater than that of current optical storage. This technology is expected to become available within this decade. Cost will range from $10 per megabyte for 1 microsecond access to 10 cents per megabyte for 100 microsecond access. While these access times are impractical for primary system memory, this type of memory could be used for large on-line storage on the order of terabytes at a cost per terabyte from $10 million down to $100,000 (US) for the slower access times. Transfer rates can be as high as 25 gigabits per second. This type of storage and bandwidth will be required when fiber optic networks support multimedia workstations on a campus-wide basis. A terabyte is 1000 gigabytes. Suppose we store NTSC quality video images. This means a resolution of 320 by 240 pixels at eight bits per pixel. Thus, one hour of video, at thirty frames per second, is 320 * 240 * 30 * 3600 (3600 seconds per hour) or 8,294,400,000 bytes per hour. Thus, one day of video would require approximately 200 gigabytes of storage. But, we can maintain a 16:1 real-time compression/decompression rate on relatively slow processors, so we could put roughly eighty days of video on a terabyte storage device provided, of course, that there was actually eighty days of educational video material of interest and that we had a fast network in place to transfer the video data on demand to the receiving unit.

2.3 Secondary Storage Capacity

Secondary storage technology is still a major component of the cost of purchasing a well-configured microcomputer. Simple application software such as word processors or spreadsheets requires the allocation of three to fifteen megabytes of disk space simply to install all the tutorial material, examples, templates, dictionaries and add-on features found in the latest version of such packages. Figure 2 shows sample prices of hard disk storage devices found in the December issues of *BYTE* from 1982 to 1991. A review of current mail-order machine configurations indicates that low-end configurations are including from 40 to 60 megabytes of disk storage while the top-end configurations, typically Intel 80486 machines, offer 150 to 300 megabytes of storage. Assuming the typical academic will use fewer than five applications, the packaging of storage appears sufficient for most users. However, for graphical and multimedia work, storage requirements will rise dramatically. While improvements, such as reductions in the mass of magnetic read/write heads and higher in-track recording densities, will continue to increase storage capacity and reduce costs, there are no dramatic breakthroughs apparent on the horizon for magnetic disk storage. Thus, other mass storage technologies, particularly improved optical storage technology, are the likely candidates for applications such as multimedia.

Figure 2

Year	Size (in megabytes)	Cost (US dollars)
1982	10	4995
1983	10	1899
1984	10/30	888/2099
1985	10/44	569/1499
1986	20/80	529/1295
1987	20/80	349/895
1988	20/80/150	268/698/1445
1989	20/80/150/330	248/598/1098/1700
1990	20/80/200/1.0GB	249/549/849/3995
1991	20/80/425/1.2GB	239/449/1649/2499

Ten Year Trend in Disk Storage for Microcomputers

2.3.1 Optical Secondary Storage

Optical storage uses a laser beam to read or write information on a recording surface. The most familiar form of optical storage is the CD-ROM used by the recording industry to store digitized sound. Each spot on an optical disk is very small, less than a micron (one-millionth of a meter) in diameter. Since it is difficult to visualize the actual engineering requirements imposed by this recording density, Olafsson makes the following comparison:

> The dimensions are so small and the movements so fast that they are unimaginable in terms of direct experience. If the whole apparatus were scaled up to more familiar dimensions, an average optical drive reading a disk would be the equivalent of a Boeing 747 cruising at an altitude of 3 miles and never deviating from that altitude by more than 12 feet, while accurately following a flight line 16 feet wide at an unvarying speed of 123 million miles per hour. (Olafsson 1991:242)

2.3.1.1 Compact Disk Read-Only Memory (CD-ROM)

The common form of optical storage, compact disk read-only memory (CD-ROM), provides approximately 650 megabytes of read only storage. Access times are slow, the fastest drives being about 325 milliseconds. Transfer rates are also slow at peak rates of 153 kilobytes per second. CD-ROM technology uses audio CD mechanisms and these rates are sufficient for audio. Hence, the result is inexpensive storage with CD-ROM drives selling for as little as $350 (US), but with low performance. However, the technology is reliable and CD disks are inexpensive to produce in quantity. Since disks are mass-produced using injection molding at per unit costs below $2, the technology is used for distribution of software and multimedia materials. Alternative forms of optical storage have and are being developed to add functionality and performance.

2.3.1.2 Floptical Storage

Two companies, Brier Technology and Insite Technology, market twenty megabyte 3.5 inch removable disk drives (Ryan 1992:166). The Insite drive uses an optical mechanism for head positioning and is downward compatible with conventional 720 kilobyte and 1.44 megabyte disks. The Brier drive will have this compatibility in the near future and a fifty megabyte capacity. Both of these products are non-standard and the setting of standards for these technologies is an important issue because users will want to carry the removable disks to machines from other manufacturers. To this end Insite has licensed its technology to Iomega to provide a second source of its drives and has arranged for the magnetic-media manufacturers 3M and Maxell to make the diskettes. These companies have formed the Floptical Technology Association to promote the Floptical drive as an industry standard. They have since obtained the support of several SCSI adapter makers and OEM drive makers.

2.4 Advanced Technologies

Advances in interactive multimedia technologies will bring about the realization of the ultimate information "appliance" which will include high-resolution images, high-fidelity audio, high quality text and high definition full-motion video. The availability of such technology will enliven and enhance educational applications. Video conferencing and audio/video mail will change the way education is delivered.

This will require innovations in many areas of hardware and software such as graphics systems, cybernetics, operating systems, object-oriented programming, information storage and retrieval, hypertext and hypermedia, scripting languages, parallel processing, complex architectures for distributed systems, fast processors, high speed networks and large and fast storage devices (Fox 1991).

2.4.1 Technology in the Classroom and Laboratory

So, what technology is currently to be found in the classroom or laboratory? Before we discuss innovations such as multimedia and the elusive ultimate information "appliance," a pause to reflect on the possible answers to this question is appropriate. Assume that the context is a standard lecture hall or classroom where a relationship or bond exists between the instructor and student. The discussions in this chapter do not focus on this fact, but it is the foundation of the learning experience. The case studies in Chapter 3 reveal just how individual and personal this experience is and how varied the reaction can be to the use, aid, or intrusion of technology between the instructor and student. The key to effective incorporation of technology is to augment the instruction, not to distract from it and, certainly, not to lessen the effectiveness of the instructor. Teachers communicate and, thus, teach in different ways and with different styles. Students learn in different ways; some learn most effectively from a lecture; some from a "hands-on" experience; some from a textbook.

Technology may enhance the process or not. Technology may work in some contexts and not in others, for some individuals and not for others. This chapter does not attempt to resolve these important issues.

Returning to the question of what is in the classroom, how many instructors carry chalk to the lecture hall? For that matter, imagine the surprise of the teacher and students arriving at a classroom to find a note saying "class canceled since the blackboard is down." Appropriate and familiar technology is invisible; we use it and forget it. It is just there when needed. Overhead projection systems are fast becoming the most popular display technology in classrooms, including large lecture halls. In part, the reason is because the liquid crystal display (LCD) overhead tablet is viewed as a simple extension of an existing technology. The overhead projector is familiar technology; it has become as much a part of the classroom environment as the blackboard. Overhead projection of transparencies offers many of the advantages that delineate what the instructor wants for the classroom:

1. Availability: The projector unit is generally available in classrooms without any need to make prior arrangements for its delivery;
2. Ease of operation: Verify that the unit is plugged in and turn on the power switch, typically the only control on the unit;
3. Nothing to go wrong[2];
4. Portability: The transparency material is light and is dealt with in the same manner as ordinary lecture notes;
5. One size fits all: The overhead projector works with a small audience or in a large lecture hall;
6. Reusable: The transparencies can be used repeatedly and can be mixed and matched for use in different classes or lectures;
7. Existing sources: Many textbook publishers provide transparencies covering the textbook content upon adoption of a text.

There are, of course, several disadvantages, especially the preparation time required for the graphics. Since material is prepared in advance of the class, the instructor is likely to invest extra time in preparing pictures and diagrams (relative to drawings done on the blackboard during class time). Additionally, individual transparencies are difficult to update. Unfortunately, using the overhead projector extensively can change the style or atmosphere in the classroom. The instructor may be less spontaneous. The instructor is seen more as the presenter, rather than the originator, of information and ideas. The classroom experience may become less intimate with less face to face communication between students and the instructor.

The LCD tablet retains or enhances most of these advantages and can

---

[2] Actually the bulb can burn out (and it will at the most inappropriate time). Also, if the display screen is pulled down using a long piece of rope or string, someone will think to tie the string in knots so it dangles just outside the reach of even the tallest instructor.

minimize some of the disadvantages. For example, the computer material being displayed can be stored, edited and replicated easily on the computer. It can be mailed electronically to students or colleagues. The whole range of capabilities of the computer is available, from access to on-line services to multimedia presentations.

2.4.2 Interactive Videodiscs

Each side of a videodisc can hold 54,000 still pictures or 30 minutes of full motion video at 30 frames per second and 30 minutes of stereo sound. The access time is approximately one second which is inappropriate for normal data storage applications but, in an interactive tutoring or simulation context, this delay can be accommodated. Advantages of the videodisc are the random access to video images and the fact that, under computer control through a serial interface, the videodisc player can continuously display a selected still picture or run through motion sequences as needed in the interactive session. While there are now over 6,400 discs available, most of these are film releases (Laser Video File 1992). However, organizations such as the National Geographic Society, that have archives of video material, are releasing much of this material on videodisc. Moreover, since the material is randomly accessible by frame number, it is possible for instructors to develop hypertext materials that will reference existing materials. That is, individual instructors can plan lesson sequences that may never have been imagined when the material was originally mastered.

2.4.3 Voice Recognition

The ability to communicate verbally with a computer has been a research objective almost as long as it has been a central theme of science fiction. Voice synthesis and digitized voice playback capabilities already enliven educational material, simulations and computer games. However, the science fiction vision has the user conversing freely with the computer. Of course, even if the computer could recognize the word elements present in the speech, major breakthroughs in natural language processing and artificial intelligence are needed to allow the computer to respond intelligently. Researchers will require access to the type of processing power expected by the end of the decade before such breakthroughs occur. However, we can expect, within the next several years, to have voice input capabilities that will allow us to control the user interface and direct the execution of application packages. For example, Apple has demonstrated its Caspar voice input system (Gore February 1992:1). This technology requires a high-end processor to handle a vocabulary of 100,000 words. A top quality microphone must be used in order to reduce interference from background noise. DSP (digital signal processor) hardware is also required to digitize the speech accurately and quickly. Apple expects to deliver the hardware and software on its top-end systems by the end of 1993. However, the user will only be able to communicate known commands to the system. For example, it will be possible to say something like, "Find 'Intel 4004'"; it will not be possible to say, "See if you can find whether I've indicated who built the 4004."

So, we will not be able to hold intelligent conversations with our technology just yet. Moreover, it is not clear what use education will make of this technology. The primary improvements in voice recognition technology this decade will be lower costs and the elimination of the need to train the voice recognition system to recognize different voices. Thus, it will be possible to incorporate the technology in the lab or classroom because this training period will be eliminated. It will then be practical to expand CAI applications and role simulations packages to make it appear to the student that a conversation is possible. Of course, when the student soon goes beyond the limited command structure of the software, the machine will once again be responding with, "Sorry, I do not understand you."

2.5 Obsolescence and Maintenance Considerations

The maintenance of equipment is a long term cost issue that tends to be overlooked and, consequently, omitted from the budget process when the equipment is purchased. There are numerous issues to consider such as the long-term budget implications of maintaining service contracts on equipment that, as it ages, appears to be worth less and less relative to its maintenance contract cost. Self-maintenance is a viable and often necessary option, particularly if the vendor does not have local service staff. Training service staff is costly and trained staff become valuable commodities in the market; they may seek other employment based on their enhanced abilities. Issues such as service contracts versus in-house service are related to "build versus buy" software issues covered in Chapter 5. The Computer Science Department at the University of Regina still uses numerous cathode ray tubes (CRTs) which were purchased ten to fifteen years earlier. Computer technology tends to fade away rather than wear out, especially if the equipment is being maintained in-house. When replacement parts are not available, failed units will be used to supply parts. The result is likely to be an uneven mixture of equipment purchased over a long period. There will always be pressure to replace "old" equipment with new technology. However, there is very little demand for used computer equipment unless it is of quite recent manufacture.

2.5.1 Reusing "Old" Technology

The problem is what to do with the older, but still functional systems. For example, many current application packages require an Intel 80386 processor to run satisfactorily. What is the utility of the older 80286 systems purchased only a few years earlier? Elementary and secondary school systems have often chosen to move older equipment into the lower grades as newer technology moves into the higher grades. Formalized procedures are not in place at the university level, but it may be appropriate to attempt to develop or promote equivalent procedures. However, it would be akin to being the youngest child of several in a family. You begin to wonder if you will ever have any new clothes instead of the castoffs from your older siblings. The relatively high degree of autonomy between the senior university administration and the various faculties and units would make it difficult to impose such a strategy.

2.5.2 Upgrading Existing Equipment

The modern microcomputer has considerable expansion capacity in that disk drives can be replaced with larger units, memory can be expanded, display controllers and displays can be replaced and coprocessors can be added. Modular manufacturing and assembly processes allow vendors to sell a wide range of machines by varying the building blocks used in different machine configurations. This approach facilitates later expansion of the machine. There is also a very active market for third-party expansion. Users can readily purchase upgrades from companies who specialize in microprocessor or memory upgrades, for example.

2.6 Influence on Teaching and Research

New technology has the potential to invigorate the university classroom. This may occur because a particular technology offers a new or improved way of teaching certain subjects or simply because the new technology rekindles the instructor's interest in teaching. There is a possibility that new technologies will lead to increased expectations for faculty, notably by students reacting to the use of technology by some faculty and perceiving the lack of use as a negative mark against others.

Technology such as multimedia applications will not be easy to learn. Training and production requirements will increase with the incorporation of multimedia technology. By comparison, in the publishing of a textbook, it is unlikely that the finished diagrams, professional photographs and similar illustrations were produced by the author. Yet, the material presented in the classroom is usually prepared by the person presenting the material. Authoring packages and presentation tools will help but this software is not trivial to learn. Additionally, working with several types of media still means, at present, that the individual needs several software packages. The ability of authoring and hypertext packages to incorporate pictures and animation sequences, prepared with other packages, is often stated as a positive feature. However, in reality, the user must learn to use these additional packages; learning one package will not suffice.

Once you know the mechanics of how the software works, you could be compared to someone who has just learned to use a typewriter or word processor; there is no assurance that you will be successful in writing something worth reading. The ability to choose correct colours for computer presentations, to build the appropriate links into hypertext documents or to use sound when it works, is a new skill set required to prepare good computer presentations. It will not be necessary to train all faculty as instructional designers, but some appreciation and ability in instructional design will be required of those using technology. There are alternatives, provided the resources are available. For example, Athabasca University uses a team approach where several instructional designers work with the content expert, the faculty member, in the preparation of new courses (*cf.* below, 3.6).

3. Software Trends

The software running on a computer personifies the computer for the majority of users. While there may be the occasional discussion of processor capabilities or cache memory or other hardware features amongst more technically oriented users, the real debates take place over whether or not to use a graphical user interface and mouse or a keyboard, or over why this or that application does not seem to understand what you really wanted to do when you entered the last command. This relationship with a microcomputer can be very strong and very personal for many users. Perhaps this is to be expected since the microcomputer is rapidly becoming the primary tool for the individual's academic efforts, whether this be the use of a word processor to prepare a research paper or electronic mail to arrange a committee meeting or a graphics package to prepare a diagram for the next lecture. At present most of this software operates on text, with the occasional picture. This relationship will change with the increasing use of video and sound in the coming decade.

3.1 Software Development Lags Behind Hardware

No matter how much effort vendors apply to providing software with the release of a new processor or a new innovation, it is axiomatic that software, modified or upgraded to take full advantage of the new hardware, will be delivered later than the hardware. Manufacturers rush technology to market as quickly as possible in order to remain competitive. Prototype units are provided to major software developers during the final stages of development, but only a limited distribution is feasible for reasons of security and cost and because only larger developers can afford to undertake development on incomplete and unfinished, usually poorly documented, equipment. Moreover, equipment manufacturers often cannot visualize the innovative uses that will be made of new technology. To quote Vladimir Nabokov, "Genius is an African who dreams up snow" (Fitzhenry 1986:139). The original genius of the engineer or scientist who developed the ideas for the innovative product has long been replaced by the concerns of the sales and marketing staff before final product release.

3.2 Graphical User Interfaces

At present the need or desire for a graphical user interface is being hotly debated in the trade literature. Actually the debate centers more on the best graphical user interface amongst competitors such as Windows 3.1, the Macintosh Finder, OS/2 Presentation Manager and numerous other offerings.

Few comments appear supporting the DOS style of command line or text-based interface.

3.2.1 Ease of Use

It is difficult to understand why application packages, operating systems, the user interface and, in general, the whole computer system can be so complex to use at times. Experienced software developers and engineers are familiar with the initial reaction of users to their designs. Norman explains that the designer has a design model, a conceptual model of the system (for the original discussion, *cf.* Chapter 6, Norman 1986). Similarly, the user has a conceptual model of the system acquired through its use. The designer expects the user's model to be the same as the design model, but it often is not. The user's model is actually based on the image the system presents to the user. The UNIX operating system is a favourite operating system for many programmers although it is commonly described as having a very terse command line interface. The answer lies in the fact that the original designers of the operating system used early implementations of the system as the system grew and evolved. In fact, it is the very terseness that experienced programmers appreciate.

The phrase "user-friendly" is often used in a very imprecise manner by computer users to describe software or systems that they like and which are easy to use. This phrase might also be applied to a thousand objects, devices or tools we use every day. Norman explains the use or control of an object in terms of visibility:

> The user needs help. Just the right things have to be visible. . . . It is the lack of visibility that makes so many computer controlled devices so difficult to operate. And it is an excess of visibility that makes the gadget-ridden, feature-laden modern audio set or video cassette recorder (VCR) so intimidating. (Norman 1988:8)

3.3 Hypertext

Jakob Nielsen offers this description of hypertext:

> The simplest way to define hypertext is to contrast it with traditional text like this book. All traditional text, whether in printed form or in computer files, is *sequential*, meaning that there is a single linear sequence defining the order in which the text is to be read. First you read page one. Then you read page two. Then you read page three. . . . Hypertext is *nonsequential*; There is no single order that determines the sequence in which the text is to be read. . . . Hypertext presents several different options to the readers, and the *individual* reader determines which of them to follow *at the time* of reading the text. (Nielsen 1990:1)

There are numerous more formal definitions of hypertext but they all have in common the concept of nodes containing information tied together by links that permit the reader flexibility in reading or moving through the document. Systems such as Apple's HyperCard use a stack of note cards as a metaphor (Apple Computer 1989:7), while Asymetrix uses pages from a book in its TOOLBOOK software (Pierce 1990:19).

3.4 MULTIMEDIA Trends and Implications

Interactive multimedia is a "collection of computer-centered technologies that give a user the capability to access and manipulate text, audio and video" (Ambron and Hooper 1990:*xi*). Today's technology allows the user to combine text and graphics. Recent developments in optical storage technology, faster processors and compression techniques are making it possible to integrate music, sound effects, still pictures, computer generated animation and full-motion video into interactive multimedia presentations. According to Ambron and Hooper:

> [W]hat is clear is that learning in schools, businesses, and homes will take on a new dimension when integrated hardware is less expensive and when easy-to-use and 'capable' multimedia software is readily available. (Ambron and Hooper 1990:xi).

It is difficult to disagree with this statement given the requirement that the software must be "easy-to-use." Perhaps one might conclude that, if this new dimension has not arrived, it is because the software is still too difficult. The potential of multimedia software is significant and exciting, but Saettler (1990:466) offers a more cautionary comment in saying that "although there is no question that the computer can contribute to the educational process in many ways, it is only a tool. Its ultimate educational potential depends on how it is used and how effectively it can be integrated into the total instructional process."

3.5 Courseware Authoring Software

The topic of courseware and courseware authoring was covered in detail in Chapter 3. Recent authoring software packages, such as Authorware Professional, support new technologies such as hypertext and videodisc (Authorware 1990:1-10).

3.6 New Skill Requirements

Athabasca University uses instructional design teams with faculty members as the curriculum content experts when creating new classes. Athabasca has almost no in-house students since it is a distance education institute delivering most of its classes by correspondence. There are typically more instructional design specialists than faculty members on each team. The faculty members on the team will decide what material to cover in the new class and the instructional designers will decide the best methods to present this material to the students. The team also includes support staff concerned with the actual packaging and distribution of class materials. Often the content expert will be a faculty member from another university, contracted to deliver the subject content of the new class for arrangement by the rest of the team. However, Athabasca is in a unique situation, having no in-house students, and has adopted this approach to maximize the production of printed support materials for distance education students. Saettler (1990:470) goes much further in saying that:

> [I]t is important to realize that the *majority* of the instructional system staff should be *nonteaching* members. The nonteaching staff would assist the teaching members in specialized functions: graphic art, film and television production, photography, secretarial, engineering, computer programming, etc.

It certainly appears that Saettler is anticipating accurately the potential skill requirements of interactive multimedia. The problem is that the resources he describes are simply not going to be available to most faculty. Outside of the product champions described in Chapter 3, few faculty are likely to develop the skills of the programmer-*cum*-instructional designer. Fortunately, advances such as graphical user interfaces have resulted in viable alternatives such as authoring software and hypertext.

4. Alternative Delivery Options

Alternatives related to communication between students and teachers or between researchers themselves generally split into questions of distance delivery to remote students or campuses and network facilities.

4.1 Distance Education

The University of Regina's experiences with distance education, detailed in Chapter 3, introduced the alternatives currently in use to deliver classes to students at a distance. The University uses the Saskatchewan Communications Network (SCN) service to deliver televised lectures from a classroom equipped for that purpose. Instructors may also travel from the University to the remote site to give the class, for example, on Saturday mornings. While the University of Regina does not use the correspondence-school model, Athabasca University in Alberta uses this approach extensively and other universities offer this approach through their extension departments. The University of Calgary uses audio conferencing extensively for distance education. Thus, there is a wide range of traditional methods in place for distance delivery. Technologies such as multimedia and others described throughout this chapter will definitely be incorporated into the various approaches. Some disciplines will be affected more than others.

In the past, the Computer Science Department and University Extension had to provide for microcomputer access for off-campus classes. In fact, this author received the "NorthStar Award of Merit" from his 1983 Melville Computer Science 102 class, presumably in sympathy for having to teach BASIC programming to a class that was split into small groups using a wide array of different makes of microcomputers, one of which was called a NorthStar. It is now practical to assume that many of the class members will own or have access to a microcomputer. It is conceivable that many of these students will own CD-ROM drives in a few years and the University could be distributing lesson material in CD-ROM format. Language classes could use the same format with packages such as Hanzi Assistant, a CD-ROM containing a HyperCard dictionary of 2500 *hanzi*[3] (Dartmouth 1991). This software displays animation sequences of writing each *hanzi* in correct stroke order and provides pronunciation of each in both male and female voice. The several hundred megabytes required to do all this could not readily be distributed on floppy diskettes.

4.2 Networks

Section 3.5 of Chapter 4 describes the current state of network technology within North America and how the University of Regina is connected to CA*net, which is connected to the array of networks that make up the Internet (Frey 1989:118). The major enhancements to wide-area networking, CA*net and Internet, in this decade will be speed improvements as described in Chapter 4. Speeds of one to two gigabits per second will be widely available by the year 2000. These speeds will be necessary to allow rapid communication of the large files generated by multimedia and graphical applications. Local-area networking speeds will improve simultaneously. The FDDI network being installed at the University of Regina will use a fibre optics backbone with 100 megabit per second transfer speed. Most of the 1600 connections will be limited to ten megabits per second initially. However, this is a function of the cost of a direct FDDI interface connection which, at several thousand dollars, is more expensive than the microcomputer being connected. Moreover, with today's hardware only a fast workstation would be able to cope with the FDDI transfer speed. With increases in processor power and reduced connection costs, it will be possible to upgrade the campus network to allow 100 megabit or higher connections to everyone.

4.3 Telecommunications Technology and Portabilty

A modem providing up to 57,600 bits per second data transfer with error correction over unconditioned telephone lines can be purchased for $399 (US) today (*BYTE* 1992:398). The most attractive feature of current modem technology is the automatic sensing of transmission problems such that the device continuously varies the speed of data transmission to suit the quality of the connection. It is possible to use these speeds to extend the campus local-area network to the home of students and faculty. Apple, for example, includes software called AppleTalk Remote with each of its PowerBook portable

---

[3]*Hanzi* refers to Chinese characters or, more generally, to the set of characters composing the Chinese alphabet.

computers. The user can dial into any Macintosh on campus connected to the campus local-area network and have the same access to printers, file servers and other network connections as the on-campus machine. The distinction between wide-area networking and local-area networking will disappear as communication speeds increase. Integrated Services Data Networking (ISDN) will become part of the standard offerings of all North American telephone companies this decade. With ISDN will come 64,000 bits per second circuits. This speed is sufficient to carry real-time compressed video, and such technology could, for example, replace the use of satellites in offering two-way televised classes.

Wireless modems, such as the Motorola RPM415, are also available using cellular telephone technology (Gore March 1992:1). These units are currently limited to 9600 baud but they can turn a portable computer into a truly portable working environment. It is conceivable that students, while sitting in their classroom desks, could retrieve the professor's lecture notes or access an on-line database to check for information on a point relevant to the current class discussion or play a flight simulator game, for that matter. As research into collaborative computing environments produces results, it will be feasible for individual students to incorporate their suggestions into the model or program or poem being developed and, presumably, being displayed and instantaneously updated for all to see.

5. Summary

Management of technology is difficult. It requires skills and insights into technology trends as well as the ability to judge which technologies will work in the university context. Additionally, the managers must be able to facilitate the adoption of the technology by faculty and staff who are already coping with heavy workload and limited budgets and may not be the most receptive audience.

5.1 Identifiable Issues

This chapter tried to identify areas or issues related to technological innovation that can affect teaching, research and administration at universities. It is impractical to offer a checklist of solutions corresponding to problems that may arise from these issues given the individual nature and circumstances of each university. Well informed teachers, researchers and administrators will provide the needed solutions. The difficulty lies in identifying, motivating and informing these individuals. The main issues raised in this chapter are:

1. Technological innovations are occurring rapidly and continuously;
2. Computer hardware will become so powerful that, later in this decade, microcomputers will be used for most existing research, including much of

which is currently carried out on supercomputers;

3. Universities are acquiring a growing base of aging microcomputers that will function for many more years but will not be attractive to users wishing to obtain newer machines;
4. New voice recognition, hypertext and multimedia technologies will offer opportunities to invigorate the learning process;
5. A significant effort is required to learn to use these technologies effectively and faculty and staff training requirements will increase;
6. Optical technology will provide quick access to massive amounts of information but will require new approaches to the presentation and use of this information;
7. The cost of technology will allow students to bring their computers into the classroom and, while in the classroom, students will access on-line databases and hypertext information sources.

These issues were part of the discussions between the Indian and Canadian teams that led to the recommendations to be found in Volume I, *An Overview*.

6. Acknowledgments

I would like to thank my Winter 1992 Computer Science 822 students, especially Burt Christian, for their direct and indirect help in the writing of this chapter.

References

Ambron, Susan and Kristina Hooper. (ed.). *Learning with Interactive Multimedia: Developing and Using Multimedia Tools in Education.* Redmond, Washington: Microsoft Press, 1990.

Apple Computer. *HyperCard Stack Design Guidelines.* Reading, Massachusetts: Addison-Wesley, 1989.

Augarten, Stan. *BIT by BIT: An Illustrated History of Computers.* New York: Ticknor & Fields, 1984.

Authorware, Inc. *Authorware Professional for Macintosh Reference.* Minneapolis, Minnesota, 1990.

BYTE. Business Instruments advertisement, 17.6 (1992).

Burger, Robert M. and William C. Holton. "Reshaping the Microchip." *BYTE* 17.2 (1992), 137-138, 142, 146-148.

Dartmouth College. Hanzi Assistant 2.0. Distributed by Panda Software, 101 Bartlett Hall, Hanover, NH 03755-1870, 1991.

Fitzhenry, Robert I. (ed.). *The Fitzhenry & Whiteside Book of Quotations.* Markham, Ontario: Fitzhenry & Whiteside Limited, 1986.

Fox, Edward A. "Advances in Interactive Digital Multimedia Systems." *Computer* 24.10 (1991), 9-21.

Frey, Donnalyn and Rick Adams. *!%@:: A Directory of Electronic Mail Addressing and Networks.* Sebastopol, California: O'Reilly & Associates, 1989.

Gazis, Denos C. "Brief Time, Long March: The Forward Drive of Computer Technology." In Leebaert (ed.), 1991, 41-76.

Gelsinger, Patrick., Paolo Gargini, Gerhard Parker, and Albert Yu. "2001: A Microprocessor Odyssey." In Leebaert (ed.), 1991, 95-113.

Gibson, Cyrus F. and Richard L. Nolan, "Managing the four stages of EDP growth." *Harvard Business Review* 52.1 (1974), 76-88.

Gore, Andrew. "Pen, voice will shape interface." *MacWeek* 6.5, 3 February 1992.

— "PowerBook turns wireless page." *MacWeek* 6.11, 16 March 1992.

Herriot, Jim. "Software is the key to Wafer-scale RAM." *High Performance Systems* 11.1, (1990), 36-37.

Laser Video File. 4.1, Spring/Summer 1992. Westwood, NJ: NewVisions.

Leebaert, Derek. (ed.). *Technology 2001: The Future of Computing and Communications.* Cambridge, Massachusetts: MIT Press, 1991.

Myers, Ware. "Faster . . . Caltech dedicates world's most powerful supercomputer." *Computer* 24.7 (1991), 96-98.

Nielsen, Jakob. *Hypertext and Hypermedia.* San Diego, California: Academic Press, 1990.

Nolan, Richard L. "Managing the crisis in data processing." *Harvard Business Review* 57.2 (1979), 115-126.

Norman, D. A. and S. W. Draper. (ed.). *User centered system design: New perspectives on human-computer interaction.* Hillsdale, NJ: Erlbaum

Associates, 1986.
Norman, D. A. *The Psychology of Everyday Things*. New York, NY: Basic Books, 1988.
Olafsson, Olaf. "The Multiplier: Future Productivity in the Light of Optical Storage." In Leebaert (ed.), 1991, 240-267.
Pierce, Joseph R. *TOOLBOOK Companion*. Redmond, Washington: Microsoft Press, 1990.
Poole, Gary Andrew. "An Unsung Academic." *UnixWorld*, June 1992, 57-58.
Ryan, Bob. "Scaling the Memory Pyramid." *BYTE* 17.3, March 1992, 161-170.
Saettler, Paul. *The Evolution of American Educational Technology*. Englewood, Colorado: Libraries Unlimited, 1990.
Stein, Richard Marlon. "Terabyte Memories with the Speed of Light." *BYTE*, 17.3 (1992), 168-169.

INDEX

APPENDIX A

HISTORY OF COMPUTING AT THE UNIVERSITY OF REGINA

1. Early Developments

When the first computer was installed at the University of Regina, the institution was one of two campuses of the University of Saskatchewan. In 1962 the Province decided to change the status of Regina College, which had been created in 1911, as a junior college, to that of a degree-granting institution. Further, it combined this new degree-granting institution with the other degree-granting institution, the University of Saskatchewan, which had been granted its charter in 1907, to form the University of Saskatchewan system, with two campuses–the Saskatoon Campus, in Saskatoon, and the Regina Campus, in Regina.

In November 1963, the first computer was installed at the Regina Campus, an International Business Machines (IBM[1]) 1620. The machine was acquired with the aid of grants from the National Research Council (NRC) and Producer's Pipelines Incorporated.

The National Research Council, an arm of the Government of Canada, had, at that time, a policy of funding computing activities at universities across the country, to stimulate computing-related research activities in Canadian universities.

Producer's Pipelines Inc. contributed $7,500 to support the installation of the IBM 1620 at the Regina Campus. This contribution amounted to half of the cost of installation of the machine (Carter 1992). They further supported Campus computing by agreeing to purchase 44 hours per month for 12 months at a rate of $1,000 per month. In addition, they were provided with the option to purchase computer time after that period on a price per hour basis which would not exceed the IBM service bureau rate (Arc63).

In less than three years the IBM 1620 could not keep up with demand and was replaced in August 1966 by a larger and more powerful IBM 1130. However, by early 1967 (Arc67a) the 1130 was also experiencing great difficulty keeping up with the rapidly increasing demands from users. Below is a section from a February 21, 1967 memo to W. A. Riddell, Principal of Regina Campus, from L. L. Achtemichuk, Director of the Computer Centre,

---

[1]IBM is a registered trademark of International Business Machines Corporation.

which provides a glimpse of some of the pressures being experienced by the computer centre in its attempt to provide service to its academic and administrative users:

> There are many reasons for these increases, some of which are
>
> 1. Increased utilization for scientific projects.
>
> During the past few months, the number of scientific programs which have been written and run has increased by several hundred percent. The 1130 has greatly expanded the range of potential use and the number of graduate students, as well as faculty members utilizing our services is increasing every week. I feel that in this respect, the situation is very encouraging.
>
> 2. The initiation of the Science Stores system.
>
> This complete system of inventory and departmental billing was started in August to provide a much needed improvement in the manner of operation of the central science store-room. After an initial orientation and experimental period, the system is now almost up-to-date with monthly billings. Large savings resulting from the improved inventory control have been the most dramatic advantage of the system.
>
> 3. Programming instruction.
>
> The recently started series of Computer Science courses in mathematics has in a short time, become rather popular. The result is that a significant amount of computer time is utilized by the students in these courses for their laboratory assignments. Last fall, the Computer Centre sometimes ran over 100 student programs in a day. The first course in the series will be given every semester with an expected enrolment of 40 students for the September semester.
>
> 4. The Payroll system.
>
> The random-access disk storage of the 1130 has made it feasible to implement a relatively comprehensive payroll system with the facility for easily producing the many reports and summaries required by the Controller's Office. The initial design was based on a figure of 300 employees, but in fact the current monthly payroll involves over 600 persons.
>
> 5. Program development and testing.
>
> Every new program required for an application requires an often under-estimated amount of computer and programmer's time for its development, testing and debugging. In this sense, computer utilization grows, exponentially since each new program requires time for development, testing and debugging. Once the program is in production, time is required to do the regular production runs and in almost every case the situation is then created where another program is required to extend the system being developed.
>
> 6. The Registrar's Office.
>
> This office is the major user of the computer facility. The system has been expanded in many directions and made more comprehensive and complete than before. Numerous programs have

been developed and are still being written to improve and expand the system. The increased enrolment has provided a situation with immense processing volumes. The new semester system has increased the workload and decreased the lead-time many-fold in almost every segment of the system.

- - - - -

As you all know, the Producer's Pipelines [Inc.] Company has for the past number of years made a generous donation to the university in return for a certain amount of computer time. Since the 1130 arrived, this company has used less than 5 hours of time. I have been informed that Producer's Pipelines recently ordered two disk cartridges for our computer which indicates that they soon intend to utilize part of their share of the computer. I am at a loss to suggest what we should do if they suddenly demand 15 hours a week.

In the same vein, the Computer Centre has found itself in a position of having absolutely no reserve capacity left. We are unable to deal with an emergency or crisis and cannot provide the extra service required during the many peak periods of the university term. This is a very disturbing and unsatisfactory situation.

I do not believe that there can be any doubt in your mind that something significant must be done to remedy the situation. I'm sure you are all aware that an IBM 360 computer has been ordered for delivery in 1968. I must urge you to seriously consider and support my previous proposal moving the delivery date from June to January, 1968. More immediate steps are required, however, to solve our current problem.

What alternatives do we have? The first and simplest is that we do nothing. Let us briefly consider what will be the results.

The Computer Centre staff are unable to continue devoting so much of their own time to the centre. After seven months of working from 60-90 hours per week, one cannot be expected to maintain the high level of efficiency required.

Major systems will have to be eliminated from our schedule of operations.

No academic programs will be run.

Students in programming classes will be limited to 2 or 3 runs per assignment, making it commonplace for students to have completed a course without writing a working program.

All system development will be frozen and no changes or improvements possible.

I have no doubt that you will agree that this situation should never be allowed to develop. An <u>immediate</u> solution must be found.

> The solution I am suggesting is that the university contract for the delivery of a second IBM 1130 computer system immediately. A second computer would provide the following advantages.
>
> an immediate doubling of throughput
> no reprogramming will be necessary
> no data conversion is required
> it would provide an important reserve capacity to deal with peak loads
> more efficient use of operators
> provides the least expensive solution
> provides the most rapid implementation
>
> It is therefore proposed that an immediate decision be made on this matter and that our proposals be approved in full, including the recommendations relating to computer operators and the IBM 360 computer. The approval of these recommendations will allow the Computer Centre to provide the quality of service that this university has the right to expect.

By April 1967 (Arc67b) the University had made arrangements with IBM to rent time on an 1130 at their Data Centre in Regina to handle some of the increase in demand and had ordered some equipment upgrades for the University's 1130.

The 1130 was replaced in August 1969 by an IBM 360/40. The primary rationale for this change and for all other changes was increasing demand (Mack 1991) from the three user bodies–students, faculty and administrators–coupled with price reductions and functionality increases that occurred.

1.1 Structure of the Central Facility

Over time, as the user base and the demand for service changed, the structure of the "computer centre" at the University was modified in an attempt to ensure that it continually met the needs of its users. An overview of these changes is reflected in Table 1 which lists the individuals who have been responsible for the central computing facility along with their job titles and the dates of their appointments.

Mr. L. L. Achtemichuk, the first Director of the Computer Centre, came to the University from the (Saskatchewan) Government Computer Centre (Achtemichuk 1992). When he joined the University in 1963 the user base was dominated by academics, as administrative systems had yet to be developed. Hence, advisory bodies and the official reporting structure reflected this. However, by March 1967 the administrative users had increased in numbers and importance to such a degree that when they expressed their displeasure with the type and level of service that they were receiving the reaction of the University was to transfer the Centre from academic to administrative control (Kaller 1992, Arc67c).

Table 1

DATE	TITLE	INDIVIDUAL
Dec. 63 - June 67	Director, Computer Centre	Mr. L. L. Achtemichuk
July 67 - June 69	Director, Computer Centre	Mr. P. Gross
July 69 - July 70	Acting Director, Computer Centre	Dr. E. Stanley
July 70 - June 75	Director, Computer Centre	Dr. L. R. Symes
July 75 - July 80	Manager, Computing Services	Mr. C. Turnbull
July 80 - Sept. 83	Director, Systems and Analytical Services	Mr. N. Southam
July 80 - Dec. 81	Director, Academic Computing	Dr. L. R. Symes
Jan. 82 - Sept. 83	Director, Academic Computing	Dr. R. B. Maguire
Oct. 83 - April 84	Acting Director, Computing Services	Mr. N. Southam
May 84 -	Director, Computing Services	Mr. G. Peardon

In the system of governance under which Canadian Universities operate, academic and academic-related matters are dealt with by the academic bodies which report through an Academic Vice-President, while financial and other support services are handled by the administrative units which report through an Administrative Vice-President. The two groups ultimately report to the President (Vice-Chancellor).

The proposed change in reporting structure was seen by the academic community as a significant shift in direction and was viewed by many as a potential threat. Ultimately, the proposed change was not enacted but it did provoke a great deal of debate within the institution.

1.2 Saskatoon Campus

The first computer acquired by the University of Saskatchewan, in Saskatoon, was an LPG 30 in the late 1950's. Its acquisition required the combined support of the Saskatchewan Research Council, the National Research Council and the University. The machine was located in the Mathematics Department. This machine was succeeded by an IBM 1620 in the fall of 1963. The 1620 was replaced by an IBM 7040 in the fall of 1965, and this, in turn, was replaced by an IBM 360/50 in 1967.

2. IBM System /360 Era

The two campuses had no sooner acquired their respective 360's when they again began to experience problems in meeting user demands. While a considerable amount of the growth was the result of increased demands from research and administrative users, the primary cause was that both institutions introduced undergraduate computer science programs in the late 1960's, and as a result experienced a tremendous increase in demand from students who entered these programs. Consequently, each campus was forced to introduce a number of different measures in an attempt to control growth.

At the Saskatoon Campus it was felt that the management of computing was not satisfactory (Barber 1991). The Vice-President of the University of Saskatchewan, Ken McCallum, asked Dr. Lloyd Barber to set up a tripartite arrangement among the three user groups in order to manage computing so that individuals from all groups could have better access and obtain more satisfactory service.

The tripartite arrangement was worked out and managed by a committee of three people, Dr. Lloyd Barber, Dr. John Cooke and Blaine Holmlund (Barber 1991, Peardon 1991). Later Glenn Peardon joined and became the equivalent of Chief Executive Officer of the operation. This committee consolidated administrative computing with the academic computing so that greater capacity could be afforded and efficiency attained.

2.1 Charging Policies

In order to account for the system's utilization, a charging system for computer utilization was implemented at the Saskatoon Campus. The users were provided nominal dollars, "funny money", so that there was some record of who was using computing resources and for what. While computing dollars could not be spent on other goods or services, budgeting for computing utilization was done in departments where those responsible had an understanding of the work being done and its relative importance. Further, the charge back system indicated to users and others in a direct way that computing was not a free good. This system encountered opposition and resentment from a number of users (Barber 1991).

At the Regina Campus the debate over charging policies was affected by the grant that the Campus, as all other universities in the country, received from the National Research Council. This grant funded approximately 50% (Arc66) of the operating costs of the Computer Centre. The academic users put forward the argument that it would be unfair to charge them or their graduate students for computing as it would amount to double billing. NRC would first be paying through the grant it gave the university directly and again through charges levied against research grants. Indeed, this argument had considerable validity, for NRC was responsible for funding research in the sciences and engineering and this group of academics was the largest group of research users. Ultimately in the mid 1960's NRC, which by then had become the Natural Sciences and Engineering Research Council (NSERC), dropped block grants to universities in support of computing and replaced the grant to the institution with funding for computing in research grants given directly to individual researchers. While this changed the argument put forward by researchers as to why they should not be charged for computing, it did not diminish it. For now they argued that when they received their grant (which was never as much as they had requested), it was always the computing budget which had been trimmed from their grant request.

While a policy of budgeting and direct billing for computing was not implemented on the Regina Campus, rates were established and users were given bills which reflected their consumption. This permitted research users to estimate the cost of their computing needs so that they could request funding from their granting agency. Further, it allowed the institution to account for the computing costs of the various constituencies–administrative, instructional and research users. In the case of administrative and instructional users, each month their computing costs were assigned to their monthly budget statements. As the rate structure was not intended to produce either a surplus or a deficit in the computer centre's budget, an adjustment was required at year's end to balance the books. This was done by either reducing or increasing the charge for computing which had appeared in the user statements when the final statements for the fiscal year were produced.

2.2 Regina Campus

At Regina Campus three major actions were initiated in an attempt to provide the level of service required. They involved a removal of time-sharing equipment and ordering of additional resources to support batch users, extension of the hours of operation to three full shifts a day, seven days a week, and the development of a link between the two campuses so that load-sharing could be initiated (Dennis 1991, Holden 1991).

The initial configuration of the IBM 360/40 included a controller[2] which was used to support four terminals for time sharing. While time sharing was something that some of the users wanted to become involved with, it was not particularly functional on the model 40, given the power of the machine and the state (of the art) of time-sharing software. With the tremendous increase in demand for batch cycles from the students, in particular, it was decided to exchange this equipment and replace it with additional memory which would permit the Centre to change the version of the operating system (OS), from PCP (Primary Control Program) to MFT (Multiple Fixed Tasks). This switch allowed batch jobs to be run, printed and read simultaneously, whereas with PCP, jobs were read, processed and then printed.

The second action involved adding a third shift to the normal work week and the introduction of weekend shifts. The third shift was primarily devoted to large research jobs which would take several hours to complete and consequently did not require the presence of an operator, and therefore did not involve any new staff (Holden 1991). To minimize the possibility of problems occurring during unattended hours of operation, the printer was

---

[2]The cost of the IBM 2705 controller and the IBM 2741 terminals was equivalent to the cost of doubling the memory which was required to support the upgrade of the operating system from PCP to MFT.

shut down so that these jobs would not be printed until the morning shift arrived. The weekend operations, however, required the hiring of additional operators for two of three shifts each day. These shifts were devoted almost exclusively to the processing of student jobs. The third shifts on Saturday and Sunday were again devoted to large research jobs as was done during the week.

While the increased hours of operation were instituted to increase student access, other measures were introduced to control access. For example, schedules were posted for the processing of student jobs, and the next batch of jobs would be picked up from the student work area before the previous batch of jobs had been returned. The purpose of this policy was to stop a student from submitting the same job on consecutive collections of student jobs. A student did not receive the output of the previously submitted job until after the next batch of jobs was collected, thereby, theoretically, limiting a student to submitting the "same" job with every second batch of jobs processed.

The third action was the development of a telecommunication link between the two campuses (Dennis 1991). This included the development of a software[3] package, for communication between two HASP[4] systems at each campus, and the establishment of a high-speed (for late 1970s) communications link. This project was supported by SaskTel, the provincially-owned telecommunication company, which provided a 4.8 kilo bits per second line between Regina and Saskatoon, a distance of approximately 220km. With the aid of this link, research jobs could be off-loaded to the larger machine in Saskatoon. With the equipment available at this time, the Centre would frequently get research jobs which would run for several evenings before completion. These jobs would require much less time to complete when shipped to the larger facility in Saskatoon for processing. The link also provided an opportunity to investigate the sharing of administrative systems software.

3. Computer Rationalization

Incremental changes would not solve the problems that each campus' computer centre was experiencing. As a result both initiated a process to investigate long-term needs and subsequently to initiate the selection of replacement equipment.

---

[3]The system was an intelligent remote job entry/spooling system running under OS MFT or OS MVT. It expanded HASP's Remote Terminal Access Method and utilized HASP's multileaving philosophy to transmit data between a HASP queue and a remote HASP station.

[4]HASP provides spooling support for Operating System 360.

The central office of the University, to which each campus reported, became concerned with the projected costs of computing upgrades after the initial responses to the call for tenders were received. In an effort to force some rationalization into the process, a committee was formed in 1971. The committee was chaired by Dr. Lloyd Barber, then Vice-President of the University of Saskatchewan, and included three representatives from each campus and support staff from the University Systems Study Group, which reported to Dr. Barber.

The efforts of this committee were in themselves not particularly successful as applied to the two campuses of the University, for each campus looked at the exercise of computer rationalization as a "zero sum game", in which the available funding was very limited; as a result each felt that any increase in computing capacity which one campus obtained would come at the expense of the other.

One effort initiated during this period, which remained after the two campus structure was abandoned and was replaced by two separate universities (The University of Regina from Regina Campus and the University of Saskatchewan from Saskatoon Campus) in 1974, was the implementation of UNIFACTS (University of Toronto Financial Accounting System).

The University purchased the UNIFACTS system, a general ledger and accounts payable system, from the University of Toronto and adapted it for use by the two campuses. The system was run on the machine at the Saskatoon Campus. The telecommunications link was used to transfer input from Regina to Saskatoon for processing and to return output to Regina for printing.

3.1 Tenders - Regina Campus

In response to the call for proposals (tender) for a computing system to replace the IBM 360/40 put out by Regina Campus, four bids were received. They were from UNIVAC, a UNIVAC 1106, from IBM, an IBM 370/145, from Digital Equipment Corporation, a DEC[5] System 10 and from Xerox Corporation, a Xerox Sigma[6] 6. The initial ranking assigned to the bids was, from high to low, DEC, Xerox, IBM, and UNIVAC. The DEC System 10 was approximately the same price as a 360/40 as was Xerox Sigma 6. However, the Xerox configuration did not have the same power as the DEC System 10. Consequently, Xerox repackaged their bid and offered a Sigma 9 without a

---

[5]DEC is a registered trademark of Digital Equipment Corporation

[6]Sigma is a registered trademark of Xerox Corporation.

RAD[7], and IBM replaced their bid of the 370/145 with the newly announced 370/148. The Xerox bid was one of their first systems bids to be offered to a customer without a RAD which until then was the only device to be used for high speed swapping on their systems. The new bid used disks for swapping. The advantage of the Sigma 9 over the previously bid Sigma 6 was a substantial increase in CPU power. In fact, by some measures, the Sigma 9 had the processing power of an IBM 370/155, the next machine up in the 370 family after the 370/145.

3.1.1 The Xerox Bid

The Sigma 9 was actually designed by SDS–a small start-up company that designed basic architecture that formed a good foundation for time-sharing. Xerox, wanting to get into the computing business, bought the company and changed its name to XDS–Xerox Data Systems. The Sigma Series had sound time-sharing facilities and good support for batch processing.

3.1.2 The IBM Bid

The IBM system had very primitive time-sharing capability. The DEC System 10 and the Xerox Sigma Series were much superior in that respect. IBM proposed TSO (Time-Sharing Option) to provide time-sharing on the 370. The disadvantage with TSO was that it consumed a tremendous amount of CPU cycles just to support time-sharing. While the campus wanted time-sharing, it needed significant additional cycles for its batch processing load. It was judged that the 370/148 did not have enough power to support both.

3.1.3 The DEC Bid

The DEC System 10 with the KI processor was more powerful than the Sigma 6 but less powerful than a Sigma 9. A major concern that the campus had with the bid from Digital was the lack of maturity of their TOPS-10 operating system and the degree of maintenance support the campus would receive given its relative degree of isolation from other major Digital customers. Xerox, on the other hand, being new to the computer business, was investing heavily in maintenance and related support activities. Consequently, they were developing a very good rapport with their user community.

3.2 The Evaluation

The performance evaluation of these systems was carried out by members of both the Computer Centre and the Computer Science

[7]Rapid-Access Data Storage System from Xerox. The RAD Storage Unit employs fixed read/write heads, minimizing access times which improved access time. This combined with its high data transfer rate minimized system swapping time.

Department. A complex set of evaluation criteria was developed and, based upon these criteria, benchmark tests and on-site demonstrations were planned and conducted.

Dr. Symes and Dr. Lee, members of the Computer Science Department, prepared a paper study of each configuration proposed by the vendors, including those received by the Saskatoon Campus. The paper study was based upon the work of K. E. Knight (Knight 1963), and others (Hillegass 1965; Grenberger 1966; Solomon 1966; Arbuckle 1966; Sharpe 1969; Joslin 1968), and predicted the theoretical power of each configuration, later borne out by benchmark tests that were conducted.

The choice was narrowed to one between Sigma 9 and DEC System 10 which were quite close on paper. The major issue was reduced to which company would provide better support and deliver quality software. As time sharing was new, customers required a great deal of support from the vendor. As a result of this concern Mr. Colin Turnbull, Manager of the Computer Centre, travelled to a few carefully chosen sites with the objective of evaluating customer support and their general level of satisfaction with the vendor. He came back clearly leaning towards Xerox. Xerox's support did turn out to be exceptional. Subsequently, however, the level of support received was reduced considerably when Honeywell[8] took over Xerox's computer operations.

3.3 The Acquisition

Ultimately, the Sigma 9 was selected. Although the price of the system was approximately $1,000,000, Xerox financed the acquisition by means of a 6 year lease to purchase agreement which kept the financial arrangements the same, on a monthly basis, as they had been for the IBM 360/40 it replaced–$17,000 per month. The combination of the system's multi-processing capability and the good price was a significant factor in the selection of the Sigma 9. Its acquisition was a major step forward for the University in terms of the sophistication of technology and capacity.

The Sigma 9 was purchased, with the concurrence of SaskComp (*cf.* section 3.4). From October 1973 until February 1974, when it was brought under the management of SaskComp, the machine was operated by the University alone.

A major concern during the evaluation phase was the fact that the Sigma 9, along with the other non-IBM bids, did not have a PL/1[9] compiler for their machine. The vast majority of administrative systems running on

---

[8]After all of these investigations, Xerox decided in the fall of 1975 to get out of the computer business and sold its computer operations to Honeywell. This occurred about two years after the Sigma 9 was acquired and after SaskComp had assumed control of the machine.

[9]PL/1 is a registered trademark of International Business Machines Corporation.

the 360/40 including: the Student Records system, the Library Acquisitions system, and the Library Serials system, had been developed specifically for the IBM/360 family and were coded in PL/1, a programming language developed by IBM for that family of machines and which by 1973 had not been implemented by many other vendors.

3.3.1 Software Porting from IBM to Sigma 9

The Sigma 9 launched the Campus into time-sharing, a whole new world. A time table was developed to aid in the orderly conversion of systems (Turnbull 1991). Contracting out for extra staff to help meet the deadlines was not a practical alternative. Even if money had been available, it would have been difficult to find people with Sigma Series skills or time-sharing system expertise.

The installation and conversion went well because of the dedication of the personnel involved, and the plans developed prior to delivery, which included contingency plans, arrangements for on-line access to Xerox hardware elsewhere prior to delivery of the machine, and careful monitoring of progress throughout the project. Planning records were maintained and regular meetings were held to review progress and make adjustments.

The Sigma 9 proved to be a very easy machine to learn and use. As a result staff quickly became proficient in its use. Jobs which had previously required an elaborate JCL[10] script could be accomplished on the Sigma 9 with a few commands (Purse 1991). The conversion from PL/1 to COBOL on Sigma 9 also proved to be relatively straightforward (Van Eyck 1991).

The Library had some systems that had to be converted, but at the time of the acquisition of the Sigma 9 the Library had contracted with the Library at the University of Toronto to use their UTLAS[11] system. They started using the UTLAS system for book orders and cataloguing. Arrangements were made to run the other segments of the Library Acquisitions system at the Government Computer Centre for several months after the 360/40 departed. Indeed, the conversion of Library Acquisitions System extended past the departure of the 360/40, and it was run on the Government Centre's IBM 360/50 for some time.

The Registrar's system was the major system that required conversion to Sigma 9 COBOL from PL/1 (Purse 1991). This task required a great deal of effort and put considerable stress on the individuals concerned, particularly those in the Registrar's Office.

Conversion was aided by the fact that the Sigma 9 was delivered and installed in October 1973, three months before scheduled. This provided the

---

[10]Job Control Language–language used to communicate to the operating system the resources that a job requires.

[11]University of Toronto Library Acquisition System.

University with three extra months of overlapped operation with the 360/40, at no cost. When conversion plans were developed it called for three months of parallel operation of the Sigma 9 and the IBM 360/40, from January 1974 through March 1974. By the end of the extended overlap period, Payroll, Library Serials and Student Records Systems were converted from PL/1 to Sigma 9 COBOL.

The contingency plans also included making arrangements with The Co-operators Data Services Limited, a large national corporation with its head office in Regina, so that some jobs could be run on their IBM equipment if the need arose.

By the time the Sigma 9 was acquired, financial systems had been consolidated by the University for both campuses, into a single system that was run in Saskatoon, with the aid of the computer link–UNIFACTS. This action precluded the need to transfer the financial system to the Sigma 9. This, however, required the link software which had been developed to support IBM HASP to IBM HASP communications be modified to support IBM HASP to Xerox CP-V[12] communications. Another advantage of the link was that it continued to provide researchers with access to IBM computing, again reducing the need to convert some of their software packages and programs.

Apart from use of the contingency sites for longer than had been planned, the conversion went well (Turnbull 1991). A key factor was that no major changes were attempted on any systems. The initial goal was to simply get the systems (programs) ported from IBM PL/1 to Sigma 9 COBOL. Attempts to exploit the time-sharing capabilities of the Sigma 9, for example, were not considered until all of the systems which had to be converted were functioning. Once all systems were operational, attention turned to moving student use to terminals and to modifying administrative and research applications to take advantage of the new capabilities of on-line computing.

Student access to the new machine really did not become a concern until the fall of 1974, as classes were able to continue using the IBM gear until it was removed at the end of March–almost coincident with the end of the semester. This meant that, during the conversion of administrative systems, Computer Centre personnel and those on loan from Xerox to aid with the conversion did not have to divide their attention between two groups of users.

3.4 The Formation of SaskComp

Prior to the acquisition of the Sigma 9 and concurrent with the activities of the two campuses of the University in determining their future computing needs, the provincial government found itself in a situation in which all of the major users of publicly-funded computing resources were

[12]CP-V was the name of the Sigma 9's operation system.

reassessing their needs for additional computing capacity (Barber 1991). These included the Crown Corporations[13] (such as Saskatchewan Power Corporation (SPC), Saskatchewan Telephone Company (SaskTel), Saskatchewan Government Insurance Corporation (SGIO)), the hospitals and the Government Computer Centre which supplied computing to all the government departments.

In such an environment it was unlikely that both campuses of the University, the Crown Corporations or the Government Computer Centre could get what each wanted or needed, due to the projected increase in size of the investment required–of the order of several million dollars.

As a result, the possibility of coordinating this entire acquisition activity was explored[14] to ensure that the Province would end up with the capacity and the type of computing resources it required, but not with costly excess capacity (Schroeder 1991). Without such coordination each of the user agencies would have attempted to acquire capacity for their current and projected future needs. This would have undoubtedly resulted in the acquisition of considerable excess capacity which would have increased the provincial computing bill. The other possible outcome to the non-coordinated acquisition could have been the acquisition of systems which would not at the time have met the users' needs, because the province would not have been able to afford the total bill. A number of individuals felt that the latter would have been the result of a non-coordinated approach–the acquisition of far less computing capacity in the province than the provincial needs called for.

Out of this exercise came a new Crown Corporation in April 1973, the Saskatchewan Computer Utility Corporation–SaskComp, whose mandate was to provide computing for all Government Departments, Crown Corporations, and Universities. SaskComp assumed the responsibility for operation of all of the machines possessed by this group of users, and all staff associated with the operation of these machines were transferred to SaskComp.

In February, 1974, the Sigma 9 became one of the three shared centres managed and operated by SaskComp. While SaskComp operated other centres, these other centres were intended to supply service only to the institution at which they were installed–SaskTel, SGIO, SPC. The three shared centres were created from the Government Computer Centre, located in Regina, and the Computer Centres at the two Campuses of the University–Regina and Saskatoon. These three centres under SaskComp

[13]A Crown Corporation is an enterprise which is wholly owned by the Government.

[14]The first formal meeting was held October 1, 1971. It brought together representatives from the University of Saskatchewan, the Saskatchewan Government Computer Centre and Treasury Board (Minutes of a Meeting to Discuss 'A Position Paper on University of Saskatchewan Computing as related to the Provincial Computing Community', October 1, 1971).

were to provide computing service to any government-funded agency on a fee-for-service basis. The new equipment installed at these three centres included an IBM 370/158 at what had been the Government Computer Centre and at the Saskatoon Campus, and the Xerox Sigma 9 at Regina Campus.

3.4.1 Effect of SaskComp on University Computing

At the outset, a major problem developed between the University and SaskComp due to the nature of computer utilization in an academic environment and SaskComp's desire to establish a fee-for-service contract with users based upon utilization. In a university environment there is considerable variability in utilization over time, particularly from student and research users. For example, a researcher may be a very heavy user for a period of time, then she may disappear back into her laboratory or office to obtain new data or write up the results obtained to date. Similarly, undergraduate student utilization is very dependent upon whether or not there is an assignment due or whether the university is in session.

SaskComp, upon assuming management of the University's computing, established a fee for service based upon a unit of machine time used. To do this they had taken a snapshot of the University's usage and assumed it to be representative. While this method of rate determination was satisfactory for university administrative computing, it did not reflect reality when it came to the bulk of the university's utilization–instruction and research.

With this fundamental disagreement over rates, the University and SaskComp entered into contract negotiations. While the general terms and conditions were quickly negotiated, no agreement could be reached on a rate structure. The University could not initially make the case for the uniqueness of its user community, and the rates established by SaskComp were projected to consume the University's yearly budget for computing in very much under a year's time–a budget that prior to the involvement with SaskComp was sufficient to pay for the total operation of the Sigma 9 and to restrict its use to only University users.

In an effort to demonstrate to SaskComp the uniqueness of its user base, the University contacted all its research users and asked them to postpone their computing activities for a period during these negotiations. Reluctantly, they agreed.

The effect of the University not using any computing for research was apparent to SaskComp immediately, as utilization and revenue dropped significantly. SaskComp, therefore, agreed that the university was different from its other users and this fact was incorporated into the rate structure which was agreed to in the contract. The rate for CPU utilization was based upon a variable rate structure: one rate for computing that was done in prime time (normal office hours); a discounted rate for non-prime time (evening) use; and a special rate for research users after midnight–no charge for computer time. The charge for disk usage, tape mounts and the consumption of supplies was separated from the CPU (computer time) rate and was not discounted, as these costs were essentially independent of the time of consumption.

While it took the University in Regina and SaskComp almost nine months to negotiate their contract, they reached an agreement which formed the basis of a close working relationship. The agreement distributed the usage across the day in a workable fashion and provided the University with a rate structure it could afford. The administrative computing was mainly performed during prime time. The students were, to a great extent, prime time users, but were significant users of non-prime-time computing as well. Research computing was divided into three categories: in prime time the researchers were provided with access to a small amount of time, additional access in non-prime time, with the bulk of their processing time being restricted to the after-midnight hours. Thus the majority of prime time research computing was limited to program development and debugging, with the majority of research production jobs being run after midnight.

After the University joined SaskComp, the name of the central computing facility was changed to more accurately reflect what it was involved with–service. The name was changed from Computer Centre to Department of Computing Services, for with the advent of SaskComp the University no longer operated any computing equipment, other than that associated with data entry.

At this time a number of individuals also felt that the incorporation of the word "service" into the name of the unit would act as a reminder to those involved that they were, as they had always been, a service unit for others on campus. For, regardless of the unit's name, the only reason for the creation of a computing facility, whether the unit operates equipment or purchases time, is to ensure that computing service is provided in the most effective way to the members of the institution–both academic and administrative members.

One of the largest benefits to the University derived from this contract was the access to research computing that it could not have afforded at the time, left to its own resources. The after-midnight rule was subsequently modified so that jobs were initiated in the evening after the majority of other customers had completed their work. The after-midnight arrangement for research computing was also extended to any machine in SaskComp's inventory, which as time passed extended to a number of very large and powerful machines–primarily IBM machines. Without SaskComp (and the original link between the two Campuses) the University would not have had access to these machines. This arrangement for research computing in off-peak hours survived the termination of the contract between the University and SaskComp and the transition of SaskComp from a Crown Corporation to a publicly traded company–Westbridge Computer Corporation[15]. Subsequently Westbridge has been restructured as Information Systems Management Corporation (ISM), of which IBM is the majority shareholder–51.4% (*The Globe and Mail*, June 4 1992:B2).

4. The Formation of the Computer Science Department

The creation of the Department of Computer Science was approved by Senate in 1968 (Arc68). Because of the newness of the discipline, the Department was not assigned to any of the existing Faculties; rather, it was created as a Campus Department and reported directly to the Vice Principal. The reasoning for this structure was to give the Department flexibility in the development of its programs, for the discipline affected all of the other faculties–Administration, Arts and Science, Education and Engineering. The initial appointment, Dr. Larry Symes, arrived on campus in late June, 1970. Prior to that time computing-related classes were offered by the Faculty of Administration and the Department of Mathematics (Tomkins 1991). In the fall of 1970, as an interim measure, the classes offered by Administration and Mathematics were assumed by the new Department but were offered under their old labels. An advisory committee was established that included representatives from all faculties to provide advice with respect to the creation of classes and degree programs in Computer Science. The Committee met frequently during that year and obtained approval for a package of classes and undergraduate degree programs that have essentially remained unchanged until a University-wide review of curriculum associated with the change from the 4/4 to the 5/3 Credit-Hour System, which is to be implemented in 1993.

In the spring of 1970 when Dr. Symes was considering on offer to come to Regina Campus to form a Computer Science Department, the position of Director of the Computer Centre was also vacant. This was a significant factor in his decision to come to the University. For, while he was at Purdue University, he had witnessed the result of what can occur when operational control of the Computer Centre and the Computer Science Department is divided between two individuals. At that institution when control of the Centre was separated from the Head of the Computer Science Department, albeit another member of the Department. The result was that a great deal of tension developed between the two individuals and consequently the two units. The primary reason for this tension is the different objectives of the two units.

---

[15]There was still significant participation in Westbridge through shares held by the SaskTel.

A computer science department is primarily interested in the creation and dissemination of knowledge. This requires experimentation with either the hardware or the operating system or both. On the other hand, a computer centre is primarily interested in maximizing the service it provides to the largest number of users possible. Conflict develops because computer science is just one of the user groups for which the computer centre is attempting to provide service and when the department's faculty members or students are given special attention, the overall level of service provided by the computer centre to others is likely to be diminished.

During the initial development period of both a computing centre and a computer science department, it may be beneficial to combine these units in such a way that they report to a single individual. Such a structure permits the two units to grow and develop together, thereby reducing conflict and providing time for these two units, as well as other user groups on campus, to mature.

In the fall of 1971, Dr. Lee was appointed as the second faculty member in the Department. He stayed for just one year. Then Dr. Brien Maguire joined in the fall of 1972. Subsequently, to replace Dr. Lee on a temporary basis, Mr. Peter LeQuesne was appointed for one year. In the next year, two more people were appointed, Dr. D. Pradham to replace Mr. LeQuesne and Dr. Larry Saxton to fill a newly created permanent position. By the fall of 1991 the Department had grown so that it had 14 faculty positions, four laboratory instructor positions and three technical support staff (one software system manager and two hardware technicians).

On January 1, 1972, the Department, after considerable debate, lost its status as a Campus Department and was assigned to a Faculty–the Faculty of Arts and Science. Specifically, it was placed in the Division of Natural Sciences and Mathematics[16].

The Department was successful in attracting students. It also spent a great deal of time doing off-campus work, teaching classes in Yorkton, Melville, Swift Current and various other areas in the province. These activities had a significant effect on increasing the profile, not only of the Computer Science program, but of the University.

4.1 Industry's Demand of CS Graduates

There was a considerable apprehension by some companies about the hiring of Computer Science degree holders, for it was felt in the early 1970's that such individuals were not as well trained (in the specifics such as JCL–Job Control Language), and consequently were not as useful, as the

[16]On July 1, 1974 the Faculty of Arts and Science was separated into two separate faculties. What had been the Division of Natural Sciences and Mathematics became the Faculty of Science and the balance became the Faculty of Arts.

graduates of two-year programs offered by technical institutes, which had heretofore supplied all of their demands.

A significant change occurred when SaskTel hired one of the Department's graduates. Previously they had relied completely on the graduates for one of the Province's two year technical institutes. It was not long before this individual was standing out amongst all his peers with respect to what he could and could not do. As a result this individual created a demand which led to the wider acceptance of the program's graduates.

A few years after this, another Regina-based firm, The Co-operators Data Services Limited, hired the whole graduating class of the Department. Those graduates are now scattered throughout Canada, some in very senior positions within that organization.

4.2 The Graduate Program

In 1975 the Department proposed a graduate program leading to a Master's of Science degree (Arc76). This proposal received all of the required approvals on the Campus but was subsequently turned down by the University Grants Commission. The negative decision with respect to the graduate program was a critical blow to the Department; Dr. Pradham left, and the introduction of new developments was severely retarded during the next two years.

Finally in 1985 the Department did receive approval to offer a Masters program (Maguire 1991) and in 1991 the Department received approval for the final piece of its graduate program, its Ph.D. program. The graduate program activities of the department are now amongst the largest and most vigorous at the University.

4.3 The Development of Departmental Laboratories

4.3.1 Minicomputers

In the early 1970's, the Computer Science Department was having problems in getting the type and amount of service it required from the Computer Centre, especially for introductory classes and some of the upper-level classes (Maguire 1991). At that time, access was delivered by the IBM 360/40 running MFT–a batch system. The Department wanted to get access to some form of time-sharing facility and to its own dedicated batch facility. The batch service was required because there are a number of concepts associated with, for example, operating systems, such as device drivers and scheduling algorithms, which can not be demonstrated or for which assignments can not be given if all that is available is a computing system which is used to support general computing. Hence, the Department acquired a PDP[17] 11/20 in the Fall of 1973 and a PDP 11/10 in the Spring of 1974.

---

[17]PDP is a registered trademark of Digital Equipment Corporation.

When the PDP 11/20 first arrived on campus it was used as single-user system. Later after the arrival of the PDP 11/10, the PDP 11/20 was used as a time-sharing system in support of an introductory class, CS 102, which introduced the students to on-line computing and the programming language BASIC. The operating system used to support this was RSTS (Resource-sharing Timesharing System). The PDP 11/10 was used primarily as a single user system running DOS (Disk Operating System). Its purpose was to give students direct access to hardware and related software, without the constraints that were normally placed on them when they used a shared facility such as that provided by the Computing Centre.

In practice the PDP-11/20 could also be switched to its initial use–single-user DOS from multi-user RSTS. Further, students were encouraged to do the switching on their own. To do this, they just loaded a different disk pack and rebooted the machine. This practice created a conflict between the senior students who would want to run DOS and the 100 level students who wanted to run the RSTS system.

The primary purposes of the laboratories were three:

1. BASIC and time-sharing for the introductory service class.
2. Assembler Language and Computer Architecture–second year class for majors.
3. Special projects for senior students.

As funds became available and as new members joined the PDP-11 family such machines were acquired. Some of the major acquisitions by the Computer Science Department, along with their date of acquisition, are given below[18]:

IMLAC PDS-1	Fall 1971
PDP 11/20	Fall 1972
PDP 11/10	Spring 1973
PDP 11/40	Fall 1975
PDP 11/34	Winter 1976
PDP 11/15	Winter 1977
Cromenco Z-2D	Summer 1978
Commodore PET	Summer 1978
SWTP 6800	Winter 1978
PDP 11/23[19]	Spring 1982
VAX 730	Fall 1982
Apple IIe	Summer 1983

[18]In the case of micro computers and workstations only the first of a type has been noted.

[19]The Department currently has 12 PDP-11/23's in an undergraduate laboratory.

6	PDP 11/40's	Spring 1984
	IBM PC-XT	Fall 1984
	VAX 750	Fall 1984
	SUN II Workstation	Winter 1984
3	PDP 11/44	Summer 1985
	VAX 750	Summer 1985[20]
	Apple Macintosh	Summer 1985
	IRIS 4D/20 Workstation	Summer 1988
	IRIS 4D/60 Workstation	Summer 1988
	MIPS M120 Risc	Summer 1988
	SUN Sparcstation 1+	May 1989
	IRIS 4D/25 Workstation	Summer 1989
	SUN III Workstation	Summer 1989
	MIPS M120 Risc	Summer 1989
	SUN Sparcstation 2	May 1991
	IBM RS/6000 Workstation	Summer 1991
	MIPS RC 3330	December 1991
	Indigo XS 24	April 1992

As the hardware changed, so too did the software that the Department employed. Some of the operating systems used included–RSX-11M (Real-Time Multiprogramming Executive Operating System), RT-11 (Real-Time Operating System–a small single-user system which supported foreground job execution and background interactive or batch program development) and UNIX[21] (*cf.* section 4.3.2).

When the Department started to develop its own laboratories, hardware was more expensive than it is now. At one point, 1975, the Department bought a memory upgrade for the PDP 11/20, which took the machine from 48KB (Kilo Bytes) to 56KB–the maximum memory for the machine (Maguire 1991). The cost for the upgrade was $0.50 per byte and consumed the whole of the Department's equipment budget for the year. The technology has come a long way, for today it is very common to have personal computers with 8MB (Mega Bytes) of memory and the total cost of the machine including memory, colour monitor, and hard disk is considerably less than the price of the memory upgrade for the PDP 11/20.

The high cost of maintenance was partially due to the fact that Digital did not at the time have an office in Regina, and thus a maintenance call resulted in the extra costs associated with bringing a technician in from one of the neighbouring provinces–Alberta or Manitoba. This prompted the Department to hire its own technician and to start performing its own

[20]Transferred from the Computer Centre to the Computer Science Department.

[21]UNIX is a registered trademark of AT & T Bell Laboratories.

maintenance. The development of the expertise associated with this function had the added benefit of permitting the Department to acquire hardware from third party manufacturers and from used equipment vendors.

Given the popularity of the PDP-11 family a significant number of companies entered the compatibles market, producing a number of different pieces of hardware from memory and disk drives to various controllers, at prices which were considerably below the prices of DEC supplied equivalents. In 1976 the Department purchased three 2.5MB disk drives from a supplier in Arizona, Wangco. The degree of competition in this market was demonstrated when, as it came time to deliver and install the drives, they arrived along with two company employees who did the installation (Maguire 1991).

4.3.2 UNIX

Around the time when the 11/34 and 11/40 were acquired, in 1976, the Department started running UNIX, an operating system developed at Bell Labs, and became one of the first 100 universities in the world to do so (Maguire 1991).

Initially the acquisition of UNIX was very much a word of mouth affair. The first time Dr. Maguire heard about it was in June of 1975 from Dr. Bob Kavanagh, a member of the Computational Science Department at the University of Saskatchewan. They had been one of the first 35 universities to acquire their copy of UNIX. The primary reason for acquiring UNIX, in addition to its low cost (approximately $300 US–which included the cost of the tape, documentation and other incidentals), was its functionality and ease of use. UNIX was an operating system that the student could both comprehend and modify, for while it was not extremely sophisticated, it did provide the necessary functionality and it was an open system–documentation and source code were provided. Consequently, it became the tool of choice for most operating system classes nation-wide. Its adoption was also aided by the fact that it ran on a line of affordable hardware and the cost of updates, like the initial purchase price of the software, was minimal.

The popularity of UNIX within the academic world increased markedly. Quickly almost every CS Department in North America had a copy.

5. The Re-establishment of On-Campus Computing

5.1 The VAX System for Undergraduate Computing

While the contract between the University and SaskComp did not explicitly permit the Computer Science Department to acquire hardware, the relationship which developed did. When SaskComp was created the Department already had acquired its first machines, and they were not included in the contract between the University and SaskComp at that time or later. Rather, as long as there was a sound pedagogic justification for the acquisition of a system and it did not substantially impact on SaskComp's position as a supplier to the University, the acquisition was not challenged.

In 1978, because of the growth of the Department's undergraduate program (the introductory class alone had grown to approximately 700 students per semester), the Department was forced to investigate computing alternatives. The equipment in its laboratories (PDP-11's) was not sufficient, nor was there enough money available in the budget to purchase additional time from SaskComp.

The Department explored a number of alternatives and ultimately decided that the acquisition of a PRIME 750 would be the most cost-effective solution. SaskComp was approached with the Department's needs and proposed solution. They understood the problem but were concerned with their position as supplier to all governmental departments, the Crowns and the Universities. In the time since the creation of SaskComp the functionality of systems had increased dramatically while their cost had decreased just as dramatically. This, in turn, led to pressure from more and more of the user population to be permitted to acquire their own systems.

The result was that the University was offered a very special rate for undergraduate student computing which used the Sigma 9. Undergraduate computing was not restricted to the Sigma 9, but the rates for non-Sigma 9 (IBM) computing remained unchanged. This special deal involved a fixed rate for almost unlimited Sigma 9 student computing. This could be done because the Sigma 9 had undergone several upgrades which had substantially improved its performance, thereby allowing for a substantial increase in its user base and its associated revenue generation capacity.

Finally in October 1982 the University acquired a Digital Equipment Corporation VAX 11/750, the University's first computer for general academic computing since it had obtained the Sigma 9 in the fall of 1973. By so doing and with the tacit approval of SaskComp, the University started to re-establish itself as a provider to both its academic and administrative users. The reason for the drift away from SaskComp was the high cost of mainframe computing when compared to the cost of the new mid-range and super-mini computers. Technology had reached the point where it was possible to buy computing in much smaller units and the price performance of these units was comparable to that previously provided only on large mainframe computers.

5.2 Academic Computing and Systems and Analytical Services

In the late 1970's neither the academic nor the administrative users felt that they were getting the type or the amount of service that they required. As a result the University, after an external review, decided to reorganize computing on campus. A new department of Academic Computing was given responsibility for providing computing related services to the academic community. Responsibility for major administrative systems was distributed to the three main user departments. And a second new department, Systems and Analytical Services, was created to combine the functions of Institutional Research, data administration[22] for administrative systems and coordination of administrative systems acquisition.

When this separation (Southam 1992) occurred the individuals who were working for the Department of Computing Services were assigned to one or the other of the new organizations or to one of the existing three main administrative user departments, based upon where the majority of their time and effort had previously been spent. Academic Computing was given some analyst support so that it could provide consulting to the academic community. It was also given the technical personnel and responsibility for the maintenance of terminals and communications switching gear for the whole of the institution, while data-entry personnel were assigned to the Registrar's office and the Business office. The assignment of these latter two groups was based upon the fact that the majority of the terminals in place supported either teaching or research and the majority of the demand for data entry emanated from these two administrative users .

The two most radical changes were with respect to budgeting and management of personnel associated with administrative computing in an effort to control costs and to improve service (Southam 1992). At the time there were three departments primarily involved with administrative computing:

- the business office
- the registrar's office
- the Library.

Of these systems, only the student information system, run by the registrar's office, had been completely designed, built and run at the University of Regina. In the case of the business office, the major component of their system UNIFACTS, was run in conjunction with the University of Saskatchewan, in Saskatoon; the Library purchased a significant amount of its information processing needs from the University of Toronto Library–UTLAS.

The two radical changes made were:

> All of the programmer analysts, except for two, were transferred out of the central organization, Computing Services, to the user departments–the registrar's office, the business office and the Library. The two which remained were kept in Systems and

---

[22]If the University at the time had been using databases then the assigned function would have been that of "Database Administrator"

Analytical Services so that they had staff who could be used to satisfy requests from other administrative areas on campus that required, or would require, support but did not need the services of a full-time individual.

The budget for computing was also transferred to these three units. This included the funding required to pay the salaries and benefits of the transferred personnel, as well as the money required to purchase computer time. This included the money to purchase outside services such as those purchased from SaskComp, the University of Saskatchewan and the University of Toronto.

5.3 New Administrative Systems

The decision to acquire, in 1983, new systems (Southam 1992) for the registrar's office, business office and personnel office was driven primarily by deficiencies which had been identified in the registrar's student information system in the mid 1970's (after the system had been transferred to the Sigma 9). The system could barely handle the normal day-to-day demands which were placed upon it, let alone provide departments, faculties, or members of the University's senior management team with the management information they required to satisfy both their own needs and that requested of them by outside agencies. Another factor which contributed to the need to acquire new systems was the fact that systems were not integrated. For example, the student information system could not share data with the financial system run by the business office.

When the proposal for acquisition of these systems was put forward, it was proposed that the one million dollars required for both the hardware and software be capitalized over the estimated useful life of each component–the hardware over a five year period and the software over a seven year period. There was more than enough money in the computing budgets of the business office and registrar's office to annually make the required payment for the hardware. It was proposed that the annualized cost of the software be distributed to the user departments in proportion to their use and that their share of this cost be assumed by their existing budgets, as no additional funding was to be given to them to cover the cost of the software. The proposal would have required these departments to make some modifications to their budgets in order to absorb these charges.

Based upon advice from the Provincial Auditor (Southam 1992), the proposal to capitalize was not, however, implemented. This resulted in the whole cost, hardware and software, being expensed in one year. This resulted in a deficit for the University and reduced the pressure on the user departments to come up with their proposed share of the software cost.

5.4 Computing Services

After an external review of computing, conducted during the spring and summer of 1983, the University concluded that Academic Computing and Systems & Analytical Services should be rejoined into a single unit, and that the budgets and personnel to support administrative computing which had been distributed in 1980 (*cf.* section 5.2) be returned to this single unit. While the personnel were returned to the central organization for reasons which included long term planning, training, performance evaluation and backup support, they were left in the offices that they were occupying in the user departments.

In October 1983, the Department of Computing Services was re-created. Mr. N. Southam assumed the role of Acting Director, and a search was initiated to find someone from outside the institution to assume this role on a permanent basis. In May of 1984 Mr. G. Peardon, who had previously been associated with the Computer Centre at Saskatoon Campus in the 1960's and the University Systems Study Group when there were two campuses in the 1970's, rejoined the university sector from industry to head the newly re-created Department.

The review also recommended significant changes in the reporting/advisory structure for the Department. Although the Director was to continue reporting to the Vice-President Academic through the Associate Vice-President Academic, and there would continue to be committee(s) of users to advise the Director, the report recommended the establishment of a Policy Committee, to be chaired by the Associate Vice-President Academic. This committee was to aid the Director in the formulation of policy- and budget-related decisions. In addition to the Associate Vice-President Academic and the Director of Computing Services, the Committee was composed of senior academic and administrative personnel concerned with computing: the Vice-President Administrative Services, the Associate Vice-President Facilities, the Director of University Services, the Associate Vice-President Research, the Dean of Science, the Head of Computer Science and the Chair of the Academic Users Committee.

This Committee, which still exists, can be viewed as a "Board of Directors" acting on behalf of the President of the University who is the sole shareholder of the Department of Computing Services.

5.5 The Termination of the Contract with SaskComp

The contractual agreement between the University and SaskComp terminated amicably in the summer of 1984. A portion of the rationale for the creation of SaskComp had disappeared since its formation–the price of hardware decreased and its functionality increased dramatically. This was a major factor in the termination of the contract. Another factor was the poor fit between the universities and the other clients that SaskComp served. The universities' student population was always an area of concern with respect to the security of data files and unauthorized access. Another factor was the change in government in the Province in the spring of 1982. This was accompanied by philosophical change, which resulted in a reduction in the degree of central governmental control. Consequently, the Sigma 9 was returned to the University of Regina on July 1, 1984, for the nominal price of one dollar and the University reassumed the role of provider for the majority of its computing needs.

By the first of January 1985, the University was operating 5 VAX 11/750's–two in support of general academic computing with 56 terminal lines each, two in support of administrative users in the Registrar, Personnel and Business offices also with 56 terminal lines each, and one by the Computer Science Department with 48 lines in support of its laboratories (The Granule 1985).

On 14 February, 1985, over eleven years after the acquisition of the Sigma 9, Computing Services held a farewell party (*The Granule* 1985, Saunders 1991) which was attended by many of those who had been associated with the University at the time of the machine's arrival and those who had been users of it during its service bureau days with SaskComp. Larry Symes, who had been the Director of the Computer Centre when it was purchased, was given the honour of shutting the machine down for the final time. This involved having the CP-V operating system shut itself down and having the machine play "O Canada[23]" on its speaker until the power was cut off.

In the summer of 1985 the University replaced the centrally operated VAX 11/750's with two medium-sized mainframes–a DEC 8600 and an IBM 4381. One of the VAX 11/750's was transferred (and moved) to the Department of Computer Science, one was allocated to the Faculty of Engineering for its use and two were sold to Agriculture Canada. In 1992 the central facility on campus, Computing Services, operates an upgraded version of the IBM 4381, two DEC 6320's and an IBM RS/6000. However, there is more computing located elsewhere on campus which has been acquired by departments to support the teaching programs, by research groups to support their research activities, and by individuals to support their individual needs (with PC's which today are more powerful than the IBM 360/40).

5.6 Integrated Library System

After the acquisition of systems in 1984, the library system was the only major system which had not been renewed since the arrival of the Sigma 9 in 1973. Further, a significant portion of the library's system was run off campus–UTLAS. In August of 1987 requests for proposals were sent out to the vendors who supplied library systems. In October of that year a

---

[23]National Anthem of Canada.

committee, composed of librarians, academics and administrators, was brought together to evaluate the proposals which were received and in December of 1987 and January 1988 six bidders were invited to come to the campus and demonstrate their product. Shortly after these demonstrations, the number of bidders was reduced to a short list of three. The committee then made arrangements to visit a number of sites which were running these systems so that first hand experience could be obtained from other users. The committee then reviewed the library's recommendation against criteria which had been developed and a final selection was made at the end of February. The contract with the vendor was not signed, however, until August 1988, as it took until then to negotiate terms which were acceptable to both parties. Portions of the system were implemented immediately (cataloguing) but the library's data base was not functional until the end of the year. Initially, the data base consisted mainly of the records which were converted from UTLAS format to the new NOTIS system's format. (The library named its new system Murlin.) The materials acquired prior to the use of UTLAS were not in machine readable form, and for a period of time there were two catalogues in use–the old card catalogue and the machine readable catalogue which could be accessed from a terminal in the library or any other terminal or microcomputer attached to the University's network.

The conversion of the non machine readable portions of the catalogue was greatly aided by the lease of a CD-ROM based catalogue conversion system. It provided the University with CD-ROMs and software which could be used to search the CDs for catalogue records which were not previously in machine readable form.

6. Data Communications and Computer Networks

6.1 Data Communications

The first computer network was installed on campus shortly after the installation of the Sigma 9. Prior to the arrival of the Sigma 9, the Computer Centre was allocated a block of one hundred telephone lines on the University's telephone exchange. It was intended that users who required on-line access would either have their terminal hard-wired to the computer or (if they were not heavy users) have an acoustic coupler to make their connection through their telephone. Those connected by hard-wiring would have their terminal connected to the computer by a dedicated line and they would continually tie up a terminal port on the computer. Those connected by an acoustic coupler would connect to the computer by means of the telephone in their work area, so that the port on the computer would only be assigned to them when they needed it and consequently the port could be shared amongst users. The one hundred telephone lines were thought to be more than adequate for some time as the initial configuration would permit fewer than one hundred terminals to be connected to it. This assumption was incorrect, because it was quickly determined that the campus telephone switch was designed to accommodate only sixteen active lines per block of one hundred lines (numbers) and as a result only sixteen users could use this method to access the machine at one time.

Consequently, an alternative had to be found. It involved the installation of a second communications switch, a PACX unit from Gandalf, which did not have the above limitation, and a second set of lines to points where terminal access to computing was required. Although this was a costly and time-consuming project, in part because buildings had not been designed to accommodate two communications networks, there were the advantages of greater speed, reliability and convenience–the telephone was still available for voice communications. Further, the system permitted users to access any computer from any terminal. Initially this was a feature used only by the members of the Computer Science Department, providing access to the Sigma 9 and the PDP-11/20.

This system was replaced in the early 1980's jointly by the Computer Science Department and Computing Services with a system from Develcon. Part of the rationale behind this change was the movement of the Computer Science laboratories from an area adjacent to the Computer Centre to a different building. The Develcon switches provided the ability to connect terminals in a building or area to a separate switch and then tie that switch into a network of switches, thereby eliminating the need to string each line from the terminal to the central switch and lines back from the central switch to the now widely-dispersed time-sharing systems around campus.

The Computer Science Department participated in the creation of this new network so as to allow their students to access any machine from any terminal, for until the introduction of the Develcon switches[24] the majority of the Department's terminals were hard-wired to their machines and the terminals that had been acquired by Computing Services while on the old switch could not be used to access departmental machines. As a result groups of terminals would be over subscribed while other were sitting idle.

In the mid 1980's a separate Ethernet network was installed between a limited number of locations for those users who required high-speed communication–shared file service, for the university's first workstation.

The University is currently migrating from the Develcon switch technology to packet switching and FDDI (Fiber Distributed Data Interface) network with the support of a grant from Digital Equipment Corporation (UofRnet 1992). The new network[25], which should be completely installed by early 1993, is based upon a 100 Mbits/sec (megabits per sec) FDDI backbone,

---

[24]By 1992 access to computing across computes is provided to 1,226 offices, laboratories, and work areas (Still 1992; see fn. 3 in Chapter 5).

[25]When installed the network will provide access to 1,684 offices, laboratories, classrooms and work areas.

with 10 Mbits/sec communications via IEEE 802.3 (Ethernet) standard radiating out from the backbone to classrooms, laboratories and offices. These connections will be accomplished with unshielded twisted pair (UTP) cable. Extra fiber will be laid in order to support future communication technologies such as multimedia.

6.2 Computer Networking

The HASP to HASP and later the CP-V to HASP link, which originally was used to link the two campuses of the University, was the first exposure the University had to the use of computer networks.

The second was UUCP (UNIX to UNIX CoPy), a UNIX user network. In the late 1970's, the Computer Science Department linked one of their machines into the UUCP network via a dial-up line to a machine in Saskatoon which in turn was connected again via a dial-up line to a machine at the University of Alberta in Edmonton. This permitted daily connection to other UNIX machines connected to the network across North America. This network was primarily used to share software, exchange information concerning the status of UNIX, and act as a conduit for E-mail. A great deal of the traffic on the network was between members of Computer Science Departments–particularly between their graduate students.

The reason for the once-a-day access to the network was cost. Instead of leasing dedicated lines to connect the Universities of Regina and Saskatchewan to the network, the two institutions used a coordinated dial-up arrangement to access a machine at the University of Alberta which was connected to the network via a dedicated line. At a pre-specified time in the early morning the machine at the University of Saskatchewan would dial-up the machine at the University of Alberta and retrieve all the mail for itself and the University of Regina and would transmit all queued outgoing mail. Later, the machine at Regina would connect itself to the machine at the University of Saskatchewan and receive and send its mail.

In October 1985, the University of Regina joined NetNorth, a cross-Canada network designed to link universities and research institutes in Canada together and to their counterparts world-wide. NetNorth was connected to other national and regional networks (in the USA, Europe and Japan) via a gateway at Guelph University in Ontario. IBM aided the establishment of NetNorth by providing a grant to cover the cost of line charges for the first three years.

In March 1991 the connection was changed from NetNorth on Bitnet to Sask#net on CA*net on Internet. The national CA*net and the various provincial sub-networks had expanded functionality and speed when compared to NetNorth. For example, the maximum speed of NetNorth was 9.6 kilo bits per second while the speed of CA*net is 56 kilo bits per second.

General access by members of the University to such a national/international network greatly changed the working habits and needs of a significant number of individuals who previously neither wanted nor required access to a computer. Access to the central facility from almost all offices and laboratories now became a requirement, so that faculty and staff could use the University's central computer as a gateway and hence have access to networks, electronic mail, and the various subscription services they desired.

7. Summary–Major Equipment

Below is a list of the major pieces of computing equipment (mainframes and minicomputers) which have been installed at the University of Regina, the date of acquisition and the unit which placed the order if other than the central organization–computing services:

- Nov. 1963 IBM 1620
- Aug. 1966 IBM 1130 (replaced 1620)
- Aug. 1969 IBM 360/40 (replaced 1130)
- Oct. 1973 Xerox Sigma 9 (replaced 360/40)
- Oct. 1982 Digital VAX 750
- Nov. 1982 Digital VAX 730 Computer Science
- Fall 1983 3 Digital VAX 750's
- Fall 1984 1 Digital VAX 750 Computer Science
- Feb. 1985 Digital VAX 785
- Aug. 1985 IBM 4381 Digital 8600 (together replaced 4 VAX 750's)
- Apr. 1987 Prime 9650[26] Geography/Engineering/ Physical Plant
- Apr. 1988 IBM 4381 upgraded
- Jul. 1988 Digital VAX 6310 (replaced VAX 785)
- June 1989 2 Digital VAX 6320's (replaced 8600 and VAX 6310)

Current diversification and penetration of computing is shown by the following list of computer-based laboratory facilities which are in existence now on campus:

[26]Upgraded in 1988 to a model 9755.

Biology Department
- 5 - 8088 based PCs

Chemistry Department
- 5 80486 based PCs
- 5 80386 based PCs
- 1 80286 based PCs

Computer Science Department
- 34 - Zenith, 8086's
- 13 - Packard Bell, 80386's
- 31 - DEC, 80386's
- 15 - Macintosh, SE's
- 5 - Macintosh, Quadra's

Computing Services
- 16 - Zenith 8086's

German and Slavic Studies
- 5 - 8088 based PC's

Faculty of Administration
- 30 - Zenith 8088's

Faculty of Arts
- 18 - Cougar[27] 80486's (Networked - 17 + 1 server)

Faculty of Art Language Laboratory
- 21 - Zenith 80286's
- 1 - Zenith 80386
- 1 - 80486 based PC.

Faculty of Engineering

Industrial Systems Engineering
- 4 - 8088 based PCs
- 4 - 80386 based PCs
- 1 - 80486 based PC
- 15 - IBM 286's in Autodesk supported AutoCAD lab.
- 12 - IBM 386's in Autodesk supported AutoCAD lab.

Electronic Information Systems Engineering
- 10 - 80286 based PC's
- 2 - 80386 based PC's
- 1 - 80486 based PC
- 3 - Sun SPARC workstations

Regional Systems Engineering
- 1 - 8088 based PC
- 3 - 80386 based PCs
- 1 - 80486 based PCs

Faculty of Education

---

[27]The Cougar is assembled by the Computing Services Department, University of Regina (*cf.* Chapter 5, Section 3.4).

- 20 - 8088 based PCs
- 2 - 80286 based PCs
- 2 - Macintosh

Geography Department

- 4 - 80286 based PCs
- 5 - 80386 based PCs
- 1 - 80486 based PC

Saskatchewan Indian Federated College

- 13 - IBM 80386's (Networked - 12 + 1 server)

University Extension

- 10 - 8088 based Laptops (for a Distance Education Class)
- 16 - 80386 based PC's

Bibliography

1. References

Arbuckle, R. A. "Computer Analysis and Throughput Evaluation." *Computer and Automation*, Jan. 1966, 13-15,19. (Arbuckle 1966).

Grenberger, F. "Are Small Free-standing Computers Here to Stay?" *DATAMATION*, April 1966, 67-68. (Grenberger 1966).

Hillegass, J. R. "Hardware Evaluation". *DPMA Proceedings* VIII (1965), 391-392. (Hillegass 1965).

Joslin, E. O. *Computer Selection*. Reading, Mass.: Addison-Wesley Publications Inc., 1968. (Joslin 1968).

Knight, K. E. *A Study of Technological Innovation - The Evaluation of Digital Computers*. Doctoral dissertation, Carnegie Inst. of Technology, IV-5, IV-6, IV-7. Nov. 1963. (Knight 1963).

Sharpe, W. *The Economics of Computers.* New York: Columbia University Press, 1969. (Sharpe 1969).

Solomon, M. B. Jr. "Economics of Scale and IBM System/360". *Communications of the ACM*, June 1966, 435-440.(Solomon 1966).

2. Interviews

Barber, 1991	Interview with Dr. Lloyd Barber, Dec. 2, 1991.
Carter, 1992	Interview with Bob Carter, Feb. 13, 1992.
Dennis, 1991	Interview with Al Dennis, July 16, 1991.
Holden, 1991	Interview with Liz Holden, July 3, 1991.
Maguire, 1991	Interview with Dr. R. Brien Maguire, July 22, 1991.
Peardon, 1991	Interview with Glenn Peardon, July 2, 1991.
Purse, 1991	Interview with Ross Purse, Oct. 7, 1991.
Schroeder, 1991	Interview with Iann Schroeder, Sept. 10, 1991.
Tomkins, 1991	Interview with R. J. Tomkins, July 11, 1991.
Van Eyck, 1991	Interview with Peter van Eyck, Sept. 9, 1991.

3. Other sources

Achtemichuk, Larry L. Correspondence to L. R. Symes, Mar. 9, 1992. (Achtemichuk 1992).

Item C, Minutes of Division of Natural Sciences, University of Saskatchewan, Regina Campus, December 4, 1963. (Arc63).

Memo. No. 106.09.01(8) from A. B. van Cleave to W. A. Riddell regarding computer time charges for graduate students, Oct. 3, 1966. (Arc66).

Memo. No. 06.09.01 (30) from L. L. Achtemichuk to W.A. Riddell regarding computer centre operations, Feb. 21, 1967. (Arc67a).

Memo. No. 106.09.01(49) from W. A. Riddell to A. B. van Cleave regarding rental of time and higher speed units, Apr. 24, 1967. (Arc67b).

Memo. No. 106.09.01(39) from W. A. Riddell to S. G. Mann regarding administrative control of computer centre, Mar. 13, 1967. (Arc67c).

Item 13, University of Saskatchewan Senate Minutes, Nov. 1, 1968. (Arc68).

Item 6.7.1, University of Regina Council Minutes, Jan. 14, 1976. (Arc76).

Personal communication between L. R. Symes and N. Southam. (Southam 1992).

Kaller, Cecil. Correspondence, CIDA/INDIA Project 101.07 and 106.09.02, May 1, 1992. (Kaller 1992).

Mack, Tony. Correspondence, CIDA/INDIA Project 101.07, Aug. 19, 1991. (Mack 1991).

The Granule, (Computing Services Newsletter), 11, 1 (Feb. 1985). (The Granule 1985).

UofRnet News, March 1992. (UofRnet 1992).

Saunders, Eileen. Paper by third year Journalism student, CIDA/India Project 101.07, March 19, 1991. (Saunders 1991).

Turnbull, Colin C. Correspondence, Aug. 31, 1991. (Turnbull 1991).

Acknowledgements

I would like to express my appreciation to Mr. N. Wang, Mr. V. Gupta, and Mr. B. S. Christian, graduate students in the Computer Science Department at the University of Regina, for their efforts in collecting information from personnel files and the University Archives, and to Ms. Shelley Sweeney of the University Archives for all of her invaluable assistance. Special recognition must be noted of Mr. Christian for the preparation of an early draft of this history of computing at the University of Regina and his interviewing of a large number of the people who had been associated with computing at the University.

APPENDIX B

UNIVERSITY OF REGINA SPRING TRAINING PROGRAMMES

Introduction

Ideally, all institutions undergoing a process of computerization will have a cadre of product champions, or at least personnel with some degree of knowledge of and competence in the use of a variety of hardware and applications software. To ensure that this was the case with some of the universities in India that are in the process of computerization, the University of Regina, in collaboration with the team from India, developed a training programme at the University of Regina.

Three training sessions, each lasting about six weeks, were held at the University of Regina in May and June of 1990, 1991 and 1992. For each session thirteen individuals came to the University of Regina; twelve were trainees and one was a member of the Indian research team. Tables 1 and 2 give the areas and the institutions that the trainees were drawn from. Twenty four came from the State of Gujarat while twelve were from elsewhere in India.

Table 1

Area	1990	1991	1992	Total
Computer Systems/ Computer Science	5	2	1	8
Natural Sciences	4			4
Social Sciences	3	2	2	7
Languages		2		2
Education		2	3	5
Librarians		4		4
Business			2	2
Mathematics			2	2
Administrators			2	2

Table 2

Institution	1990	1991	1992	Total
Gujarat University	5	4	6	15
Indian Space Research Organization	1	1	1	3
Bharathiar University	2	1	1	4
Aligarh Muslim University	1	1	1	3
M.S. University of Baroda		1	1	2
Sardar Patel University			1	1
North East Hill University	1	1	1	3
Gujarat Vidyapith		1		1
Central Institute of Indian Languages		1		1
SNDT Women's University		1		1
Vikram Sarabhai Science Center	1			1
South Gujarat University	1			1

Objectives of Training Programme

The programme was designed with several goals in mind and these determined, to a large extent, the content and organization of the sessions. The key objectives or goals were:

1. To introduce the Project.
2. To introduce the university system in Canada, thus providing a context for the computerization process at the University of Regina.
3. To familiarize participants with the role played by computers in teaching, research, library services and administration at a Canadian university.
4. To introduce and teach some of the important microcomputer software packages presently available and useful for academics.

5. To have the participants attempt some practical application of one or more software packages by requiring them to undertake a small project and to present it in a seminar setting.
6. To broaden the cultural, social, geographical and educational horizons of the participants through a number of "extra curricular" tours, social events and outings.

Typical Organization

The precise organizational and scheduling details of the training sessions varied somewhat from year to year as the Regina team learned from the previous year's session as well as to meet needs of the specific group of trainees. The following organizational pattern was typical:

1. Introduction to the University of Regina, the goals of the project, and university education in Canada.
2. Familiarization with University facilities including computing facilities, networks, and the libraries.
3. Training sessions in the use of networks and E-mail.
4. Hands-on training sessions in a variety of microcomputer software packages such as word processing (Microsoft Word), spreadsheets (Lotus 1-2-3), data bases (dBase IV), presentation packages (Harvard Graphics), authoring packages (ToolBook). Instruction in software installation was also carried out.
5. Encouragement and support to participants as they developed a proposal for their individual projects. Assistance was given to the trainees to facilitate work in their disciplines or areas of interest by linking them with others in similar fields at the University, or outside if necessary.
6. Presentation of a series of formal sessions with University of Regina employees involved in virtually every area of the administrative use of computing, including registration, student counselling, admissions, budgeting, accounting, personnel and payroll. A number of the administrative systems were demonstrated to trainees and, in some cases, panels of users as well as individuals from Computing Services were called on to provide as many voices and perspectives as possible.
7. Panel discussions and presentations with a variety of academics from different disciplines and faculties to illustrate the use of computing in teaching and research. The participants were able to learn about some special computerized projects, and to see various computer laboratories and multi-media rooms.
8. Presentations by computer professionals from the business community to discuss current trends and the likely future in computer hardware and software.

9. Provision of afternoon sessions for individual project preparation in weeks 3, 4 and 5 of the training programme, with assistance from the Canadian team when required. In the last week three days were allocated for individual project presentations and discussions.
10. Intermingling social events, tours, and special outings throughout the training programme to encourage a broad range of educational, social and cultural experiences.
11. Provision of a general discussion of the training programme at the end of the session to allow the participants an opportunity to provide feedback to the Canadian team.
12. Presentation of formal certificates of participation by the President of the University of Regina.

Evaluating the Training Programmes

The true effectiveness of the Training Programme can only be evaluated by examining its impact on the individuals involved and their subsequent contributions to their institutions. Although there is preliminary anecdotal information indicating that the participants have indeed been able to have an impact in their home institutions, it is too early to conclude that the programme was a success.

In order to assist the Canadian team in its on-going attempts to improve the training programme, the trainees were encouraged to complete questionnaire evaluations of each part of the programme using a five point scale (1=poor, 2=fair, 3=average, 4=good, 5=excellent). Prior to the detailed planning for each year's programme the results from the previous year were evaluated along with the overall objectives of the programme. Most aspects of the programme were positively received. For example, the Quality and Organization of the training programme received ratings from 3.50 to 4.64 with the rating generally improving each year. There were some sessions, particularly those involving administrative uses of computers, that most trainees did not find relevant to their roles as academics. For example, the registration and financial systems sessions received ratings under 3.5, often below 3.0. In contrast, the sessions on specific software packages usually ranked well above 4.0. Nonetheless, the team felt that it was important that as many individuals as possible should have a broad overview of computer use in a computerized university.

A final word is in order. The Canadian Team would have been unable to mount a successful training programme of this magnitude without assistance from the University of Regina. A great deal of help was received from the President's Office, Computing Services, the Registrar's Office, the Business Office, the Department of Personnel, the Library, the Department of Computer Science, the Faculty of Engineering, the Geography Department, the Electronic

Learning Centre, Luther College, the Chemistry Department, the Sample Survey and Data Bank Unit and from individual faculty members in many disciplines. IBM Canada and DEC Canada also provided experts for special sessions.

APPENDIX C

A SURVEY OF ACADEMIC COMPUTING IN CANADIAN UNIVERSITIES

I. Introduction

In the Fall of 1989 a questionnaire dealing with academic computing was sent to 957 academics at 13 Canadian universities. The process of selecting the questionnaire's recipients was as follows: The 80 Colleges and Universities that are members of the A.U.C.C. were divided into four groups based on number of faculty - the University of Toronto, large universities, medium-sized universities and small universities. Four universities were chosen from each of the three size-related categories so that the total sample maintained a reasonable geographical and linguistic balance. The number of faculty chosen from each university was made proportional to the fraction that university's faculty complement is of the group from which it was chosen. To ensure a reasonable sample from small universities, the minimum number of faculty chosen for any university was set at 10. Table 1.1 gives the number of questionnaires sent out, by institution, and the number returned.

Table 1.1
Number of Questionnaires sent out and returned

Institution	Number Sent	Number Returned
University of British Columbia	163	34
Brock University	10	3
University of Calgary	82	24
Concordia University	71	17
University of Lethbridge	11	4
McMaster University	67	12
Memorial University of Newfoundland	61	12
Université de Moncton	10	1
Mount Allison University	10	3
Royal Military College	10	0
Université de Sherbrooke	32	4
University of Toronto	323	80
University of Waterloo	101	28
Total	957	222

The distribution of returned questionnaires by academic unit is presented in Table 1.2.

Table 1.2
Returned Questionnaires by Academic Unit

Academic Unit	% Returned
Fine Arts	4.2
Humanities	7.9
Social Sciences	13.6
Natural Sciences	12.0
Mathematics	3.7
Administration/Commerce	6.3
Education	5.2
Engineering	10.5
Medicine	12.6
Others	22.0

The next few pages of this appendix are devoted to a summary of the questions asked as part of the questionnaire, and an analysis of the responses. The last two parts contain the questionnaire used (pages C 12-18) and a partial summary of the data from the responses (pages C 19-43).

II. General Background

Fewer than 1 % of the undergraduate academic units in Canadian universities require their undergraduate students to purchase a microcomputer. A greater number (22%) **encourage** computer purchase. The Arts and Sciences are below average in this regard (12 to 17%) while Engineering (60%) and Administration/Commerce (50%) are much above average.

Computer classes are not generally required by the Fine Arts, Humanities, Social Sciences or Medicine. In these areas computer literacy is more likely to be achieved as part of regular instruction or elective classes. The Fine Arts consider computer literacy to be unimportant (63%). Engineering (95%), Administration and Mathematics are much more likely to require formal classes of their students while the Education (50%) and the Sciences tend to **encourage** computer classes as electives rather than requiring them. Faculty at small universities and the University of Toronto are nearly twice as likely to consider instruction in the use of computers unimportant as their colleagues at larger or medium-sized universities.

Slightly less than half the respondents indicated that their University provides free access to a mainframe computer. Interestingly, academics at the University of Toronto (23%) appear much less likely to have free access than their peers at large or medium-sized universities (59%) or even small universities. Access to a minicomputer is most likely in Administration (58%), Mathematics and Engineering. Shared microcomputer facilities are most prevalent in the Fine Arts (50%), Humanities, Education and Medicine. Only 8% of all academics are provided with terminals. While overall about 11% are **provided** with microcomputers the percentages are much less in the Humanities, Social Sciences and Natural Sciences (0 to 4%) and are much higher in Administration (33%), Mathematics and Medicine.

It is extremely interesting that nearly 75% of all faculty have a microcomputer of their own. The numbers are slightly lower in small universities (67%) and significantly lower in Mathematics (57%) and Engineering. The Social Sciences (85%), Natural Sciences, Administration, Education and the Humanities are slightly more likely to have faculty with their own micros. Several respondents indicated that they possessed more than one microcomputer. Those in small universities are much more likely to have their computers purchased by the academic unit or university (50%) and much less likely to have purchased them using a grant or contract (10%). The University of Toronto does not encourage institutional purchase of personal computers (18%). Approximately 40% of academics in the Fine Arts, Humanities and Social Sciences who have computers have purchased their own; those in the Engineering (75%), Mathematics and the Sciences have been more likely to use grants or contracts while those in Administration and Education have had the greatest luck in having their microcomputers provided by the academic unit (50%). 17% in Administration shared the cost of their computer with the university or academic unit.

58% and 75% of the respondents indicated that computer training courses and consulting services respectively are readily available. Large universities are most likely to provide training courses (72%) and consulting services (86%); small universities are least likely (38 and 56% respectively). The Sciences (86%), Mathematics, Administration, Education and the Social Sciences appear to have greater access to readily-available consulting services, in particular, than other academic units. Fine Arts, Medicine and Engineering have the poorest access.

Large and medium-sized universities have provided for more faculty input (around 80%) into university computing policy. The University of Toronto and small universities appear to have provided less. The Fine Arts and Social Sciences (42%) are least likely to have unit computer advisory committees whereas Engineering (79%), Administration, Mathematics, Education, the Humanities and Sciences are more likely to have advisory committees.

III. Preparation of Class Materials

Roughly 70 to 75% of the respondents said that computers are used by **some** faculty in their academic unit to prepare materials and to analyze data for class use; slightly less than 50% indicated there is some use to prepare tests or exams. Between 30 and 50% of those indicating use of computers in these areas said the use was in **all types of classes** - graduate as well as senior and lower-level undergraduate classes. Faculty in the large universities make considerably greater use of computers in this regard than do faculty at medium-sized universities which, in turn, make more use than their colleagues in small universities. Medicine (90%), Education and the Sciences are most likely to have computer-prepared AV materials; Administration (87%) and the Sciences make greatest use of data analysis. Administration (75%), and to a lesser extent, the Social Sciences (64%), Sciences and Medicine are most likely to use computer-prepared tests or exams. The Fine Arts make rather limited use of computers for preparation of class materials as do faculty in Mathematics **except** to analyze data for classroom use (71%).

Overall, for preparing materials large universities have slightly better technical and support services than medium-sized universities and considerably more than small universities and the University of Toronto. Small universities have little technical support but, interestingly, are more likely to have consultants to call upon. The Humanities, Sciences, Education and Medicine seem to be best served by technical support. The Fine Arts are poorest in this regard although the Social Sciences and Mathematics are also well below average.

IV. In-Class Use (An instructor is normally present)

Between 30 and 50% of those indicating use of computers in these areas said they were being used in **all types of classes** - graduate as well as senior and lower-level undergraduate classes. Approximately equal use (45%) is made in classes of less than 25 and in classes between 25 and 100. Much less use of computers occurs in larger sized classes. 40% of the use involves MS-DOS computers, 17% Macintoshes, 24% mainframes, 13% mini-computers and 6% other types of computer. Commercially available software makes up about 75% of all software used. Evaluation is carried out routinely in about a quarter of the uses and occasionally or rarely three quarters of the time. About in-class use of computers students are said to be enthusiastic (46%), show mild acceptance (52%) or are indifferent (2%).

There is moderate use of computers in the classroom to analyze data (67%), for graphics and simulations (48%), and for electronic presentation. (43%). Much less use is made of computers for other purposes such as simulation of laboratory equipment and distance education (about 20%). For most of these purposes large universities make greatest use of computers in the classroom with little real differences among the other groups. The one exception to this generalization involves the use of computers to simulate laboratory training; about two thirds of the respondents from small universities indicated some use of computers for laboratory simulation as opposed to the average of 20%. The most widespread use of computers for electronic presentation is in Education (88%), Administration, Engineering and Medicine, for graphics or design capabilities is in Education (78%), Medicine, Engineering, Administration, Mathematics, and the Sciences, for modelling and simulations is in Engineering (80%), Administration, the Sciences and the Social Sciences, for data analysis is in Education (up to 100%) ,

Administration, the Sciences, Engineering and the Social Sciences, with other devices is in Education (67%), for laboratory simulation is in Engineering (44%), Education, the Sciences, the Social Sciences and Medicine, for distance education is in Education, Administration and Medicine. With the exception of design (Fine Arts), and simulations and data analysis (Humanities) the Fine Arts and Humanities do not make as much use as other academic areas or faculties of computers in the classroom.

Research in the use of computers for teaching purposes is not a major undertaking. Research is greatest in CAI/CMI/CAL (40%), followed closely by simulation/modelling and electronic presentation (32%) then graphics/design (24%), use in multi-media presentations (20%), laboratory simulation (18%) and distance education (12%). Small universities are involved much less than the average in every one of these research areas **except** simulation of laboratory equipment where they are more heavily involved (50%) than larger universities. The Humanities (54%) and Administration tend to be most involved in research into electronic presentation, the Fine Arts (43%) and Administration in research in graphics or design uses, Administration (50%) in simulation/modelling research, Engineering (35%) and the Sciences in laboratory equipment simulation, Medicine (32%) and Education in distance education, the Humanities (69%) and Medicine in CAI/CMI/CAL, Education (44%) and Medicine in computer multi-media instruction. It is interesting that Administration is least likely by far to be involved in research into CAI/CMI/CAL while the Social Sciences, Mathematics and Administration have little interest in multimedia instruction involving computers.

V. Out-Of-Class Use (An Instructor is normally not present)

Between 30 and 50% of those indicating use of computers in these areas said they were being used in **all types of classes** - graduate as well as senior and lower-level undergraduate classes. Approximately equal use (41%) is made in classes of less than 25 and classes between 25 and 100, 7% in classes between 100 and 250. Much less use is made of computers for classes of larger size. 40% of the use involves MS-DOS computers, 13% Macintoshes, 31% mainframes, 12% mini-computers and 4% other computers. Commercially available software makes up about 75% of all software used. Evaluation is carried out routinely (30%), occasionally and rarely (70%). About out-of-class use of computers, students are said to be enthusiastic (49%), show mild acceptance (47%), are indifferent (3%) or express disapproval (1%).

There is moderate use of computers outside the classroom to facilitate data analysis (66%), and for simulations or modelling (50%). Much less use is made of computers for other purposes such as computer-assisted review or drill (36%), replacement of all or part of a lecture class or to provide access to an expert system (20%). For most purposes large universities make greatest use of computers outside the classroom followed by medium-sized universities, small universities and the

University of Toronto although differences are not large. Medium-sized universities appear to use computers more for modelling and simulations. The most likely use of computer-assisted drill is in Engineering (54%), Education, Medicine, Administration and the Humanities, of computers replacing lectures is in Education (50%), Medicine and Engineering, of computer simulation or modelling is in Engineering (93%), Education, the Sciences and Administration, of data analysis is in Education (up to 100%), Engineering, the Sciences and Administration, of expert systems is in Engineering (40%), Administration, Education, the Sciences and Medicine. With the exception of computer-assisted drill and data analysis in the Humanities, the Humanities, Fine Arts, Social Sciences and Mathematics tend to use computers for out-of-class purposes much less than the average.

VI. Computerized Support Systems

Over 85% of those responding to the questionnaire indicated their library has a computerized catalogue system. Libraries in the large universities are more likely to be computerized (93%) while those of small universities are much less likely (33%). However, a third of the respondents from small universities noted that computerization **was coming**. Social Science (69%), Medical, Fine Arts and Humanities libraries are least likely to be computerized; Mathematics (up to 100%), Engineering, Natural Sciences and Education libraries are most computerized.

Computerized bibliographical, informational or library data bases are most prevalent in Medicine, Education, the Sciences, Humanities and Engineering. They are least available in Administration and Mathematics. Large Universities are much more likely to provide computerized access to data bases.

Mathematics (43%), the Sciences and the Humanities provide the greatest likelihood of access to these databases from locations outside the library. Large universities are more likely to provide this privilege than medium-sized universities or the University of Toronto; small universities have very little computerized access to data bases.

Large universities provide a greater opportunity of accessing library indexes from faculty offices (61%) than medium-sized universities or the University of Toronto; there is very little access in small universities (11%). By discipline, the access is greater in Education (78%), the Sciences, Engineering, the Fine Arts and the Social Sciences; it is least likely in Medicine (13%).

Only about 12% indicated that no faculty use electronic mail for local or national/international communication. The small universities have a larger percentage (25%) not using national or international E-mail while medium-sized universities have 18-20% not using E-mail for either purpose. In large universities only 6-7% don't use E-mail. The apparent use of E-mail is greatest in Education (up to 100%), Engineering and Administration. It is least used in Medicine (up to 30% don't use it in any form) and the Fine Arts. E-mail is not used much to communicate with students; when it is so used it is most likely to be in Engineering (up to 78%), Education and Administration.

Between 70 and 75% of the respondents indicated that word processing facilities are provided for students. Interestingly there was an inverse size correlation; the smaller the institution the more likely it is to provide these facilities. For the most part, computers as word processors, when provided are placed in a few locations. Medium-sized universities do the best job of making word processors widely available. Engineering students are most likely to have access to word processors (90%), Mathematics (57%), and Medicine students least likely. Generally, the Arts and Sciences are all about equally good in providing facilities although Science students will probably find word processors in only a very few locations.

VII. General Comments

99% of all administrative offices now have word processors. About 42% of these were introduced in each half of the last decade. They and the attendant hardware were most likely to have been purchased by the academic unit from its own operating or equipment funds (61%). 40% used money provided specifically by the University for that purpose.

76% of the respondents are convinced that faculty are doing substantially more of the preparation of manuscripts as the result of the widespread availability of word processors. This feeling is most widely held in Administration (92%), the Sciences, Engineering and the Social Sciences. It is less prevalent in Medicine (58%) and Education. A significant number of faculty, especially in Education (30%), Medicine and the Humanities, are not certain whether academics are doing more of their own manuscript preparation.

Faculty in Education (6/1), Administration, Engineering, Medicine, the Humanities and the Sciences are more likely to agree than to disagree that the use of computers has permitted an improvement in the quality of education. Those in the Fine Arts tend to disagree by a two to one ratio. Their colleagues in the Social Sciences and Mathematics were about equally divided on the question. Interesting is the large number of faculty who either had no opinion or simply couldn't decide: as high as 57% in the Fine Arts and 35% in Medicine. Those offering an explanation for their opinion were more likely to explain why computers had improved quality (68%). The most common reasons dealt with more efficient use of time and better preparation of courses and class material (Table 6.1).

Table 6.1
Comments on Computers and quality in education

Comment	Frequency
Allow better use of time	13
Courses are better prepared	9
Allow better presentation of class material	9
Not used enough to know	8
They have simplified analysis	8
They improve writing	8
Computers are tools only	7
Too early to tell	7

A significant number of faculty (41%) do not feel that the use of computers has provided them with more time to devote to academic pursuits although a large number didn't express any opinion (as high a 60% in Education and 40% in the Humanities). Only in the Social Sciences and Engineering did the No/Yes ratio become low approaching unity. There was an oft-stated view that there may be a gain in **productivity**, calculation power and time from manuscript preparation but that does not translate to an overall saving in time (Table 6.2).

Table 6.2
Comments on Computers and time for teaching and scholarly activity

Comment	Frequency
Their use actually requires more time	15
There is a gain in productivity but no saving in time	13
There are fewer secretaries hired	10
Less time wasted in manuscript preparation	8
There is a gain in calculation power	7

Faculty generally are favorably disposed towards the use of computers in instruction at the university level. Overall, there is slightly more agreement than disagreement that lecture content and presentation are improved through the use of computers. Greatest support appears to come from Medicine, Engineering, Education, Administration and the Humanities with strongest disagreement from the Fine Arts and Mathematics. The Sciences and Social Sciences are close to being evenly split. Those under 40 are most positive, those over 50 most negative. There is general agreement that student motivation is increased. While the greatest agreement comes from Medicine, Education, Engineering, Administration and the Humanities there is more disagreement than agreement from the Fine Arts, Mathematics and Social Sciences. Those under 40 are not as positive as group aged 40-60. There is strong disagreement with the notion that the cost of education is lowered by increased use of computers. Faculty in Education and those under 40 are least negative. There is general disagreement with the proposal that communication between instructor and student is improved. Disagreement is greatest in the Arts and Sciences and least in the professional colleges where there are almost equal numbers of faculty agreeing as disagreeing. Although there aren't large differences based on age, those under 40 are least likely to disagree. There is wide-spread agreement that out-of-class learning opportunities are improved. There is also strong agreement that students can obtain access to information they might not otherwise get through the use of computers. There is no disagreement from faculty in Administration while those in the Fine Arts and Mathematics are more evenly divided. Those under 40 are most likely to agree strongly. There is very strong agreement that calculation-intensive operations such as simulations become possible as a teaching strategy. Strong agreement was most in evidence from Engineering, Administration and the Humanities. There is general agreement that computers can remove the drudgery of drill and repetition. Faculty in Engineering, the Natural Sciences, Administration and Medicine are most likely to agree. Academics in the Fine Arts and Mathematics disagreed. Those in Education, the Humanities, the Social Sciences and those 60 and older tended to agree with those in disagreement making up a sizeable proportion (up to around 40%). There is general agreement that young people are computer oriented and computer literate although faculty in Mathematics were about equally divided on the subject. Surprisingly, a large percentage of faculty held no opinion on most of these questions. Percentages in the 25-35 range were quite common and on occasion were as high as 64%.

In responding to perceived disadvantages in the use of computers there was general disagreement with the notion that computers diminish the role of faculty as teachers. The strongest disagreement came from Education, Mathematics, Administration and Medicine. The Fine Arts, Natural Sciences, Engineering, Humanities and Social Sciences are more likely to agree than disagree that computers do deemphasize personal teaching. There is general disagreement with the assertion that the cost of computers does not justify their use. The Fine Arts, Mathematics, and to a lesser extent, Engineering are more likely to see cost as a disadvantage. Those over 50, particularly those over 60, tend to more concerned about cost as well. There is disagreement in all areas that the use of computers causes less communication between instructors and students. While the Fine Arts, Natural Sciences, Medicine and Mathematics indicated the most concern with potential loss of communication there was virtually no concern in Administration and Education. Again, those over 50 are least likely to disagree with the proposed disadvantage. There is fairly general agreement that faculty don't get adequate training in the use of computer hardware and software. The Social Sciences, Mathematics and Engineering are most likely to disagree with training as a disadvantage. It is interesting that faculty feel this way since 58% and 75% of the respondents to an earlier question had indicated that computer training courses and consulting services are readily available. The obvious conclusions are that the training is available but inadequate or faculty simply don't avail themselves of the training in its present form. There was a general disagreement that computers cater too much to a desire by students for entertainment. Faculty in Mathematics, Engineering and the Social Sciences were more likely to agree with the disadvantage than their peers although, overall, they too disagreed. There was a general agreement that computers do not make education too impersonal with the

Sciences, Medicine and the Fine Arts most likely to feel that they do. Those over 60 also have a greater tendency to be concerned about impersonalization. Opinions were more equally divided over whether mastering hardware and software gets in the way of learning. Overall, there was a small tendency to disagree that this concern is a disadvantage. Mathematics and Administration agreed quite markedly that this is a disadvantage; Engineering was almost equally divided; The Fine Arts, Social Sciences and Education are most likely to disagree. A moderate percentage of faculty hold no opinion on most of these questions. Percentages in the 25-30 range were quite common and on occasion went as high as 55%.

Cost is a major constraint on academic computing for 70% of the respondents. Those in the Sciences (91%), Education, Mathematics, Administration and Engineering are most likely to see it as a constraint. The Humanities (54%), Social Sciences, Medicine and those 60 or older seem to be less concerned with cost as a major constraint. Space is a major constraint for 41%. The percentage is highest in Administration (64%), the Sciences, Mathematics and Engineering, lowest in the Fine Arts (29%) and Education. Computer or terminal availability is a major constraint for 42% with the greatest concern in the Sciences (59%), Education, Humanities, Social Sciences, Mathematics and Administration. Faculty in Fine Arts (17%), Engineering and those under 40 are significantly less concerned. Software availability is a major constraint for 31% with the greatest concern in Mathematics (50%), Administration and Medicine. It is least likely to be a major constraint in the Humanities (23%) and the Sciences. Computer and system compatibility represents a major constraint for 29%. Medicine (44%), the Humanities, the Fine Arts, Administration and Mathematics are most likely to see this as a major concern; Education (11%), Engineering, the Social Sciences, the Sciences and those under 40 are less likely to be concerned. Only 14% consider capacity of and available time on mainframe computers as a major constraint. Mathematics (33%), Administration and Education are more likely to see this as a problem. Engineering (6%) and the Sciences are least likely to find this a major constraint. Training of faculty is a major constraint for 45%. It is most likely to be a concern for Administration (73%), Medicine and Education but is less likely for Mathematics (14%), the Sciences, Engineering, the Fine Arts and the Social Sciences. Training of students is a major constraint for 29%, primarily those faculty in Education (56%), Administration and Medicine. As a major constraint it is less important in Mathematics (as low as 0%), the Sciences, Fine Arts, Humanities and the group aged 40 to 49. Faculty inertia is a major constraint for 52%. The areas most likely to view inertia as a problem are Education (78%), Fine Arts, the Social Sciences and Administration. Only in Mathematics is there little likelihood to see this as a major concern (17%). Lack of transparent technology is seen as a major constraint by 29%. This is most of concern in the Fine Arts (50%), the Humanities, Medicine and Administration. As a major constraint it is least important in the Sciences (18%), Social Sciences, Education and Engineering. The inadequacy of available software is a major constraint for 41% most notably in Education (78%), Mathematics, the Sciences and Fine Arts. It is least likely to be viewed as a problem in the Social Sciences (23%), Administration, the Humanities and Medicine. It is a major concern for those over 60 more than those under 40 (55% to 32%).

The consensus is that, within five years, all faculty will have a computer in their offices (63%), students will see a need to own a microcomputer (59%), computer access to libraries from all faculty offices will be possible (57%) and all faculty will make use of by E-mail (50%). Engineering (80%), Medicine, Administration, the Sciences and Mathematics were are likely to predict all faculty having a microcomputer; the percentage for the Fine Arts was only 13%. Administration (75%) and Education see a greater likelihood of students needing to have their own microcomputer; the percentage in Mathematics is 43%. Mathematics (71%), Education and Engineering predict a greater likelihood of faculty accessing the library from their offices; for Administration the figure is 42%. Mathematics (71%), Engineering and Education are more optimistic about all faculty using E-mail; the percentage in the Social Sciences is only 35%. Only 7% foresee students being required to own microcomputers, 8% see computer simulation replacing actual laboratory experience, and 20% believe that all faculty will use computers in some manner in classroom instruction within five years. Engineering students (30%) are most likely to be required to have computers. Engineering (20%) and Medicine predict the greatest use of lab simulation. Engineering (40%), Medicine and Administration are more likely to predict widespread use of computers in the classroom. The Fine Arts, Humanities, Social Sciences and Mathematics have no or little confidence that all faculty will use computers in the classroom. Faculty under 40 are more likely than the average to predict all the proposed requirements and uses will occur in the next 5 years. Those over 50 are less likely to predict them all with the exception that students will see a need to have their own microcomputers.

94% of all respondents claimed that they presently use computers in their scholarly activity. The highest percentages (100%) were for the Sciences, Engineering and Education, the lowest occurred in the Fine Arts (75%), Mathematics, Humanities, Administration and Medicine. There were no significant differences based on age. Of the computers used for research, microcomputers make up 63%, mainframes 21%, mini-computers 15% and supercomputers 2%. Respondents in Administration indicated use of microcomputers only. Engineering and Science respondents are less likely than the average to use microcomputers but are more likely to use mainframes (all the use of super computers occurred in the Sciences). While Education, the Humanities and the Social Sciences use minicomputers less than the average Medicine uses them more than the average. Faculty under 40 are less likely to use microcomputers (49%) but are more likely to use minicomputers (21%), mainframes (26%) and super computers (4%). The major research uses of computers are summarized in Table 6.3

Table 6.3
Major research uses of computers

Use	Frequency (% of total)
Word processing	121 (63%)
Data analysis	104 (53%)
Database operations	52 (27%)
Graphics	48 (25%)
E mail	33 (17%)
Modelling	26 (14%)
Numeric calculations	17 (9%)
Spreadsheets	13 (7%)
Development of teaching methods	11 (6%)
Bibliographic retrieval	10 (5%)
Data collection	10 (5%)
Software development	9 (5%)

Word processing is a major use for all faculty. Data analysis is most important in Education, Medicine, the Sciences, Social Sciences and Administration. Database operations represent a major use in the Fine Arts, Education, Medicine and the Humanities. Graphics use is most important in the Sciences, Engineering, Medicine, the Fine Arts and the Humanities. E-mail is most important in the Fine Arts, Mathematics, the Social Sciences, Humanities and Education. Modelling is most important for the Sciences and Engineering. Numeric calculations are most important for Mathematics and Engineering. Spreadsheet use is most important in Administration and Engineering. CAI and development of teaching methods are most important in the Humanities and the Social Sciences.

There is a general feeling that research use of large mainframe computers will decrease (75%), with an attendant increase in the use of work stations (73%) and microcomputers (93%). Administration, Education, Engineering and the Humanities are most likely to predict decrease use in mainframe computers, Social Sciences, Medicine, Mathematics and the Sciences are least likely. Engineering and the Sciences foresee the greatest increase in research use of work stations, Administration, Social Sciences, education and the Humanities the least. Faculty under 40 also predict a greater use of workstations than their colleagues.

The greatest impact of computers on the academic process is seen to be in word processing, communications, information access, visual presentations, self-learning, replacing labs, data analysis, improved administrative efficiency, simulation, complex calculations and preparation of learning materials (Table 6.4).

Table 6.4
Areas of greatest impact of computers

Area	Frequency
Word processing	26
Communications	24
Information access	21
Visual presentations	17
Self-learning	16
Replacing laboratories	12
Data analysis	11
Improved administrative efficiency	10
Simulation	9
Complex calculations	8
Preparation of learning materials	8
Teaching problem solving	7
Reducing repetitive tasks	5
Distance education	4

Only 38% said that their views on the role and importance of computers have changed over the past 5 years. The greatest change has occurred in Education (67%) and Administration (60%). The smallest change is in Engineering (28%), Medicine (29%) and the Sciences (31%). Those under 40 have changed their minds least (30%). Those who have changed their minds are now preponderantly more positive about computers. That is true in all academic areas and age groups except for Mathematics where those more positive and those less positive are about equal in number, and in Administration where the ratio is 3/1. For those under 40 the ratio is 6/1. Faculty who have not changed their minds have, for the most part, always been positive except in Education where the numbers of those who have been positive equal those who have been negative.

QUESTIONNAIRE
ACADEMIC COMPUTING

University of Regina
Regina, Saskatchewan
S4S 0A2

Name of University or College ______________________________

Academic Unit ______________________________

In order to faciliate comparisons with the data collected in India we would like to ask you to provide some personal data:

Respondent' position within university ____________________
Respondent's age ____________
Educational level ____________

If possible we would like the name and telephone number of an individual we could call for further information or follow up question

Name ______________________________

Telephone Number ____________

Please send a copy of the report of the survey results to:

Name ______________________________
Address ______________________________
____
____

I. Background

1. a) Are undergraduate students in your unit **required** to purchase a microcomputer? Yes___ No___

   b) If you answered 'No' for question 1 a)
   are undergraduate students in your unit **encouraged** to purchase a microcomputer? Yes___ No___

   c) Which of the following best reflects the policy of your unit regarding instruction in the use of computers?
   i. students are required to take at least one credit computer class ___
   ii. students are required to take a non-credit computer class offered by a teaching department ___
   iii. students are required to take a non-credit computer class offered by a central computing facility ___
   iv. students are encouraged to take a computer class for elective credit ___
   v. students are encouraged to take a non-credit elective computer class ___
   vi. computer literacy is taught through components of regular instruction ___
   vii. instruction in the use of computers is not considered important ___

2. a) Indicate which of the following are current policies of the University or Academic Unit to provide faculty with computer resources:
   i. faculty are provided with free access to a mainframe computer ___
   ii. faculty must pay for access to a mainframe computer ___
   iii. faculty are provided with access to a minicomputer within the unit ___
   iv. faculty are provided with access to shared microcomputer facilities within the unit ___
   v. every faculty office is provided with a terminal ___
   vi. every faculty office is provided with a microcomputer ___

   b) If there is no policy of providing a terminal or microcomputer for every faculty member do you
   i. have a terminal? Yes___
   ii. have a microcomputer? Yes___

   c) If you obtained a terminal or microcomputer indicate which of the following applies:
   i. you paid for it personally ___
   ii. you paid for it out of a grant or contract ___
   iii. it was purchased for you by the University or Unit ___
   iv. you paid part of the cost while the University or Unit paid the remainder ___

   d) Check the options that best describe the situation at your University for providing faculty with instruction in the use of computers and common software:

	Readily	Occasionally	Never
i. courses are available	___	___	___
ii. consulting services are available	___	___	___

3. Is there a University-level committee with faculty representation to set or advise on policy with respect to academic computing? Yes___ No___ Don't know___

4. Is there a committee in your Academic Unit to set or advise on policy with respect to academic computing?
   Yes___ No___ Don't know___

5. Is anyone in your Unit carrying out research in the use of computers for the following purposes?

		Yes	No	Don't know
i.	for in-class electronic presentation	___	___	___
ii.	to provide in-class graphics or design capabilities	___	___	___
iii.	to allow in-class simulations or model manipulations	___	___	___
iv.	to simulate equipment in laboratory training	___	___	___
v.	to aid in off-campus or distance education	___	___	___
vi.	for computer assisted or mediated instruction	___	___	___
vii.	in conjunction with video tape, video disk, CD ROM or CDI for computer assisted instruction	___	___	___
viii.	other (please specify) ______________________			

II. Preparation of Class Materials

1. Indicate which of the following apply in your Unit with respect to the use of computers in preparation of class materials for various levels of classes:

	By all faculty			By a few faculty			By no faculty
	Grad	Senior	Junior	Grad	Senior	Junior	
i. to prepare AV materials for class use?	___	___	___	___	___	___	___
ii. to access data bases and analyze data for classroom use?	___	___	___	___	___	___	___
iii. to access test banks for preparation of tests and exams?	___	___	___	___	___	___	___
iv. other (please specify) ______________________	___	___	___	___	___	___	___

2. Indicate which of the following technical or other support services, if any, are provided to aid faculty in computer-assisted preparation of class materials:

i. faculty have access to instructional designers	___
ii. faculty have access to technicians who prepare graphics	___
iii. technicians are available to set up and maintain equipment	___
iv. faculty have access to trainers/consulting support in use of technology	___

III. In-Class Use (An instructor is normally present)

1. Indicate which of the following apply in your Unit with respect to the use of computers in the classroom or laboratory for various types of classes:

		By all faculty			By a few faculty			By no faculty
		Grad	Senior	Junior	Grad	Senior	Junior	
i.	for electronic presentation	___	___	___	___	___	___	___
ii.	to provide graphics or design capabilities	___	___	___	___	___	___	___
iii.	to allow simulations or model manipulation	___	___	___	___	___	___	___
iv.	to analyze data	___	___	___	___	___	___	___
v.	in conjunction with other devices such as video tape	___	___	___	___	___	___	___
	video disk	___	___	___	___	___	___	___
	CD ROM	___	___	___	___	___	___	___
	CDI	___	___	___	___	___	___	___
vi.	to **simulate** equipment in laboratory training	___	___	___	___	___	___	___
vii.	to aid in off-campus or distance education	___	___	___	___	___	___	___
viii.	other (please specify) ______________________	___	___	___	___	___	___	___

2. For those above that are being used extensively please indicate:

	i	ii	iii	iv	v	vi	vii	viii
a) size of class(es)								
>250	___	___	___	___	___	___	___	___
100 - 250	___	___	___	___	___	___	___	___
25 - 100	___	___	___	___	___	___	___	___
<25	___	___	___	___	___	___	___	___
b) computer systems used								
mainframe	___	___	___	___	___	___	___	___
mini	___	___	___	___	___	___	___	___
MS-DOS	___	___	___	___	___	___	___	___
Macintosh	___	___	___	___	___	___	___	___
Apple II	___	___	___	___	___	___	___	___
C-64	___	___	___	___	___	___	___	___
other	___	___	___	___	___	___	___	___
c) software								
commercially available	___	___	___	___	___	___	___	___
developed on site	___	___	___	___	___	___	___	___
d) evaluation of effectiveness								
routinely	___	___	___	___	___	___	___	___
occasionally	___	___	___	___	___	___	___	___
rarely	___	___	___	___	___	___	___	___
e) student response								
enthusiastic	___	___	___	___	___	___	___	___
mild acceptance	___	___	___	___	___	___	___	___
indifference	___	___	___	___	___	___	___	___
disapproval	___	___	___	___	___	___	___	___

IV. Out-Of-Class Use (An Instructor is normally not present)

1. Indicate which of the following apply in your Unit with respect to the use of computers outside the classroom or laboratory for various types of classes:

	By all faculty			By a few faculty			By no faculty
	Grad	Senior	Junior	Grad	Senior	Junior	
i. to provide students with self-paced, computer-assisted review or drill?	___	___	___	___	___	___	___
ii. to replace some or all of a more formal lecture-type class?	___	___	___	___	___	___	___
iii. to provide students access to "an expert system"?	___	___	___	___	___	___	___
iv. to provide access to mathematical modelling or simulation?	___	___	___	___	___	___	___
v. to facilitate data analysis?	___	___	___	___	___	___	___
vi. other (please specify) ______________________	___	___	___	___	___	___	___

2. For those above that are being used extensively please indicate:

	i	ii	iii	iv	v	vi
a) size of class(es)						
>250	___	___	___	___	___	___
100 - 250	___	___	___	___	___	___
25 - 100	___	___	___	___	___	___
<25	___	___	___	___	___	___
b) computer systems used						
mainframe	___	___	___	___	___	___
mini	___	___	___	___	___	___
MS-DOS	___	___	___	___	___	___
Macintosh	___	___	___	___	___	___
Apple II	___	___	___	___	___	___
C-64	___	___	___	___	___	___
other	___	___	___	___	___	___
c) software						
commercially available	___	___	___	___	___	___
developed on site	___	___	___	___	___	___
d) evaluation of effectiveness						
routinely	___	___	___	___	___	___
occasionally	___	___	___	___	___	___
rarely	___	___	___	___	___	___
e) student response						
enthusiastic	___	___	___	___	___	___
mild acceptance	___	___	___	___	___	___
indifference	___	___	___	___	___	___
disapproval	___	___	___	___	___	___

V. Computerized Support Systems

1. Does your library have a computerized catalogue system? Yes___ No___ Don't know___

2. a) What bibliographical, informational or library data bases can be accessed through your library?

b) Which of these data bases can be accessed from faculty offices or from other locations **outside** the library?

	Yes	No	Don't know
3. i. Can the library indexes be accessed from faculty offices?	___	___	___
ii. Can the library indexes be accessed from locations, other than faculty offices, outside the library?	___	___	___

4. Indicate the use of the following:	By all faculty	By most faculty	By a few faculty	By no faculty
i. an international or national network such as BITNET or NETNORTH	___	___	___	___
ii. electronic mail to communicate with other faculty on campus	___	___	___	___
iii. electronic mail to communicate with students in class	___	___	___	___

5. a) Are word processing facilities **provided** for students to prepare theses, papers and assignments? Yes____ No____ Don't know____

b) If your answer is 'Yes', indicate which of the following best describes the situation:

i. facilities are widely available to all student ___
ii. facilities are available in a few locations ___

VI. General Comments

1. In what year were word processors first introduced into the administrative offices of your Unit? 19____

2. How were (are) computers and associated hardware purchased for administrators?

i. with money provided by the University specially for that purpose ___
ii. out of the Unit's operating or equipment funds ___
iii. other (please specify) ______________________________ ___

3. Has the use of personal computers as word processors led to faculty doing substantially more of the preparation of manuscripts for publication? Yes___ No___ Not certain___

4. a) Has the use of computers improved the quality of education in your Unit? Yes___ No___ No Opinion___

b) Please explain.

5. a) Has the use of computers provided your faculty with **more time** to devote to teaching and scholarly activity?
Yes___ No___ Don't know___ No opinion___

b) Please explain.

6. The following are major advantage(s) of computers in instruction at a university level:

		Strongly Agree	Agree	Disagree	Strongly Disagree	No opinion
i.	lecture content and presentation are improved	___	___	___	___	___
ii.	student motivation and self-learning are increased	___	___	___	___	___
iii.	the cost of instruction is lowered	___	___	___	___	___
iv.	there is improved communication between instructor and student	___	___	___	___	___
v.	out-of-class learning opportunities are improved	___	___	___	___	___
vi.	students are provided access to information they might not otherwise get	___	___	___	___	___
vii.	calculation-intensive operations such as simulations become possible	___	___	___	___	___
viii.	computers can remove from faculty the drudgery of drill and repetition	___	___	___	___	___
ix.	the youth of today are generally computer-oriented and computer literate	___	___	___	___	___

7. The following are major disadvantage(s) of computers in instruction at a university level:

	Strongly Agree	Agree	Disagree	Strongly Disagree	No opinion
i. less emphasis is placed on the role of faculty as teachers	___	___	___	___	___
ii. the cost does not justify their use	___	___	___	___	___
iii. there is less communication between instructor and students	___	___	___	___	___
iv. faculty are not adequately trained in their use	___	___	___	___	___
v. they cater to an excessive need for entertainment	___	___	___	___	___
vi. they make education too impersonal	___	___	___	___	___
vii. mastering computer hardware and software gets in the way of learning	___	___	___	___	___

8. What constraints do you see on increased use of academic computing:

		Major	Minor	None	Don't know
i.	cost	___	___	___	___
ii.	space	___	___	___	___
iii.	availability of computers or terminals	___	___	___	___
iv.	availability of software	___	___	___	___
v.	compatability of computers or of computer systems	___	___	___	___
vi.	capacity of or available time on mainframe computers	___	___	___	___
vii.	training of faculty	___	___	___	___
viii.	training of students	___	___	___	___
ix.	faculty inertia	___	___	___	___
x.	difficulty using hardware or software (the technology isn't transparent)	___	___	___	___
xi.	inadequacy of software for computer-assisted instruction	___	___	___	___
xii.	other (please specify) ______________________________	___	___	___	___

9. Check those of the following that you believe will occur in your Unit within five years:

i. all faculty will have a microcomputer in their offices ___
ii. all faculty will be able to access the library from their offices ___
iii. all faculty will communicate by electronic mail ___
iv. all faculty will use computers in some way in classroom instruction ___
v. simulation will replace actual laboratory experience ___
vi. all students will see a need to have their own microcomputers ___
vii. all students will be required to have their own microcomputers ___

10. a) Do you presently use computers in your research or scholarly activity?. Yes___ No___

b) If you answered 'Yes', please elaborate on the type(s) of computer(s) and how they are utilized:

11. Which of the following describe the likely future of research computing in your Unit?

	Increase	Decrease
i. use of large, central mainframe computer(s)	___	___
ii. use of work station(s)	___	___
iii. use of dedicated minicomputer(s)	___	___
iv. use of microcomputers	___	___

12. Where do you see computers making the greatest impact on the academic enterprise (not including research)?

13. a) Have your views changed over the last 5 years on the role and importance of computers? Yes___ No___

b) Explain.

In the final section of this questionnaire we would like to ask you some general opinion questions concerning the role and impact of the computer in the university and society as a whole. Please be reassured that the data will be treated as an aggregate and no individual responses will be identified.

QUESTIONNAIRE RESULTS

ACADEMIC COMPUTING

Comparison of Results by Institution, Academic Unit and Ag

Number of Questionnaires sent out	957
Number of Questionnaires or responses returned	222 (23.2%)
Number of Questionnaires used in analysis	191 (20.0%)
From University of Toronto	62 (32.5%)
From large universities	73 (38.2%)
From medium-sized universities	46 (24.1%)
From small universities	10 (5.2%)
Male	62 (32.5%)
Female	17 (8.9%)
Not known	113 (59.2%0
Age:	
In 20's	2 (1.0%)
In 30's	47 (24.6%)
In 40's	68 (35.6%)
In 50's	47 (24.6%)
In 60's	12 (6.3%)
>69	3 (1.6%)
Highest Degree:	
Bachelors	6 (3.1%)
Masters	27 (14.1%)
Doctorate	147 (77.0%)
Position:	
Assistant Professor	36 (18.8%)
Associate Professor	41 (21.4%)
Professor	61 (31.8%)
Department Head	8 (4.2%)
Associate Dean	6 (3.1%)
Academic Unit:	
Fine Arts	8 (4.2%)
Humanities	15 (7.9%)
Social Sciences	26 (13.6%)
Natural Sciences	23 (12.0%)
Mathematics	7 (3.7%)
Computer Science	1 (0.5%)
Administration/Commerce	12 (6.3%)
Education	10 (5.2%)
Engineering	20 (10.5%)
Medicine	24 (12.6%)

I. Background

1. a) Are undergraduate students in your unit **required** to purchase a microcomputer

	Yes (%)	No (%)	Not applicable (%)
Total	1.0	94.2	4.7
University Size			
Toronto		88.5	11.5
Large		97.3	2.7
Medium	4.3	95.7	
Small		100.0	
Academic Unit			
Fine Arts		100.0	
Humanities		100.0	
Social Sciences	3.8	96.2	
Natural Sciences		100.0	
Mathematics	14.3	85.7	
Admin/Commerce		100.0	
Education		90.0	10.0
Engineering		100.0	
Medicine		87.5	12.5
Others		88.1	11.9

b) If you answered 'No' for question 1 a)
are undergraduate students in your unit **encouraged** to purchase a microcomputer?

	Yes (%)	No (%)
Total	21.6	78.4
University Size		
Toronto	24.1	75.9
Large	19.1	80.9
Medium	18.2	81.8
Small	37.5	62.5
Academic Unit		
Fine Arts	12.5	87.5
Humanities	15.4	84.6
Social Sciences	16.0	84.0
Natural Sciences	17.4	82.6
Mathematics	16.7	83.3
Admin/Commerce	50.0	50.0
Education	22.2	77.8
Engineering	60.0	40.0
Medicine	14.3	85.7
Others	8.3	91.7

c) Which of the following best reflects the policy of your unit regarding instruction in the use of computers?

i. students are required to take at least one credit computer class
ii. students are required to take a non-credit computer class offered by a teaching department
iii. students are required to take a non-credit computer class offered by a central computing facility
iv. students are encouraged to take a computer class for elective credit
v. students are encouraged to take a non-credit elective computer class
vi. computer literacy is taught through components of regular instruction
vii. instruction in the use of computers is not considered important

(Some people checked more than one answer)

	i (%)	ii (%)	iii (%)	iv (%)	v (%)	vi (%)	vii (%)
Total	31.3	1.1	0.5	18.1	11.0	27.5	21.4
University Size							
Toronto	22.2	1.9	1.9	11.1	7.4	31.5	27.8
Large	28.2	1.4		25.4	12.7	25.4	18.3
Medium	50.0			13.0	8.7	23.9	17.4
Small	11.1			22.2	22.2	44.4	33.3
Academic Unit							
Fine Arts				12.5			62.5
Humanities	7.1			14.3	21.4	35.7	28.5
Social Sciences	7.7			15.4	11.5	38.4	30.8
Natural Sciences	26.1			30.4	13.0	26.1	4.3
Mathematics	71.4			14.3		14.3	
Admin/Commerce	66.7	8.3	8.3			41.7	8.3
Education	40.0			30.0	20.0	20.0	10.0
Engineering	90.0	5.0				15.0	
Medicine	4.2			20.8	12.5	37.5	29.2
Others	26.2			21.4	11.9	21.4	26.2

2. a) Indicate which of the following are current policies of the University or Academic Unit to provide faculty with computer resources:

i. faculty are provided with free access to a mainframe computer
ii. faculty must pay for access to a mainframe computer
iii. faculty are provided with access to a minicomputer within the unit
iv. faculty are provided with access to shared microcomputer facilities within the unit
v. every faculty office is provided with a terminal
vi. every faculty office is provided with a microcomputer

	Yes (Modified Yes) (%)					
	i	ii	iii	iv	v	vi
Total	44.5 (5.8)	33.0 (5.2)	28.8 (2.1)	38.2	7.9 (1.6)	10.5 (5.2)
University Size						
Toronto	23.0 (3.3)	39.3 (1.7)	34.4 (3.3)	36.1	8.2 (3.3)	13.1 (6.6)
Large	53.4 (8.2)	34.2 (6.9)	23.3 (1.4)	37.0	11.0 (1.3)	11.0 (4.1)
Medium	58.7 (6.5)	23.9 (8.7)	28.3 (1.9)	43.5	4.4	6.5 (4.4)
Small	44.4	22.2	44.4	33.3		(11.1)
Academic Unit						
Fine Arts	12.5	25.0	12.5	50.0		12.5
Humanities	50.0 (14.3)	28.5 (14.3)	35.7	50.0		
Social Sciences	73.1 (3.8)	23.1	34.8 (3.8)	34.6	(3.9)	(7.7)
Natural Sciences	34.8 (4.3)	65.2	17.4	34.7	4.3	4.3 (4.3)
Mathematics	42.9	42.9	57.1	28.6		28.6
Admin/Commerce	66.7	(8.3)	58.3	25.0	8.3 (8.3)	33.3 (16.7)
Education	60.0 (20.0)	10.0 (20.0)	20.0 (10.0)	50.0	10.0	10.0 (10.0)
Engineering	40.0 (5.0)	50.0 (5.0)	40.0 (5.0)	20.0	5.0	10.0
Medicine	33.3	37.5	29.2	41.7	12.5	20.8 (4.2)
Others	35.7 (9.5)	31.0 (9.5)	16.7 (2.4)	47.6	16.7 (2.4)	7.1 (7.1)

b) If there is no policy of providing a terminal or microcomputer for every faculty member do **you**

i. have a terminal?

ii. have a microcomputer?

	i (%)	ii (%)
Total	32.5	73.3
University Size		
Toronto	29.5	70.5
Large	30.1	78.1
Medium	37.0	73.9
Small	55.6	66.7
Academic Unit		
Fine Arts		75.0
Humanities	28.6	78.6
Social Sciences	34.6	84.6
Natural Sciences	43.5	82.7
Mathematics	14.3	57.1
Admin/Commerce	25.0	83.3
Education	40.0	80.0
Engineering	45.0	60.0
Medicine	29.2	70.8
Others	33.3	69.0

c) If you obtained a terminal or microcomputer indicate which of the following applies:

i. you paid for it personally

ii. you paid for it out of a grant or contract

iii. it was purchased for you by the University or Unit

iv. you paid part of the cost while the University or Unit paid the remainder

v. other

	i (%)	ii (%)	iii (%)	iv (%)	v (%)
Total	26.4	39.4	27.9	3.4	2.9
University Size					
Toronto	32.3	43.5	17.7	4.8	1.6
Large	23.5	40.0	31.8	2.4	2.4
Medium	24.5	38.8	28.6	4.1	4.1
Small	30.0	10.0	50.0		10.0
Academic Unit					
Fine Arts	37.5	25.0	25.0		12.5
Humanities	38.9	27.8	27.8		5.6
Social Sciences	40.7	25.9	25.9		7.4
Natural Sciences	19.4	54.8	19.4	6.5	
Mathematics	16.7	66.7	16.7		
Admin/Commerce	8.3	25.0	50.0	16.7	
Education	28.6	21.4	50.0		
Engineering	5.0	75.0	10.0	5.0	5.0
Medicine	30.8	38.5	23.1	7.7	
Others	25.0	40.0	32.5		2.5

(Several respondents had more than one microcomputer)

d) Check the options that best describe the situation at your University for providing faculty with instruction in the use of computers and common software:

i. courses are available

ii. consulting services are available

	Readily		Occasionally		Never		Don't know	
	i (%)	ii (%)	i (5)	ii (%)	i (%)	ii(%)	i (%)	ii (%)
Total	58.4	74.7	34.1	19.2	4.8	3.8	2.2	1.6
University Size								
Toronto	46.6	62.1	37.9	25.9	8.6	6.9	6.9	5.2
Large	72.2	85.9	25.0	12.7	1.4			
Medium	57.8	78.6	35.6	14.3	6.7	7.1		
Small	37.5	55.6	62.5	44.4				
Academic Unit								
Fine Arts	42.9	62.5	57.1	37.5				
Humanities	57.1	76.9	42.9	23.1				
Social Sciences	58.3	79.2	37.5	16.7	4.2	4.2		
Natural Sciences	69.5	85.7	26.1	9.5				
Mathematics	71.4	83.3	14.3	16.7	14.3			
Admin/Commerce	25.0	83.3	66.7	16.7	8.3			
Education	80.0	80.0		10.0	10.0		10.0	10.0
Engineering	60.0	61.1	30.0	27.8	10.0	11.1		
Medicine	50.0	60.9	36.4	26.1	13.6	13.0		
Others	63.4	76.2	34.1	19.0		2.4	2.4	2.4

3. Is there a University-level committee with faculty representation to set or advise on policy with respect to academic computing?

	Yes (%)	No (%)	Don't know (%)
Total	72.9	8.5	18.6
University Size			
Toronto	59.0	11.5	29.5
Large	83.1	7.0	9.9
Medium	77.8	6.7	15.6
Small	66.7		33.3
Academic Unit			
Fine Arts	62.5		37.5
Humanities	78.6	7.1	14.3
Social Sciences	80.8	3.8	15.4
Natural Sciences	69.6	17.4	13.0
Mathematics	71.4	28.6	
Admin/Commerce	75.0	16.7	8.3
Education	90.0		10.0
Engineering	88.9		11.1
Medicine	54.2	12.5	33.3
Others	70.7	7.3	22.0

4. Is there a committee in your Academic Unit to set or advise on policy with respect to academic computing?

	Yes (%)	No (%)	Don't know (%)
Total	56.0	36.1	7.8
University Size			
Toronto	56.5	35.5	8.1
Large	56.9	34.7	8.3
Medium	58.7	34.8	6.5
Small	22.2	66.7	11.1
Academic Unit			
Fine Arts		87.5	12.5
Humanities	66.7	33.3	
Social Sciences	42.3	46.2	11.5
Natural Sciences	65.2	34.8	
Mathematics	71.4	28.6	
Admin/Commerce	75.0	16.7	8.3
Education	70.0	20.0	10.0
Engineering	78.9	15.8	5.3
Medicine	50.0	29.2	20.8
Others	50.0	42.9	7.1

5. Is anyone in your Unit carrying out research in the use of computers for the following purposes?
   - i. for in-class electronic presentation
   - ii. to provide in-class graphics or design capabilities
   - iii. to allow in-class simulations or model manipulations
   - iv. to simulate equipment in laboratory training
   - v. to aid in off-campus or distance education
   - vi. for computer assisted or mediated instruction
   - vii. in conjunction with video tape, video disk, CD ROM or CDI for computer assisted instruction
   - viii. other

	Yes (Don't know) (%)						
	i	ii	iii	iv	v	vi	vii
Total	32.2 (14.7)	24.4 (23.8)	32.4 (20.2)	17.5 (20.5)	12.0 (22.2)	39.5 (18.6)	20.2 (23.8)
University Size							
Toronto	28.6 (12.5)	23.6 (16.4)	27.6 (19.0)	11.1 (18.5)	7.3 (16.4)	34.5 (22.4)	14.8 (18.5)
Large	36.8 (17.6)	21.5 (30.8)	36.4 (19.7)	24.2 (21.2)	19.7 (24.2)	45.5 (16.7)	20.9 (31.4)
Medium	31.8 (11.4)	30.0 (22.5)	34.1 (19.5)	8.1 (24.3)	7.7 (25.6)	40.0 (17.5)	25.6 (17.9)
Small	14.3 (28.6)	14.3 (28.6)	28.6 (28.6)	50.0 (12.5)	0.0 (33.3)	14.3 (14.3)	0.0 (33.3)
Academic Unit							
Fine Arts	14.3 (28.6)	42.9 (14.3)	28.6 (42.9)	14.3 (14.3)	0.0 (14.3)	37.5 (12.5)	14.3 (14.3)
Humanities	53.8 (15.4)	23.1 (30.8)	38.5 (30.8)	25.0 (16.7)	7.7 (23.1)	69.2 (7.7)	16.7 (33.3)
Social Sciences	39.1 (13.0)	17.4 (21.7)	37.5 (20.8)	25.0 (20.0)	5.0 (25.0)	36.4 (18.2)	5.3 (15.8)
Natural Sciences	36.4 (9.1)	14.3 (28.6)	38.1 (9.5)	27.3 (18.2)	13.6 (22.7)	45.5 (18.2)	13.6 (27.3)
Mathematics	28.6 (0.0)	33.3 (0.0)	33.3 (0.0)	0.0 (0.0)	14.3 (0.0)	42.9 (0.0)	0.0 (16.7)
Admin/Commerce	50.0 (33.3)	36.4 (45.5)	50.0 (41.7)	0.0 (36.4)	9.1 (36.4)	9.1 (63.6)	9.1 (45.5)
Education	40.0 (20.0)	22.2 (33.3)	30.0 (20.0)	11.1 (22.2)	22.2 (33.3)	44.4 (22.2)	44.4 (22.2)
Engineering	36.8 (15.8)	29.4 (23.5)	38.9 (27.8)	35.3 (23.5)	5.9 (29.4)	23.5 (23.5)	11.8 (35.3)
Medicine	28.6 (14.3)	9.5 (33.3)	27.3 (13.6)	13.6 (22.7)	31.8 (13.6)	52.4 (14.3)	40.9 (18.2)
Others	26.3 (7.9)	35.1 (8.1)	22.2 (11.1)	11.1 (16.7)	8.6 (17.1)	39.5 (38.0)	26.3 (15.8)

II. Preparation of Class Materials

1. Indicate which of the following apply in your Unit with respect to the use of computers in preparation of class materials for various levels of classes:
   i. to prepare AV materials for class use?
   ii. to access data bases and analyze data for classroom use?
   iii. to access test banks for preparation of tests and exams?
   iv. other

	By all faculty (%)			By a few faculty (%)			By no faculty (%)			Don't know (%)		
	i	ii	iii	i	ii	iii	i	ii	iii	i	ii	iii
Total	10.9	5.9	3.8	55.6	59.4	37.2	23.0	25.9	47.4	4.0	3.5	5.1
University Size												
Toronto	11.2	5.6	7.5	47.2	50.0	26.4	22.2	25.5	49.1	5.6	5.5	3.8
Large	13.3	4.6	1.7	67.6	70.8	48.3	11.8	15.4	43.1	5.9	4.6	5.2
Medium	6.8	7.3		54.5	51.2	31.4	36.4	39.0	54.4			8.6
Small	14.3		12.5	28.6	50.0	37.5	57.1	50.0	50.0			
Academic Unit												
Fine Arts	12.5				25.0	12.5	50.0	50.0	62.5	12.5		
Humanities	7.7	8.3		53.8	58.3	45.5	30.8	25.0	45.5	7.7	8.3	9.1
Social Sciences	4.2	4.2	9.1	54.2	66.7	50.0	37.5	25.0	36.4	4.2	4.2	4.5
Natural Sciences	8.7	4.3		73.9	73.9	57.1	13.0	17.4	38.1	4.3	4.3	4.8
Mathematics				42.9	71.4	16.7	57.1	28.6	66.7			16.7
Admin/Commerce	10.0		12.5	80.0	75.0	50.0		12.5	25.0			12.5
Education				80.0	90.0	50.0	10.0		40.0			
Engineering	17.7	14.3	9.1	58.9	50.0	9.1	23.5	35.7	81.8			
Medicine	30.0	15.0	5.3	45.0	40.0	42.1	10.0	30.0	36.8	5.0	5.0	5.3
Others	10.2	5.0	2.8	59.0	55.0	25.0	17.9	27.5	55.6	5.1	5.0	5.6

2. Indicate which of the following technical or other support services, if any, are provided to aid faculty in computer-assisted preparation of class materials:
   i. faculty have access to instructional designers
   ii. faculty have access to technicians who prepare graphics
   iii. technicians are available to set up and maintain equipment
   iv. faculty have access to trainers/consulting support in use of technology

	i (%)	ii (%)	iii (%)	iv (%)
Total	15.2	28.8	48.7	46.6
University Size				
Toronto	9.8	27.9	37.7	39.3
Large	16.4	38.4	57.5	49.3
Medium	19.6	21.7	52.2	50.0
Small	11.1		33.3	55.6
Academic Unit				
Fine Arts			12.5	12.5
Humanities	28.6	28.6	50.0	64.3
Social Sciences	7.7	11.5	38.5	42.3
Natural Sciences	21.7	34.8	52.2	47.8
Mathematics		14.3	57.1	14.3
Admin/Commerce		8.3	58.3	58.3
Education	20.0	40.0	70.0	40.0
Engineering	5.0	30.0	55.0	30.0
Medicine	25.0	45.8	50.0	45.8
Others	19.0	38.1	47.6	57.1

III. In-Class Use (An instructor is normally present)

1. Indicate which of the following apply in your Unit with respect to the use of computers in the classroom or laboratory for various types of classes:
   - i. for electronic presentation
   - ii. to provide graphics or design capabilities
   - iii. to allow simulations or model manipulation
   - iv. to analyze data
   - v. in conjunction with other devices such as video tape, video disk, CD ROM, CDI etc.
   - vi. to **simulate** equipment in laboratory training
   - vii. to aid in off-campus or distance education
   - viii. other

	By all faculty (%)				By a few faculty (%)				By no faculty (%)			
	i	ii	iii	iv	i	ii	iii	iv	i	ii	iii	iv
Total	1.6	5.3	3.5	7.5	41.7	42.9	44.7	58.9	56.7	51.9	51.8	33.6
University Size												
Toronto	2.5	7.0		11.1	35.0	34.9	43.2	51.1	62.5	58.1	56.8	37.8
Large		4.3	3.7	5.3	51.1	54.3	50.0	73.7	46.8	41.3	46.3	19.3
Medium	3.1	5.4	8.1	5.3	33.3	37.8	37.8	44.7	63.6	56.8	54.1	50.0
Small					42.9	42.9	50.0	66.7	57.1	57.1	50.0	33.3
Academic Unit												
Fine Arts						33.3	16.7	33.3	100.0	66.7	83.3	66.7
Humanities			18.2	15.4	11.1	18.2	18.2	53.8	88.9	81.8	63.6	30.8
Social Sciences					50.0	38.9	52.6	71.4	50.0	61.1	47.4	28.6
Natural Sciences					40.0	56.3	63.6	85.7	60.0	43.8	36.4	14.3
Mathematics					28.6	57.1	42.9	28.6	71.4	42.9	57.1	71.4
Admin/Commerce			12.5	14.3	71.4	57.1	62.5	71.4	28.6	42.9	25.0	14.3
Education		11.1		12.5	87.5	66.7	42.9	87.5	12.5	22.2	57.1	
Engineering		8.3	6.7	6.7	58.3	50.0	73.3	66.7	41.7	41.7	20.0	26.7
Medicine		14.3		26.7	50.0	50.0	46.7	40.0	50.0	35.7	53.3	33.3
Others	6.5	9.4	3.3	6.3	29.0	31.3	23.3	46.9	64.5	59.4	73.3	46.9

	By all faculty (%)			By a few faculty (%)			By no faculty (%)		
	v	vi	vii	v	vi	vii	v	vi	vii
Total	0.9	0.8		15.3	20.3	18.8	83.8	78.8	81.2
University Size									
Toronto				10.8	15.0	7.9	89.2	85.0	92.1
Large				28.2	30.2	32.6	71.8	69.8	67.4
Medium	3.3	3.4		6.7	3.4	14.8	90.0	93.1	85.2
Small					66.7		100.0	33.3	100.0
Academic Unit									
Fine Arts				20.0			80.0	100.0	100.0
Humanities					11.1	11.1	100.0	88.9	88.9
Social Sciences					27.8	7.1	100.0	72.2	92.9
Natural Sciences				25.0	31.3	23.5	75.0	68.8	76.5
Mathematics						14.3	100.0	100.0	85.7
Admin/Commerce						40.0	100.0	100.0	60.0
Education				66.7	42.9	62.5	33.3	57.1	37.5
Engineering				22.2	44.4		77.8	55.6	100.0
Medicine				30.8	28.6	35.7	69.2	71.4	64.3
Others	3.7	3.7		7.4	7.4	10.3	88.9	88.9	89.7

IV. Out-Of-Class Use (An Instructor is normally not present)

1. Indicate which of the following apply in your Unit with respect to the use of computers outside the classroom or laboratory for various types of classes:
   i. to provide students with self-paced, computer-assisted review or drill?
   ii. to replace some or all of a more formal lecture-type class?
   iii. to provide students access to "an expert system"?
   iv. to provide access to mathematical modelling or simulation?
   v. to facilitate data analysis?
   vi. other

	By all faculty (%)					By a few faculty (%)					By no faculty (%)				
	i	ii	iii	iv	v	i	ii	iii	iv	v	i	ii	iii	iv	v
Total	6.9	2.5	2.5	6.6	11.4	29.0	15.7	17.5	43.4	55.0	64.1	81.9	80.0	50.0	33.6
University Size															
Toronto	7.3			4.5	8.9	22.0	8.1	13.9	43.2	53.3	70.7	91.9	86.1	52.3	37.8
Large	6.7	4.3	2.2	6.1	11.5	34.7	19.1	22.2	44.9	63.5	59.2	76.6	75.6	49.0	25.0
Medium	8.8	3.2	6.3	11.1	16.7	29.4	19.4	15.6	41.7	44.4	61.8	77.4	78.1	47.2	38.9
Small						28.6	16.7	14.3	42.9	57.1	71.4	83.3	85.7	57.1	42.9
Academic Unit															
Fine Arts				16.7	16.7	14.3		16.7		16.7	85.7	100.0	83.3	83.3	66.7
Humanities	10.0			10.0	15.4	30.0			10.0	53.8	60.0	100.0	100.0	80.0	30.8
Social Sciences						22.2	6.3	11.1	44.4	57.9	77.8	93.8	88.9	55.6	42.1
Natural Sciences						35.3	12.6	28.6	70.0	85.0	64.7	87.5	71.4	30.0	15.0
Mathematics					14.3	14.3			28.6	14.3	85.7	100.0	100.0	71.4	71.4
Admin/Commerce	14.3			14.3	14.3	28.6	16.7	40.0	42.9	57.1	57.1	83.3	60.0	42.9	28.6
Education			12.5		12.5	50.0	50.0	25.0	75.0	87.5	50.0	50.0	62.5	25.0	
Engineering	27.3	12.5		31.3	38.5	27.3	25.0	40.0	63.5	53.8	45.5	62.5	60.0	6.3	7.7
Medicine	18.8	12.5			13.3	31.3	25.0	26.7	33.3	53.3	50.0	62.5	73.3	66.7	33.3
Others	3.4		7.7	3.6	9.7	31.0	19.2	7.7	35.7	48.4	65.5	80.8	84.6	60.7	41.9

V. Computerized Support Systems

1. Does your library have a computerized catalogue system?

	Yes (%)	No (%)	Coming (%)	Don't know (%)
Total	85.8	7.9	2.1	4.2
University Size				
Toronto	85.2	6.6		8.2
Large	93.2	2.7	1.4	2.7
Medium	84.4	13.3		2.2
Small	33.3	33.3	33.3	
Academic Unit				
Fine Arts	75.0		12.5	12.5
Humanities	78.6	14.3		7.1
Social Sciences	69.2	23.1	7.7	
Natural Sciences	95.7			4.3
Mathematics	100.0			
Admin/Commerce	83.3			4.3
Education	90.0			10.0
Engineering	95.0	5.0		
Medicine	70.8	12.5	4.2	12.5
Others	95.2	4.8		

2. a) What bibliographical, informational or library data bases can be accessed through your library?

	1 to 5 (%)	More than 5 (%)	Don't know (%)
Total	50.8	6.2	19.4
University Size			
Toronto	44.3	13.1	11.5
Large	65.7	9.6	15.1
Medium	45.6	2.2	34.8
Small		33.3	33.3
Academic Unit			
Fine Arts	25.0	25.0	12.5
Humanities	50.0	14.3	21.4
Social Sciences	46.2	7.7	23.1
Natural Sciences	52.2	13.0	30.4
Mathematics	42.9		28.6
Admin/Commerce	16.7	16.7	33.3
Education	60.0	10.0	
Engineering	45.0	15.0	15.0
Medicine	75.0	4.2	4.2
Others	54.8	7.1	21.4

b) Which of these data bases can be accessed from faculty offices or from other locations **outside** the library?

	All (%)	Most (%)	A few (%)	None (%)	Don't know (%)
Total	21.5	4.2	10.5	15.7	17.8
University Size					
Toronto	14.8	1.6	14.8	9.8	11.5
Large	28.8	6.8	11.0	13.7	20.5
Medium	19.6	4.3	6.5	23.9	23.9
Small	11.1			33.3	11.1
Academic Unit					
Fine Arts	12.5			37.5	12.5
Humanities	28.6		14.3	21.4	7.1
Social Sciences	11.5	7.7	11.5	23.1	19.2
Natural Sciences	39.1	4.3	4.3	8.7	17.4
Mathematics	42.9				8.7
Admin/Commerce	8.3		8.3	16.7	25.0
Education	10.0	20.0	10.0	10.0	10.0
Engineering	20.0	10.0	15.0	10.0	10.0
Medicine	12.5		12.5	33.3	12.5
Others	26.2	2.4	11.9	7.1	26.2

3. i. Can the library indexes be accessed from faculty offices?
   ii. Can the library indexes be accessed from locations, other than faculty offices, outside the library?

	Yes		No		Don't know	
	i (%)	ii (%)	i (%)	ii (%)	i (%)	ii (%)
Total	50.3	51.4	32.8	20.7	14.2	24.0
University Size						
Toronto	44.3	52.6	34.4	17.5	9.8	21.1
Large	60.6	60.0	22.5	12.9	15.5	27.1
Medium	46.5	42.9	41.9	31.0	11.6	21.4
Small	11.1		44.4	62.5	44.4	37.5
Academic Unit						
Fine Arts	57.4	57.4	42.9	28.6		14.3
Humanities	41.7	63.6	41.7	18.2	8.3	9.1
Social Sciences	54.2	47.8	29.2	26.1	12.5	21.7
Natural Sciences	65.2	63.6	13.0	9.1	13.0	22.7
Mathematics	42.9	85.7	42.9		14.3	14.3
Admin/Commerce	36.4	27.3	45.5	36.4	18.2	36.4
Education	77.8	77.8	22.2	11.1		11.1
Engineering	60.0	52.6	30.0	31.6	10.0	15.8
Medicine	13.0	17.4	52.2	34.8	30.4	39.1
Others	57.1	54.8	28.6	11.9	14.3	28.6

4. Indicate the use of the following:
   i. an international or national network such as BITNET or NETNORTH
   ii. electronic mail to communicate with other faculty on campus

	By all faculty		By most faculty		By a few faculty		By no faculty		Don't know	
	i (%)	ii (%)	i (%)	ii (%)	i (%)	ii (%)	i (%)	ii (%)	i (%)	ii (%)
Total	7.8	5.0	21.1	22.9	55.3	59.2	12.8	11.7	3.4	1.1
University Size										
Toronto	11.3	9.4	15.1	17.0	54.7	60.4	15.1	13.2	3.8	
Large	2.8		29.6	35.7	56.3	57.1	7.0	5.7	4.2	1.4
Medium	13.3	8.9	13.3	13.3	53.3	55.6	17.8	20.0	2.2	2.2
Small			12.5		62.5	88.9	25.0	11.1		
Academic Unit										
Fine Arts			16.7	16.7	50.0	50.0	16.7	33.3	16.7	
Humanities			41.7	25.0	41.7	66.7	16.7	8.3		
Social Sciences	7.7	4.0	15.4	8.0	57.7	76.0	15.4	12.0	3.8	
Natural Sciences	8.7	4.3	17.4	21.7	60.9	65.2	13.0	8.7		
Mathematics	16.7	28.6	66.7	57.1		14.3	16.7			
Admin/Commerce	16.7		25.0	27.3	58.3	63.6		9.1		
Education	11.1		22.2	44.4	66.7	55.5				
Engineering	15.0	15.8	20.0	26.4	60.0	47.4		5.3	5.0	5.3
Medicine			9.1	9.1	54.5	63.6	31.8	22.7	4.5	4.5
Others	7.7	5.0	17.9	27.5	59.0	55.0	10.3	12.5	5.1	

   iii. electronic mail to communicate with students in class

	By all faculty	By most faculty	By a few faculty	By no faculty	Don't know
	iii (%)	iii (%)	iii (%)	iii (%)	iii (%)
Total	2.4	4.3	35.4	51.8	6.1
University Size					
Toronto	2.1	4.3	25.5	63.8	4.3
Large		3.1	43.8	45.3	7.8
Medium	6.8	6.8	36.4	43.2	6.8
Small			14.3	85.7	
Academic Unit					
Fine Arts			20.0	80.0	
Humanities			40.0	60.0	
Social Sciences			25.0	66.7	8.3
Natural Sciences	5.0		30.0	50.0	15.0
Mathematics	14.3	14.3	14.3	57.1	
Admin/Commerce			70.0	30.0	
Education		12.5	50.0	25.0	12.5
Engineering	5.6	5.6	61.1	22.2	5.6
Medicine			28.6	61.9	9.5
Others	2.7	10.8	32.4	51.4	2.7

5. a) Are word processing facilities **provided** for students to prepare theses, papers and assignments?

	Yes (%)	Senior undergrads and/or grads only (%)	Some cost (%)	No (%)	Don't know (%)
Total	67.0	5.3	2.1	20.2	4.3
University Size					
Toronto	52.5	5.1		32.2	6.8
Large	69.4	8.4	2.8	16.7	2.8
Medium	76.1		4.3	15.2	4.3
Small	100.0				
Academic Unit					
Fine Arts	62.5				37.5
Humanities	76.9			23.1	
Social Sciences	73.1	3.8	3.8	15.4	3.8
Naural Sciènces	65.2	13.0		21.7	
Mathematics	57.1			42.9	
Admin/Commerce	50.0	16.7	8.3	25.0	
Education	60.0	10.0		10.0	20.0
Engineering	90.0			10.0	
Medicine	59.1			36.4	4.5
Others	68.3	4.9	4.9	19.5	2.4

b) If your answer is 'Yes', indicate which of the following best describes the situation:

i. facilities are widely available to all students

ii. facilities are available in a few locations

			Limited access	
	i (%)	ii (%)	i (%)	ii (%)
Total	36.4	50.7	3.6	5.7
University Size				
Toronto	41.2	44.1	2.9	14.7
Large	29.3	53.4	6.9	3.4
Medium	48.6	48.6		
Small	22.2	55.5		11.1
Aoadomic Unit				
Fine Arts	20.0	40.0	20.0	20.0
Humanities	40.0	50.0		50.0
Social Sciences	42.9	45.5		13.7
Natural Sciences	5.6	83.3	5.6	
Mathematics	25.0	75.0		
Admin/Commerce	33.3	33.3	11.1	11.1
Education	57.1	28.6	14.3	
Engineering	50.0	33.3	5.6	11.1
Medicine	38.5	69.2		
Others	43.8	40.6		

VI. General Comments

3. Has the use of personal computers as word processors led to faculty doing substantially more of the preparation of manuscripts for publication?

	Yes (%)	No (%)	Not certain (%)
Total	76.4	8.9	14.1
Academic Unit			
Fine Arts	75.0	12.5	12.5
Humanities	73.3	6.7	20.0
Social Sciences	80.8	7.7	7.7
Natural Sciences	87.0	4.3	8.7
Mathematics	71.4	28.6	
Admin/Commerce	91.7		8.3
Education	60.0	10.0	30.0
Engineering	85.0		15.0
Medicine	58.3	20.8	20.8
Others	73.8	9.5	14.3

4. a) Has the use of computers improved the quality of education in your Unit?

	Yes (%)	No (%)	Yes and no (%)	No opinion (%)	Don't know (%)
Total	42.7	22.[illegible]	3.8	29.2	2.2
Academic Unit					
Fine Arts	14.3	28.6		42.9	14.3
Humanities	46.7	20.0	6.7	26.7	
Social Sciences	33.3	37.5		29.2	
Natural Sciences	43.6	21.7	4.3	26.1	4.3
Mathematics	42.9	42.9		14.3	
Admin/Commerce	58.3	16.7		25.0	
Education	60.0	10.0	10.0	20.0	
Engineering	66.7	22.2	5.6	5.6	
Medicine	47.8	17.4		30.4	4.3
Others	31.7	14.6	7.3	43.9	2.4

b) Please explain.

	Negative response (%)	Neutral response (%)	Positive response (%)
Total	14.0	17.8	68.2
Academic Unit			
Fine Arts			
Humanities		36.4	63.6
Social Sciences	30.0	5.0	65.0
Natural Sciences	8.3	20.8	70.8
Mathematics		33.3	66.7
Admin/Commerce	23.1	7.7	69.2
Education	9.1	9.1	81.8
Engineering	12.0	16.0	72.0
Medicine	10.5	21.1	68.4
Others	16.1	22.6	61.3

5. a) Has the use of computers provided your faculty with **more time** to devote to teaching and scholarly activity?

	Yes (%)	No (%)	No opinion (%)	Don't know (%)
Total	17.4	40.8	10.3	31.5
Academic Unit				
Fine Arts		57.1	14.3	28.6
Humanities	20.0	40.0		40.0
Social Sciences	29.2	33.3	4.2	33.3
Natural Sciences	13.6	40.9	18.2	27.3
Mathematics		85.7		14.3
Admin/Commerce	16.7	41.7	25.0	16.7
Education	10.0	30.0		60.0
Engineering	30.0	40.0	5.0	25.0
Medicine	13.6	36.4	13.6	36.4
Others	17.5	40.0	12.5	30.0

b) Please explain.

	Negative response (%)	Neutral response (%)	Positive response (%)
Total	39.8	35.0	25.2
Academic Unit			
Fine Arts			
Humanities	10.0	80.0	10.0
Social Sciences	54.5	18.2	27.3
Natural Sciences	52.6	36.8	10.5
Mathematics	66.7	33.3	
Admin/Commerce	33.3	33.3	33.3
Education		100.0	
Engineering	26.7	46.7	26.7
Medicine	57.1	14.3	28.6
Others	44.4	11.1	44.4

6. The following are major advantage(s) of computers in instruction at a university level:
   i. lecture content and presentation are improved
   ii. student motivation and self-learning are increased
   iii. the cost of instruction is lowered

	Strongly Agree			Agree			Disagree			Strongly Disagree			No opinion		
	i (%)	ii (%)	iii (%)	i (%)	ii (%)	iii (%)	i (%)	ii (%)	iii (%)	i (%)	ii (%)	iii (%)	i (%)	ii (%)	iii (%)
Total	7.2	5.4	2.7	33.1	41.1	9.3	21.5	18.9	41.8	6.1	3.8	7.9	29.8	28.6	35.2
Academic Unit															
Fine Arts	12.5				12.5	12.5	50.0	37.5	50.0	12.5	12.5		25.0	37.5	37.5
Humanities	14.3	6.7		28.6	40.0		7.1	13.3	26.7			20.0	50.0	40.0	53.3
Social Sciences	8.0			28.0	25.0	8.0	20.0	29.2	44.0	12.0	8.3	12.0	28.0	37.5	36.0
Natural Sciences				28.6	56.5	19.0	23.9	8.7	42.9	4.8		4.8	42.9	34.8	33.3
Mathematics		16.7		33.3	16.7	16.7	33.3	33.3	50.0	16.7	16.7	16.7	16.7	16.7	16.7
Admin/Commerce	18.2	9.1		27.3	63.6	18.2	18.2	18.2	63.6	9.1			27.3	9.1	18.2
Education	20.0	20.0	20.0	30.0	50.0		30.0	20.0	30.0			20.0	20.0	10.0	30.0
Engineering	11.1	11.1	5.9	38.9	55.6	17.6	27.8	16.7	41.2			11.8	22.2	16.7	23.5
Medicine	4.2	4.2		41.7	45.8	4.2	16.7	12.5	45.8	8.3	4.2	4.2	20.8	25.0	37.5
Others	2.5	4.9	5.0	40.0	34.1	2.5	17.5	19.5	37.5	2.5	2.4	7.5	35.0	36.6	45.0
Age															
Under 40	6.7	6.7	5.0	38.3	36.7	11.7	18.3	23.3	28.3	1.7	1.7	5.0	30.0	28.3	45.0
40 to 49	10.9	4.6	1.6	32.8	47.7	10.9	21.9	13.8	50.0	6.3	6.2	9.4	28.1	27.7	28.1
50 to 59	4.5	4.3		27.3	41.3	6.7	27.3	13.0	53.3	9.1	4.3	6.7	29.5	30.4	31.1
60 and over		7.1	7.7	30.8	28.6		15.4	28.6	23.1	15.4		30.8	38.5	35.7	38.5

iv. there is improved communication between instructor and student

v. out-of-class learning opportunities are improved

	Strongly Agree		Agree		Disagree		Strongly Disagree		No opinion	
	iv (%)	v (%)	iv (%)	v (%)	iv (%)	v (%)	iv (%)	v (%)	iv (%)	v (%)
Total	2.2	14.8	17.7	48.9	30.9	9.9	9.4	3.3	37.6	20.3
Academic Unit										
Fine Arts			12.5	66.7	50.0	16.7			25.0	16.7
Humanities		21.4	7.1	42.9	21.4	14.3	7.1		64.3	21.4
Social Sciences		4.2	8.0	50.0	28.0	8.3	16.0	12.5	48.0	25.0
Natural Sciences		14.3	19.0	47.6	28.6	4.8	19.0		33.3	33.3
Mathematics		16.7	16.7	33.3	33.3		16.7	16.7	33.3	33.3
Admin/Commerce		18.2	36.4	72.7	36.4		9.1		18.2	9.1
Education		20.0	40.0	50.0	40.0	20.0			20.0	10.0
Engineering	11.1	26.3	22.2	42.1	27.8	10.5	5.6		33.3	21.1
Medicine		12.5	20.8	58.3	20.8		12.5	4.2	37.5	16.7
Others	5.0	12.2	15.0	48.8	32.5	14.6	2.5	2.4	42.5	19.5
Age										
Under 40	3.4	13.6	16.9	42.4	32.2	8.5	3.4	3.4	39.0	27.1
40 to 49		18.5	20.0	49.2	30.8	10.8	10.8	3.1	38.5	18.5
50 to 59	2.3	13.6	15.9	52.3	34.1	9.1	9.1	4.5	36.4	15.9
60 and over	7.7	7.1	15.4	64.3	15.4	14.3	30.8		30.8	14.3

vi. students get access to information they might not otherwise get

vii. calculation-intensive operations such as simulations become possible

	Strongly Agree		Agree		Disagree		Strongly Disagree		No opinion	
	vi (%)	vii (%)	vi (%)	vii (%)	vi (%)	vii (%)	vi (%)	vii (%)	vi (%)	vii (%)
Total	13.0	29.6	51.6	45.2	11.4	3.8	3.8	2.2	17.9	17.2
Academic Unit										
Fine Arts		12.5	37.5	37.5	50.0	12.5			12.5	37.5
Humanities	21.4	35.7	42.9	28.6	7.1	7.1	7.1		21.4	28.6
Social Sciences	12.0	20.0	48.0	52.0	4.0	4.0	8.0	4.0	28.0	20.0
Natural Sciences	4.8	23.8	57.1	71.4	4.8		4.8		28.6	4.8
Mathematics	16.7	14.3	33.3	71.4	16.7		16.7	14.3	16.7	
Admin/Commerce	18.2	54.5	81.8	45.5						
Education	20.0	30.0	60.0	50.0	10.0	10.0			10.0	10.0
Engineering	27.8	52.6	33.3	42.1	16.7				22.2	5.3
Medicine	8.3	25.0	62.5	33.3	4.2		8.3	8.3	8.3	25.0
Others	11.9	31.0	52.4	35.7	14.3	7.1			19.0	23.8
Age										
Under 40	19.7	32.3	44.3	39.7	11.5	6.5	1.6	1.6	18.0	29.3
40 to 49	12.3	32.3	58.5	46.2	10.8	3.1	4.6	1.5	13.8	18.5
50 to 59	8.9	24.4	53.3	34.1	11.1	2.2	4.4	2.2	20.0	38.6
60 and over		21.4	46.1	35.7	15.4		7.7	7.1	30.8	35.7

viii. computers can remove from faculty the drudgery of drill and repetition

ix. the youth of today are generally computer-oriented and computer literate

	Strongly Agree		Agree		Disagree		Strongly Disagree		No opinion	
	viii (%)	ix (%)	viii (%)	ix (%)	viii (%)	ix (%)	viii (%)	ix (%)	viii (%)	ix (%)
Total	7.2	12.6	40.3	53.0	17.7	19.1	4.4	2.2	28.2	10.4
Academic Unit										
Fine Arts			25.0	87.5	62.5	12.5			12.5	
Humanities	14.3	28.6	21.4	28.6	14.3	28.6	7.1		42.9	14.3
Social Sciences		4.3	40.0	43.5	20.0	17.4	8.0	13.0	32.0	17.4
Natural Sciences	4.8	4.8	47.6	66.7	14.3	23.8			33.3	4.8
Mathematics	16.7		16.7	42.9	50.0	42.9	16.7			14.3
Admin/Commerce	9.1	18.2	54.5	54.5	18.2	18.2			18.2	9.1
Education		11.1	40.0	66.7	20.0	11.1	10.0		30.0	11.1
Engineering	11.1	21.1	55.6	63.2	5.6	10.5			27.8	5.3
Medicine	8.3	20.8	41.7	50.0	12.5	8.3	4.2	4.2	25.0	8.3
Others	10.0	11.9	40.0	50.0	12.5	21.4	2.5		32.5	14.3
Age										
Under 40	8.6	16.7	39.7	46.7	15.5	18.3	1.7	3.3	29.3	8.3
40 to 49	9.2	9.2	46.2	56.9	20.0	24.6	6.2	1.5	18.5	7.7
50 to 59	4.5	11.6	34.1	51.2	15.9	14.0	4.5	2.3	38.6	18.6
60 and over		13.3	35.7	66.7	21.4	13.3	7.1		35.7	6.7

The following are major disadvantage(s) of computers in instruction at a university level:

i. less emphasis is placed on the role of faculty as teachers

ii. the cost does not justify their use

iii. there is less communication between instructor and students

	Strongly Agree			Agree			Disagree			Strongly Disagree			No opinion		
	i (%)	ii (%)	iii (%)	i (%)	ii (%)	iii (%)	i (%)	ii (%)	iii (%)	i (%)	ii (%)	iii (%)	i (%)	ii (%)	iii (%)
Total	2.2	2.2	3.3	11.0	8.2	10.4	54.7	53.8	52.2	9.9	13.7	7.1	20.4	19.8	24.7
Academic Unit															
Fine Arts	14.3		14.3	14.3	28.6	14.3	28.6	42.9	42.9	14.3			28.6	28.6	28.6
Humanities				13.3	6.7	13.3	46.7	60.0	66.7	13.3	6.7		26.7	26.7	20.0
Social Sciences	4.0			8.0	8.0	12.0	48.0	56.0	48.0	8.0	8.0	8.0	20.0	24.0	28.0
Natural Sciences				22.7	4.5	22.7	45.5	63.6	40.9	4.5	13.6	4.5	27.3	18.2	31.8
Mathematics		16.7	16.7				50.0	33.3	33.3	16.7	16.7	16.7	33.3	33.3	33.3
Admin/Commerce				9.1	9.1		72.7	63.6	81.8	9.1	18.2	9.1	9.1	9.1	9.1
Education							80.0	60.0	60.0	10.0	30.0	20.0	10.0	10.0	20.0
Engineering				22.2	17.6	5.6	50.0	52.9	50.0	11.1	17.6	11.1	16.7	11.8	33.3
Medicine			4.2	8.3	8.3	16.7	58.3	58.3	45.8	8.3	12.5	8.3	20.8	16.7	20.8
Others		5.0	5.0	7.7	7.5	7.5	61.5	45.0	55.0	12.8	17.5	5.0	15.4	22.5	25.0
Age															
Under 40	1.7			10.2	8.5	8.5	55.9	57.6	47.5	6.8	10.2	8.5	22.0	20.3	32.2
40 to 49	1.6	3.1	4.6	12.5	4.6	7.7	56.3	56.9	64.6	14.1	18.5	6.2	15.6	16.9	16.9
50 to 59	2.2	2.2	4.3	10.9	10.9	17.4	47.8	50.0	41.3	10.9	13.0	8.7	23.9	19.6	23.9
60 and over	7.7	8.3	8.3	7.7	16.7	8.3	61.5	33.3	50.0		8.3		23.1	33.3	33.3

iv. faculty are not adequately trained in their use
v. they cater to an excessive need for entertainment

	Strongly Agree		Agree		Disagree		Strongly Disagree		No opinion	
	iv (%)	v (%)	iv (%)	v (%)	iv (%)	v (%)	iv (%)	v (%)	iv (%)	v (%)
Total	16.1	2.2	52.2	12.5	16.1	40.2	1.1	11.4	12.4	31.5
Academic Unit										
Fine Arts	14.3		57.1		14.3	57.1		14.3	14.3	28.6
Humanities	6.7		66.7	13.3	13.3	46.7		13.3	13.3	26.7
Social Sciences	20.0	4.0	36.0	12.0	32.0	28.0		16.0	8.0	36.0
Natural Sciences	13.6		45.5	4.5	13.6	31.8		9.1	27.3	54.5
Mathematics	14.3		42.9	28.6	28.6	42.9			14.3	28.6
Admin/Commerce	18.2		54.5	9.1	18.2	45.5		27.3	9.1	18.2
Education	10.0		60.0		20.0	50.0		20.0	10.0	30.0
Engineering	36.8		31.6	22.2	21.1	33.3	5.3		5.3	44.4
Medicine	20.8		45.8	12.5	16.7	45.8	4.2	12.5	8.3	25.0
Others	9.8	5.0	68.3	15.0	4.9	42.5		10.0	14.6	25.0
Age										
Under 40	11.5	3.3	50.8	13.3	16.4	43.3	3.3	6.7	14.8	30.0
40 to 49	15.4	1.5	60.0	9.2	16.9	41.5		15.4	7.7	32.3
50 to 59	15.2		52.2	17.4	13.0	34.8		13.0	15.2	30.4
60 and over	42.9	7.7	21.4	7.7	21.4	38.5		7.7	14.3	38.5

vi. they make education too impersonal
vii.mastering computer hardware and software gets in the way of learning

	Strongly Agree		Agree		Disagree		Strongly Disagree		No opinion	
	vi (%)	vii (%)	vi (%)	vii (%)	vi (%)	vii (%)	vi (%)	vii (%)	vi (%)	vii (%)
Total	2.7	4.9	14.3	27.9	49.5	40.5	11.5	7.7	19.8	16.4
Academic Unit										
Fine Arts	14.3		14.3	14.3	28.6	57.1	14.3		28.6	28.6
Humanities			6.7	33.3	60.0	26.7	6.7	20.0	26.7	20.0
Social Sciences	4.0	4.0	12.0	16.0	32.0	44.0	20.0	12.0	28.0	20.0
Natural Sciences		4.5	31.8	31.8	45.5	40.9		4.5	22.7	18.2
Mathematics		14.3	16.7	57.1	33.3	14.3	16.7		33.3	14.3
Admin/Commerce		9.1	9.1	63.6	81.8	18.2	9.1			9.1
Education	10.0	10.0		10.0	50.0	50.0	20.0		20.0	20.0
Engineering			11.1	33.3	50.0	27.8	11.1	11.1	27.8	27.8
Medicine		4.2	29.2	20.8	45.8	45.8	8.3	12.5	12.5	12.5
Others	2.5	5.0	5.0	25.0	57.5	52.5	15.0	5.0	15.0	10.0
Age										
Under 40		1.7	18.6	35.6	45.8	33.9	10.2	8.5	22.0	16.9
40 to 49	4.7	9.2	10.9	26.2	54.7	46.2	14.1	7.7	15.6	10.8
50 to 59	2.2		10.9	21.7	50.0	41.3	10.9	8.7	21.7	21.7
60 and over	7.7	15.4	23.1	23.1	38.5	38.5	7.7		23.1	23.1

8. What constraints do you see on increased use of academic computing:

i. cost

ii. space

iii. availability of computers or terminals

	Major			Minor			None			Don't know		
	i (%)	ii (%)	iii (%)	i (%)	ii (%)	iii (%)	i (%)	ii (%)	iii (%)	i (%)	ii (%)	iii (%)
Total	69.6	40.9	41.5	25.4	43.2	42.6	2.8	12.5	10.8	2.2	3.4	5.1
Academic Unit												
Fine Arts	71.4	28.6	16.7	14.3	42.9	33.3		14.3		14.3	14.3	50.0
Humanities	53.8	35.7	50.0	46.1	50.0	33.3		14.3	16.7			
Social Sciences	60.0	39.1	50.0	36.0	47.8	37.5	4.0	8.7	12.5		4.3	
Natural Sciences	90.9	52.3	59.1	9.1	28.6	31.8		14.3	4.5		4.8	4.5
Mathematics	83.3	50.0	50.0	16.7	33.3	33.3		16.7	16.7			
Admin/Commerce	81.8	63.6	45.5	18.2	36.4	45.5			9.1			
Education	88.9	33.3	55.6		55.6	33.3	11.1	11.1				11.1
Engineering	75.0	42.1	21.1	20.0	47.2	68.4		5.3	5.3	5.0	5.3	5.3
Medicine	56.5	34.8	39.1	34.8	43.5	47.8	4.3	17.4	8.7	4.3	4.3	4.3
Others	63.4	35.8	35.0	29.3	43.6	42.5	4.9	17.9	17.5	2.4	2.6	5.0
Age												
Under 40	70.2	49.1	29.6	26.3	31.6	53.7		14.0	11.1	3.5	5.3	5.6
40 to 49	69.7	35.5	50.8	27.3	53.2	38.5	3.0	9.7	6.2		1.7	4.6
50 to 59	75.6	35.6	43.2	20.0	51.1	36.4	4.4	13.3	18.2			2.3
60 and over	46.2	50.0	38.5	30.8	16.7	38.5	7.7	16.7	7.7	15.4	16.7	15.4

iv. availability of software

v. compatibility of computers or of computer sys...

	Major		Minor		None		Don't know	
	iv (%)	v (%)	iv (%)	v (%)	iv (%)	v (%)	iv (%)	v (%)
Total	30.6	28.6	45.9	56.6	19.4	10.3	4.1	4.6
Academic Unit								
Fine Arts	33.3	42.9	16.7	42.9	16.7		33.3	14.3
Humanities	23.1	42.9	53.8	42.9	23.1	14.3		
Social Sciences	28.6	19.0	38.1	71.4	28.6	9.5	4.7	
Natural Sciences	23.8	21.7	61.9	69.6	9.5	8.7	4.8	
Mathematics	50.0	33.3	16.7	33.3	33.3	33.3		
Admin/Commerce	45.5	36.4	36.4	63.6	18.2			
Education	33.3	11.1	55.6	66.7	11.1	11.1		11.1
Engineering	27.8	16.7	50.0	61.1	16.7	16.7	5.6	5.6
Medicine	34.8	43.5	43.5	30.4	17.4	13.0	4.3	13.0
Others	28.9	30.8	52.6	59.0	15.8	5.1	2.6	5.1
Age								
Under 40	28.3	21.4	45.3	57.1	22.6	10.7	3.8	8.9
40 to 49	36.1	33.3	45.9	54.0	14.8	12.7	3.3	
50 to 59	27.3	31.8	45.5	56.8	25.0	9.1	2.3	2.3
60 and over	25.0	23.1	50.0	61.5	8.3		16.7	15.4

vi. capacity of or available time on mainframe computers
vii. training of faculty

	Major		Minor		None		Don't know	
	vi (%)	vii (%)	vi (%)	vii (%)	vi (%)	vii (%)	vi (%)	vii (%)
Total	13.6	45.1	37.3	45.1	35.5	6.4	13.6	3.5
Academic Unit								
Fine Arts	16.7	33.3	33.3	50.0	16.7		33.3	16.7
Humanities	15.4	46.2	30.8	46.2	38.5	7.7	15.4	
Social Sciences	14.3	36.4	38.1	54.5	42.9	9.1	4.8	
Natural Sciences	9.1	31.3	45.5	54.5	45.5	13.6		
Mathematics	33.3	14.3	16.7	85.7	50.0			
Admin/Commerce	27.3	72.7	54.5	27.3	18.2			
Education	22.2	55.6	11.1	33.3	66.6	11.1		
Engineering	5.6	33.3	44.4	55.5	33.3	5.6	16.7	5.6
Medicine	8.7	60.9	30.4	17.4	30.4	8.7	30.4	13.0
Others	5.6	47.4	44.4	47.4	27.8	2.6	22.2	2.6
Age								
Under 40	15.1	50.0	35.8	40.7	35.8	3.7	17.0	5.6
40 to 49	14.8	36.5	42.6	57.1	34.4	6.3	8.2	
50 to 59	11.6	48.8	34.9	39.5	44.2	11.6	9.3	
60 and over	8.3	53.8	25.0	23.1	25.0		41.7	23.1

viii. training of students
ix. faculty inertia

	Major		Minor		None		Don't know	
	viii (%)	ix (%)	viii (%)	ix (%)	viii (%)	ix (%)	viii (%)	ix (%)
Total	29.2	51.5	58.5	34.5	8.8	7.6	3.5	6.4
Academic Unit								
Fine Arts	16.7	71.4	66.7	14.3			16.7	14.3
Humanities	23.1	53.8	69.2	38.5	7.7	7.7		
Social Sciences	31.8	63.6	54.5	31.8	9.1	4.5	4.6	
Natural Sciences	9.1	50.0	77.3	40.9	13.6	9.1		
Mathematics		16.7	100.0	50.0		16.7		16.7
Admin/Commerce	36.4	63.6	54.5	27.3	9.1			9.1
Education	55.6	77.8	44.4	11.1		11.1		
Engineering	27.8	43.8	50.0	43.8	16.7	6.3	5.6	6.3
Medicine	36.4	47.8	45.5	34.8	9.1	4.3	9.1	13.0
Others	35.1	42.1	54.1	34.2	8.1	13.2	2.7	10.5
Age								
Under 40	32.7	56.4	60.0	20.0	3.6	12.7	3.6	10.9
40 to 49	20.3	47.5	71.2	47.5	8.5	3.3		1.6
50 to 59	34.1	51.1	43.2	37.2	18.5	9.3	4.5	2.3
60 and over	38.5	50.0	46.2	25.0			15.4	25.0

x. difficulty using hardware or software (the technology isn't transparent)
xi. inadequacy of software for computer-assisted instruction
xii. other

	Major		Minor		None		Don't know	
	x (%)	xi (%)	x (%)	xi (%)	x (%)	xi (%)	x (%)	xi (%)
Total	29.2	41.3	57.7	34.1	5.4	9.0	7.7	15.6
Academic Unit								
Fine Arts	50.0	50.0	33.3				16.7	50.0
Humanities	46.2	33.3	46.2	25.0	7.7	25.0		16.7
Social Sciences	20.0	22.7	50.0	40.9	20.0	18.2	10.0	18.2
Natural Sciences	18.2	57.1	77.3	28.6	4.5	9.5		4.8
Mathematics	28.6	71.4	71.4	28.6				
Admin/Commerce	36.4	27.3	63.6	45.5		9.1		18.2
Education	22.2	77.8	70.0	25.0		12.5		12.5
Engineering	25.0	37.5	56.3	50.0	6.3		12.5	12.5
Medicine	36.4	31.8	40.9	45.5	4.5		18.2	22.7
Others	26.3	44.7	65.8	31.6		7.9	7.9	15.8
Age								
Under 40	28.8	32.1	55.8	35.8	5.8	13.2	9.6	18.9
40 to 49	25.8	46.7	69.4	41.7	3.2	3.3	1.6	8.3
50 to 59	35.7	41.9	45.2	27.9	9.5	14.0	9.5	16.3
60 and over	25.0	54.5	50.0	9.1			25.0	36.4

9. Check those of the following that you believe will occur in your Unit within five years:
   i. all faculty will have a microcomputer in their offices
   ii. all faculty will be able to access the library from their offices
   iii. all faculty will communicate by electronic mail
   iv. all faculty will use computers in some way in classroom instruction
   v. simulation will replace actual laboratory experience
   vi. all students will see a need to have their own microcomputers
   vii. all students will be required to have their own microcomputers

	i (%)	ii (%)	iii (%)	iv (%)	v (%)	vi (%)	vii (%)
Total	63.4	57.1	49.7	19.9	8.4	58.6	6.8
Academic Unit							
Fine Arts	12.5	50.0	37.5			50.0	
Humanities	53.3	53.3	46.7		13.3	53.3	6.7
Social Sciences	46.2	57.7	34.6	7.7	7.7	46.2	
Natural Sciences	73.9	60.9	43.5	17.4	4.3	60.9	4.3
Mathematics	71.4	71.4	71.4			42.9	
Admin/Commerce	75.0	41.7	50.0	33.3		75.0	16.7
Education	60.0	70.0	60.0	20.0	10.0	70.0	10.0
Engineering	80.0	65.0	70.0	40.0	20.0	60.0	30.0
Medicine	75.0	45.8	41.7	33.3	16.7	62.5	4.2
Others	66.7	59.5	57.1	21.4	4.8	59.5	2.3
Age							
Under 40	73.8	59.0	63.9	26.2	14.8	60.7	9.8
40 to 49	66.7	60.6	51.5	15.2	7.6	59.1	4.5
50 to 59	51.1	51.1	34.0	17.8	4.3	61.7	6.4
60 and over	53.3	60.0	40.0	26.7		46.7	6.7

10. a) Do you presently use computers in your research or scholarly activity?

	Yes (%)	No (%)	Not applicable (%)
Total	93.7	4.8	1.6
Academic Unit			
Fine Arts	75.0	12.5	12.5
Humanities	85.7	14.3	
Social Sciences	96.0		4.0
Natural Sciences	100.0		
Mathematics	85.7	14.3	
Admin/Commerce	90.9		9.1
Education	100.0		
Engineering	100.0		
Medicine	91.7	8.3	
Others	95.2	4.8	
Age			
Under 40	91.9	3.2	4.8
40 to 49	95.5	4.5	
50 to 59	93.5	6.5	
60 and over	93.3	6.7	

b) If you answered 'Yes', please elaborate on the type(s) of computer(s) and how they are utilized:

	Personal computer (%)	Mini computer (%)	Mainframe (%)	Super computer (%)
Total	62.5	14.9	20.7	1.9
Academic Unit				
Fine Arts	50.0	50.0		
Humanities	64.3	7.1	28.6	
Social Sciences	67.9	10.7	21.4	
Natural Sciences	53.3	15.6	22.2	8.9
Mathematics	55.6	22.2	22.2	
Admin/Commerce	100.0			
Education	71.4	7.1	21.4	
Engineering	42.9	23.8	33.3	
Medicine	73.7	21.1	5.3	
Others	65.3	14.3	20.4	
Age				
Under 40	49.3	20.5	26.0	4.1
40 to 49	68.4	10.5	19.7	1.3
50 to 59	72.0	10.0	18.0	
60 and over	72.7	9.1	18.2	

	Word proces. (%)	Graphics (%)	Data analys. (%)	Databases (%)	Modelling (%)	Calculations (%)	E-mail (%)
Academic Unit							
Fine Arts	55.6	11.1		22.2			11.1
Humanities	28.2	10.3	17.9	12.8	2.6	2.6	7.7
Social Sciences	32.7	8.2	26.5	8.2		2.0	8.2
Natural Sciences	23.0	13.8	26.4	5.7	19.5	2.3	3.4
Mathematics	15.8	5.3	10.5	5.3		26.3	10.5
Admin/Commerce	29.2	4.2	25.0	4.2	4.2		4.2
Education	30.8	3.8	30.8	15.4			7.7
Engineering	18.2	11.4	9.1	9.1	9.1	18.2	4.5
Medicine	20.4	11.1	25.9	14.1			5.6
Others	26.4	10.9	24.5	10.9	3.6	1.0	10.0
Age							
Under 40	22.6	12.9	21.3	9.0	7.7	5.8	6.5
40 to 49	24.1	9.7	27.2	10.8	4.6	2.1	7.7
50 to 59	34.5	6.9	16.1	12.6	4.6	2.3	6.9
60 and over	28.6	10.7	14.3	21.4	3.6	7.1	7.1

	Spreadsheets (%)	CAI/CAL (%)	Softw. dev. (%)	Dev. teach. methods (%)	Biblio retrieval (%)	Data collection (%)
Academic Unit						
Fine Arts						
Humanities	5.1	2.6	2.6	5.1		2.6
Social Sciences	2.0		2.0	6.1	2.0	2.0
Natural Sciences	1.1		1.1	1.1	1.1	1.1
Mathematics			15.8	5.3		5.3
Admin/Commerce	12.5			4.2	8.3	4.2
Education	3.8	3.8			3.8	
Engineering	9.1	2.3	2.3	2.3		2.3
Medicine	1.9	3.7			3.7	1.9
Others		1.0	1.8	1.8	3.6	1.0
Age						
Under 40	1.9	1.3	3.9	0.6	1.3	2.6
40 to 49	3.1	0.5	1.0	3.1	3.1	2.6
50 to 59	3.4	1.1	1.1	4.6	2.3	1.1
60 and over	3.6	3.6				

	CAD (%)	Harw. dev. (%)	Expert systems (%)	Artificial intel. (%)
Academic Unit				
Fine Arts				
Humanities				
Social Sciences				
Natural Sciences				
Mathematics				
Admin/Commerce				
Education				
Engineering		4.5		
Medicine			1.9	
Others	1.8		1.0	1.0
Age				
Under 40	1.3	1.3		
40 to 49			0.5	
50 to 59			1.1	1.1
60 and over				

11. Which of the following describe the likely future of research computing in your Unit?

i. use of large, central mainframe computer(s)

ii. use of work station(s)

iii. use of dedicated minicomputer(s)

iv. use of microcomputers

	Increase (%)				Decrease (%)				No change (%)				Don't know (%)			
	i	ii	iii	iv	i	ii	iii	iv	i	ii	iii	iv	i	ii	iii	iv
Total	14.1	51.8	34.6	86.9	56.5	11.0	19.9	0.5	3.1	4.2	3.1	0.5	1.6	3.7	4.7	0.5
Academic Unit																
Fine Arts	12.5	25.0		87.5	25.0								12.5	12.5	12.5	
Humanities	6.7	33.3	26.7	80.0	53.3	13.3	6.7		6.7	6.7	6.7	6.7			6.7	
Social Sciences	23.1	26.9	26.9	88.5	46.2	15.4	11.5			7.7	7.7					
Natural Sciences	21.7	73.9	47.8	95.7	60.9		17.4		4.3	4.3	4.3			4.3	4.3	
Mathematics	28.6	71.4	57.1	71.4	57.1	14.3	14.3	14.3	14.3	14.3						
Admin/Commerce		33.3	25.0	83.3	75.0	25.0	33.3							16.7	16.7	
Education	10.0	50.0	20.0	100.0	90.0	40.0	50.0									
Engineering	10.0	90.0	50.0	100.0	75.0		25.0						5.0	5.0	10.0	
Medicine	16.7	37.5	45.8	79.2	37.5	12.5	16.7							4.2	4.2	
Others	9.5	61.9	31.0	81.0	59.5	7.1	23.8		7.1	7.1	4.8		2.4	2.4	2.4	2.3
Age																
Under 40	16.4	67.2	39.4	83.7	59.0	8.2	19.7		3.3	1.6			1.6	3.3	4.9	1.6
40 to 49	16.7	50.0	39.4	90.9	59.1	10.6	18.2	1.5	4.5	6.1	6.1	1.5		3.0	3.0	
50 to 59	10.6	42.6	25.5	91.5	57.4	17.0	25.5		2.1	6.4	4.3		2.1	4.3	6.4	
60 and over	6.7	33.3	26.7	80.0	40.0	6.7	13.3		6.7	6.7			6.7	6.7	6.7	

12. Where do you see computers making the greatest impact on the academic enterprise (not including research)?

Total	word processing > info access > communications > visual presentations > self-learning > replacing labs
Academic Unit	
Fine Arts	data analysis > calculations = word processing = teach prob. solving = prep. learning materials = repetitive tasks
Humanities	word processing > admin efficiency = replacing labs = distance ed = repetitive tasks
Social Sciences	word processing > communications = visual presentations > data analysis = simulations = prep. learn. materials
Natural Sciences	admin. efficiency = self-learning > word processing = information access = communications = teach prob solving
Mathematics	word processing = information access = communications = teach prob solv. = integ. academ. management
Admin/Commerce	information access = communications > word processing >complex calcn > visual presentations = self-learning
Education	communications > prep learn materials > word processing = info access = self-learning = replacing labs.
Engineering	visual presentations > calcns = word processing = self-learning = replacing labs
Medicine	visual presentations = information access = self-learning > communications
Others	information access = communications > visual presentations = word processing > data analysis = self-learning
Age	
Under 40	information access > visual present >communications > simulations > word processing > calculations
40 to 49	word processing > self-learning >communications > information access = replacing labs > visual presentations
50 to 59	communications > word processing > information access > admin. efficiency > calculation = visual presentations
60 and over	word processing = self-learning > data analysis = visual present. > calculations = info. access = admin efficiency

13. a) Have your views changed over the last 5 years on the role and importance of computers?

	Yes (%)	No (%)
Total	38.3	61.1
Academic Unit		
Fine Arts	42.9	57.1
Humanities	46.7	53.3
Social Sciences	36.4	63.6
Natural Sciences	31.8	68.2
Mathematics	42.9	57.1
Admin/Commerce	60.0	40.0
Education	66.7	33.3
Engineering	27.8	72.2
Medicine	28.6	71.4
Others	40.0	57.5
Age		
Under 40	30.2	67.9
40 to 49	43.8	56.3
50 to 59	38.6	61.4
60 and over	42.9	57.1

b) Explain.

	Now more positive (%)	Now less positive (%)	Always been positive (%)	Always been negative (%)	Never had opinion (%,
Total	45.6	3.5	39.5	2.6	6.1
Academic Unit					
Fine Arts	40.0		20.0		40.0
Humanities	54.5		45.5		
Social Sciences	33.3		46.7		20.0
Natural Sciences	33.3		66.7		
Mathematics	25.0	25.0	50.0		
Admin/Commerce	37.5	12.5	50.0		
Education	71.4		14.3	14.3	
Engineering	33.3		66.7		
Medicine	58.3	8.3	33.3		
Others	36.6	2.4	9.8	2.4	4.9
Age					
Under 40	40.8	6.7	43.3	3.3	6.6
40 to 49	56.4	5.1	33.3	5.1	5.1
50 to 59	39.4		51.5		9.1
60 and over	71.4		28.6		

APPENDIX D

SURVEY OF ADMINISTRATIVE COMPUTING

RESULTS

General Information

University Size

Large	7 (25.0%)
Medium	6 (21.4%)
Small	15 (53.0%)

Respondent's Academic Unit

Administration/Commerce/Business/ Management	2 (7.1%)
Other	22 (78.6%)
Not applicable	2 (7.1%)
No response	2 (7.1%)

Respondent's Position Within Institution

Technical or Professional Position	2 (7.1%)
Director/Supervisor/ Manager Computer Facility	16 (57.1%)
Other	7 (25.0%)
No response	3 (10.7%)

Respondent's Age

No response	28 (100%)

Respondent's Education Level

Completed bachelor's degree	6 (21.4%)
Completed master's degree	8 (28.6%)
Completed doctoral degree	8 (28.6%)
Other	1 (3.6%)
No response	5 (17.8%)

Respondent's Sex

Male	25 (89.3%)
Not known	3 (10.7%)

I. PAYROLL SYSTEM

1. Year computerized 19__

63	1 (3.6%)
66	1 (3.6%)
68	2 (7.1%)
69	2 (7.1%)
70	2 (7.1%)
72	3 (10.7%)
73	1 (3.6%)
74	1 (3.6%)
75	1 (3.6%)
78	1 (3.6%)
79	1 (3.6%)
80	2 (7.1%)
84	2 (7.1%)
86	1 (3.6%)
87	3 (10.7%)
Not installed	1 (3.6%)
Don't know	2 (7.1%)
No response	1 (3.6%)

2. Indicate which of the following apply:

i. Current system built in house

Yes	14 (50.0%)
No	9 (32.1%)
Don't Know	1 (3.6%)
No Response	4 (14.3%)

ii. Part of an integrated system

Yes	14 (50.0%)
No	9 (32.1%)
Don't Know	1 (3.6%)
No Response	4 (14..3%)

iii. Faculty have direct access to system

Yes	1 (3.6%)
No	22 (78.6%)
Don't Know	1 (3.6%)
No Response	4 (14.3%)

iv. Department offices have direct access to system

Yes	4 (14.3%)
No	19 (67.9%)
Don't Know	1 (3.6%)
No Response	4 (14.3%)

v. Dean's offices have direct access to system

Yes	2 (7.1%)
No	21 (75.0%)
Don't Know	1 (3.6%)
No Response	4 (14.3%)

vi. Payroll Office has direct access to system

Yes	22 (78.6%)
No	1 (3.6%)
Don't Know	1 (3.6%)
No Response	4 (14.3%)

vii. In-house maintenance

Yes	13 (46.4%)
No	9 (32.1%)
Don't Know	2 (7.1%)
No Response	4 (14.3%)

viii. Contract maintenance

Yes	5 (17.9%)
No	17 (60.7%)
Don't Know	2 (7.1%)
No Response	4 (14.3%)

ix. Combination of in-house and contract maintenance

Yes	5 (17.9%)
No	18 (64.3%)
Don't Know	1 (3.6%)
No Response	4 (14.3%)

x. Support staff is increasing

Yes	5 (17.9%)
No	18 (64.3%)
Don't Know	1 (3.6%)
No Response	4 (14.3%)

xi. Support staff is decreasing

Yes	3 (10.7%)
No	20 (71.4%)
Don't Know	1 (3.6%)
No Response	4 (14.3%)

3. What is the typical time (in months) required to:

i. have a minor modification done?

less than 1 month	13 (46.4%)
1 to 3 months	5 (17.9%)
Don't know	4 (14.3%)
No response	6 (21.4%)

ii. have a major modification done?

less than 4 months	8 (28.6%)
4 to 6 months	6 (21.4%)
7 to 9 months	1 (3.6%)
10 to 12 months	1 (3.6%)
13 to 15 months	2 (7.1%)
Don't Know	4 (14.3%)
No response	6 (21.4%)

4. What are the outstanding issues or problems with the current system?

- Old, (out-of-date, based on batch processing. lack of functionality) 11 (39.3%)
- Need to be integrated with Personal System/Human Resource System 4 (14.3%)
- System runs at a service bureau. 3 (10.7%)
- No problems 1 (3.6%)
- Not have enough flexibility 1 (3.6%)
- Need experienced analysts to modify 1 (3.6%)
- Don't know 1 (3.6%)
- No response 6 (21.4%)

5. What are your institution's future plans with respect to the payroll system?

- Use service bureau whose payroll system is integrated with their personal system 7 (25.0%)
- On-line integrated with personal system and accessible from user departments 11 (39.3%)
- Rewrite the system using 4GL 1 (3.6%)
- Upgrade: converted from VSAM-based to DB2-based system 1 (3.6%)
- Let it develop as demand requires 3 (10.7%)
- Re-implementation under a different platform 1 (3.6%)
- Don't know 1 (3.6%)
- No response 3 (10.7%)

II. ACCOUNTING SYSTEM

1. Year computerized 19__

64	1 (3.6%)
66	2 (7.1%)
68	3 (10.7%)
69	1 (3.6%)
70	2 (7.1%)
72	4 (14.3%)
79	1 (3.6%)
80	1 (3.6%)
82	2 (7.1%)
83	1 (3.6%)
84	2 (7.1%)
85	1 (3.6%)
86	1 (3.6%)
87	3 (10.7%)
88	1 (3.6%)
Don't know	2 (7.1%)

2. Indicate which of the following apply:

i. Current system built in house

Yes	14 (50.0%)
No	14 (50.0%)

ii. Part of an integrated system

Yes	20 (71.4%)
No	7 (25.0%)
Don't Know	1 (3.6%)

iii. faculty have direct access to system

Yes	8 (28.6%)
No	19 (67.9%)
Don't Know	1 (3.6%)

iv. Department offices have direct access to system

Yes	15 (53.6%)
No	12 (42.9%)
Don't Know	1 (3.6%)

v. Dean's offices have direct access to system

Yes	13 (46.4%)
No	15 (53.6%)

vi. Payroll Office has direct access to system

Yes	27 (96.4%)
No	1 (3.6%)

vii. In-house maintenance

Yes	16 (57.1%)
No	11 (39.3%)
Don't Know	1 (3.6%)

viii. Contract maintenance

Yes	5 (17.9%)
No	21 (75.0%)
Don't Know	2 (7.1%)

ix. Combination of in-house and contract maintenance

Yes	7 (25.0%)
No	20 (71.4%)
Don't Know	1 (3.6%)

x. Support staff is increasing

Yes	3 (10.7%)
No	22 (78.6%)
Don't Know	3 (10.7%)

xi. Support staff is decreasing

Yes	1 (3.6%)
No	24 (85.7%)
Don't Know	3 (10.7%)

3. What is the typical time (in months) required to:

i. have a minor modification done

less than 1 month	17 (60.7%)
1 to 3 months	6 (21.4%)
Don't know	3 (10.7%)
No response	2 (7.1%)

ii. have a major modification done

less than 4 months	9 (32.1%)
4 to 6 months	6 (21.4%)
7 to 9 months	2 (7.1%)
10 to 12 months	1 (3.6%)
13 to 15 months	1 (3.6%)
16 to 18 months	1 (3.6%)
greater than 2 years	1 (3.6%)
Don't know	4 (14.3%)
No response	2 (7.1%)

4. What are the outstanding issues or problems with the current system?

- Inadequately meet functional needs; reporting form does not meet nood	9 (32.1%)
- It is based on batch processing	3 (10.7%)
- Not integrated with purchasing system; Student Information System; budget office	2 (7.1%)
- Need to expand on-line capability with 4GL	3 (10.7%)
- Age of system	1 (3.6%)
- No problems	3 (10.7%)

- Don't know 1 (3.6%)

- No response 6 (21.4%)

5. What are your institution's plans with respect to the accounting system?

   - Develop an on-line system distribute to departments 9 (32.1%)

   - Upgrade 5 (17.9%)

   - Convert from mainframe system to a micro or a different platform 2 (7.1%)

   - Keep it 2 (7.1%)

   - Use relational database system 2 (7.1%)

   - Review 1 (3.6%)

   - Don't know 2 (7.1%)

   - No response 5 (17.9%)

III. HUMAN RESOURCE SYSTEM

1. Year computerized 19__

68	1 (3.6%)
69	1 (3.6%)
70	1 (3.6%)
71	1 (3.6%)
72	1 (3.6%)
76	1 (3.6%)
79	1 (3.6%)
80	1 (3.6%)
82	2 (7.1%)
84	1 (3.6%)
85	1 (3.6%)
86	1 (3.6%)
88	1 (3.6%)
89	2 (7.1%)
90	1 (3.6%)
Not installed	7 (25.0%)
No response	4 (14.3%)

2. Indicate which of the following apply:

i. Current system built in house

Yes	11 (39.3%)
No	6 (21.4%)
No response	11 (39.3%)

ii. Part of an integrated system

Yes	14 (50.0%)
No	3 (10.7%)
No response	11 (39.3%)

iii. Faculty have direct access to system

Yes	4 (14.3%)
No	12 (42.9%)
Don't know	1 (3.6%)
No response	11 (39.3%)

iv. Department offices have direct access to system

Yes	7 (25.0%)
No	9 (32.1%)
Don't know	1 (3.6%)
No response	11 (39.3%)

v. Dean s offices have direct access to system

Yes	4 (14.3%)
No	12 (42.9%)
Don t know	1 (3.6%)
No response	11 (39.3%)

vi. Payroll Office has direct access to system

Yes	16 (57.1%)
Don't know	1 (3.6%)
No response	11 (39.3%)

vii. In-house maintenance

Yes	11 (39.3%)
No	4 (14.3%)
Don't know	2 (7.1%)
No response	11 (39.3%)

viii. Contract maintenance

No	15 (53.6%)
Don't know	2 (7.1%)
No response	11 (39.3%)

ix. Combination of in-house and contract maintenance

Yes	4 (14.3%)
No	12 (42.9%)
Don't know	1 (3.6%)
No response	11 (39.3%)

x. Support staff is increasing

Yes	6 (21.4%)
No	7 (25.0%)
Don't know	4 (14.3%)
No response	11 (39.3%)

xi. Support staff is decreasing

Yes	1 (3.6%)
No	12 (42.9%)
Don't know	4 (14.3%)
No response	11 (39.3%)

3. What is the typical time (in months) required to:

i. have a minor modification done

less than 1 month	12 (42.9%)
1 to 3 months	1 (3.6%)
Don't know	3 (10.7%)
No response	12 (42.9%)

ii. have a major modification done

less than 4 months	7 (25.0%)
4 to 6 months	3 (10.7%)
7 to 9 months	1 (3.6%)
13 to 15 months	2 (7.1%)
22 to 24 months	1 (3.6%)
Don't Know	2 (7.1%)
No response	12 (43.9%)

4. What are the outstanding issues or problems with the current system?

- All manual	2 (7.1%)
- Does not meet current functional needs	6 (21.4%)
- Hardware limitation	1 (3.6%)
- Integrated with payroll system	3 (10.7%)
- Ad hoc reporting and security of data	3 (10.7%)
- Need experienced analysts to modify	1 (3.6%)
- Not installed	1 (3.6%)
- Don't know	2 (7.1%)
- No response	9 (32.1%)

5. What are your institution's future plans with respect to the human resource system?

- Integrated with the payroll system	9 (32.1%)
- Implement relational data model or a different platform	3 (10.7%)
- Purchase a new system to be run internally	3 (10.7%)
- Have HRS run by a service bureau	1 (3.6%)
- Minor development using micro-computer database	1 (3.6%)
- Distribute on-line updating	2 (7.1%)
- Don't know	3 (10.7%)
- No response	6 (21.4%)

IV. ENERGY CONTROL SYSTEM

1. Year computerized 19__

74	1 (3.6%)
75	3 (10.7%)
77	1 (3.6%)
84	1 (3.6%)
85	1 (3.6%)
86	2 (7.1%)
87	1 (3.6%)
Not installed	9 (32.1%)
Don't know	8 (28.6%)
No response	1 (3.6%)

2. Indicate which of the following apply:

i. Current system built in house

Yes	4 (14.3%)
No	5 (17.9%)
Don't know	1 (3.6%)
No response	18 (64.3%)

ii. Part of an integrated system

Yes	2 (7.1%)
No	7 (25.0%)
Don't know	1 (3.6%)
No response	18 (64.3%)

iii. Faculty have direct access to system

No	9 (32.1%)
Don't Know	2 (7.1%)
No response	17 (60.7%)

iv. Department offices have direct access to system

No	9 (32.1%)
Don't know	1 (3.6%)
No response	18 (64.3%)

v. Dean's offices have direct access to system

No	9 (32.1%)
Don't Know	1 (3.6%)
No response	18 (64.3%)

vi. Payroll Office has direct access to system

Yes	8 (28.6%)
No	1 (3.6%)
Don't know	1 (3.6%)
No response	18 (64.3%)

vii. In-house maintenance

Yes	5 (17.9%)
No	3 (10.7%)
Don't know	2 (7.1%)
No response	18 (64.3%)

viii. Contract maintenance

Yes	3 (10.7%)
No	5 (17.9%)
Don't know	2 (7.1%)
No response	18 (64.3%)

ix. Combination of in-house and contract maintenance

Yes	5 (17.9%)
No	4 (14.3%)
Don't know	1 (3.6%)
No response	18 (64.3%)

x. Support staff is increasing

Yes	3 (10.7%)
No	6 (21.4%)
Don't know	1 (3.6%)
No response	18 (64.3%)

xi. Support staff is decreasing

No	9 (32.1%)
Don't know	1 (3.6%)
No response	18 (64.3%)

3. What is the typical time (in months) required to:
    i. have a minor modification done

less than 1 month	5 (17.9%)
Don't know	3 (10.7%)
No response	20 (71.4%)

    ii. have a major modification done

less than 4 months	5 (17.9%)
Don't Know	3 (10.7%)
No response	20 (71.4%)

4. What are the outstanding issues or problems with the current system?

- Information available to monitor energy management and real time control	4 (14.3%)
- Age of system	2 (7.1%)
- No problems at present	1 (3.6%)
- Don't know	1 (3.6%)
- No response	20 (71.4%)

5. What are your institution's future plans with respect to the energy control system?

- Upgrade system	3 (10.7%)
- Select new system	2 (7.1%)
- Expand system	1 (3.6%)
- Redevelop real time system control	1 (3.6%)
- None	1 (3.6%)
- Don't know	3 (10.7%)
- No response	17 (60.7%)

V. INVENTORY CONTROL SYSTEM

1. Year computerized 19__

72	1 (3.6%)
73	1 (3.6%)
79	1 (3.6%)
80	1 (3.6%)
82	1 (3.6%)
85	2 (7.1%)
87	2 (7.1%)
Not installed	16 (57.1%)
Don't know	2 (7.1%)
No response	1 (3.6%)

2. Indicate which of the following apply:

i. Current system built in house

Yes	8 (28.6%)
No	1 (3.6%)
No response	19 (67.9%)

ii. Part of an integrated system

Yes	3 (10.7%)
No	6 (21.4%)
No response	19 (67.9%)

iii. Faculty have direct access to system

No	9 (32.1%)
No response	19 (67.9%)

iv. Department offices have direct access to system

No	9 (32.1%)
No response	19 (67.9%)

v. Dean's offices have direct access to system

No	9 (32.1%)
No response	19 (67.9%)

vi. Payroll Office has direct access to system

Yes	6 (21.4%)
No	3 (10.7%)
No response	19 (67.9%)

vii. In-house maintenance

Yes	8 (28.6%)
No	1 (3.6%)
No response	19 (67.9%)

viii. Contract maintenance

No	9 (32.1%)
No response	19 (67.9%)

ix. Combination of in-house and contract maintenance
- Yes 1 (3.6%)
- No 8 (28.6%)
- No response 19 (67.9%)

x. Support staff is increasing
- Yes 1 (3.6%)
- No 8 (28.6%)
- No response 19 (67.9%)

xi. Support staff is decreasing
- No 9 (32.1%)
- No response 19 (67.9%)

3. What is the typical time (in months) required to:

i. have a minor modification done
- less than 1 month 5 (17.9%)
- 1 to 3 months 1 (3.6%)
- 4 to 6 months 1 (3.6%)
- Don't know 2 (7.1%)
- No response 19 (67.9%)

ii. have a major modification done
- less than 4 months 3 (10.7%)
- 7 to 9 months 1 (3.6%)
- 13 to 15 months 1 (3.6%)
- 16 to 18 months 1 (3.6%)
- 22 to 24 months 1 (3.6%)
- Don't Know 2 (7.1%)
- No response 19 (67.9%)

4. What are the outstanding issues or problems with the current system?

- Out-of-date, needs to be enhanced or replaced with a new system 3 (10.7%)
- Integration of inventory system and purchasing system 2 (7.1%)
- Maintain system 1 (3.6%)
- PC based with a limited list of items 1 (3.6%)
- Not installed 1 (3.6%)
- Don't know 1 (3.6%)
- No response 18 (64.3%)

5. Do departments/faculties have their own computerized inventory control systems?

- Yes	11 (39.3%)
- No	10 (35.7%)
- Don't know	1 (3.6%)
- No response	6 (21.4%)

6. What are your institution's future plans with respect to the inventory control system?

- Leave to individual departments	2 (7.1%)
- Explore the area of artificial intelligence	1 (3.6%)
- Purchase a system	4 (14.3%)
- Implement bar code stickers	1 (3.6%)
- None at present	7 (25.0%)
- Low priority --- no changes for next 3-5 years	1 (3.6%)
- Don't know	5 (17.9%)
- No response	7 (25.0%)

APPENDIX E

SURVEY OF DIRECTORS OF COMPUTER CENTRES

RESULTS

General Information

University size

Large	2 (16.7%)
Medium	3 (25.0%)
Small	7 (58.3%)

Respondent's Position within university

Director/Manager/ Supervisor Computer Facilities	3 (25.0%)
Director/Manager Computer Center	7 (58.3%)
Associate/Vice President Administration	2 (16.7%)

Respondent's Educational Level

Completed bachelors degree	7 (58.3%)
Completed masters degree	2 (16.7%)
Completed doctoral degree	2 (16.7%)
No response	1 (8.3%)

Respondent's Sex

Male	12 (100%)

I. Background

1. Total university budget in dollars

Budget <= 15 M	1 (8.3%)
15 < Budget <= 30 M	5 (41.7%)
30 < Budget <= 60 M	1 (8.3%)
90 < Budget <= 120 M	1 (8.3%)
120 < Budget <= 150 M	1 (8.3%)
180 < Budget	1 (8.3%)
No response	2 (16.7%)

2. Percentage of university budget spent on:

i. Academic computing

0 <= 1	3 (25.0%)
1 <= 2	3 (25.0%)
8 <= 9	1 (8.3%)
11 <= 12	1 (8.3%)
No response	4 (33.3%)

ii. Administrative computing

0 <= 1	3 (25.0%)
1 <= 2	3 (25.0%)
8 <= 9	1 (8.3%)
9 <= 10	1 (8.3%)
No response	4 (33.3%)

iii. Library computing

0 <= 1	3 (25.0%)
1 <= 2	2 (16.7%)
8 <= 9	1 (8.3%)
Included in administrative computing budget	1 (8.3%)
No response	5 (41.7%)

3a. Computer centre's operating budget in dollars.

Budget <= 500 K	2 (16.7%)
500 K < Budget <= 1 M	2 (16.7%)
1 M < Budget <= 1.5 M	3 (25.0%)
1.5 M < Budget <= 2.0 M	1 (8.3%)
3.5 M < Budget <= 4.0 M	1 (8.3%)
4.5 M < Budget <= 5.0 M	1 (8.3%)
No response	2 (16.7%)

b. Computer centre's capital budget in dollars.

Budget <= 500 K	5 (41.7%)
500 K < Budget <= 1 M	1 (8.3%)
1.5 M < Budget <= 2.0 M	1 (8.3%)
2.0 M < Budget <= 2.5 M	1 (8.3%)
3.5 M < Budget <= 4.0 M	1 (8.3%)
No response	3 (25.0%)

c. Percentage of computer centre's operating budget

i. Derived from grants and contracts

0 <= 2	6 (50.0%)
4 <= 6	1 (8.3%)
24 <= 26	1 (8.3%)
No response	4 (33.3%)

ii. Spent on maintenance

6 <= 8	1 (8.3%)
8 <= 10	4 (33.3%)
18 <= 20	1 (8.3%)
20 <= 22	2 (16.7%)
24 <= 26	1 (8.3%)
28 <= 30	1 (8.3%)
No response	2 (16.7%)

iii. Spent on software

0 <= 2	1 (8.3%)
2 <= 4	2 (16.7%)
4 <= 6	1 (8.3%)
6 <= 8	1 (8.3%)
8 <= 10	4 (33.3%)
14 <= 16	1 (8.3%)
No response	2 (16.7%)

4. How is the budget reviewed and approved

1. First to Advisory Committee	7 (58.3%)
2. Directly to Budget Committee	4 (33.3%)
3. No response	1 (8.3%)

II. The Present Computing Environment

5. Software - Considering value, and excluding micro computer software, what is the:

a. Percentage of software packages developed in house

0 <= 5	4 (33.3%)
15 <= 20	1 (8.3%)
25 <= 30	1 (8.3%)
45 <= 50	1 (8.3%)
60 <= 65	1 (8.3%)
70 <= 75	1 (8.3%)
75 <= 80	1 (8.3%)
No response	2 (16.7%)

b. Percentage of software packages acquired from vendors

15 <= 20	1 (8.3%)
20 <= 25	1 (8.3%)
30 <= 35	1 (8.3%)
45 <= 50	1 (8.3%)
65 <= 70	2 (16.7%)
90 <= 95	1 (8.3%)
95 <= 100	2 (16.7%)
No response	2 (16.7%)

6. What is the campus policy with respect to the organization, operation and maintenance of microcomputers on campus?

(Note: There was a maximum of two responses of this question.)

	1st Response	2nd Response
- PC's must be IBM compatible	1 (8.3%)	1 (8.3%)
- Computer Center maintains public micro computor	8 (66.7%)	1 (8.3%)
- User maintains micro computer	1 (8.3%)	1 (8.3%)
- Decentralised User Department furnishes space and equipment	1 (8.3%)	----------
- No response	1 (8.3%)	9 (75.0%)

7a. Have any problem arisen between employees and management with regard to computerization?

Yes	3 (25.0%)
No	6 (50.0%)
No response	3 (25.0%)

b. If so, please describe the problem and how they were resolved?

- In process of solution; not following standards	2 (16.7%)
- One person still uses a hard copy terminal, refuses to use video terminal	1 (8.3%)
- No problem	5 (41.7%)
- No response	4 (33.3%)

8. Of your total (installed base of) computing approximately what percentage is consumed by

i. Research computing

0 <= 5	2 (16.7%)
5 <= 10	3 (25.0%)
10 <= 15	1 (8.3%)
15 <= 20	1 (8.3%)
25 <= 30	1 (8.3%)
35 <= 40	1 (8.3%)
45 <= 50	1 (8.3%)
No response	2 (16.7%)

ii. Teaching computing

5 <= 10	1 (8.3%)
15 <= 20	4 (33.3%)
25 <= 30	3 (25.0%)
35 <= 40	1 (8.3%)
55 <= 60	1 (8.3%)
No response	2 (16.7%)

iii. Administrative computing

10 <= 15	1 (8.3%)
15 <= 20	1 (8.3%)
25 <= 30	1 (8.3%)
30 <= 35	1 (8.3%)
35 <= 40	1 (8.3%)
45 <= 50	1 (8.3%)
50 <= 55	1 (8.3%)
75 <= 80	1 (8.3%)
No response	2 (16.7%)

iv. Library computing

0 <= 5	4 (33.3%)
5 <= 10	2 (16.7%)
10 <= 15	2 (16.7%)
15 <= 20	1 (8.3%)
No response	3 (25.0%)

v. Non-University computing

0 <= 5	10 (83.3%)
No response	2 (16.7%)

9. Staff

i. Number of operation staff

0	1 (8.3%)
1 to 4	6 (50.0%)
5 to 8	3 (25.0%)
9 to 12	1 (8.3%)
No response	1 (8.3%)

ii. Number of systems staff

0	2 (16.7%)
1 to 4	5 (41.7%)
5 to 8	3 (25.0%)
9 to 12	1 (8.3%)
No response	1 (8.3%)

iii. Number of hardware technicians

0	1 (8.3%)
1 to 4	8 (66.7%)
5 to 8	2 (16.7%)
No response	1 (8.3%)

iv. Number of applications staff, analysts and programmers

0	1 (8.3%)
1 to 4	3 (25.0%)
5 to 8	3 (25.0%)
17 to 20	3 (25.0%)
33 to 36	1 (8.3%)
No response	1 (8.3%)

v. Number of data entry staff

0	8 (66.7%)
1 to 4	1 (8.3%)
5 to 8	2 (16.7%)
No response	1 (8.3%)

vi. Number of management supporting campus computing

1	3 (25.0%)
2	3 (25.0%)
3	2 (16.7%)
4	1 (8.3%)
8	1 (8.3%)
More than 10	1 (8.3%)
No response	1 (8.3%)

vi. Number of other staff members supporting campus computing

0	2 (16.7%)
1 to 4	4 (33.3%)
5 to 8	2 (16.7%)
9 to 12	1 (8.3%)
More than 20	1 (8.3%)
Don't know	1 (8.3%)
No response	1 (8.3%)

III. Planning and Strategies for Computing

1. During the next three years what changes are you planning in your academic computing system, and why? Please list and explain them in priority order.

PRIORITY	1	2	3
- Move work to PC and workstation	3 (25.0%)	----------	1 (8.3%)
- Upgrade	4 (33.3%)	2 (16.7%)	----------
- Standardize Micro	1 (8.3%)	----------	----------
- Network - Ethernet Backbone	1 (8.3%)	----------	2 (16.7%)
- Convert mainframe to UNIX	----------	1 (8.3%)	1 (8.3%)
- Develop file server facility for network	----------	3 (25.0%)	----------
- Develop Plan	1 (8.3%)	----------	----------
- Add new mainframe or micro lab	----------	1 (8.3%)	1 (8.3%)
- No response	2 (16.7%)	4 (33.0%)	7 (58.3%)

2a. Is your library circulation system computerized?

Yes, with an in-house	3 (25.0%)
Yes, with a purchase system	5 (41.7%)
Yes, with an extensively modified purchased system	1 (8.3%)
No	2 (16.7%)
No response	1 (8.3%)

b. During the next three years what changes are you planning with respect to your library system, and why? Please list and describe them in priority order.

PRIORITY	1	2	3
- Purchase full system	3 (25.0%)	----------	----------
- Purchase PC based system	1 (8.3%)	----------	----------
- Expand system functionality	2 (16.7%)	1 (8.3%)	----------
- Convert system to UNIX	1 (8.3%)	----------	----------
- Review	1 (8.3%)	----------	----------
- Integrate library system with financial system	----------	1 (8.3%)	----------
- Expand access to library	2 (16.7%)	1 (8.3%)	1 (8.3%)
- No response	2 (16.7%)	9 (75.0%)	11 (91.7%)

3. During the next three years what changes are you planning in your administrative computing system, and why? Please list and explain them in priority order.

PRIORITY	1	2	3
- Inventory system	1 (8.3%)	----------	----------
- Student information system	1 (8.3%)	3 (25.0%)	----------
- Move system to new hardware	2 (16.7%)	----------	----------
- Convert in-house to relational database	2 (16.7%)	----------	1 (8.3%)
- Purchase new fully integrate administrative system	1 (8.3%)	1 (8.3%)	----------
- Increase processing capacity	----------	2 (16.7%)	----------
- Add Capacity	1 (8.3%)	----------	----------
- Develop existing system	3 (25.0%)	----------	1 (8.3%)
- No response	1 (8.3%)	6 (50.0%)	10 (83.3%)

4. During the next three years what are you planning with respect to microcomputers on campus, and why? Please list and explain them in priority order.

PRIORITY	1	2
- Acquire more workstations	6 (50.0%)	-----------
- Replace aging hardware	2 (16.7%)	-----------
- Network with file serve support	-----------	4 (33.3%)
- Not applicable	1 (8.3%)	-----------
- No response	3 (25.0%)	8 (67.7%)

5. During the next three years what are you planning to do with respect to computing networks?

- Install campus-wide fiber optic backbone	4 (33.3%)
- Connect micro to centralized computer	2 (16.7%)
- Expand network	5 (41.7%)
- No response	1 (8.3%)

6. What problem do you think must be solved, if these plans are to be realized?
(Note: There was a maximum of two responses of this question.)

	1st Response	2nd Response
- Money	7 (58.3%)	-----------
- Need more staff resources	1 (8.3%)	2 (16.7%)
- Conversion of administrative computing	1 (8.3%)	-----------
- Meet user's requirements	-----------	2 (16.7%)
- No response	3 (25.0%)	8 (67.6%)

IV. Organizational Structures for Computing

1a. Do you separate the computer centre into an academic center and an administrative center?

- Yes	------------
- No	10 (83.3%)
- Not applicable	1 (8.3%)
- No response	1 (8.3%)

b. Would you please explain the rationale for your structure?

- One computing centre	5 (41.7%)
- Separate on functional groups	3 (25.0%)
- Not applicable	1 (8.3%)
- No response	3 (25.0%)

2. What recent changes have you made, and what changes will you make in the organizational structure of campus computing, and why?

- Merge academic and administrative computing 2 (16.7%)
- Define a new position responsible for academic computing 1 (8.3%)
- Put telephone system on the responsibly of computing centre 1 (8.3%)
- Define a new position responsible for networking and communication 1 (8.3%)
- Not applicable 4 (33.3%)
- No response 3 (25.0%)

3. How are decision made with respect to coordinating computing activities/acquisitions on campus?

- Advisory Committee reviews Director's plan 7 (58.3%)
- Non-PC administrative computing decisions made by Director and/or V.P. 2 (16.7%)
- Vetted by Budget Committee 1 (8.3%)
- By department affected 1 (8.3%)
- No response 1 (8.3%)

4a. Do you employ the services of contract programming personnel?

- Yes 7 (58.3%)
- No 4 (33.3%)
- No response 1 (8.3%)

b. If your answer is 'yes', please describe the reasons and the degree to which contract programming is employed.

- Major project sufficient expertise not available in house 3 (25.0%)
- 50% of staff is contract 1 (8.3%)
- Occasionally 2 (16.7%)
- A few of staff is contract 1 (8.3%)
- No Response 5 (41.7%)

5. How are policy items debated and approved?

- Within the Advisory Committee 7 (58.3%)
- With a meeting of those affected 2 (16.7%)
- Very ad hoc 1 (8.3%)
- No Response 2 (16.7%)

APPENDIX F

SURVEY OF REGISTRARS

RESULTS

Number of Questionnaires sent out	76
Number of Questionnaires or responses returned	35
Number of Questionnaires used in analysis	35

Name of University or College:

From large universities	3 (8.6%)
From medium-sized universities	10 (28.6%)
From small universities	22 (62.9%)

1. Respondent's position within university:

Registrar	29 (82.9%)
Admissions Officer	1 (2.9%)
Director	4 (11.4%)
No Response	1 (2.9%)

2. Respondent's Age:

In 30s	4 (11.4%)
In 40s	15 (42.9%)
In 50s	8 (22.9%)
In 60s	2 (5.7%)
>69	1 (2.9%)
No Response	5 (14.3%)

3. Respondent's Educational Level:

High School	2 (5.7%)
Bachelors	13 (37.1%)
Masters	13 (37.1%)
Doctorate	2 (5.7%)
Other	2 (5.7%)
No Response	3 (8.6%)

4. Respondent's Gender:

Male	19 (54.3%)
Female	14 (40.0%)
Not Known	2 (5.7%)

I. ADMISSIONS

1. a) Does your province provide a central admitting service for all universities in the province?

   Yes 11 (31.4%) No 22 (62.9%) No Response 2 (5.7%)

   b) If you answered 'Yes' please explain how the system works.

   Not coded on codesheet.

2. Does your university have a central admissions office for all undergraduate students?

   Yes 31 (88.6%) No 3 (8.6%) No Response 1 (2.9%)

3. What faculties/colleges/schools does your university have?

i.	Arts	31 (88.6%)
ii.	Science	29 (82.9%)
iii.	Administration/Commerce	27 (77.1%)
iv.	Engineering	17 (48.6%)
v.	Education	21 (60.0%)
vi.	Medicine	4 (11.4%)
vii.	Agriculture	2 (5.7%)
viii.	Pharmacy	2 (5.7%)
ix.	Library Science	2 (5.7%)
x.	Nursing	7 (20.0%)
xi.	Social Work	12 (34.3%)
xii.	Law	9 (25.7%)
xiii.	Architecture	3 (8.6%)
xiv.	Journalism/Communications	5 (14.3%)
xv.	Dentistry	3 (8.6%)
xvi.	Veterinary Medicine	2 (5.7%)
xvii.	Grad. Studies	3 (8.6%)
xviii.	Environmental Studies	3 (8.6%)
xix.	Fine Arts/Music	8 (22.9%)
xx.	Theology/Religious Studies	2 (5.7%)
xxi.	Home Economics	2 (5.7%)
xxii.	Phys./Occ. Therapy	2 (5.7%)
xxiii.	Phys. Ed./Studies	6 (17.1%)
xxiv.	Recreation Studies	3 (8.6%)
xxv.	Health Studies	5 (14.3%)

4. What is the role of these faculties/colleges/schools in the admission of students?

	Not Applicable	4 (11.4%)
i.	Represented on admissions committees	7 (13.7%)
ii.	Set admissions policies	8 (15.7%)
iii.	Set class size/enrolment limits/quotas	4 (7.8%)
iv.	Decide on individual problems or special cases	6 (11.8%)
v.	Set entrance standards/requirements	6 (11.8%)
vi.	Interview and rank applicants	1 (2.0%)
vii.	No role	6 (11.8%)
viii.	Available for consultation/advice	11(21.6%)
ix.	Review files	1 (2.0%)
x.	Other	1 (2.0%)

5.a) Does your university have "associated or federated or member" colleges such as those affiliated with a church?

Yes 14 (40.0%) No (20 (57.1%) No Response 1 (2.9%)

b) If you answered 'Yes' please list and indicate the nature of the affiliated college (i.e. Lutheran Church affiliated college).

Not coded on codesheet.

c) Do those "associated or federated" colleges have their own admissions offices?

Yes 9 (25.7%) No 5 (14.3%)
Not Applicable 20 (57.1%) No Response 1 (2.9%)

d) Do these "associated or federated" colleges maintain their own computer systems for the purpose of registration and admissions?

Yes 5 (14.3%) No 8 (22.9%)
Not Applicable 20 (57.1%) No Response 2 (5.7%)

6.a) Are the student's previous educational records and documents entered into your university computer system?

Yes 26 (74.3%) No 8 (22.9%) No Response 1 (2.9%)

b) If you answered 'Yes' please indicate what sort of information is entered.

	Not Applicable	11 (31.4%)
i.	high school classes	9 (17.3%)
ii.	address	2 (3.8%)
iii.	basic biographical	5 (9.6%)
iv.	transfer credits	10 (19.2%)
v.	schools previously attended	10 (19.2%)
vi.	documents received	4 (7.7%)
vii.	basis of admission	10 (19.2%)
viii.	other	2 (3.8%)

7.a) Does your university have any provisions or programs for the admission of students without the "normal" admission requirements?

Yes 29 (82.9%) No 4 (11.4%) No Response 2 (5.7%)

b) If you aswered 'Yes' please explain.

	Not Applicable	4 (11.4%)
i.	Adult student over 21 years	10 (25.0%)
ii.	Admission by interview	2 (5.0%)
iii.	Dean/director special permission	1 (2.5%)
iv.	Admissions committee approve	9 (22.5%)
v.	Mature admission-out of school 1-5 yrs	13 (32.5%)
vi.	Mature students on probation	5 (12.5%)

8. Please explain how those in your university responsible for student registration and billing are informed once a student has been admitted. How is the computer involved in this process?

Not coded on codesheet.

II. REPORTING OF GRADES

1. Please explain in a step-by-step manner the typical procedures for the approval and submission of final grades?

Not coded on codesheet.

2. How soon after final examinations are written are instructors required to submit their final grades?

i.	1-7 days	24 (68.6%)
ii.	8-14 days	5 (14.3%)
iii.	>15 days	2 (5.7%)
iv.	No Response	4 (11.4%)

3. **How long does it typically take from the time instructors submit their final grades until students are notified of the results?**

i.	1-7 days	13 (37.1%)
ii.	8-14 days	12 (34.3%)
iii.	>15 days	7 (20.0%)
iv.	No Response	3 (8.6%)

4. **What sort of final grade notification are students provided with? If possible include a sample.**

i.	statement in mail	19 (54.3%)
ii.	statement is speedmailer	2 (5.7%)
iii.	teaching units each send	1 (2.9%)
iv.	report of standing	4 (11.4%)
v.	statement of average & ran	1 (2.9%)
vi.	term end transcripts	4 (11.4%)
vii.	no response	4 (11.4%)

III. CLASS SCHEDULING

1. **Please describe the procedures your university utilizes in establishing and changing your class schedules.**

Not coded on codesheet.

2. **How long before the beginning of the term is the class schedule available?**

i.	less than 5 weeks	7 (20.0%)
ii.	5-8 weeks	8 (22.9%)
iii.	9-12 weeks	5 (14.3%)
iv.	13-16 weeks	1 (2.9%)
v.	more than 16 weeks	6 (17.1%)
vi.	uncertain/variable	2 (5.7%)
vii.	no response	5 (14.3%)

3. **Please comment on the strengths and weaknesses of your particular system of establishing the class timetable.**

Not coded on codesheet.

IV. EXAMINATION SCHEDULING

1. Please describe the procedures your university utilizes in establishing the final examination schedule.

Not coded on codesheet.

2. How long before the final examinations is the schedule available? weeks

i.	less than 5 weeks	8 (22.9%)
ii.	5-8 weeks	14 (40.%)
iii.	9-12 weeks	3 (8.6%)
iv.	13-16 weeks	1 (2.9%)
v.	more than 16 weeks	3 (8.6%)
vi.	uncertain/variable	3 (8.6%)
vii.	no response	2 (5.7%)

3.a) Do you make allowances for instructor-initiated special requests for specific dates, times, etc.?

Yes 24 (68.6%) No 7 (20.0%) No Response 4 (11.4%)

b) If you asnwered 'Yes' who is responsible for approving and monitoring such special requests?

	Not Applicable	11 (31.4%)
i.	Registrar	8 (22.9%)
ii.	Associate Registrar	6 (17.1%)
iii.	Department Head	3 (8.6%)
iv.	Dean	3 (8.6%)
v.	Assistant Dean	1 (2.9%)
vi.	Committee	1 (2.9%)
vii.	Exam Supervisor	2 (5.7%)

4. Please comment on the strengths and weaknesses of your particular system of scheduling final examinations?

Strengths - Not Applicable		12 (34.3%)
i.	Minimizes consecutive exams	1 (2.4%)
ii.	Schedule available early	5 (12.2%)
iii.	Students and faculty involved	4 (9.8%)
iv.	Flexible	7 (17.1%)
v.	Simple	3 (7.3%)
vi.	Individual needs accommodated	5 (12.2%)
vii.	Avoids conflict	12 (29.3%)
viii.	Fast	3 (7.3%)
ix.	Large classes write first	1 (2.4%)

<u>Weaknesses</u> - Not Applicable	6 (17.1%)
i. Too labour intensive	4 (8.2%)
ii. Does not prevent back to back exams	7 (14.3%)
iii. Exam dates not available early	5 (10.2%)
iv. No flexibility	8 (16.3%)
v. Too formal	2 (4.1%)
vi. Exam hall approach difficult	2 (4.1%)
vii. Uneven distribution of exams	7 (14.3%)
viii. Exam period too long	5 (10.2%)
ix. Uses too much computer time	2 (4.1%)
x. Too time consuming for staff	7 (14.3%)

V. CLASS LISTS

1.a) Are class lists provided to instructors?

Yes 34 (97.1%) No 0 (0.0%) No Response 1 (2.9%)

b) If you answered 'Yes' at what point in time during the term are such lists provided?

Not Applicable	2 (5.7%)
i. First 1 to 3 days of class	18 (30.0%)
ii. End of class add/drop period	17 (28.3%)
iii. As grade sheet for mid-terms	1 (1.7%)
iv. 1 week before end of classes	1 (1.7%)
v. Prior to final exams	3 (5.0%)
vi. On request	4 (6.7%)
vii. 1-3 weeks after classes begin	9 (15.0%)
viii. At term end for grade submission	3 (5.0%)
ix. Various points during term	4 (6.7%)

2. What is the primary purpose of such lists?

Not Applicable	3 (8.6%)
i. Provide information for instructor	7 (11.5%)
ii. Verify registrations	26 (42.6%)
iii. Assist grade reporting	15 (24.6%)
iv. Check attendance	8 (13.1%)
v. Check room size	2 (3.3%)
vi. Keep track of wait list	2 (3.3%)
vii. Other	1 (2.9%)

VI. CLASSROOM ALLOCATION

1. Please describe the procedures utilized in your university for the allocation of classrooms for classes.

Not coded on codesheet.

VII. USES OF COMPUTERS

1. Have you implemented or planned for any of the following:

		Implemented	Not Implemented	Planned	Don't Know
i.	automated creation of computer accounts for students in class	20(57.1)	6(17.1)	4(11.4)	2 (5.7)
ii.	automated creation of electronic mail accounts for students in class	7(20.0)	16(45.7)		9(25.7)
iii.	automated creation of electronic mail dist. lists for faculty and teaching assistants	6(17.1)	15(42.9)	2 (5.7)	9(25.7)
iv.	electronic class lists	26(74.3)	6(17.1)	1 (2.9)	
v.	electronic submission of grades	6(17.1)	19(54.3)	6(17.1)	1 (2.9)
vi.	no response = 3 (8.6%) except (iv) = 2 (5.7%)				

VIII. GENERAL COMPUTER USE INFORMATION

1. Please provide the appropriate information to indicate the extent and type of computer use for the following activities:

A = i. admissions
B = ii. student registration
C = iii. telephone registration
D = iv. exam scheduling
E = v. time-tabling
F = vi. classroom allocation
G = vii. student records

	Comput erized	Not Comput erized	Main frame	Mini	PC	Commer cial	Devel oped
A	31 (88.6)	2 (5.7)	26 (74.3)	3 (8.6)	7 (20.0)	3 (8.6)	28 (80.0)
B	30 (85.7)	3 (8.6)	24 (68.6)	4 (11.4)	6 (17.1)	3 (8.6)	27 (77.1)
C	10 (28.6)	23 (65.7)	9 (25.7)	2 (5.7)	3 (8.6)	4 (11.4)	7 (20.0)
D	20 (57.1)	13 (37.1)	20(57.1)	1 (2.9)	2 (5.7)	3 (8.6)	15 (42.9)
E	14 (40.0)	19 (54.3)	13(37.1)	1 (2.9)	2 (5.7)	3 (8.6)	11 (31.4)
F	14 (40.0)	19 (54.3)	12(34.3)	1 (2.9)	4 (11.4)	4 (11.4)	7 (20.0)
G	30 (85.7)	3 (8.6)	26(74.3)	4(11.4)	4 (11.4)	1 (2.9)	24 (68.6)

APPENDIX G

SURVEY OF DEANS/STUDENT COUNSELLORS

RESULTS

Number of Questionnaires sent out	99
Number of Questionnaires or responses returned	49
Number of Questionnaires used in analysis	44

Name of University of College:

From University of Toronto	11 (25.0%)
From large universities	20 (45.5%)
From medium-sized universities	10 (22.7%)
From small universities	3 (6.8%)

1. Respondent position within university:

Associate Professor	1 (2.3%)
Professor	1 (2.3%)
Dean	8 (18.2%)
Registrar	10 (22.7%)
Admissions Officer	2 (4.5%)
Director	2 (4.5%)
Assistant Dean	15 (34.1%)
Associate V-P Academics	1 (2.3%)
Admin. Assistant	1 (2.3%)
Other	2 (4.5%)
No Response	1 (2.3%)

2. Respondent's Age:

In 20s	1 (2.3%)
In 30s	7 (15.9%)
In 40s	18 (40.9%)
In 50s	9 (20.5%)
In 60s	1 (2.3%)
No Response	8 (18.2%)

3. Respondent's Educational Level:

High School	5 (11.4%)
Bachelors	10 (22.7%)
Masters	4 (9.1%)
Doctorate	20 (45.5%)
Other	1 (2.3%)
No Response	4 (9.1%)

4. Respondent's Gender:

Male	15 (34.1%)
Female	13 (29.5%)
Not Known	16 (36.4%)

5. Respondent's Academic Unit:

Arts	7 (15.9%)
Science	4 (9.1%)
Arts and Science	1 (2.3%)
Education	3 (6.8%)
Administration	2 (4.5%)
Engineering	3 (6.8%)
Social Work	1 (2.3%)
Law	3 (6.8%)
Nursing	1 (2.3%)
Medicine	1 (2.3%)
Pharmacy	2 (4.5%)
Commerce	1 (2.3%)
Forestry	2 (4.5%)
Grad. Studies	3 (6.8%)
Other	4 (9.1%)
No Response	6 (13.6%)

I. TELEPHONE REGISTRATION

1. Does your university utilize an automated telephone or 'touch tone' registration system?

   Yes 11 (25.0%) (Please answer Part A)
   No 31 (70.5%) (Please proceed to Part B, question 10)
   No Response 2 (4.5%)

PART A (To be completed by universities with automated 'touch tone' registration systems)

2. In what year was telephone registration system first used? 19___

1987	3 (6.8%)
1988	6 (13.6%)
1989	2 (4.5%)
No Response	2(4.5%)

3. What were the most important reasons for the adoption of telephone registration system?

	Not Applicable	35 (79.5%)
a)	Convenient for students	3 (7.9%)
b)	Efficient for Administrators	4 (10.5%)
c)	Provides more accurate data	8 (21.1%)
d)	Avoids arena style registration	1 (2.6%)
e)	Makes planning easier	1 (2.6%)
f)	Prevents early September rush	1 (2.6%)
g)	More class time	3 (7.9%)
h)	Efficient fee collection	1 (2.6%)
i)	Students commit earlier	1 (2.6%)
j)	Efficient room allocation	1 (2.6%)
k)	Fairer to all students	3 (7.9%)
l)	Reduced labour required	4 (10.5%)
m)	Easier to monitor requirements	1 (2.6%)
n)	More flexible	1 (2.6%)
o)	Replaced old technology	1 (2.6%)
p)	Faster service for all	4 (10.5%)

4. What specific problems in your previous registration system did you hope to overcome by adopting a telephone registration system?

	Not Applicable	33 (75.0%)
a)	Students had to line up	6 (18.8%)
b)	Enrolment data not available early	3 (9.4%)
c)	Lots of time spent on registration	3 (9.4%)
d)	Old system too confusing	1 (3.1%)
e)	Lack of control over class changes	3 (9.4%)
f)	Old system slow	4 (12.5%)
g)	Data not accurate	2 (6.3%)
h)	Time consuming for all	5 (15.6%)
i)	Registration system not enforced	1 (3.1%)
j)	Students registered without prerequisites	2 (6.4%)
k)	Student manipulation of system	1 (3.1%)
l)	Previous equipment obsolete	1 (3.1%)

5. What do you see as the primary advantages of a telephone registration system?

	Not Applicable	33 (75.0%)
a)	Student has time to choose	2 (5.0%)
b)	Early enrolment data avalaible	5 (12.5%)
c)	Off-campus registration	2 (5.0%)
d)	Saves students' time	2 (5.0%)
e)	Saves administration time	2 (5.0%)
f)	Saves faculty time	4 (10.0%)
g)	Better data on students not showing up	1 (2.5%)
h)	Allows control of registration	2 (5.0%)
i)	More efficient	6 (15.0%)
j)	Allows classes to start earlier	2 (5.0%)
k)	Faster for students	2 (5.0%)
l)	Fewer errors in registration	3 (7.5%)
m)	Greater fairness	2 (5.0%)
n)	Easier for students to change classes	4 (10.0%)
o)	System capable of multiple use	1 (2.5%)

6. What do you see as the primary disadvantage of a telephone registration system?

	Not Applicable	33 (75.0%)
a)	Impersonal	4 (19.0%)
b)	Registration period longer	1 (4.8%)
c)	Can't accommodate special needs	3 (14.3%)
d)	Students can manipulate system	1 (4.8%)
e)	Access to touch-tone phone required	3 (14.3%)
f)	Changed work flow patterns	3 (14.3%)
g)	Personnel training required	1 (4.8%)
h)	Register without advisor	2 (9.5%)
i)	Process confusing	2 (9.5%)
j)	No disadvantages	1 (4.8%)

7. What, if any, are the major problems you encountered in the transition to a telephone registration system?

	Not Applicable	33 (75.0%)
a)	Telephone and line failure	2 (8.0%)
b)	Faculty unfamiliar with system	4 (16.0%)
c)	Student manipulation of system	1 (4.0%)
d)	Long distance phone costs	3 (12.0%)
e)	Academic units resist change	3 (12.0%)
f)	No major problems	1 (4.0%)
g)	Work patterns require redesign	2 (8.0%)
h)	Lack of phone lines	4 (16.0%)
i)	Schedules must be prepared earlier	2 (8.0%)
j)	Faculty & dept. head workload increases	2 (8.0%)
k)	Users require training	1 (4.0%)

8.a) Do Students have the option of not using the telephone registration system?

Yes 5 (11.4%)	No 6 (13.6%)
No Response 2 (4.5%)	Not Applicable 31 (70.5%)

b) If you answered 'Yes' please explain how students not using the telephone registration system register.

Not coded on the codesheet.

9. Please outline in a step-by-step manner the procedures a student would follow in registering using the telephone system.

Not coded on the codesheet.

Those answering PART A should now skip to II. STUDENT RECORDS.

PART B (To be completed by universities <u>not using</u> an automated 'touch tone' registration system)

10.a) Does your university plan on adopting an automated telephone registration system within the next 3 years?

Yes	13 (29.5%)
No	14 (31.8%)
Uncertain	1 (2.3%)
Don't Know	1 (2.3%)
No Response	4 (9.1%)
Not Applicable	11 (25.0%)

b) If you answered 'Yes' please indicate when.

1990	6 (13.6%)
1991	3 (6.8%)
Don't Know	5 (11.4%)
No Response	4 (9.1%)
Not Applicable	27 (61.4%)

11. Please explain why your university has made this decision.

a) If you are not planning to adopt telephone registration system, please explain why?

	Not Applicable	36 (81.8%)
i.	Cost - lack of funding	4 (28.6%)
ii.	Present system adequate	4 (28.6%)
iii.	Enrolment too small	2 (14.3%)
iv.	Never considered	1 (7.1%)
v.	Most students from local area	1 (7.1%)
vi.	Block register makes easier timetabling	1 (7.1%)
vii.	Needs of unit too specialized	1 (7.1%)

b) If you are planning to adopt telephone registration system, please explain why?

	Not Applicable	35 (79.5%)
i.	Other universities using the system	2 (6.5%)
ii.	Convenient for students	5 (16.1%)
iii.	Lack of personnel	1 (3.2%)
iv.	Current system complicated	2 (6.5%)
v.	Technology now available	1 (3.2%)
vi.	Less work for faculty	1 (3.2%)
vii.	More efficient for registrar's office	2 (6.5%)
viii.	Reduced administration	1 (3.2%)
ix.	Reduced student frustration	1 (3.2%)
x.	Reduced staff frustration	1 (3.2%)
xi.	Enrolment growth requires new system	2 (6.5%)
xii.	Reduces line-ups	5 (16.1%)
xiii.	Equipment can have multi-uses	1 (3.2%)
xiv.	Allows easier class change method	2 (6.5%)
xv.	Will speed up registration	1 (3.2%)
xvi.	Data on enrolment available faster	2 (6.5%)
xvii.	Eliminates human error	1 (3.2%)

II. STUDENT RECORDS

We would now like to ask you some questions about how your university maintains a student's records.

1. Where are master or main files of a student's academic record kept?

i.	university mainframe computer	35 (47.3%)
ii.	Faculty Office	10 (13.5%)
iii.	Registrar's Office	22 (29.7%)
iv.	Department Office	3 (4.1%)
v.	other (please specify)	4 (5.4%)

2.a) Is the datá in the student's record shared with other computer systems outside the central computer system?

Yes 9 (20.5%) No 33 (75.0%) No Response 2 (4.5%)

b) If you answered 'Yes' please elaborate.

Not coded on codesheet.

3. Please explain the role of your computer system in maintaining these records.

Not coded on codesheet.

4. Are 'hard'copy' (non-computer based) copies of a student's records kept?

Yes 33 (75.0%) No 4 (9.1%) No Response 7 (15.9%)

5. Please indicate what information about a student is typically found in his or her computer-based record.

		Yes	No	Don't Know	No Response
i.	high school grades	28 (63.6)	11 (25.0)	1 (2.3)	4 (9.1)
ii.	home address	39 (88.6)	0 (0.0)	1 (2.3)	4 (9.1)
iii.	home phone number	37 (84.1)	2 (4.5)	1 (2.3)	4 (9.1)
iv.	classes completed at university	38 (86.4)	1 (2.3)	1 (2.3)	4 (9.1)
v.	university grades	37 (84.1)	2 (4.5)	1 (2.3)	4 (9.1)
vi.	degrees received	38 (86.4)	1 (2.3)	1 (2.3)	4 (9.1)
vii.	marital status	33 (75.0)	6 (13.6)	1 (2.3)	4 (9.1)
viii.	name of next of kin	20 (45.5)	19 (43.2)	1 (2.3)	4 (9.1)
ix.	social insurance no.	32 (72.7)	7 (15.9)	1 (2.3)	4 (9.1)
x.	financial record (student's univ. acc.)	22 (50.0)	15 (34.1)	2 (4.5)	5 (11.4)
xi.	sex	36 (81.8)	3 (6.8)	1 (2.3)	4 (9.1)
xii.	birth date	39 (88.6)	0 (0.0)	1 (2.3)	4 (9.1)
xiii.	any handicaps	5 (11.4)	32 (72.7)	2 (4.5)	5 (11.4)
xiv.	transfer credits	30 (68.2)	7 (15.9)	1 (2.3)	5 (11.4)
xv.	visa information	30 (68.2)	9 (20.5)	1 (2.3)	4 (9.1)
xvi.	nationality	29 (65.9)	9 (20.5)	1 (2.3)	5 (11.4)
xvii.	grade point average	3 (6.8)	36 (81.8)	1 (2.3)	4 (9.1)
xviii.	faculty registered in	39 (88.6)	0 (0.0)	1 (2.3)	4 (9.1)
xix.	major	34 (77.3)	5 (11.4)	1 (2.3)	4 (9.1)
xx.	year of program	39 (88.6)	0 (0.0)	1 (2.3)	4 (9.1)
xxi.	original name if changed	2 (4.5)	37 (84.1)	1 (2.3)	4 (9.1)
xxii.	academic awards	2 (4.5)	37 (84.1)	1 (2.3)	4 (9.1)
xxiii.	Dean's list status	1 (2.3)	38 (86.4)	1 (2.3)	4 (9.1)
xxiv.	academic eligibility	5 (11.4)	34 (77.3)	1 (2.3)	4 (9.1)
xxv.	financial eligibility	3 (6.8)	36 (81.8)	1 (2.3)	4 (9.1)

6. Who, in the university, normally has access to a student's file?

		Yes	No	Don't Know	No Response
i.	univ. administrators	39 (88.6)	1 (2.3)	1 (2.3)	3 (6.8)
ii.	university faculty	25 (56.8)	14 (31.8)	2 (4.5)	3 (6.8)
iii.	the students herself/himself	24 (54.5)	16 (36.4)	1 (2.3)	3 (6.8)
iv.	other students	0 (0.0)	40 (90.9)	1 (2.3)	3 (6.8)
v.	next of kin	1 (2.3)	39 (88.6)	1 (2.3)	3 (6.8)
vi.	police	5 (11.4)	34 (77.3)	2 (4.5)	3 (6.8)
vii.	police/others with court order	7 (15.9)	33 (75.0)	1 (2.3)	3 (6.8)
viii.	department heads	2 (4.5)	38 (86.4)	1 (2.3)	3 (6.8)

7. Does anyone outside the university have access to information from a student's file?

Yes 3 (6.8%) No 37 (84.1%) No Response 4 (9.1%)

8. What measures are undertaken to ensure confidentiality

Not coded on codesheets.

APPENDIX H

SURVEY OF UNIVERSITY ADMISSIONS OFFICERS

RESULTS

Number of Questionnaires sent out	78
Number of Questionnaires or responses returned	34
Number of Questionnaires used in analysis	29

Name of University or College:

From large universities	3 (10.3%)
From medium-sized universities	10 (34.5%)
From small universities	16 (55.2%)

1. Respondent position within university:

Dean	1 (3.4%)
Registrar	15 (51.7%)
Admissions Officer	6 (20.7%)
Director	5 (17.2%)
Admin. Assistant	1 (3.4%)
No Response	1 (3.4%)

2. Respondent's Age:

In 30s	7 (24.1%)
In 40s	12 (41.4%)
In 50s	2 (6.9%)
In 60s	1 (3.4%)
>69	1 (3.4%)
No Response	4 (13.8%)

3. Respondent's Educational Level:

Bachelors	8 (27.6%)
Masters	13 (44.8%)
Doctorate	5 (17.2%)
Other	1 (3.4%)
No Response	3 (6.9%)

4. Respondent's Gender:

Male	8 (27.6%)
Female	9 (31.0%)
Not Known	12 (41.4%)

I. STUDENT ACADEMIC COUNSELLING

First Year Students

1.a) Are first year students required to meet with a counsellor "in person" prior to their first registration?

Yes 10 (34.5%) No 17 (58.6%) No Response 1 (3.4%)

b) If you answered 'Yes' who provides the counselling services?

	Not Applicable	13 (44.8%)
i.	regular teaching faculty	11 (32.4%)
ii.	Assistant Dean	6 (17.6%)
iii.	Administrative Assistants	5 (14.7%)
iv.	Faculty Office Staff	3 (8.8%)
v.	Admissions Officer	3 (8.8%)
vi.	Program Co-ordinator	1 (2.9%)
vii.	Registrar's Staff	5 (14.7%)

c) How are such "in person" counselling sessions arranged?

	Not Applicable	12 (41.4%)
i.	Through Student Services	4 (17.4%)
ii.	Students call	11 (47.8%)
iii.	Students drop in	4 (17.4%)
iv.	Admission Office school visits	1 (4.3%)
v.	Computerized scheduling system	3 (13.0%)

d) On average, how long would such a first year student's counselling appointment take?

	Not Applicable	12 (41.4%)
i.	less than 15 min.	7 (36,8%)
ii.	15-30 min.	9 (47.4%)
iii.	over 30 min.	2 (10.5%)
iv.	varies	1 (5.3%)

2.a) Do basic program requirements influence the selection of first year/term courses?

Yes 20 (69.0%) No 5 (17.2%) No Response 2 (6.9%)

b) If you answered 'Yes' please explain how.

	Not Applicable	8 (27.6%)
i.	Pre-requisites for 2nd yr.	6 (24.0%)
ii.	Must include basic requirements	10 (40.0%)
iii.	Common 1st yr. in liberal arts	1 (4.0%)
iv.	Basic program requirements dictate	8 (32.0%)

3.a) Do all counsellors have access to computer-based information on the student's academic background?

Yes 17 (58.6%) No 9 (31.0%) No Response 2 (6.9%)

b) If you answered 'Yes' please indicate what information concerning the student's academic background would be available:

		Yes	No
	Not Applicable	12 (41.4%)	
i.	high school grades	9 (31.0%)	8 (27.6%)
ii.	home address	16 (55.2%)	1 (3.4%)
iii.	home phone number	16 (55.2%)	1 (3.4%)
iv.	classes completed at university	15 (51.7%)	2 (6.9%)
v.	university grades	13 (44.8%)	4 (13.8%)
vi.	degrees received	14 (48.3%)	3 (10.3%)
vii.	marital status	9 (31.0%)	8 (27.6%)
viii.	name of next of kin	4 (13.8%)	13 (44.8%)
ix.	social insurance number	11 (37.9%)	6 (20.7%)
x.	financial record (student's univ. accounts)	3 (10.3%)	14 (48.3%)
xi.	sex	13 (44.8%)	4 (13.8%)
xii.	birth date	15 (51.7%)	2 (6.9%)
xiii.	any handicaps	4 (13.8%)	13 (44.8%)
xiv.	transfer credits	15 (51.7%)	2 (6.9%)
xv.	visa data	10 (34.5%)	7 (24.1%)
xvi.	nationality	10 (34.5%)	7 (24.2%)
xvii.	basis of admission	4 (13.8%)	13 (44.8%)
xviii.	parents' name	2 (6.9%)	15 (51.7%)
xix.	parents' address	2 (6.9%)	15 (51.7%)
xx.	local address	2 (6.9%)	15 (51.7%)
xxi.	other	3 (10.3%)	14 (48.3%)

4.a) Do all counsellors have access to computer-based information on class schedules and class availability?

Yes 9 (31.0%) No 17 (58.6%) No Response 2 (6.9%)

b) If you answered 'Yes' please indicate what information is available on the computer system:

	Not Applicable	20 (69.0%)
i.	time	7 (18.4%)
ii.	day	7 (18.4%)
iii.	instructor	5 (13.2%)
iv.	lecture hours	7 (18.4%)
v.	lab/seminar hours	8 (21.1%)
vi.	course title	2 (5.3%)
vii.	enrolment per section	2 (5.3%)

5. What measures are taken to ensure the confidentiality of information concerning students?

	Not Applicable	6 (20.7%)
i.	University policy document as control	6 (20.7%)
ii.	Computer access codes and security system	11 (37.9%)
iii.	No formal measures	3 (10.3%)
iv.	Data not released from registrar's office	6 (20.7%)
v.	Those with access under oath	1 (3.4%)
vi.	Student permission required	2 (6.9%)

6. What other counselling options (ie. Expert System) do students have access to?

	Not Applicable	12 (41.4%)
i.	None	8 (38.1%)
ii.	Telephone registration	1 (4.8%)
iii.	Student services office	1 (4.8%)
iv.	Personal counselling	4 (19.0%)
v.	Academic advice center	4 (19.0%)
vi.	Planning computer based system	1 (4.8%)
vii.	Other	2 (9.5%)

Student Academic Counselling in Second and Subsequent Years

7. Are students required to see a counsellor "in person" during their second and subsequent years?

Yes 17 (57.6%) No 10 (34.5%) No Response 2 (6.9%)

PART A

8. Who provides student academic counselling for students in their second and subsequent years?

	Not Applicable	9 (31.0%)
i.	regular teaching faculty	16 (35.6%)
ii.	Assistant Dean	10 (22.2%)
iii.	Administrative Assistants	6 (13.3%)
iv.	Faculty Office Staff	5 (11.1%)
v.	Registrar's Office	6 (13.3%)
vi.	Other	2 (4.4%)

9. How long would these academic counselling appointments typically take?

	Not Applicable	10 (34.5%)
i.	less than 15 min.	5 (17.2%)
ii.	15-30 min.	12 (41.4%)
iii.	over 30 min.	0 (0.0%)
iv.	varies	2 (6.9%)

PART B

10. If students do not see a counsellor prior to registration, how do you ensure that the student registers in the correct classes?

	Not Applicable	8 (27.6%)
i.	Student expected to read calendar and know	8 (25.8%)
ii.	Administrator contacts if there's a problem	3 (9.7%)
iii.	Voluntary counselling available	3 (9.7%)
iv.	Student has no choices	1 (3.2%)
v.	Faculty member checks	8 (25.8%)
vi.	Student must get form signed	2 (6.5%)
vii.	Computer checks systems	5 (16.1%)
viii.	Other means	1 (3.2%)

II. GENERAL REGISTRATION PROCEDURES

The following questions are designed to provide some general information about the overall registration process at your university.

1. Please describe in a step-by-step fashion a typical first year student's registration procedures.

Not coded on codesheet.

2. Please describe in a step-by-step fashion a typical upper year student's registration procedures.

Not coded on codesheet.

3. How has the adoption of computer based technology changed student registration procedures over the past 10 years?

	Not Applicable	6 (20.7%)
i.	Made faster/sped up all aspects	11 (16.7%)
ii.	Increased need to check data	1 (1.5%)
iii.	Sped up data production	5 (7.6%)
iv.	Made data more accurate	7 (10.6%)
v.	Made data more available	7 (10.6%)
vi.	Made class changes easier	2 (3.0%)
vii.	No real impact/none	4 (6.1%)
viii.	Eliminated line-ups	4 (6.1%)
ix.	Makes control of class size easier	3 (4.5%)
x.	Allows easier check of student files and records	9 (13.6%)
xi.	Less staff/personnel required	4 (6.1%)
xii.	Allows better service	9 (13.6%)

4. What future changes and developments in your registration procedures do you anticipate? Please indicate the role computers are expected to play in these changes.

	Not Applicable	7 (24.1%)
i.	Telephone registration system being considered	15 (40.5%)
ii.	Computer program/conflict check system coming	4 (10.8%)
iii.	Computers will free time from registration work	6 (16.2%)
iv.	No changes anticipated	2 (5.4%)
v.	Class and exam schedules to be computerized	5 (10.8%)
vi.	Degree requirement audit system in planning	5 (13.5%)
vii.	Mail registration system being planned	1 (2.7%)

5. Please provide a sample copy of your registration forms, time tables, and other documents used by students and counsellors in registration.

Not coded on codesheet.

APPENDIX I

ATTITUDE SURVEY

The data used here are part of the Canada-wide survey on university computerization conducted in the autumn of 1989. Each of the six different questionnaires (for faculty, deans, admissions officers, registrars, computer centre directors, and academic vice-presidents) included the same questions on attitudes. There were three hundred and forty responses to the attitude portion of the survey. The relatively low response rate, particularly among faculty and computer centre directors, means that we must be cautious in making generalizations.

A thirty-question, 5-point Likert scale was used to determine attitudes. The level of differences in attitudes were ascertained through analysis of variance (ANOVA) and t-tests of significance as well as the Chi-Square measure of association, using the SPSS-X statistical package. Discussion of the findings is presented in chapter two. Having a positive attitude about computers means that one supports claims about the beneficial influence of computers in pedagogical and social situations.

The attitude portion of the survey was coordinated with the Indian team, and the two sets of questions are as similar as the different circumstances of the two countries, and differences in language, permit. Analysis of the Indian results can be found in the second volume of this study. In general, Indians are significantly more positive towards computers than are Canadians. The reasons for this are not clear, although the different levels of experience with computerization could be suggested as one possible explanation. Full analysis of national differences awaits further study.

Attitude Survey Questionnaire

Please rate the following statements by circling the number that represents the response closest to your opinion.

1 = strongly disagree 2 = disagree 3 = undecided 4 = agree 5 = strongly agree

1.	Computers help to increase productivity in the educational process.	1 2 3 4 5
2.	Computers can help to achieve a higher quality of learning.	1 2 3 4 5
3.	Computers can help to individualize instruction to better meet the needs of particular students.	1 2 3 4 5
4.	Computers help to lay the foundation of primary and secondary education.	1 2 3 4 5
5.	Computers help to motivate students.	1 2 3 4 5
6.	Computers can prevent social isolation.	1 2 3 4 5
7.	Computers can help weaker students.	1 2 3 4 5
8.	Teaching with computers is too expensive and time consuming to be worth the effort.	1 2 3 4 5
9.	Computers will widen the gap between rural and urban students.	1 2 3 4 5
10.	Computers will reduce differences in the quality of universities.	1 2 3 4 5
11.	There is a lot of politics involved in the introduction of computers in higher education.	1 2 3 4 5
12.	Computerization will disproportionately benefit better funded universities.	1 2 3 4 5
13.	Computers will bring about a pedagogical revolution in higher education.	1 2 3 4 5
14.	Computers are only really useful in science and technical education.	1 2 3 4 5
15.	Computerization generally creates new jobs.	1 2 3 4 5
16.	Computers improve university administration.	1 2 3 4 5
17.	Computerization fosters fair and equitable admission to higher education.	1 2 3 4 5
18.	In education, computers are gender neutral.	1 2 3 4 5
19.	Computers adversely affect students' analytical abilities.	1 2 3 4 5
20.	Computers increase creativity.	1 2 3 4 5
21.	Computers make humans machine dependent.	1 2 3 4 5
22.	Computers widen the gap between rich and poor students.	1 2 3 4 5
23.	Computers are expensive toys.	1 2 3 4 5
24.	The introduction of computers into teaching threatens teachers.	1 2 3 4 5
25.	Computerization makes university administrators' jobs easier.	1 2 3 4 5
26.	Computers threaten workers' health.	1 2 3 4 5
27.	Studying computers will guarantee a higher paying job.	1 2 3 4 5
28.	Computers will widen the gap between men and women.	1 2 3 4 5
29.	Those with power in the university make all major decisions about computers.	1 2 3 4 5
30.	Computerization leads to the loss of jobs.	1 2 3 4 5

Attitude Survey Results

QUESTION		Frequency Distribution Percentages						
		ST DISAGREE	DISAGREE	UNDECIDED	AGREE	ST AGREE	MEAN	N
#1	Computers help to increase productivity in the educational process.							
	ALL FACULTY	2.2	9.3	23.6	47.3	17.6	3.69	182
	DEANS	2.6	2.6	5.1	51.3	38.5	4.21	39
	ADMISSIONS	0	0	5.3	42.1	52.6	4.47	19
	REGISTRARS	0	0	9.7	35.5	54.8	4.45	31
	COM. CENTRE	0	0	18.2	72.7	9.1	3.91	11
	ACADEMIC VP	0	0	3.8	46.2	50	4.46	26
	ALL ADMIN	0.8	0.8	7.1	46.8	44.4	4.33	126
	ALL CANADA	1.6	5.8	16.9	47.1	28.6	3.95	308
#2	Computers can help to achieve a higher quality of learning.							
	ALL FACULTY	3.8	8.7	27.7	45.7	14.1	3.58	184
	DEANS	0	2.6	20.5	53.8	23.1	3.97	39
	ADMISSIONS	0	5.3	31.6	47.4	15.8	3.74	19
	REGISTRARS	0	3.2	12.9	48.4	35.5	4.16	31
	COM. CENTRE	0	0	36.4	54.5	9.1	3.73	11
	ACADEMIC VP	0	0	11.5	42.3	46.2	4.35	26
	ALL ADMIN	0	2.4	19.8	49.2	28.6	4.04	126
	ALL CANADA	2.3	6.1	24.5	47.1	20	3.77	310
#3	Computers can help to individualize instruction to better meet the needs of particular students.							
	ALL FACULTY	2.7	14.1	30.8	36.2	16.2	3.49	185
	DEANS	0	0	16.2	59.5	24.3	4.08	37
	ADMISSIONS	0	10.5	26.3	42.1	21.1	3.74	19
	REGISTRARS	0	0	26.7	50	23.3	3.97	30
	COM. CENTRE	0	0	36.4	54.5	9.1	3.73	11
	ACADEMIC VP	0	0	26.9	46.2	26.9	4.00	26
	ALL ADMIN	0	1.6	24.4	51.2	22.8	3.95	123
	ALL CANADA	1.6	9.1	28.2	42.2	18.8	3.68	308
#4	Computers help to lay the foundation of primary and secondary education.							
	ALL FACULTY	14.1	22.9	36.5	16.7	4.7	2.74	182
	DEANS	10.5	13.2	36.8	28.9	10.5	3.16	38
	ADMISSIONS	10.5	31.6	31.6	15.8	10.5	2.84	19
	REGISTRARS	10.3	31	37.9	13.8	6.9	2.76	29
	COM. CENTRE	9.1	45.5	27.3	9.1	9.1	2.64	11
	ACADEMIC VP	8	8	56	20	8	3.12	25
	ALL ADMIN	9.8	2.1	39.3	19.7	9	2.96	122
	ALL CANADA	12.8	23.4	38.8	18.4	6.6	2.83	304

# 5	Computers help to motivate students.						
	ALL FACULTY	3.8	16.1	34.9	41.4	3.8	3.25	186
	DEANS	2.6	7.9	36.8	47.4	5.3	3.45	38
	ADMISSIONS	0	5.6	44.4	50	0	3.44	18
	REGISTRARS	0	10	40	40	10	3.50	30
	COM. CENTRE	9.1	0	63.6	27.3	0	3.09	11
	ACADEMIC VP	0	8	32	44	16	3.68	25
	ALL ADMIN	1.6	7.4	40.2	43.4	7.4	3.48	122
	ALL CANADA	2.9	12.7	37	42.2	5.2	3.34	308
# 6	Computers can prevent social isolation.							
	ALL FACULTY	18.1	33.5	37.4	8.8	2.2	2.43	182
	DEANS	16.2	24.3	43.2	13.5	2.7	2.62	37
	ADMISSIONS	15.8	42.1	36.8	5.3	0	2.32	19
	REGISTRARS	3.3	46.7	33.3	16.7	0	2.63	30
	COM. CENTRE	18.2	45.5	9.1	27.3	0	2.46	11
	ACADEMIC VP	8	32	48	12	0	2.64	25
	ALL ADMIN	11.5	36.1	37.7	13.9	0.8	2.57	122
	ALL CANADA	15.5	34.5	37.5	10.9	1.6	2.49	304
# 7	Computers can help weaker students.							
	ALL FACULTY	4.9	14.8	37.2	37.7	5.5	3.24	183
	DEANS	0	10.8	29.7	51.4	8.1	3.57	37
	ADMISSIONS	10.5	5.3	26.3	52.6	5.3	3.37	19
	REGISTRARS	3.3	3.3	36.7	46.7	10	3.57	30
	COM. CENTRE	0	9.1	36.4	45.5	9.1	3.55	11
	ACADEMIC VP	0	8	36	36	20	3.68	25
	ALL ADMIN	2.5	7.4	32.8	46.7	10.7	3.56	122
	ALL CANADA	3.9	11.8	35.4	41.3	7.5	3.37	305
# 8	Teaching with computers is too expensive and time consuming to be worth the effort.							
	ALL FACULTY	19.7	41	29.5	7.7	2.2	2.32	183
	DEANS	34.2	47.4	13.2	0	5.3	1.95	38
	ADMISSIONS	21.1	42.1	31.6	5.3	0	2.21	19
	REGISTRARS	27.6	51.7	13.8	6.9	0	2.00	29
	COM. CENTRE	27.3	45.5	27.3	0	0	2.00	11
	ACADEMIC VP	15.4	65.4	19.2	0	0	2.04	26
	ALL ADMIN	26	51.2	18.7	2.4	1.6	2.02	123
	ALL CANADA	22.2	45.1	25.2	5.6	2	2.20	306
# 9	Computers will widen the gap between rural and urban students.							
	ALL FACULTY	12.5	38.6	29.9	14.7	4.3	2.60	184
	DEANS	18.4	31.6	42.1	7.9	0	2.40	38
	ADMISSIONS	10.5	31.6	31.6	21.1	5.3	2.79	19
	REGISTRARS	22.6	29	25.8	19.4	3.2	2.52	31
	COM. CENTRE	0	54.5	45.5	0	0	2.46	11
	ACADEMIC VP	7.7	42.3	30.8	11.5	7.7	2.69	26
	ALL ADMIN	14.4	35.2	34.4	12.8	3.2	2.55	125
	ALL CANADA	13.3	37.2	31.7	13.9	3.9	2.58	309

#10	Computers will reduce the differences in the quality of universities.							
	ALL FACULTY	17.9	42.9	26.6	10.9	1.6	2.35	184
	DEANS	23.7	18.4	42.1	15.8	0	2.50	38
	ADMISSIONS	15.8	31.6	42.1	10.5	0	2.47	19
	REGISTRARS	10	40	26.7	20	3.3	2.67	30
	COM. CENTRE	9.1	63.6	18.2	9.1	0	2.27	11
	ACADEMIC VP	7.7	30.8	42.3	19.2	0	2.73	26
	ALL ADMIN	14.5	32.3	36.3	16.1	0.8	2.57	124
	ALL CANADA	16.6	38.6	30.5	13	1.3	2.44	308
#11	There is a lot of politics involved in the introduction of computers in higher education.							
	ALL FACULTY	3.9	21.5	32	30.4	12.2	3.25	181
	DEANS	7.9	28.9	26.3	28.9	7.9	3.00	38
	ADMISSIONS	0	42.1	26.3	26.3	5.3	2.95	19
	REGISTRARS	6.9	27.6	20.7	34.5	10.3	3.14	29
	COM. CENTRE	0	0	27.3	63.6	9.1	3.82	11
	ACADEMIC VP	3.8	19.2	19.2	46.2	11.5	3.42	26
	ALL ADMIN	4.9	26	23.6	36.6	8.9	3.19	123
	ALL CANADA	4.3	23.4	28.6	32.9	10.9	3.23	304
#12	Computerization will disproportionately benefit better funded universities.							
	ALL FACULTY	4.3	21.7	27.2	37.5	9.2	3.26	184
	DEANS	2.6	15.8	36.8	36.8	7.9	3.32	38
	ADMISSIONS	0	26.3	36.8	36.8	0	3.11	19
	REGISTRARS	3.2	19.4	19.4	48.4	9.7	3.42	31
	COM. CENTRE	0	0	18.2	72.7	9.1	3.91	11
	ACADEMIC VP	0	23.1	30.8	38.5	7.7	3.31	26
	ALL ADMIN	1.6	18.4	29.6	43.2	7.2	3.36	125
	ALL CANADA	3.2	20.4	28.2	39.8	8.4	3.30	309
#13	Computers will bring about a pedagogical revolution in higher education.							
	ALL FACULTY	12.1	31.9	35.7	17.6	2.7	2.67	182
	DEANS	8.1	10.8	48.6	32.4	0	3.05	37
	ADMISSIONS	0	27.8	33.3	33.3	5.6	3.17	18
	REGISTRARS	0	10	43.3	43.3	3.3	3.40	30
	COM. CENTRE	0	0	72.7	27.3	0	3.27	11
	ACADEMIC VP	0	7.7	46.2	34.6	11.5	3.50	26
	ALL ADMIN	2.5	11.5	46.7	35.2	4.1	3.27	122
	ALL CANADA	8.2	23.7	40.1	24.7	3.3	2.91	304
#14	Computers are only really useful in science education.							
	ALL FACULTY	24.9	53	13	7	2.2	2.09	185
	DEANS	36.8	55.3	2.6	2.6	2.6	1.79	38
	ADMISSIONS	42.1	36.8	10.5	10.5	0	1.90	19
	REGISTRARS	46.7	50	0	3.3	0	1.60	30
	COM. CENTRE	45.5	45.5	9.1	0	0	1.64	11
	ACADEMIC VP	46.2	53.8	0	0	0	1.54	26
	ALL ADMIN	42.7	50	3.2	3.2	0.8	1.69	124
	ALL CANADA	32	51.8	9.1	5.5	1.6	1.93	309

#15	Computerization generally creates new jobs.							
	ALL FACULTY	6	13.1	42.1	35.5	3.3	3.17	183
	DEANS	2.6	7.7	28.2	51.3	10.3	3.59	39
	ADMISSIONS	5.3	26.3	31.6	31.6	5.3	3.05	19
	REGISTRARS	0	26.7	16.7	53.3	3.3	3.33	30
	COM. CENTRE	0	9.1	36.4	54.5	0	3.46	11
	ACADEMIC VP	0	23.1	42.3	30.8	3.8	3.15	26
	ALL ADMIN	1.6	18.4	29.6	44.8	5.6	3.34	125
	ALL CANADA	4.2	15.3	37	39.3	4.2	3.24	308
#16	Computers improve university administration.							
	ALL FACULTY	7.6	10.9	20.7	41.8	19	3.54	184
	DEANS	0	5.3	7.9	55.3	31.6	4.13	38
	ADMISSIONS	0	5.3	0	36.8	57.9	4.47	19
	REGISTRARS	0	3.4	3.4	44.8	48.3	4.38	29
	COM. CENTRE	0	0	18.2	63.6	18.2	4.00	11
	ACADEMIC VP	0	3.8	7.7	46.2	42.3	4.27	26
	ALL ADMIN	0	4.1	6.5	48.8	40.7	4.26	123
	ALL CANADA	4.6	8.1	15	44.6	27.7	3.83	307
#17	Computerization fosters fair and equitable admission to higher education.							
	ALL FACULTY	10.4	29	49.2	10.4	1.1	2.63	183
	DEANS	10.5	13.2	42.1	28.9	5.3	3.05	38
	ADMISSIONS	0	31.6	15.8	47.4	5.3	3.26	19
	REGISTRARS	6.7	26.7	26.7	40	0	3.00	30
	COM. CENTRE	0	27.3	63.6	9.1	0	2.82	11
	ACADEMIC VP	0	24	60	12	4	2.96	25
	ALL ADMIN	4.9	22.8	39.8	29.3	3.3	3.03	123
	ALL CANADA	8.2	26.5	45.4	18	2	2.79	306
#18	In education, computers are gender neutral.							
	ALL FACULTY	6.1	12.2	36.5	35.4	9.9	3.31	181
	DEANS	2.8	8.3	33.3	47.2	8.3	3.50	36
	ADMISSIONS	5.6	11.1	44.4	33.3	5.6	3.22	18
	REGISTRARS	6.5	9.7	35.5	41.9	6.5	3.32	31
	COM. CENTRE	0	0	27.3	63.6	9.1	3.82	11
	ACADEMIC VP	4	0	40	48	8	3.56	25
	ALL ADMIN	4.1	6.6	36.4	45.5	7.4	3.46	121
	ALL CANADA	5.3	9.9	36.4	39.4	8.9	3.37	302
#19	Computers adversly affect students' analytical abilities.							
	ALL FACULTY	16	35.9	28.7	13.3	6.1	2.58	181
	DEANS	13.2	44.7	18.4	18.4	5.3	2.58	38
	ADMISSIONS	10.5	57.9	26.3	0	5.3	2.32	19
	REGISTRARS	20.7	31	27.6	17.2	3.4	2.52	29
	COM. CENTRE	9.1	63.6	18.2	9.1	0	2.18	11
	ACADEMIC VP	15.4	61.5	19.2	3.8	0	2.12	26
	ALL ADMIN	13.8	48.8	22	11.4	3.3	2.39	123
	ALL CANADA	15.1	41.1	26	12.5	4.9	2.50	304

#20	Computers increase creativity.							
	ALL FACULTY	7.6	23.4	36.4	26.1	6.5	3.01	184
	DEANS	2.6	10.5	55.3	31.6	0	3.16	38
	ADMISSIONS	0	11.1	44.4	38.9	5.6	3.39	18
	REGISTRARS	0	13.8	31	55.2	0	3.41	29
	COM. CENTRE	9.1	9.1	63.6	18.2	0	2.91	11
	ACADEMIC VP	0	7.7	46.2	38.5	7.7	3.46	26
	ALL ADMIN	1.6	10.7	46.7	38.5	2.5	3.30	122
	ALL CANADA	5.2	18.3	40.5	31	4.9	3.12	306
#21	Computers make humans machine dependent.							
	ALL FACULTY	8.2	38.6	18.5	32.1	2.7	2.83	184
	DEANS	7.9	23.7	15.8	44.7	7.9	3.21	38
	ADMISSIONS	21.1	21.1	15.8	42.1	0	2.79	19
	REGISTRARS	6.9	24.1	10.3	58.6	0	3.21	29
	COM. CENTRE	9.1	18.2	27.3	45.5	0	3.09	11
	ACADEMIC VP	0	42.3	11.5	42.3	3.8	3.08	26
	ALL ADMIN	8.1	26.8	14.6	47.2	3.3	3.11	123
	ALL CANADA	8.1	33.9	16.9	38.1	2.9	2.94	307
#22	Computers widen the gap between rich and poor students.							
	ALL FACULTY	5.5	27.1	28.7	29.8	8.8	3.09	181
	DEANS	5.4	18.9	37.8	35.1	2.7	3.11	37
	ADMISSIONS	10.5	31.6	31.6	21.1	5.3	2.79	19
	REGISTRARS	0	29	32.3	25.8	12.9	3.23	31
	COM. CENTRE	0	9.1	36.4	54.5	0	3.46	11
	ACADEMIC VP	3.8	30.8	34.6	26.9	3.8	2.96	26
	ALL ADMIN	4	25	34.7	30.6	5.6	3.09	124
	ALL CANADA	4.9	26.2	31.1	30.2	7.5	3.09	305
#23	Computers are expensive toys.							
	ALL FACULTY	28.2	42	12.2	15.5	2.2	2.22	181
	DEANS	29.7	56.8	5.4	8.1	0	1.92	37
	ADMISSIONS	42.1	42.1	10.5	5.3	0	1.79	19
	REGISTRARS	25	42.9	10.7	7.1	14.3	2.43	28
	COM. CENTRE	36.4	36.4	18.2	0	9.1	2.09	11
	ACADEMIC VP	23.1	57.7	7.7	1.5	0	2.08	26
	ALL ADMIN	29.8	49.6	9.1	7.4	4.1	2.07	121
	ALL CANADA	28.8	45	10.9	12.3	3	2.16	302
#24	The introduction of computers into teaching threatens teachers.							
	ALL FACULTY	30.9	50.8	8.8	7.2	2.2	1.99	181
	DEANS	23.7	42.1	10.5	21.1	2.6	2.37	38
	ADMISSIONS	21.1	47.4	15.8	15.8	0	2.26	19
	REGISTRARS	26.7	50	10	13.3	0	2.10	30
	COM. CENTRE	40	40	10	10	0	1.90	10
	ACADEMIC VP	15.4	57.7	15.4	11.5	0	2.23	26
	ALL ADMIN	23.6	48	12.2	15.4	0.8	2.22	123
	ALL CANADA	28	49.7	10.2	10.5	1.6	2.08	304

#25	Computerization makes university administrator's jobs easier.							
	ALL FACULTY	4.9	15.8	19.7	44.3	15.3	3.49	183
	DEANS	2.6	15.8	13.2	42.1	26.3	3.74	38
	ADMISSIONS	0	10.5	0	57.9	31.6	4.11	19
	REGISTRARS	7.4	22.2	11.1	18.5	40.7	3.63	27
	COM. CENTRE	0	45.5	9.1	27.3	18.2	3.18	11
	ACADEMIC VP	0	19.2	15.4	46.2	19.2	3.65	26
	ALL ADMIN	2.5	19.8	10.7	38.8	28.1	3.70	121
	ALL CANADA	3.9	17.4	16.1	42.1	20.4	3.58	304
#26	Computers threaten workers health.							
	ALL FACULTY	23	33.3	31.1	9.8	2.7	2.36	183
	DEANS	18.4	36.8	31.6	13.2	0	2.40	38
	ADMISSIONS	15.8	52.6	26.3	5.3	0	2.21	19
	REGISTRARS	20	50	26.7	3.3	0	2.13	30
	COM. CENTRE	36.4	27.3	27.3	9.1	0	2.09	11
	ACADEMIC VP	30.8	42.3	23.1	3.8	0	2.00	26
	ALL ADMIN	22.6	42.7	27.4	7.3	0	2.19	124
	ALL CANADA	22.8	37.1	29.6	8.8	1.6	2.29	307
#27	Studying computers will guarantee a higher paying job.							
	ALL FACULTY	7.6	29.9	32.6	25	4.9	2.90	184
	DEANS	5.3	39.5	15.8	34.2	5.3	2.95	38
	ADMISSIONS	10.5	36.8	10.5	42.1	0	2.84	19
	REGISTRARS	0	36.7	33.3	30	0	2.93	30
	COM. CENTRE	18.2	54.5	9.1	18.2	0	2.27	11
	ACADEMIC VP	11.5	15.4	38.5	30.8	3.8	3.00	26
	ALL ADMIN	7.3	34.7	23.4	32.3	2.4	2.88	124
	ALL CANADA	7.5	31.8	28.9	27.9	3.9	2.89	308
#28	Computers will widen the gap between men and women.							
	ALL FACULTY	25.1	44.3	25.1	2.7	2.7	2.14	183
	DEANS	16.2	62.2	10.8	10.8	0	2.16	37
	ADMISSIONS	26.3	52.6	15.8	5.3	0	2.00	19
	REGISTRARS	20	50	20	3.3	6.7	2.27	30
	COM. CENTRE	27.3	45.5	18.2	9.1	0	2.09	11
	ACADEMIC VP	26.9	50	23.1	0	0	1.96	26
	ALL ADMIN	22	53.7	17.1	5.7	1.6	2.11	123
	ALL CANADA	23.9	48	21.9	3.9	2.3	2.13	306
#29	Those with power in the university make all major decisions about computers.							
	ALL FACULTY	10.5	34.8	18.8	27.1	8.8	2.89	181
	DEANS	2.6	39.5	15.8	31.6	10.5	3.08	38
	ADMISSIONS	5.6	33.3	16.7	44.4	0	3.00	18
	REGISTRARS	9.7	38.7	0	38.7	12.9	3.07	31
	COM. CENTRE	9.1	27.3	9.1	54.5	0	3.09	11
	ACADEMIC VP	11.5	50	15.4	19.2	3.8	2.54	26
	ALL ADMIN	7.3	39.5	11.3	34.7	7.3	2.95	124
	ALL CANADA	9.2	36.7	15.7	30.2	8.2	2.92	305

#30	Computerization leads to the loss of jobs.						
	ALL FACULTY	15.6	38.9	32.2	10.6	2.8	2.46	180
	DEANS	21.1	52.6	21.1	5.3	0	2.11	38
	ADMISSIONS	5.6	44.4	33.3	16.7	0	2.61	18
	REGISTRARS	3.4	69	13.8	13.8	0	2.38	29
	COM. CENTRE	9.1	63.6	27.3	0	0	2.18	11
	ACADEMIC VP	23.1	53.8	11.5	7.7	3.8	2.15	26
	ALL ADMIN	13.9	56.6	19.7	9	0.8	2.26	122
	ALL CANADA	14.9	46	27.2	9.9	2	2.38	302

APPENDIX J

This appendix contains a listing of the applications implemented by the 452 institutions surveyed by the Professional Association for Computing and Information Technology in Higher Education and reported in their 1985 Profile of Administrative Systems (Thomas, Charles R. and Dana S. van Hoesen. *Administrative Information Systems: The 1985 Profile and Five-Year Trends*. CAUSE Publications, 1986). The survey of the 452 institutions categories the 157 different administrative applications into eleven categories. Section 1 gives the eleven categories along with an abbreviation used to denote the category. Section 2. and 3. list the applications. In section 2. the applications are listed by category and in section 2. they are sorted by the number of institutions which have implemented the application, beginning with the application which was implemented by the largest number of the 452 institutions and ending with the application which the fewest to the institutions have implemented. The number appearing at the after each application is the number of institutions which had implemented the application.

1. Application Categories

Admissions & Records Applications Analysis - ARAA
Financial Management Applications Analysis - FMAA
Planning Mgmt & Institutional Research Applications Analysis - PMIRAA
Logistics and Related Services Applications Analysis - LRSAA
Faculty/Staff/Student Services Applications Analysis - FSSSAA
General Administrative Services Applications Analysis - GASAA
Auxiliary Services Applications Analysis - ASAA
Library Application Analysis - LAA
Physical Plant Operations Applications Analysis - PPOAA
Computing Installation Management Applications Analysis - CIMAA
Hospital Applications Analysis - HAA

2. Applications by Applications Category

Admissions & Records Applications Analysis - ARAA

Application	Number
Undergraduate Admissions Process	427
Graduate Admissions Process	272
High School Testing Records	289
Course Catalog Records	355
Schedule of Classes Prep	377
Student Class Scheduling	359
Tuition & Fees Assessment	391

Student Registration Process	442
Class Rosters	436
Term Student Records & Reports	396
Course Add & Drop Processing	432
Enrollment Reporting	433
Enrollment Statistics	432
Student Ethnic Group Reporting	388
Term Grade Reporting	430
Honors Program Records	252
Student Transcript Records	351
Degree Requirements Evaluation	174
Correspondence Course Records	70
Academic Advisement Records	192
Career Planning	143
Student Recruitment	253
Continuing Education Units	173
Grade Distributions	356
Classroom Assignment	225
Veterans Reporting	237
Foreign Student Reporting	236
Final Exam Scheduling	79

Financial Management Applications Analysis - FMAA

General Fund Ledger	412
General Fund Expenditure	399
Departmental Expenditures	390
General Accounts Receivable	341
Student Accounts Receivable	397
Accounts Payable	386
Payroll	385
Employee Benefit Accounting	260
Retirement System Accounting	180
Bank Account Reconciliation	280
Cash Flow Analysis/Projection	151
Investment Records	124
Investment Evaluation	84
Grant & Contract Administration	191
Research Project Accounting	140
Research Proposal Monitoring	69
Financial Aid Accounting	376
Tuition & Fees Accounting	384
Residence Hall Accounting	228
Stores Accounting	158
Telephone Accounting	255
Travel Accounting	193

Planning Mgmt & Institutional Research Applications Analysis - PMIRAA	
Budget Forecasting	249
Budget Preparation	345
Budget Analysis	282
Budget Position Control	228
Institutional Cost Studies	198
Faculty Salary Analysis	287
Support Staff Salary Analysis	231
Faculty Activity Analysis	163
Support Staff Activity Analysis	56
Resource Requirements Modeling	50
Student Flow Modeling	65
Financial Modeling	125
Long Range Planning	77
Enrollment Forecasting	142
HEGIS Reporting	287
Data Element Dictionary	180
Institutional Code Control	55
ICLM/Cross-over Studies	51
Project Management	88

Logistics and Related Services Applications Analysis - LRSAA	
Purchase Order Follow-up	142
Purchasing Information	182
Vendor Information	251
Stores Inventory	163
Office Machine Repair	38
Automobile Registration	166
Parking Lot Space Assignment	60
Traffic Violation Records	163
Crime Reporting	40
Car Pool Matching	39
Motor Pool Records	40
Equipment Inventory	291

Faculty/Staff/Student Services Applications Analysis - FSSSAA	
Faculty/Staff Directory Prep	314
Student Directory Prep	304
Student Housing Reports	269
Teacher & Job Placement	62
Student Counseling Records	64
Fraternity/Sorority Rush	57
Staff Ethnic Group Reporting	170
Student Psychological Tests	27

Instructor Evaluation	212
Financial Aid Evaluation	259
Financial Aid Rewards	355
Student Employment Records	247
Work Study Records	279

General Administrative Services Applications Analysis - GASAA

Facilities Inventory	251
Facilities Utilization Analysis	160
Classroom Utilization Analysis	186
Personnel Records	344
Personnel Evaluation	86
Personnel Placement	52
Federal Compliance Reporting	198
Civil Service Position Records	47
Skills/Interest Inventory	30
Alumni Records	366
Foundation & Gift Records	297
Curriculum Planning	41
Test Scoring & Analysis	218

Auxiliary Services Applications Analysis - ASAA

Residence Hall Billing	192
Faculty Club Billing	31
Food Service Menu & Inventory	78
Bookstore Inventory & Operations	131
Events Calendar & Prep	55
Room Reservations	95
Audio/Visual Booking/Billing	50
College/University Press	40
General Mailing List System	270
Computer Billing System	161
Health Service System	44
Athletic Event Ticket System	72
Sports Information System	41

Library Application Analysis - LAA

Acquisitions	142
Cataloging	182
Card & Mat'l Prep & Control	251
Circulation Control	163
Serials Holdings	38
Bibliographic Search Service	166
Fugitive Material Indexing	60
Educational Media Services	163

Physical Plant Operations Applications Analysis - PPOAA

Physical Plant Accounting	133
Physical Plant Job Schedule	117
Building Maintenance Costs	102
Equipment Preventive Maintenance	90
Key Inventory	103
Building Access Control	38
Energy Monitoring System	166

Computing Installation Management Applications Analysis - CIMAA

Hardware Inventory/Accounting	132
Chargeback System	125
Hardware Performance Monitor	139
Storage Media Management	85
Forms Inventory	65
Project Management	107

Hospital Applications Analysis - HAA

Patient Registration/Admission	40
Hospital Census	34
Medical Records	34
Appointments & Scheduling	29
Central Supply Inventory	25
Communications & Order Inventory	11
Dietary Food Service	19
Housekeeping	7
Laboratory Information System	29
Radiology Information System	22
Pharmacy Information System	25
Nursing Station Support System	17
Physician Support System	16
Patient Billing/Accts Rec	42
Hospital Financial Info System	31
Bloodbank Records	13

3. Applications in Order of Implementation

ARAA	Student Registration Process	442
ARAA	Class Rosters	436
ARAA	Enrollment Reporting	433
ARAA	Course Add & Drop Processing	432
ARAA	Enrollment Statistics	432
ARAA	Term Grade Reporting	430

ARAA	Undergraduate Admissions Process	427
FMAA	General Fund Ledger	412
FMAA	General Fund Expenditures	399
FMAA	Student Accounts Receivable	397
ARAA	Term Student Records & Reports	396
ARAA	Tuition & Fees Assessment	391
FMAA	Departmental Expenditures	390
ARAA	Student Ethnic Group Reporting	388
FMAA	Accounts Payable	386
FMAA	Payroll	385
FMAA	Tuition & Fees Accounting	384
ARAA	Schedule of Classes Preparation	377
FMAA	Financial Aid Accounting	376
GASAA	Alumni Records	366
ARAA	Student Class Scheduling	359
ARAA	Grade Distributions	356
ARAA	Course Catalog Records	355
FSSSAA	Financial Aid Rewards	355
ARAA	Student Transcript Records	351
PMIRAA	Budget Preparation	345
FMAA	General Accounts Receivable	341
GASAA	Personnel Records	344
FSSSAA	Faculty/Staff Directory Prep	314
FSSSAA	Student Directory Prep	304
GASAA	Foundation & Gift Records	297
LRSAA	Equipment Inventory	291
ARAA	High School Testing Records	289
PMIRAA	Faculty Salary Analysis	287
PMIRAA	HEGIS Reporting	287
PMIRAA	Budget Analysis	282
FMAA	Bank Account Reconciliation	280
FSSSAA	Work Study Records	279
ARAA	Graduate Admissions Process	272
ASAA	General Mailing List System	270
FSSSAA	Student Housing Reports	269
FMAA	Employee Benefit Accounting	260
FSSSAA	Financial Aid Evaluation	259
FMAA	Telephone Accounting	255
ARAA	Student Recruitment	253
ARAA	Honors Program Records	252
LAA	Card & Mat'l Prep & Control	251
GASAA	Facilities Inventory	251
LRSAA	Vendor Information	251
PMIRAA	Budget Forecasting	249
FSSSAA	Student Employment Records	247

ARAA	Veterans Reporting	237
ARAA	Foreign Student Reporting	236
PMIRAA	Support Staff Salary Analysis	231
FMAA	Residence Hall Accounting	228
PMIRAA	Budget Position Control	228
ARAA	Classroom Assignment	225
GASAA	Test Scoring & Analysis	218
FSSSAA	Instructor Evaluation	212
GASAA	Federal Compliance Reporting	198
PMIRAA	Institutional Cost Studies	198
FMAA	Travel Accounting	193
ARAA	Academic Advisement Records	192
ASAA	Residence Hall Billing	192
FMAA	Grant & Contract Administration	191
GASAA	Classroom Utilization Analysis	186
LAA	Cataloging	182
LRSAA	Purchasing Information	182
FMAA	Retirement System Accounting	180
PMIRAA	Data Element Dictionary	180
ARAA	Degree Requirements Evaluation	174
ARAA	Continuing Education Units	173
FSSSAA	Staff Ethnic Group Reporting	170
LAA	Bibliographic Search Service	166
LRSAA	Automobile Registration	166
PPOAA	Energy Monitoring System	166
LAA	Circulation Control	163
LAA	Educational Media Services	163
LRSAA	Stores Inventory	163
LRSAA	Traffic Violation Records	163
PMIRAA	Faculty Activity Analysis	163
ASAA	Computer Billing System	161
GASAA	Facilities Utilization Analysis	160
FMAA	Stores Accounting	158
FMAA	Cash Flow Analysis/Projection	151
ARAA	Career Planning	143
LAA	Acquisitions	142
LRSAA	Purchase Order Follow-up	142
PMIRAA	Enrollment Forecasting	142
FMAA	Research Project Accounting	140
CIMAA	Hardware Performance Monitor	139
PPOAA	Physical Plant Accounting	133
CIMAA	Hardware Inventory/Accounting	132
ASAA	Bookstore Inventory & Operations	131
CIMAA	Chargeback System	125
PMIRAA	Financial Modeling	125

FMAA	Investment Records	124
PPOAA	Physical Plant Job Schedule	117
CIMAA	Project Management	107
PPOAA	Key Inventory	103
PPOAA	Building Maintenance Costs	102
ASAA	Room Reservations	95
PPOAA	Equipment Preventive Maintenance	90
PMIRAA	Project Management	88
GASAA	Personnel Evaluation	86
CIMAA	Storage Media Management	85
FMAA	Investment Evaluation	84
ARAA	Final Exam Scheduling	79
ASAA	Food Service Menu & Inventory	78
PMIRAA	Long Range Planning	77
ASAA	Athletic Event Ticket System	72
ARAA	Correspondence Course Records	70
FMAA	Research Proposal Monitoring	69
CIMAA	Forms Inventory	65
PMIRAA	Student Flow Modeling	65
FSSSAA	Student Counseling Records	64
FSSSAA	Teacher & Job Placement	62
LAA	Fugitive Material Indexing	60
LRSAA	Parking Lot Space Assignment	60
FSSSAA	Fraternity/Sorority Rush	57
PMIRAA	Support Staff Activity Analysis	56
ASAA	Events Calendar & Prep	55
PMIRAA	Institutional Code Control	55
GASAA	Personnel Placement	52
PMIRAA	ICLM/Cross-over Studies	51
ASAA	Audio/Visual Booking/Billing	50
PMIRAA	Resource Requirements Modeling	50
GASAA	Civil Service Position Records	47
ASAA	Health Service System	44
HAA	Patient Billing/Accts Rec	42
ASAA	Sports Information System	41
GASAA	Curriculum Planning	41
ASAA	College/University Press	40
HAA	Patient Registration/Admission	40
LRSAA	Crime Reporting	40
LRSAA	Motor Pool Records	40
LRSAA	Car Pool Matching	39
LAA	Serials Holdings	38
LRSAA	Office Machine Repair	38
PPOAA	Building Access Control	38
HAA	Hospital Census	34

HAA	Medical Records	34
ASAA	Faculty Club Billing	31
HAA	Hospital Financial Info System	31
GASAA	Skills/Interest Inventory	30
HAA	Appointments & Scheduling	29
HAA	Laboratory Information System	29
FSSSAA	Student Psychological Tests	27
HAA	Pharmacy Info System	25
HAA	Central Supply Inventory	25
HAA	Radiology Info System	22
HAA	Dietary Food Service	19
HAA	Nursing Station Support System	17
HAA	Physician Support System	16
HAA	Bloodbank Records	13
HAA	Communications & Order Inventory	11
HAA	Housekeeping	7